THE VARANGIANS OF BYZANTIUM

BASIL II

Emperor of the East, 976–1025
Founder of the Varangian Regiment

THE VARANGIANS
OF BYZANTIUM

Sigfús Blöndal

An aspect of Byzantine military history
translated, revised and rewritten by
Benedikt S. Benedikz

CAMBRIDGE UNIVERSITY PRESS

CAMBRIDGE

LONDON · NEW YORK · MELBOURNE

Published by the Syndics of the Cambridge University Press
The Pitt Building, Trumpington Street, Cambridge CB2 1RP
Bentley House, 200 Euston Road, London NW1 2DB
32 East 57th Street, New York, NY 10022, USA
296 Beaconsfield Parade, Middle Park, Melbourne 3206, Australia

First published 1978

Printed in Great Britain
at the University Press, Cambridge

Library of Congress Cataloguing in Publication Data
Blöndal, Sigfús Benedikt Bjarnarson, 1874–1950.
The Varangians of Byzantium.
A revised translation of Væringjasaga.
Includes bibliographical references and index.
1. Byzantine Empire – History, Military.
2. Varangians in the Byzantine Empire – History.
I. Benedikz, Benedikt S., 1932– II. Title. DF543.B5513
1978   949.5   77–82486   ISBN 0 521 21745 8

LIBRUM FELICITER ABSOLUTUM

· HILDUR BLÖNDAL

ET

PHYLLIDI MARIAE BENEDIKZ

UXORIBUS EIUS GENERATIONEM PASSIS

LONGOS PER QUINQUAGINTA ANNOS

PRO SE ET AUCTORE

DEDICAT

EDITOR

Contents

Illustrations and Maps

Preface

On the title-page of this book stand two names. That of Sigfús Blöndal stands in the place of honour, and this is right, for the giant labour of gathering the widely scattered sources of information and attempting to make a coherent story out of them was his in the first instance. As he is not as well known to the English-speaking world as he should be, it is proper to give a brief summary of his life and career here.

Sigfús Benedikt Bjarnarson Blöndal was born on 2 October 1874 at Hjallaland in Vatnsdalur in Northern Iceland, the son of Björn Blöndal, the farmer there, a man of a well-connected family, and his wife Guðrún, also born of a family of parsons and officials. In 1883 Björn Blöndal moved to Reykjavík, and Sigfús entered the Latin School there in 1886. The family had to struggle for their existence against poverty and grievous loss, for Björn was drowned at sea in a gale in 1887, but friends came to their help, and found the means to see Sigfús through the Latin School course, which he accomplished with distinction, being dimitted at the top of the School in 1892. He sailed to Copenhagen the same autumn, and read for the degree of *candidatus magisterii* in Latin, Greek and English, taking his degree in 1898. After doing various jobs he was given a postgraduate grant to spend the year 1900–1 in England, and was appointed Assistant in the Royal Library, Copenhagen in 1901, where he was to spend his entire working life, being promoted to Assistant Librarian, and ending his days as Chief Cataloguer, having among his colleagues a reputation for vast erudition in numerous fields, and a super-pedantic temper in matters of cataloguing practice.[1] He also found time, after the death of Professor

[1] I. Koefod *et al.* (ed.), *Med Birkelund pa forperronen*, Copenhagen, 1972, esp. 44ff.

Valtýr Guðmundsson, to teach Modern Icelandic in Copenhagen University from 1931 to 1946.

The labours of a full-time member of staff in a great national library are not often such as to leave the worker with the energy to spare for the compilation of major works of scholarship, but there have been exceptions in every generation, and Sigfús Blöndal was one of them. Almost as soon as he had settled into his post in the Royal Library he began to organize the first of the two great works on which his reputation rests, the *Icelandic–Danish Dictionary*. Over a period of twenty years he directed the small team of enthusiastic scholars whose names appear on the title-page of that work,[1] and the completion of the work in 1924 was hailed by philologists as the greatest advance so far made in Icelandic lexicography. This is not the place to assess the *Dictionary*, and it must suffice to refer to Dr Jakob Benediktsson's survey of the growth of lexicography up to Blöndal.[2]

Even as he laboured at the *Dictionary*, however, Blöndal was developing a second interest which was to come to absorb his energies entirely during the last third of his life. The roots of his Byzantine work may be seen as early as 1910, when he published a popular article on Byzantine science and culture in *Berlingske Tidende*,[3] and it stemmed clearly from his lifelong love of Greek language and literature, which no amount of scholastic pedantry at Reykjavík Latin School could drive out, and which had been greatly strengthened by his youthful friendship with the poet Grímur Thomsen.[4] Throughout his life he found things Greek congenial inspirations to verse, whether in translating classical poets (he published a small volume of these translations in 1901)[5] or in direct poetical outpourings such as *Væringjar á verði*,[6] printed in his last collection of verses, where we also find translations, made over many years, of Sappho, Theocritus, Tyrtaeus, Anacreon, Euripides and the modern poet Aristoteles Valaoritis. The absorbing theme was, however, the one for which Blöndal's rare combination of classical and Norse scholarship fitted him singularly well to investigate: the Varangians of the Eastern Roman Empire. For twenty-five years he searched assiduously through a wide range of Western and Eastern

1 Sigfús Blöndal (ed.), *Islandsk-dansk ordbog*, redaktør Sigfús Blöndal; hoved-medarbejdere Björg Thorláksson Blöndal, Jón Ófeigsson og Holger Wiehe, Copenhagen, 1920-4.
2 Jakob Benediktsson, 'Íslenzk orðabókargerð á 19 öld', *Andvari*, 1969, 96–108; cf. also Jón Helgason, *Ritgerðakorn og ræðustúfar*, Reykjavík, 1959, 237–43.
3 Sigfús Blöndal, 'Den byzantiske Kultur og Videnskaben', *Berlingske Tidende*, 7 March 1910.
4 Sigfús Blöndal, *Endurminningar*, Reykjavík, 1960, 226ff.
5 Sigfús Blöndal (trsl.), *Nokkur forngrísk kvæði*, Copenhagen, 1901.
6 Sigfús Blöndal, *Sunnan yfir sæ*, Reykjavík, 1949, 54–8.

historical literature for evidences of their existence, and wrote the Icelandic text of the book in which he wanted to bring his results to the eyes of others. It is sad indeed to have to record that he barely finished this part; he had written out the text and noted roughly the references for the Icelandic text when he died on 19 March 1950, but had not yet reshuffled it to his liking, nor had he even begun to think of the book in English in which he had intended to present his work to a wider audience. The Icelandic version was seen through the press under great difficulties by his friend Dr Jakob Benediktsson, and appeared in Reykjavík in 1954, but did not attract the attention of the larger scholarly world because of the language barrier.

Væringja saga is the base on which the present book is built; but it is not the present book, and it is only proper to account both for the revision and for the second name on the title-page. In 1960 Mrs Hildur Blöndal, Sigfús Blöndal's widow, offered the reviser the opportunity to translate or to revise *Væringja saga*, as his judgment suggested, and this offer was accepted – little did the reviser know what he was letting himself in for! It soon became apparent that a simple translation was out of the question, as the book was not written for an audience already well-supplied with handbooks on virtually every aspect of Byzantine studies. The reviser therefore embarked upon the long, slow task of checking everything from the roots and endeavouring to scour the vast literature in both fields that had appeared since Dr Blöndal's death for new materials. What is now laid before the reader is the result of fifteen years of much-interrupted, but tenaciously continued labour. To anyone who compares the two volumes it will be readily apparent how much has been altered, how much of the old has been excised, and how much new has been put in; it will also be apparent that though Dr Blöndal's book underpins it at every stage, it is not the book that Dr Blöndal left that he or she is reading: hence the second name on the title-page.

That the revision is completed at last is thanks to unselfish help by the numerous friends and colleagues who have come so readily to the aid of the pygmy trying to balance on the giant's shoulders. Four institutions have contributed vital help to the eventual accomplishment of the venture: the British Academy provided a generous grant to enable the reviser to put the book through the crucial stage of checking and final rewriting; the University of Durham provided much-needed help towards research in the early stages. Leeds Polytechnic and Birmingham University provided the vital time without which the script of the book could not have been put together from the innumerable scattered scraps which had accumulated on individual points over the years; the latter also provided the additional stimulus of learned and enthusiastic colleagues in Byzantine Studies, whose zest and activity gave the reviser the final injection of energy to drive the task through to its end.

To come from behind the façade of impersonality, I would also like to express thanks *in propria persona* to the many individuals who helped with both great and small problems over the years. Firstly, my most grateful thanks are due to Hildur Blöndal for her generosity in giving me the privilege of tackling what has been an ensnaring labour; it is a peculiar pleasure that she has been able to see the work brought to an end, and her husband's last ambition fulfilled, by however unworthy a surrogate. I am also grateful to Professor Peter Foote and Sir Steven Runciman for their generous help and constant encouragement; for support in difficult times I owe much to Professors H. S. Offler, W. V. Wallace and J. H. Delargy; for rescue at a singularly hard time, and for understanding help in a tight corner, my debt to Mr D. E. Davinson is very great indeed. Many others have given unselfish help over a host of problems; so many now that their list would begin to approach that made by the compiler of the Epistle to the Hebrews; but I cannot omit to mention the generous way in which the late Professor Sigurður Nordal, Professor Einar Ól. Sveinsson, Professor Jón Helgason, Dr A. A. M. Bryer, Mr Arnold Taylor, Mr D. M. Pursglove, Mr John Townsend, Dr Mirjam Foot and Dr Jonathan Shepard have all helped with the utmost cheerfulness and readiness when pestered. It would also be ungracious for a librarian to fail to express his thanks to his numerous colleagues in the many libraries in which he has had to search for his materials: most especially the hard-pressed staffs of Det Kongelige Bibliothek, Copenhagen, the National Library of Iceland, that 'arsenal of divine vengeance' the Bodleian Library, the Arnamagnæan Institute, Copenhagen, and my long-suffering colleagues in Durham University Library, The New University of Ulster Library, the Library of the Department of Librarianship, Leeds Polytechnic, the Brotherton Library, Leeds, the libraries of University College and King's College, London, and the Bibliothèque Nationale, Paris, and not least my chiefs and colleagues of Birmingham University Library, particularly Miss Christine Penney, on whom so much extra labour has fallen as a result of my Varangian adventures. It is a sincere pleasure for the latest and least of 'their' authors to thank the staff of the printing and publishing divisions of the Cambridge University Press for the exemplary scholarliness, courtesy and patience with which they have supported him through the last and worst stage of the gestation of this book. And, lastly, I cannot end without recording my gratitude to my wife: she married with seeing eyes into the project, and has lived with it with unfailing interest ever since, borne all the upheavals of the stormy passage of this book with exemplary patience, and seen it reach completion without jealousy. Yet neither she nor anyone else is responsible for mistakes that will doubtless be found, even after my best endeavours: there the buck stops with me alone.

Birmingham   Benedikt S. Benedikz
8 January 1978

NOTE

For general reference, whenever the words 'the author' or 'the present author' appear in the text or the notes, the opinion expressed is that of Dr Blöndal, the reviser not feeling certain enough either to endorse or contradict it, but feeling that it should be made available for the consideration of others. Whenever the words 'the reviser' appear, the opinion is that of B. S. Benedikz, and Dr Blöndal either expressed a different opinion or none at all. All citations of Greek and Russian from actual texts are left in the Greek and Cyrillic alphabets; individual titles or other single words in the main text have been transliterated into Roman letters.

B. S. B.

I

Varangians and their origins

This book is intended to examine the history of the section of the
Byzantine armed forces which went in its heyday under the name of
Væringjar (Varangians). It is, however, necessary to precede the main
history with a brief outline of their origins, and especially to outline
the historical and geographical conditions which led to their appearance
in the East Roman army.

From the earliest known times Scandinavians have been attracted to
Russia on commercial enterprises, especially in search of furs for
clothing and, for a long period, of slaves. This traffic originated mainly
in Sweden, the country with the most direct access to Russia, especially
from Uppland, East Götland and the island of Gotland; the maritime
districts of Uppland and East Götland being known in early times as
Roþer or *Roþin*, and later as *Roslagen* (W. Norse *Róðrslög*), and the inhabitants were named *Róðskarlar*, *Róðsmen*, and lastly, *Roðspiggar*. These
people formed the bulk of the Russia traders and they began in time to
form settlements in the East; thus the part of the Finnish coast nearest
to Sweden was originally settled from there, and is still the Swedish-
speaking portion of Finland, whose inhabitants are known in Finnish
as *Ruotsalaiset*, and in Swedish as *Ruotsi*. As time went by their numbers
increased in Russia proper so that Norse writings refer to the northern
and central parts of Russia as *Svíþjóð en mikla* (Great Sweden) or
Svíþjóð en kalda (Cold Sweden) to distinguish them from Sweden
proper. The Slavonic peoples in Russia then took up this name for
the Norsemen from the Finns, and called them *Rus*, and from this form
it came into Mediaeval Greek as *Rhos*, and found an Arabic form as *Rûs*.[1]

---

[1] V. Thomsen, *Ryska rikets grunnläggning genom Skandinaverna*, Stockholm, 1882 (hereafter
referred to as *Grunnläggning*), 83ff. A survey of the voluminous controversial literature

The great majority of the original inhabitants of Russia were of Slavonic origin, though a number of Finno-Ugrian tribes such as the Permians and the Estonians were to be found in the North-West regions. The Swedes came most often as merchants, and, then as later, merchants had to carry arms for their own protection, and so what had begun as trading journeys often became piratical excursions. Those Vikings who went *í Austrvíking*, abducted people and sold them into slavery in one country, had perhaps a sanctuary and friendly relations with the next-door state, where they behaved as peaceful merchants, and the situation will have been similar in many parts of Russia where the Norsemen were common visitors.

As time passed social and political organization in the eastern lands became more settled, and the trade voyages of the Norsemen more regular and more important economically, and it became necessary to secure the principal trading posts against attack, especially when Swedes began to settle permanently in them. This process was not dissimilar to the immigrant movements in the United States during the latter half of the eighteenth and the first three quarters of the nineteenth centuries, when the white men built fortified trading posts in the Indian territories which gradually grew into the cities of today. It was, however, considerably easier to do this in the Russian plains, because the Slavs were far more accustomed to the Westerners' ways than were the American Indians of the eighteenth and nineteenth centuries, and the two races had comparatively little difficulty in amalgamating. In due course, when the Swedes established their 'garths' (Russ. *goroda*), these were only fortified trading posts to begin with, but peace-loving local inhabitants soon realized the advantages of living in the comparative safety of the *gorod*, and of being on friendly terms with the inhabitants, and these fortified towns gradually increased in numbers and importance, as in time the Slavs founded their own *goroda*. The name *Garðaríki* became a synonym for Russia in Scandinavia, sometimes for the whole complex of widespread states, sometimes for an individual kingdom that was formed there. Often the Slavs had already formed a petty state (*volosti*) around a fortified city when the Norsemen (who often gained eventual control) came and took up residence. The Slavonic chieftains also made frequent use of their services as allies or

up to 1930 is to be found in V. A. Mosyin, *Варяго-Русскій Вопрос, Slavia*, x (1931) 109–36, 343–79, 501–37; for subsequent argument see A. Stender-Petersen, *Varangica*, Aarhus, 1953; D. Obolensky, *The Byzantine Commonwealth*, London, 1969; P. H. Sawyer, *The Age of the Vikings*, 2nd ed., London, 1971 (esp. chs 1–2, 9). F. E. Wozniak, *The nature of Byzantine foreign policy toward Kievan Russia in the first half of the 10th century* (Ph.D., Stanford University, California, 1973), is only a conscientious summary of older work, and provides no new evidence or any really fresh assessment.

mercenaries, especially as guards for merchants against robber bands or as supporters in a civil conflict.

It is usually reckoned[1] that the Norse states in Russia began with the coming of Rurik and his brothers to Novgorod in 862, but there are various bits of evidence to show that Norse-ruled petty states existed along the great rivers long before then. It is likely that both Novgorod and Kiev had been established as independent towns some time before the Rusi came and strengthened and fortified them. The first element (*NOV(YI)*) of Novgorod is, for instance, a Slavonic vocable, while its Norse name of *Hólmgarðr* was formed through a part of the town being situated on an island in the adjacent lake. *Kænugarðr* was also formed as a name from a corruption of the Old Russian name for the inhabitants of the district (*Kiyane gorod*).[2] As the Norse sagas also show clearly, there was a close contact between the rulers of these principates and the kings of early Scandinavia, often through marriage contacts and subsequent blood-relationships. The Great Princes of Kiev and Novgorod were known in Old Russian as *stolnyi knyazi* (great princes), which became corrupted into Old Norse as *stólkonungr*, and this became in turn the customary title for the East Roman emperors in Norse sources once our proper period under investigation begins.

The *Rusi* gradually became the ruling class of the area from Ladoga to Odessa, and as time passed they gradually lost their specifically Norse characteristic, though the name remained, until the great and powerful Slavonic people whom they governed took up the name Russians, which they bear to this day.

It is only fair to point out that other explanations of the name *Rus* have been provided, particularly by historians of the Slavophil school. For the purposes of this non-specialist introduction it is enough to refer to the works of F. Knauer, S. Vernadskii, and P. Smirnov.[3]

---

[1] Cf. G. Vernadskii, *A History of Russia*, New Haven, Conn., 1943–69, I, 275–6 and refs. there.

[2] Thus S. Rozniecki, *Varægiske Minder i den russiske Heltedigtning*, Copenhagen, 1914 (hereafter referred to as Rozniecki, *Minder*), 284. Another explanation of the name Hólmgarðr has been advanced by H. Rydzevskaya, 'Холм и новгороде и древнесеверный Hólmgarðr', *Известия Академии Истории Материальной Культуры*, 1922, II; her argument is that Холм, 'the height', was the oldest part of Novgorod and that the Norsemen changed it to Hólm. For the Kievian civilization generally, see B. D. Grekov, *La culture de la Russie de Kiev*, Moscow, 1947.

[3] F. Knauer, О происшодении имена народа 'Руси', *Труди XI Археологического сёзда в Кёве*, II, 1901; see also the same author's articles on the subject in *Indogermanische Forschungen*, XXXXI (1912) and XXXXIII (1914); also P. Smirnov, Волжкии шлах и стародавни Руси, *Украинска Академия Наук: сборник ист. фил. Виддилу*, Kiev, 75 (1928); a survey by B. Briem, Alt-Skandinavien in der neueren russischen wissenschaftlichen Litteratur (1918–28), *Acta Philologica Scandinavica*, V (1930–1), 211–36; G. Vernadskii, *A History of Russia*, I, 76, 96–8; N. S. Derzhavin, *Произведении Русского Народа*, Moscow, 1944.

Smirnov and Knauer argued that it is more likely that the name derives eventually from the Greek name R*ha* for the river Volga, and the Norsemen who used that river as a highway towards the Caspian Sea had their appellation from the river's name, while Vernadskii argued that it is derived from a branch of the Alani, referred to in a Syrian annal of the sixth century as the R*os* (? R*oxolani*, 'fair Alans').

The common reaction by a Western European reader to the name *Varangian* is to think of the Byzantine Emperor's famous guards, but it is only right to point out that the name is not solely connected with them, since both before and after the creation of the regiment it was used in another, much wider meaning, both in Russia and elsewhere.[1] It has been interpreted in various ways, of which only the most widely circulated need be mentioned here. There is now a general agreement that the derivation is from the O.N. word *vár*, pl. *várar*, 'confidence (in)', 'faith (in)', 'vow of fidelity', in Proto-Norse therefore* *väringr*, then *väringi*, *væringi*. Related words in other Germanic languages are O.E. *wærgenga*, Lombardic *waregang*, O.F. *wargengus*, all derived from a West Germanic prototype *wäreganga (-u)* and meaning 'a foreigner who has taken service with a new lord by a treaty of fealty to him', or 'protégé'. Since there were in the army of the undivided Roman Empire, and in the earliest Byzantine armies, special units of *foederati*, allied troops who were used at times as the imperial life-guards, it was not unnatural that the word *væringi* would take on this meaning, especially as the imperial guards of the third and fourth centuries A.D. were largely composed of Goths.[2]

Since, however, the word appeared in Russia long before it was known to the Greeks, this explanation cannot be used. In Russian it appears as *Varyag*, O.Russ. *Varegu*. Vilhelm Thomsen has argued that this word was used of Norse merchants and soldiers who entered the protection of Russian rulers, either to do business within their territories or as mercenaries in their forces,[3] and this explanation has been commonly accepted until recent times, when Professor Adolph Stender-Petersen has propounded a new solution which is even more likely to be correct.[4] He accepts the older explanation, that the word *varar* is the base of the word *væringi*, but instead of interpreting it as 'protégé', he maintains that *Væringjar* should be understood as 'men who plight each other troth, who enter a fellowship'. *Varar* then refers to their common liability, one for all and all for one, of all goods and ships in

[1] *Grunnläggning*, 97ff.
[2] This explanation is found in J. Ihre, *Glossarium Suiogothicum*, Stockholm, 1769, II, 1069–70.
[3] *Grunnläggning*, 103–6.
[4] A. Stender-Petersen, 'Zur Bedeutungsgeschichte des Wortes Vaeringi; russ. Варагъ' *Acta Philologica Scandinavica*, VI (1931), 27–30; reprinted in *Varangica*, 89ff.

their possession. In the meaning 'security', *varar* appears in a stanza by Ólafr Þórðarson the White Poet (ob. 1259).

> Allt þá lagði frömuðr frægða
> Fekk sætt af því stillir rekka,
> Snildar skýrs ok *seldi várar*
> Sitt mál í kné lituðs stála.

He, the doer of famous acts [i.e. Earl Skúli], laid all his case in the lap of the eloquent warrior [i.e. King Haakon] and gave security; in return the warlord was given reconciliation.[1]

Finnur Jónsson translates this as *afgav edelige Løfter*, 'gave promises on oath', while Vilhelm Thomsen interprets it *Jarlen gav Kongen ganske sin Sag i Vold og stillede Sikkerhed*, 'the Earl surrendered his case completely to the King's mercy, and gave security'.[2] We also have a reference to this action in *Hákonar saga*, ch. 177 *seldi jarl þar festu til*, 'the Earl gave security for this'.[3]

The word has therefore been used primarily by men who entered into a mercantile fellowship and *seldu várar* or *veittu várar* to one another. These merchants were, or needed to be, well supplied with arms, and normally travelled in companies. *Væringi* therefore meant 'companion', a man who has entered into a contractual fellowship of merchants and soldiers, and gives security, accepts responsibility towards his companions, as they accept responsibility for him. Stender-Petersen also adds that the word came to have a wider meaning, first 'merchant from Scandinavia', then, later, 'itinerant merchant', generally a pedlar, without regard to nationality. The northernmost Russians did, however, retain the term as a specific name for a Norseman; thus, in the dialect of Archangelsk, the name *Varyaza* is still used in the meaning 'foreigner', or 'man from beyond the sea',[4] while in Southern Russia the Varangians were more usually soldiers; hence the word came gradually to mean 'Norseman' (in Byelo-Russian *varag* is habitually

---

[1] F. Jónsson, *Den norsk-islandske Skjaldedigtning*, Copenhagen, 1912–15. Hereafter referred to as FJ *Skjald*, A II, 93, B II, 105.

[2] V. Thomsen, *Samlede Afhandlinger*, Copenhagen, 1928–31, I, 435–6.

[3] *Hákonar saga*, ch. 177 (the version of *Flateyjarbók*, ed. G. Vigfússon and C. R. Unger, Christiania, 1860–9, III, 108).

[4] Cf. V. I. Dal, *Толковый Словарь Живого Велико-Русскаго Языка*, 4th ed., Saint Petersburg, 1912, I, 404–5, where Варег, Варега, Варежа, Варуги, are given with the meaning 'mittens', the provenances being (?)Karelia and Olonets. Similarly the *Словарь Русский Народных Говоров*, 4th ed., Soviet Academy of Sciences, 1969, II, 46–9, repeats Dal's tentative Karelian provenance and adds among others Perm, Yaroslavl', Vladimir, Kostroma, Vologda, Tver, Nizhnyi Novgorod, Voronezh, Olonets, Arkhangel and Kazan'. This dictionary also stresses the mercantile origin of Варар, giving (I, 64) Варар, 'pedlar' (from ?Вор, 'thief'); Варяга, 'a cunning man'. M. Vasmer, *Russisches Etymologisches Wörterbuch*, Heidelberg, 1953 (under Варар) denies this connection; see also Rozniecki, *Minder*, 210 and 41 fn. 2. (I am very much obliged to my former colleague Mr D. M. Pursglove for help with this note – BSB.)

used to mean 'tall, burly man'). Gradually too, the Russians began to differentiate between themselves and the Varangians. Thus an annal from Novgorod that mentions Varangians for the last time in 1201 refers to a treaty made with them in 1195: article ten of this treaty states 'If a Varangian demands his goods from a Russian, or a Russian from a Varangian, and the debtor denies the debt, then the creditor shall bring twelve men as witnesses and have them swear an oath (to the truth of the original transaction), and then seize his property.'[1] Later the word was largely used in Russia of Germans, or Roman Catholics generally, *vera varyazhkaya* equalling *vera latinskaya*, 'faith of the Varangians', i.e. in opposition to Greek Orthodoxy.[2] We should also note that the Arabs learnt the word in Russia, and it appears in Arabic in the form *varank*, and is used as a generic name for Scandinavians or denizens of the Norse world, while the Baltic Sea is named *Bahr Varank*, 'Varangian Sea' by Arab writers.[3]

In Greek the word *Varangos* was first used in the meaning 'Norseman', but since the regiment of life-guards from that race became especially well-known in the Empire the meaning narrowed to 'mercenary of Norse origin'.[4] Later it was used generally of Germanic mercenaries, especially of Englishmen, as will be explained.[5]

Stender-Petersen has also produced a similar explanation of the name *Kylfingar* (Russ. *Kolbyag(i)*), which he connects with the Norse word *kolfr*, 'association' (cf. *hjúkólfr*), and the *Kylfingar* will therefore have been a company of Norse merchants who operated in Russia, though the term never became as widespread there as *Væringjar*.[6] There is evidence, however, that they reached as far south as Byzantium, where they were known by this name (Gr. *Kulpingoi*), and entered the Emperor's service.[7] The late eleventh century law codex *Russkaya Pravda* shows that Varangians and Kylfings had certain privileges; thus their word was more readily believed than that of Slavonic subjects of the Russian prince; thus they could sometimes free themselves by a

---

[1] M. Vladimirskii-Budanov, *Хрестоматия по истории Русскаго Права*, Kiev, 1871, 1, 96; 'Мирная грамота Новгородцев с немцами 1195, вип. 10: Ожо емоти скот варягоу на Роусин, или Роусини на варяз а ся евозаприт то 12 миж Послухи идет роте взмет свое.' The word *væringi* is used in *Þiðreks saga* (ed. H. Bertelsen, Copenhagen, 1904, 1, 30–1, 40, 105, 347–8, 360) of a Norse or Scandinavian itinerant merchant.

[2] Mosyin, *Варяго-Русский вопрос*, *Slavia* x, 117; on Varangian Christianity in the eleventh century cf. Rozniecki, *Minder*, 197ff.   [3] *Grunnläggning*, 99.

[4] The first recorded use in Greek sources is by Cedrenus; *G. Cedrenus Ioannis Scylitzae Ope*, ed. I. Bekker (CSHB), Bonn, 1838–9, 11, 509, in 1034.

[5] See below, pp. 141ff.

[6] So A. Stender-Petersen, *Varangica*, 89ff. One of the most notable older interpretations is that by B. Briem, 'Kylfingar', *Acta Philologica Scandinavica*, iv (1928), 40–8. Briem assumes that it is a Norse translation of the name of an obscure Finno-Ugrian tribe, the *Vota* (O. Russ. води, Finn. *Vadjalaiset*) because the *vadja* (Finn. *vaaja*) means *Kylfa*, 'club' in O.N.   [7] See below, p. 82, n. 3 for yet another explanation.

simple oath where others had to bring witnesses to be freed of accusation.

There is one other possibility to explain the word *Varangian*. It is sometimes used in modern Icelandic in the meaning 'cheerful, lively youth',[1] and the feminine plural form *væringar* is used to mean 'discord, quarrel'. It is by no means impossible that these meanings existed in Old Icelandic, whatever their origins, and *Væringi* then meant at first 'quarrelsome fellow', and then attained the less pejorative meaning. I do not think, however, that this explanation is better than Stender-Petersen's.

Finally the most recent attempt at explanation must be mentioned. This is made by the Russian scholar J. D. Bruckus, who considers that the word *Væringi* (*Varangos*, *Varyag*, etc.) is derived from the Turkish word *varmak* or *barmak* (participial form *varan*), 'walk' 'to travel on foot', and that it was originally used of Norse merchants and vikings; right from the time when, in the eighth century, they began to make frequent journeys down the Volga, and that it originated with the Bulgars who at one stage held lands along that river: in turn the word spread to Kiev, which was ruled by the Khazars, and then further south. Similarly *Kylfingr* (*Kolbyag'*, *Kulpingos*) was a transliteration of the Turkish translation *köl-beg*, pl. *köl-begler*, for 'sea-king'.[2] This interpretation has found favour with F. Dölger, but it may be objected that though Bruckus rightly observes that the Varangians are most often observed as merchants in Old Russia, there is no need to search in such an unrelated language as Turkish to explain a word which can easily be explained from the Varangians' and Kylfings' own tongue, from which Stender-Petersen's explanations are perfectly satisfactory in the opinion of the present writers.

The custom whereby Varangians became mercenaries in the service of Russian princes gradually became more wisdepread. In the first instance they entered the service of the Swedish princes who founded and ruled for many generations over Norse kingdoms in the East, in Novgorod, Kiev, and other places. There they are sometimes referred to as special 'friendly troops' (Russ. *Druzhina* from *drug*, 'friend'), probably by analogy with the *Hetairia* frequently referred to in Byzantine military phraseology in the sense of mercenaries in the Imperial service. The Khazar kings on the north side of the Black Sea are also said to have *Rusi* (Varangians) and *Slavi* (Russians) in their service.

---

[1] B. Halldórsson, *Lexicon islandico-latino-danicum*, ed. R. Rask, Copenhagen, 1814; also S. Blöndal, *Islandsk-Dansk Ordbog*, Copenhagen, 1920–4, both under *væringi*.

[2] J. D. Bruckus, 'Warjager und Kolbjager', *Acta Seminarii Kondakov*, 1935, 81–102; see also a notice of this article by F. Dölger, *Byzantinische Zeitschrift* (hereafter referred to as *BZ*), 35 (1935), 480.

Besides entering the service of others, it will have happened not infrequently that Norsemen went on purely piratical excursions on their own account along the great rivers of Russia, all the way south to the Black Sea and the Caspian Sea, and made depredations there. Early in the ninth century there is mention of 'Russians' who are engaged in piracy both on the northern and southern side of the Black Sea.[1] Regular piratical expeditions on a large scale to the East Roman empire failed, however, as did open warfare against the emperors, as the Byzantine state, even after the disasters in the Bulgar wars in the early ninth century, was still too powerful a military organization for little sea-forces, and moreover several of the emperors and their leading generals were warriors of a quality that made privateers and small hostile groups – and indeed quite formidable opponents – give them a wide berth. We shall return to the Russian contacts with Byzantium later. The commercial contacts were, however, both more frequent and more important than the warlike expeditions, and stretched as far as Arab countries and even the Chinese empire, as may be seen from the great number of Arabic coins found in Scandinavian hoards in Russia (especially in Sweden) and from Chinese writers of the great epoch of the T'ang dynasty when (in the ninth and tenth centuries) the Chinese empire reached all the way to the Caspian Sea, who refer to tall, blue-eyed, red-haired men living in the area, who may well have been Norsemen.[2]

The advances of the Norsemen will, as has been stated, have been along the great Russian rivers to begin with, as the way was easiest by water, along the Duna and the Neva to begin with, then via Novgorod to Volchov, and then along the Volga to the lands of the Bulgars and the Khazars. Next would be the advance along the Dnieper to Byzantium, via Kiev, which, after the Rusi of Kiev had overthrown the Khazars in the 960s (Itil, the capital, was conquered in 969) became the main route to the Empire.[3] It is along this road that we find the place-name evidences that testify to the unquestionably Norse character of the Varangians.

---

[1] For references to Russian piracy in Byzantine Asia in the early ninth century, see the *Vita* of St Gregory of Amastris in V. G. Vasilevskii, *Русско-Византийская Исследования*, Saint Petersburg, 1893, 1–73, esp. 61ff.; also *Acta Sanctorum*, Februarius III 21 Februarii, 278–9; also the *Vita* of St Stefan of Sourozh (or Sugdaea) in Vasilevskii, *Исследования* 77–9. For two extensive studies of the earliest collisions between Byzantium and the *Rusi* see A. A. Vasilev, *The Russian Attack on Constantinople* in 860, Cambridge, Mass., 1946 and, by the same author, 'The Second Russian Attack on Constantinople', *Dumbarton Oaks Papers*, 6 (1961), 161–225.

[2] C. P. Fitzgerald, *Son of Heaven*, London, 1933, 199–201.

[3] F. Braun, 'Das historische Russland im nordischen Schrifttum des 10. bis 14. Jahrhundert', *Festschrift Eugen Mogk*, Halle am Saale, 1924, 150–96.

Along the lower part of the Dnieper, to the south of Ekaterinoslav, are mighty waterfalls which are named пороги ('thresholds') in Russian if they extend right across the river, and заборы ('fences') if they only straddle a part of it.[1] There are in all eleven of these 'thresholds' and six of the 'fences' over a distance of some fifty miles, and in the last fifty years they have been harnessed by the Soviet authorities to supply driving-power for great hydroelectric works. In the Middle Ages, however, they were regarded as great traffic hazards. Constantine VII makes several references to them in *De Administrando Imperio*,[2] where he gives the names of the principal ones ῥωσιστί ('in Russian', i.e. Norse) and σκλαβιστί ('in Slavonic', i.e. in Old Russian), and his evidence removes all doubt as to what people are meant when at that time a reference is made to the *Rhos*.

Constantine first describes how the ships of the Rhos come all the way from Nemogarda (Novgorod) and other towns, and gather into a fleet at Kioava (Kiev), also called Sambatas (O.N. *Sandbakki*, 'sand-shore'). The Slavs who are subjects to the Rusi cut great trees down in the winter and make canoes of them, transport them down the Dnieper and sell them to the Rusi in Kiev. The Russians then embark on their new boats and break up the ships on which they came to Kiev, removing from them oars, thwarts and any other useful loose articles. Then, in the month of June, they travel down the Dnieper to *Vitizevi* (Vytichev) and thence down to the cataracts. There they leave their goods on board and wade along the shallows themselves, dragging the boats, or pushing them over the difficult patches.[3]

The emperor calls the first cataract Ἐσσουπῆ, which he says means in both Russian and Slavonic 'Do not sleep'. According to this interpretation it should be called не спи, and V. Thomsen postulates that Constantine's original MS had Νεσσουπῆ. Eiríkur Magnússon has conjectured that the Norse name was originally *Nes uppi* (lit. 'upper promontory'), which is quite a likely solution, though Karlgren interprets it as *Súpandi* (lit. 'slurping').[4]

Constantine's cataract is called by him Οὐλβορσί in Russian, but

---

[1] The Varangians sometimes called the river Népr or Nípr; Rozniecki, *Minder*, 292.

[2] Constantine Porphyrogennetos, *De Administrando Imperio*, ed. G. Moravcik and R. J. H. Jenkins, London and Dumbarton Oaks, 1949–62 (hereafter called *DAI*, 58ff. The excellent commentary on this chapter by Professor Obolensky (*DAI*, II, 16–61) gathers together a mass of detail and provides a wise discussion to which the reviser feels it sufficient to refer here once and for all.

[3] *DAI*, 58–59. A full examination is given by Thomsen (*Grunnläggning*, 50–64); more recent investigations of this topic are by J. Sahlgren, Vikingar i osterled, *Namn och Bygd*, XVIII (1930), 131–48, and A. Karlgren, *Dneprfosserners nordisk-slaviske navne*, Copenhagen, 1947 (hereafter referred to as Karlgren: *Dneprfosserne*); see also *DAI*, II.

[4] *DAI*, 58–9; *Grunnläggning*, 56; Karlgren, *Dneprfosserne*, 106.

'Οστροβουνιπράχ in Slavonic, which he interprets as 'island of the waterfall'. This name may be interpreted as O.N. *Úlfarsey* or possibly *Hólmsey* (?) and O.Russ. островний праг (mod. порог), 'island waterfall'. This probably refers to two waterfalls, nowadays named Сурский and Лочанский; Thomsen conjectures that the name was *Hólmfoss* and derived from three rocks just above the Lochanskii fall, or else from a tree-covered islet just by the Surskii fall, though the former is more likely.[1]

The third cataract mentioned by the emperor is the Γελανδρί, which he interprets as meaning in Slavonic ἦχος φραγμοῦ, 'the sound of the fall', but he has gone astray here, since Γελανδρί is clearly the same as O.N. *Gjallandi* or *Gellandi*, 'shouter', which matches the present-day name of Звонец, an apt name for the fall, since its sound can be heard for miles.

The fourth cataract in Constantine's list is named by him 'Αειφόρ in Russian, and Νεασήτ in Slavonic, and is so named because pelicans build their nests in the rocks within the waterfall. This fall was regarded as the most dangerous one of all of them, and is named in modern Russian Ненаситецкий. Νεάσητ is the O.Russ. неясит or Mod.Russ. неясыт, which can mean 'pelican', and the emperor may have so understood it, but pelicans are not to be found in that region, and an alternative meaning could be from сыт, 'replete', as 'impossible to satisfy', as the modern name suggests, and V. Thomsen has conjectured that it is because it is the only fall where the river never quite covers all the rocks in the great spring floods. From this is also conjecturable the Norse name *Æfari*, 'never navigable', since the Rusi could never draw their ships along the river bed, but had to bypass the fall on land. Thomsen has suggested that the Norse name could be from *Eyforr* or *Æfor*, 'keen, ever excited', but it is just as likely that it derives from *Eifærr*, 'never passable', on the obvious grounds. There is also a conjecture by J. Sahlgren, that the O.N. name was *Eiðsfors*,[2] while Karlgren has pointed out that *aist*, 'stork', is also used to mean 'pelican' (originally from German).[3] Near Pilgårds, near Slite in Gotland, there has been discovered a rune-stone which states that Hegbiarn (? Heggbjörn) and his brothers, Roþuisl and Oystain (? Róðvísl and Eysteinn) raised a stone in memory of their brother Rafn at Rufstain (?Hrófsteinn) in the south, and had travelled as far as Aifur.[4]

---

[1] *DAI*, 58–9 and refs. there; Karlgren, *Dneprfosserne*, 35.
[2] Sahlgren, 'Vikingar', *Namn och Bygd*, XVIII (1930), 146–7.
[3] Karlgren, *Dneprfosserne*, 109–17.
[4] H. Pipping, 'Om Pilgaardsstenen', *Nordiska studier tillägnade Adolf Noreen*,Uppsala, 1914, 175–82. An illustration of this stone is in T. J. Arne, *Det store Svitjod*, Stockholm, 1917, 49, fig. 1, where the stone called in Russian Руаный Камень, 'the cleft stone,' is

Constantine VII names the fifth cataract Βαρουφόρος in Russian, and Βυλνηπράχ in Slavonic, 'because it forms a great maelstrom'. In O.N. this name would be *Bárufoss*, 'Wave Fall', and O.Russ. Влны праг, from влна, mod. волна, 'wave', corresponds precisely with this interpretation. The modern name is Волный or Волнынский. Karlgren wants to read this according to common pronunciation as Βάργφορος, and maintains that it is connected with the O.Swed. *vara*, 'stony shore', which occurs in Danish and Swedish placenames as *ora*.[1]

The sixth fall is called Λεάντι in Russian, and Βερούτζη in Slavonic which Constantine interprets as 'surge of water'. Βερούτζη corresponds to O.Ch.Slav. Враштий, 'whirler' from врети, 'to boil, simmer', mod. Russ. вручий, while Λεάντι is unquestionably O.N. *Hlæjandi*, 'laughing', 'laughter'. Thomsen thinks that this is the cataract now known as Таволжанский, where the river is about one kilometre wide, and the bed strewn with rocks, and the water is covered with foam and makes a curious simmering sound. Karlgren thinks that it is the cataract now known as Вилный, which is actually two cataracts, the main one being known as Волчигорла, 'wolf's mouth', or волчок, 'wolf cub'.[2]

Constantine's seventh and last cataract is called by him Στρούκουν in Russian and Ναπρεζή in Slavonic, which he interprets as 'the little fall'. These names are difficult to interpret; Thomsen thinks that Ναπρεζή is the adjective набрзый, 'rather quick' in O.Ch.Slav., while Στρούκουν is O.N. *Strjúkandi*, 'stroker, delicately touching'. The cataract is a small one, and this might have been the reason for Constantine's interpretation.[3] Sahlgren has however pointed out that *Strukn* is found as a placename in Sweden, for a small waterfall. Karlgren agrees with this, but points out that the Russians will have understood this word as the imperative of the O.Russ. verb стуркнути, mod. туркнуть, and so ought to mean 'push off'. Instead, however, they have replaced it with the imperative of another verb, O.Russ. напрязи, O.Bulg. напрези, 'strain harder'. It is certainly true, even at the present time, that it takes a great effort to keep the vessel from running on to the rocks on the eastern side of the water when one passes through this fall. The

shown. This stone contains circular bowls or indentations which Arne thinks were used for sacrifice to local spirits, in order to secure a safe passage through the cataract (*Svitjod*, 39–40). He translates the name as meaning 'impassable', stating (p. 38) that the cataract is 410 fathoms long, and is reckoned to be accompanied by seven waterfalls, the total length of cataract and waterfalls combined being 2577 fathoms (rather more than 3 English miles).

[1] *DAI*, 60–1; Karlgren, *Dneprfosserne*, 118–21.
[2] Karlgren, *Dneprfosserne*, 72–3 and 121–5.
[3] *DAI*, 60–1; cf. *Grunnläggning*, 62–3; Sahlgren, 'Vikingar,' 143–5; Karlgren, *Dneprfosserne*, 130–5.

emperor's description 'the little fall' suggests that he is referring to the passage now known as Школа, 'The School', which is a passage where the banks of the river are steep and high, and the passageway is narrower than elsewhere; the name has come about because this spot is a regular test of the ability of a skipper. In the other falls (except at Holmfoss) it was possible to hug the bank and push the boats on by pushing on the bank, but here they had to be steered along the middle of the water-race, and the bank had to be avoided at all costs. The emperor will have been told of this necessity, and therefore he assumed that the fall was only a small one.

In all these cases Karlgren has produced convincing proofs that the Norse names are older than the Slavonic ones.

Constantine refers next to the continuation of the journey and the dangers that await the travellers, especially attacks by the Pechenegs, who looked for opportunities to attack the Rusi, especially when they were passing through the falls, and the travellers were therefore obliged to have bands of armed men pass along the banks to protect the ship and those who dragged or carried them from assault. Further on, in an island which later became known as St Gregory's Island, the travellers would rest and feed, and offer thank-offerings to the gods under a huge oak-tree, as from there on they did not need to fear the Pechenegs. The next stop was then in Berezany (formerly St Aetherius's Island), in the mouth of the Dnieper. By treaty with the Empire the Russians were not permitted to have winter quarters there, nor yet at the neighbouring town of Belobrezhie, though this rule appears to have been broken at times; thus a rune-stone was found in Berezany which has the inscription 'Grani made this grave for Karl, his companion.'[1] The journey was then continued into the Black Sea, and broken at Mesembria before reaching Constantinople, the real goal of the travellers.[2]

By a treaty with the Emperor the Rusi had a sanctuary and a dwelling near the monastery of St Mamas, and the harbour named after the same saint was allocated to them for their ships (this is now called *Besiktas*, and is situated near the Bagce Saraj palace).[3]

The treaty made between Leo VI and the Russian chief Oleg (Helgi) in 907 stipulated that the Byzantines paid a stated sum, as well as journey monies for their return, to Russian merchants who traded the

---

[1] Illustrated in Arne, *Svitjod*, 48.

[2] See G. Schlumberger, *Un empereur de Byzance: Nicéphore Phocas*, Paris, 1890 (hereafter referred to as *Nicéphore*), 552.

[3] J. Pargoire, 'Le Saint Mame de Constantinople', *Bulletin de l'Institut Russe à Constantinople* IX (1914), 281–316, has proved that the quarters of the Rusi were there and not on the Bosphorus outside the city walls, where there was also a church dedicated to St Mamas, which Ducange (*Constantinopolis Christiana*, Paris, 1680, II, 185) and others after him took to be the place allocated to the Rusi.

Grand Prince's goods for him, and provided them with six months' board as well. The Byzantines looked on this as a convenient way of hiring an army to guard the North-West frontier against raiders, and they were also anxious to get Russians to join their regular forces, while the Russians came to look on it as a tribute to which they had a right, and disagreement over this led to the new treaty between Constantine VII and Igor (Ingvar) in 945. On the other hand, this certain lodging in Constantinople was of the utmost importance for the Russians' trade, and Klyuchevskii is quite justified in stating

when he [the Grand Prince of Kiev] became a king, and a ruler of a nation, he did not cease to be a Varangian, an armed merchantman. He gave his retinue a certain portion of his revenues, and they remained the ruling class of the nation, and assisted him in the government. During the winter season these members of the governing class took part in the rule, going round the country to collect taxes, and in the summer they went abroad to trade with their winter takings.[1]

These tax-gatherings were named by the name полуде, and as will be discussed later on, it is not impossible that the term entered the jargon of the Byzantine Varangians in the word *pólútasvarf*.[2]

There are much-discussed descriptions of these earliest Norse aristocrats, the Rusi, by Arab travellers who visited them. Ibn Dustah went to Russia in A.D. 921, and Ibn Fadhlan was the ambassador of the Caliph Mukhtadir with the Bulgars of the Volga region in 921–2, when he met Russians who came there to trade. The latter's narrative is abridged in the work of the geographer Yakut (fl. 1179–1229), though a fuller manuscript has been discovered since Yakut's work became known to the Western world.[3] It may be seen from these descriptions that the Rusi to which they refer were of Norse stock, though it is equally clear that though they were Norse by origin, they had begun to adapt themselves to Oriental ways, especially to those of their neighbours, the Slav and Finno-Ugrian tribes. The descriptions are very obviously exaggerated (especially Ibn Fadhlan's); in particular those of items reported at second hand and not actually seen; slovenliness and boorishness are described in gross terms, as is their

---

[1] V. O. Klyuchevskii, *A History of Russia*, London, 1911–31, 1, 80.

[2] See below, pp. 79ff.

[3] Ibn Dustah was edited by D. A. Khwolson, *Известия Козарах...Славянах и Русах Ибн Даста*, Saint Petersburg, 1869; there is a partial translation into Swedish in *Grunnläggning*, 34–6; another partial translation is in H. Birkelund, *Nordens Historie i Middelalderen efter arabiske Kilder*, Oslo, 1954, 14ff. An edition and German translation of Ibn Foszlan is provided by C. M. Frähn, *Ibn Foszlan und andere Araber Berichte über die Russen älterer Zeit*, Saint Petersburg, 1823; a more recent German translation is in *Ibn Fadlans Reisebericht*, tr. A. Z. V. Togau, Leipzig, 1939 (reprinted 1966); a much shortened Swedish translation is in *Grunnläggning*, 38–44.

shameless womanizing, and one is obliged to suspect that the truthfulness of these tales is on a par with descriptions of Iceland by foreign writers of the calibre of Ditmar Blefken.[1]

Even though one must acknowledge that these Norsemen played a large part in the creation of the great, widespread Russian state, this part must not be exaggerated. For one thing they did not appear as a nation of settlers, but as groups of warriors who were eventually absorbed into the populace over whom they had gained a temporary mastery. By the time of the reign of St Vladimir the two races were largely unified and, though Norse speech and nomenclature survived better in some of the noble families, it may be seen how the Slavonic elements were gradually ousting the intruders; thus a great lord would often have both a Norse and a Slavonic name (e.g. Haraldr and Mstislav were one and the same person).[2] The process was slowest in the court and in the Norse *Druzhiny*, 'friendly battalions' in the service of the Grand Princes. One may reasonably surmise that the 6000 Varangians who helped St Vladimir to his throne, and whom he sent later to the assistance of Basil II, would have spoken Norse, as one knows that Haraldr Sigurðarson, later King of Norway, and his regiment of Northerners in the service of Michael IV, did. The last record of Varangians in the service of the Russian princes is in fact of that time, in the year 1043.[3]

---

[1] See P. E. Ólason, *Menn og menntir á Íslandi á siðaskiptaöld*, Reykjavík, 1919–26, IV, 120–37; J. Benediktsson, *Arngrímur Jónsson and his works* (Bibliotheca Arnamagnæana XII), Copenhagen, 1957, 358–78.

[2] The author has given no evidence for this curious statement, presented thus baldly in the Icelandic version of this book, and the reviser can find no possible historical or philological backing for it, unless the list of names in the Russo-Byzantine treaty of 911 (see Ch. 3 below and p. 36, n. 3 there) were intended as such. Certainly the reviser has found no reference to Haraldr Sigurðarsson being called *Mstislav*, nor do the names bear even a remotely similar meaning, *Haraldr* being an elided form of *her-valdr*, 'ruler of soldiers', 'general', while Мстислав is a compound of мстить, 'to avenge', and слава, 'glory,' and hence bears the basic meaning 'glorious avenger', which would have to be more than a little twisted to mean anything remotely analogous to *Haraldr*. Nor can the Мстислав mentioned in *Повесть Временных Лет* (*Полное Собрание Летописей*), ed. E. F. Karskii, Leningrad, 1926–9 (reprinted 1962), under the years 1022–37, possibly be Haraldr, as he would have been seven years old on the first occasion when the other is referred to as a mature general!

[3] Cf. Braun, 'Historisches Russland' as above, p. 8, n. 3.

2

The army and navy of the High Byzantine Empire

The following chapter is by way of a brief introductory sketch to help readers assess the position of the Varangians in the military organization of the Empire, and as such it lays no claim to originality of either information or interpretation.[1]

The military organization of the High Byzantine empire was based on its political division. During our period (from *c.* 800 onwards) the Empire was divided by themes which, in the reign of Theophilus (829–42) numbered 11 in Asia and 12 in Europe. Each theme provided its corps of soldiers, and the term was sometimes used both of the district and the force supplied by it, the soldiers being known as

---

[1] The principal works consulted in the composition and revision of this chapter have been: F. Ausserasses, 'L'armée byzantine à la fin du VI siècle d'après le *Stratégicon* de l'Empereur Maurice', *Bibliothèque des Universités du Midi*, XIV, 1909; L. Bréhier, *Les institutions de l'Empire Byzantin*, Paris, 1949; J. B. Bury, *A History of the Eastern Roman Empire*, London, 1912 (hereafter referred to as *ERE*); H. Gelzer, *Die Genesis der byzantinischen Themen* (Abhandlungen der Königl. Sächs. Gesellsch. d. Wissenschaften, Philos.-Hist. Klasse XVIII), Dresden, 1899; H. Glykatzi-Ahrweiler, *Byzance et la mer*, Paris, 1965; the same, *Études sur les structures administratives et sociales de Byzance*, London, 1971; J. M. Hussey (ed.), *The Byzantine Empire* (Cambridge Medieval History, vol. IV), London, 1962–4 (hereafter referred to as *CMH*); Ibn Khurdadhbeh, *Liber viarum et regnorum*, ed. M. J. de Goeje, Leiden, 1889; N. Kalomenopoulos, 'Η στρατιωτικὴ ὀργάνωσις τῆς Ἑλληνικῆς ἀβτοκρατορίας τοῦ Βυζαντίου, Athens, 1937; P. Mutafciev, *Войнжки земи и Воиниси ъ Византия през XIII–XIV*вв. (Израни Произведения I), Sofia, 1973, 518–652; C. Neumann, 'Die byzantinische Marine', *Historische Zeitschrift*, 81 (1898), 1–23; N. Oikonomides, *Les listes de préséance byzantines des IXe et Xe siècles*, Paris, 1972; C. W. C. Oman, *A history of the art of war in the Middle Ages*, 2nd edn., London, 1898; G. Ostrogorskii, *History of the Byzantine Empire*, trsl. J. M. Hussey, 2nd edn., London, 1968; E. Stein, *Untersuchungen zur spätbyzantinischen Verfassungs- und Wirtschaftsgeschichte*, Hanover, 1925 (hereafter referred to as *Untersuchungen*); N. Svoronos, *Société et organisation intérieure dans l'empire Byzantin au XI siècle*, Oxford, 1966; F. J. Uspenskii, Военнии историство византиискои империи, *Извезтия Русскаго Археологическаго Института в Константинополе*, Sofia, 1900; A. Vogt, *Basile I*, Paris, 1908.

stratiotai. Two districts, the Cibirriote theme on the South coast of Asia Minor, and the theme of the Islands, were responsible for the provision of the naval force of the Mediterranean fleet.[1] In the frontier districts, moreover, there were garrison forts and heavily fortified mountain passes which were under the military control of the governors of smaller districts, the *kleisourai* (prob. derived from Lat. *clausura*). The governors of the larger themes were known as *strategoi*, and those of the smaller ones as *kleisourarchoi*, though Italy and Sicily, as long as they were Byzantine provinces (Sicily to 1043, Italy to 1071) were known as *katepanata*, and their governor as *katepano*. Military commanders of smaller districts are also found with the titles *Dux* or *Archon*.[2] The commanders of the largest themes were also patricians in rank, and the salaries of the various commanders differed greatly according to the size and importance of their commands.

The stratiotai who formed the bulk of this force lived on lands granted to them by the state, and drew their income from this property, which was hereditary, and could not be sold (except from property granted to the commanders). An especially notable class of feudal soldiers were the Akrites, a hardy and long-lasting soldier-people who occupied the border themes of the hills at the eastern end of Asia Minor, and of whose renown there has survived the great eleventh-century poem *Digenes Akritas*.[3] In the reign of the red-tape minded Constantine IX, however, this organization was overturned, and the main emphasis was laid on recruiting foreign mercenaries, and the feudal soldiery gradually declined in importance and ability.

Separate additional fiefs, the *pronoia*, were granted for outstanding services to others as well as soldiers, but in particular to military commanders, in return for which the feudatory was to supply a prescribed number of soldiers.[4] Each theme had a duty to provide two or three 'brigades', each of which was divided into a number of *droungoi* ('battalions'), and each *droungos* into five *banda* ('companies', hence mod. Eur. 'band'). There was however a considerable difference in the numbers of these units from time to time.[5] Thus it is possible to see that a *bandon* was at an early date reckoned as 200 men, while later it had risen to *c*. 400, and the *droungos* therefore fluctuated between 1000 and 2000. It also appears that the original number of *droungoi* in a *tourma* was five, but later only three; the original *tourma* was therefore at first *c*. 5000 strong, and later larger. The commander of a *tourma* was

[1] *ERE*, I, 221ff.   [2] *ERE*, I, 223.

[3] *Digenis Akritas*, ed. and tr. J. Mavrogordato, Oxford, 1956.

[4] Mutafciev, *Воинжски земи*, esp. 516ff.; Ostrogorskii, *Byzantine Empire*, 330, 371, 482 and refs. there; see also Ostrogorskii, 'La pronoia', *Byzantion*, 22 (1952), 437–518, for a weighty study of the whole problem of *pronoia*.   [5] *ERE*, I, 226.

normally of the rank of spatharocandidate, and was titled *tourmarchos*, the commander of a *droungos* a *droungarios*, the company commander a *komes* (origin of mod. Eur. 'Count'). The non-commissioned officers were respectively centurions, commanders of fifty (*pentekontarchoi*), and decurions.[1] The senior commanders were mostly men of good old noble families, who gave their best men into the service of the state. Many of these families were landowners in Asia, and some of them even provided imperial dynasties or great warrior emperors (e.g. the Phocae and the Comneni). It was not unknown, however, for a man of lowly origins to climb up the ladder of military success to the highest commands, or even to the imperial throne (e.g. Basil I).

It is reckoned that the permanent armed force kept by the Byzantine emperors of the High Byzantine period from the feudal levies was around 80,000, mostly cavalry; some argue that the number was higher, but it is not likely to have been a larger force than 120,000 men at most.

Besides this permanent levy of men from the Empire itself, there was also a second force, not tied to its territorial fiefs like the feudatories, but used in the first instance as a defensive garrison for the capital, and also as a mobile reserve for any urgent military need or other action. This was the so-called *tagmata*, 'free force'.

The *tagmata* consisted of four regiments of cavalry: the *Scholae*, the *Excubitores*, the *Arithmos* (or *Vigla*), and the *Hikanatoi*. The first three were of ancient origin, dating back to before the time of Theodosius I, but the *Hikanatoi* were of mid-Byzantine date, being founded by Nicephorus I at the beginning of the ninth century. The commanders of these regiments were named Domestics, except for the commander of the *Vigla*, who bore the title *droungarios*. Each *tagma* was divided into brigades over which there presided a *topoteretes*, the equivalent of the turmarch of a thematic regiment, and divisions of these forces were constantly around the capital as guards. At the beginning of the ninth century each regiment was composed of 4000–6000 men, but later the complement was smaller. Thus we can see in the narrative of the Cretan expedition of 949 that a brigade of Excubitores, with its topoterete and other officers, in all some 700 men, and a company of *Hikanatoi* with its complement of officers, in all some 456 men, were sent as part of this expeditionary force. Bury notes that the latter brigade had 56 officers, and 400 men; what is also noteworthy is that the regiments were

---

[1] This division approximates to that given by Ibn Khurdadhbeh, *Liber viarum*, 84. There were, of course, various changes during the long period covered by this book; cf. A. Rambaud, *L'empire grec au Xe siècle: Constantin Porphyrogennète*, Paris, 1870, 199–208, and Svoronos, *Société et organisation*, passim.

described as being 'on the other side' (i.e. of the Bosphorus), which could suggest that their quarters were over on the eastern side of the channel at that time.[1] Later on other regiments were founded, such as the 'Immortals' (*Athanatoi*), started by John I Tzimisces, who were reconstructed by Michael VII, in whose days they acquired a great reputation which they retained in the days of the succeeding emperors, being regarded as exceptionally skilful horsemen and archers;[2] other such units were the *Archontopouloi*, 'sons of officers', set up as a brigade in the days of Alexius I and manned by the sons of officers who had fallen in battle, and the *Megathymoi* 'the brave', who acquired a great reputation in the days of Michael IV and have been considered by some to have been Varangians (see below, p. 74). Generally speaking, only men of good family were admitted to these units, or young men of foreign extraction with good connections or promise, and Turks, Slavs, Arabs and other foreigners who had been brought up as Christians were often brought up as soldiers in these divisions. It was therefore natural that these four regiments became in time the especial life-guards of the emperors.

The capital had also for its defence a division of infantry which bore the Latin name *Numeri*, but must not be confused with the *Arithmos*: this division was some 4000 strong.[3] There is also reference to *optimates* as an infantry division, and finally there was a special division of guards of the city walls, which was commanded by a Count, who was also sometimes the commander of the *Numeri*, and was frequently of the rank of *protospatharios*. In the last days of the empire he was also the general supervisor of the defences of all fortified towns.

Let us now turn to look at the principal military divisions insofar as they were given duties at the Court, or as life-guards.[4]

The *Scholae* were particularly in charge of the defences of the imperial palaces, as well as generally available as guards for the city. In this regiment were young Greek noblemen, many themselves from Constantinople and its neighbourhood, and it would appear that these lived at home except when on actual guard duty at the palaces. Seven halls were assigned to them in the palace quarter, and the regiment

---

[1] Constantine Porphyrogennetos, *De Ceremoniis*, ed. I. Bekker (CSHB), Bonn, 1829, 1, 666 (hereafter referred to as *DC* (CSHB)); J. B. Bury, *The Imperial Administrative System of the 9th Century*, London, 1910, 64.

[2] Leo the Deacon, *Historiarum libri X*, ed. C. B. Hase (CSHB), Bonn, 1828, 107; Nicephorus Bryennius, *Commentarii*, ed. A. Meineke (CSHB), Bonn, 1836, 133–4; Michael Attaleiates, *Historiae*, ed. I. Bekker (CSHB), Bonn, 1835, 306.

[3] Ibn Khurdadhbeh, *Liber viarum*, 197; he also mentions another infantry regiment, the *Optimates*, as being some 4000 strong.

[4] *De Ceremoniis*, ed. A. Vogt (Classiques Budé), Paris 1935–40, 1, 19 (hereafter referred to as *DC* (Budé)); cf. also Stein, *Untersuchungen*, 42–50.

appears to have been divided originally into seven brigades – indeed, in the tenth century there appear to have been fifteen. From Constantine VII's description we can see that around 950 the *Excubitores* occupied the Third School, the so-called *candidati* (named from their white uniforms) the First and Second Schools;[1] the Fourth School was referred to as the *Triklinos ton Scholon*, the main body of the Scholae presumably inhabited it. The Fifth, Sixth and Seventh Schools were presumably allocated to the other three guards' regiments.[2]

The Domestic of the Schools was, next to the Emperor, the Commander in Chief of the Byzantine armed forces. In the later period of our study this office was divided, one being the Domestic for the Asian themes, and the other for the European themes; after the mid eleventh century we find him often referred to as the Grand Domestic (*Megas Domestikos*).

The other officers of the Guards' regiments were as a class named the *Basilikoi*, and their two senior officers (originally one) the Catepan and the Domestic, the Catepan taking precedence. The commander of the *Scholae* (the regiment, not the complex of palace guards) was also the leader of the Blue faction in the Hippodrome, and the commander of the *Excubitores* led the Greens; each of them having a civilian lieutenant, who was entitled to attend the Court on high festivals.

The *Excubitores* were, like the *Scholae*, originally the sons of the nobility. Their Domestic was next in rank after the Domestic of the Schools. The regiment consisted of eighteen or more companies; early on the Varangians appear to have entered the quarters of this division and had the use of their accommodation in the old palaces,[3] though *Excubitores* appear alongside them as late as the end of the fourteenth century.[4]

The *Vigla* (or *Arithmos*) had the duty of night-watch over the imperial palaces, and also in the military quarters. Special guides were assigned to this division in every theme that the army passed through when on an expedition away from the capital, as were representatives of the governors of the themes, to whom the Emperor sent his com-

---

[1] *DC* (CSHB), II, 77ff.   [2] *DC* (Budé), I, 54–6.

[3] We may see that the Varangians were quartered in the Excubita, and that the main route into the palaces was through or past their quarters, from the story told by Zonaras of John Comnenus' problem over entering the Imperial palaces after his father's death (Zonaras, *Annales*, ed. M. Pinder and T. Büttner-Wobst (CSHB), Bonn, 1841–97, III, 763): 'When he [John] was about to go off he was told that the Varangians had seized the route through the Excubita, where their quarters were also, and that they were permitting no one to go by that way, nor yet to approach the palace [by that route].' The term used is *Βάραγγοι*, and the phrase τὴν ἐν τοῖς ἐξκυβίτοις leaves no doubt as to the whereabouts of their guardroom.

[4] F. Miklosich and J. Müller, *Acta et diplomata graeca medii aevi*, Vienna, 1860–90, II, 50, 476, 485, 554 (Hereafter referred to as MM, *Acta*).

mands. On such expeditions the commander of the *Vigla* went his rounds at night, preceded by a torch-bearer, to make sure that watchmen were at their posts, nor could any person leave the camp without his permission. The *Vigla* survived as late as the fourteenth, and even into the fifteenth century.[1]

The *Hikanatoi* appear to have been less used for life-guard duties than the other regiments, but were much used as garrison forces. Their Domestics appear frequently at Court, however, and are referred to under that head in Constantine VII's *De Ceremoniis*.[2]

Finally the *Spatharioi Basilikoi*, the 'imperial sword-bearers', must be mentioned. In the reign of Manuel Comnenus this division had its name changed to the *Paramonai*, under which title it is mentioned in 1171.[3] The *Paramonai* were divided into two *allagia*,[4] the one infantry, the other cavalry, each commanded by a *protallagator*. This division may originally have been a section of the *Vigla*;[5] on the other hand the title of spathariote was often given as an honorific to various officials without being accompanied by any specific duties.

Besides his own troops, the Byzantine emperor had also foreign mercenaries in his service, and at times they appear to have been of more importance than the Byzantine forces. It was very common for emperors to translate the inhabitants of conquered districts to distant parts of the Empire, and settle them there, thus obtaining very good soldiers in due course; this was, for instance, done by Manuel I after his expedition to Hungary, when he moved 10,000 Hungarians into the Asiatic themes, and made them feudal farmers with a military-service duty. Men of these conquered races were organized in separate units in the army, and there are several records of their gallantry in action. Besides imperial subjects, however, there were also direct mercenaries in these units, men from nations with which the emperors had been in conflict, such as Normans, Turks, Italians, Frenchmen, Germans, Hungarians and various Caucasian tribes such as Georgians and Armenians, Arabs, Khazars, Farghans from south of the Caucasus, some Slavonic peoples, especially Russians, and last, but by no means least, Norsemen (in particular Swedes from the Russian plains), i.e. Varangians. Some divisions of this mercenary force were kept in the capital, and formed a part of the life-guard force there. The overall name for these troops was the *Hetairia*, and its Commander in Chief was the *Megas Hetairarchos*, who held the rank of *stratarchos*, and

[1] Pseudo-Codinus, *De Officiis*, ed. J. Verpeaux, Paris, 1966, 249–50 (hereafter referred to as DO). [2] *DC* (CSHB) I, 61 and II, 154–5.
[3] Nicetas Choniates, *Historia*, ed. I. Bekker (CSHB), Bonn, 1835, 224 and *passim*.
[4] Michael Attaleiates, *Historiae*, 149. [5] Stein, *Untersuchungen*, 48–50.

military science to a fine art in the time of High Byzantium, certainly
to a far more advanced degree than any other European state of that
period. Their particular strength lay both in their science, their discipline and in their constant and large choice of exceptionally able
generals and other higher officers. They looked down on the Western
barbarians with their undisciplined military habits such as wild on-
rushes before the general had given the order to attack, and had con-
tempt for such uncontrolled behaviour. They themselves considered
good discipline and skilful generalship of far more value than any
individual valour, though they knew how to value such bravery; and,
as history has shown, the Byzantine reliance on discipline and skill
gave them the victory again and again in situations where the big
battalions looked unassailable.

Our next consideration concerns the pay of the Imperial forces.[1] The
army from the themes received their main pay from their feudal grants
of land, but it is reckoned that each recruit received one nomisma
during his first year of service, two the next, and so on up to 12–18
nomismata. Over this basic rate, however, there were also takings from
expeditions, and special payments when an expedition was begun, and
these could make a lot of difference to a soldier's income. The normal
division of the booty was: one sixth to the Emperor, and the rest
divided into two parts; one for the commanders-in-chief, the other for
the soldiers. On occasions, however, the Emperor's portion was also
given to soldiers who had rendered exceptional service.[2] It is also
mentioned that sometimes the pay was only received by them every
third year, or even less frequently; at such times only a proportion of
the army would be paid each year,[3] though this will hardly have applied
to mercenary units, nor to military units which were situated close to
actual or possible theatres of war, since even civil servants know what
is good for their safety.

Officers were of course better paid than the common soldiers; the
senior generals (a *strategos* or a *patrikios*) received up to 40 pounds of
gold per annum at the highest level, and so in descending order down
to the junior generals, who received around 12 pounds of gold. It is
difficult to estimate the pay of the soldiers of the tagmata with any
certainty, though one can reckon that it was even higher in the High
Byzantine era, especially in the life-guards where those wishing to

[1] On this point see Ibn Khurdadhbeh, *Liber viarum*, 85ff.; *ERE*, 225ff.; Vogt, *Basile I*, 363–
7; Gelzer, *Genesis*, 114ff.
[2] 'Ο Πρόχειρος Νόμος, ed. C. E. Zachariae von Lingenthal, Heidelberg, 1837, 257–8.
[3] *DC* (CSHB), 1, 693; Ibn Khurdadhbeh, *Liber viarum*, 81; *ERE*, 1, 226.

join had to pay high fees to get in. Constantine VII observes[1] that anyone wanting to join the Grand Hetairia had to pay an entrance fee of at least 16 pounds of gold, for which he was to receive a *roga* (see below) of up to 40 nomismata, while if he wanted a higher one the entrance fee was raised at a rate of 1 pound of gold (72 nomismata made up the pound) for each 7 nomismata of additional *roga*. We may deduce from this that the *roga* was paid monthly; thus his additional pay of 7 nomismata per month accumulated to 84 nomismata per annum, and the soldier would thus gain 12 nomismata on his investment in the course of the year. On this reckoning the year's full ordinary *roga* would be 40 × 12, i.e. 480 nomismata, which explains the enormous entrance-fee – and at the same time we can calculate that the soldier would recoup his investment in about three years, and begin to accumulate gains after that at a very respectable rate.

The entrance fee for the Mid Hetairia was 10 pounds (720 nomismata) for each entrant, if he wished for a *roga* of 20 nomismata a month, and in proportion if he stipulated for more. In the Khazar and Farghan company (the Third Hetairia) the entrance fee was 7 pounds (504 nomismata), while the *roga* was 12 nomismata a month.

Bury calculates differently,[2] reckoning that the entrance fee was to bring an annual reimbursement at a rate of $2\frac{2}{5}$ to 4 per cent, and gives as an example a Khazar receiving 12 nomismata (at Bury's rate of exchange £7.20), having paid as entrance fee £302.40 (504 nomismata). On this rate (1 nomisma = £0.60), 7 pounds (504 nomismata) is correctly worked out, but this payment was a *once for all* payment, and Bury reckons the sum of 12 nomismata as the *annual* pay of the soldier, whereas this rate was the *monthly* one; multiplied by twelve his income of £86.40 accords much better with the scale of the entrance fee, since, among other things, the Byzantine authorities did not expect a man to spend between 25 and 40 years in recouping his expenses in joining their forces – nor would they have attracted many able foreigners into their service on that scale. (To obtain the sterling equivalent of the mid-1970s it is necessary to multiply by at least 10).

It was the custom at one point during the High Byzantine period for the Emperor to distribute the *roga* in person during Passion Week to the highest military officers, and their salaries to the high court officers, at the same time giving them robes of honour, while the Grand Chamberlain (*Parakoimomenos*) did the distribution to the lower ranks of civil and military officials. This activity lasted right through Holy Week as well, as has been attested by Liutprand of Cremona.[3]

[1] *DC* (CSHB), I, 692–3; *ERE*, I, 227 and 228, n. 5.   [2] *ERE*, I, as above.
[3] Liutprand, *Antapodosis* (MGH), Hanover, 1877, VI, 10.

It must be noted that the word *roga* has not always been interpreted in the same way, and can be found as meaning additional payments, as presents or as direct preparatory expenses in connection with an expedition, or else special bonus payments to the soldiery on special occasions. Thus the description in *De Ceremoniis*[1] of the preparations for the naval expedition to Crete in 902 refers to 700 *Rhosi* who took part in the operation, and were paid between them 7200 nomismata in *roga* which suggests an ex gratia payment averaging 11 nomismata each, though one must recollect that commissioned and non-commissioned officers will have received 2–3 times as much as the common soldiery. This payment is a little below the ordinary pay of the members of the Third Hetairia, though some soldiers there appear to have received no more than 5 nomismata, and Bury may well be right in his suggestion[2] that it is not a safe deduction to calculate the ordinary pay from the figures given for this expedition and the one of 949,[3] when 629 *Rhosi* were said to have taken part, since the sums given may well only refer to the extra expenses involved in these costly military expeditions, involving as they did the transport of a large army by sea over long distances. We should also note that *roga* is used as the term for the yearly pay to the garrison in Crete in the reign of Andronicus II.[4]

P. Mutafciev has maintained that the roga was regarded in the twelfth and the thirteenth centuries as an ex gratia payment to the military, paid once a year, and that from the thirteenth century onwards only the mercenaries received a *roga*. He also points out that mercenaries received feudal lands in the thirteenth century, and that this was a commonplace in the time of the Comnenian dynasty.[5] We must remember in this context that in times of prosperity, such as the reigns of the Macedonian emperors, the Empire was in a strong financial position, and could pay higher wages in general, as well as higher military salaries, while after the death of Basil II the imperial affairs, not least financial ones, were in a very disturbed state. From the words of the anonymous *Strategikon* we may infer that the pay of the foreign mercenaries of the author's day (early in the reign of Alexius Comnenus) was fairly low, since the writer reckons it quite unnecessary for the Emperor to pay them a high emolument, as there was ample evidence that the past Emperors could obtain plenty of foreign mercenaries for their food and clothing only.[6] We must not accept this

[1] *DC* (CSHB), I, 654.   [2] *ERE*, I, 227, n.   [3] *DC* (CSHB), I, 664ff.

[4] G. Pachymeres, *De Michaele et Andronico Palaeologis*, ed. I. Bekker (CSHB), Bonn, 1835, II, 209.

[5] Mutafciev, *Воинжски земи, passim*; cf. also review of the original printing by F. Dölger, *BZ*, 26 (1923), 102–13.

[6] Cecaumenus, *Strategikon*, ed. B. Vasilevskii and P. Jernstedt, Saint Petersburg, 1896, 95.

too literally, since the soldiers would always get a certain part of all booty and presents when a new Emperor succeeded to the throne, as well as on other special occasions. Further, it is certain that the pay in the life-guards would be higher than elsewhere in the army – if only for the sake of the imperial safety.

The works referred to concerning the pay of the *Rhosi* in the Cretan expeditions are the only known Greek sources which give some slight indication of the probable pay of the Varangians, besides what may be deduced from Constantine VII's explanations of the entrance fee to the life-guard units. There is, however, no indication there as to how high their emoluments could rise, nor are there any descriptions of the differences between the pay of officers, non-commissioned officers and men. We can be certain, however, that once the Varangians had become a separate military unit they would receive the highest rate going, that is, the rate of pay in the Grand Hetairia (*c.* 40 nomismata a month) and have had to purchase their places in the division when they had been in service long enough to save the entrance fee. It is however possible that Basil II, or one of his immediate successors, changed the system of purchasing entrance by either abolishing it or else lowering the charges greatly, even though the pay became less in consequence. There was also a great difference made between the 'Varangians within the city' and the 'Varangians without the City', whose emoluments were undoubtedly much lower. Schlumberger surmises that the latter received only 10–15 nomismata per month, which is not unlikely when one takes into account the rates of the *roga* in the Cretan expedition of 902 and the pay of the Farghans in the Third Hetairia.[1]

Besides the share of the booty and his presents at the accession of the new Emperor, records speak of *pólútasvarf* as a source of income peculiar to the Varangians. This term has caused a good deal of conjecture, and will be given more detailed consideration later on in this book, when we come to the exploits of Haraldr Sigurðarson.

In view of such factors as the depreciation of the coinage under Michael VII, the loss of several provinces to the Seljuks and the general financial straits of the Empire in the reign of Alexius I, we may surmise with some certainty that even the favoured life-guards will have received a lower remuneration during this period than during the heyday of Byzantium. It must have helped their prospects, however, that soldiers who had served long and well (especially, of course, officers) received lands in *pronoia* and so had their old age secured; though they had then to settle permanently in the Empire, and so never see their

[1] Schlumberger, *Nicéphore*, 49.

homelands again. In the time of the Palaeologan emperors, not least that of Manuel II and his sons, the aura of greatness has departed, however, and we find the Emperors in a state of perpetual financial embarrassment, which in turn affected the size of the mercenary forces and their quality. During this period the last remnant of the Varangian regiment will have been retained for ceremonial or palace duties only, like the Swiss guards of the Papacy of modern times, still nominally a band, but now for ornament rather than use, and even these 'show-case guards' were likely to find it difficult to draw their pay.

'Navigantium fortitudo mihi soli inest', is a remark made by Nicephorus II (as reported by Liutprand).[1] Nicephorus could make this boast in truth, since the emperors of High Byzantium succeeded gradually in building up a fleet of such power as to check the depredations of Arab pirates almost completely in the eastern Mediterranean. During the latter part of the eleventh century, however, the Venetians and the Genoans gradually caught up with the Byzantine marine power and, despite the strenuous efforts of the Comnenian emperors to increase their naval forces, these represented the stronger force by the death of Manuel I (1180), while the Byzantine naval presence after the death of Michael VIII was derisory and in time it vanished altogether, so that John VIII had to make his way to the Council of Ferrara–Florence by hired craft.

The fleet of the naval era was divided into two main sections: the Imperial fleet and the fleet of the themes. The former was organized into two divisions, one for the personal use of the Emperor and Empress, and for the defence of the capital, the other for use on regular military expeditions and for policing the seas against pirates. The fleet of the themes was kept up at the charge of various maritime themes, particularly those of the Greek islands (Aegea, Samos, Cephalonia), Greece and the Cibirriote theme in Asia Minor. The regular servicemen from these themes were paid in feudal land, as were the land forces in the army of the themes. An alteration was however made in the reign of Manuel I, whereby the monies expended by the themes on the upkeep of the fleet were diverted straight into the Imperial treasury, and the Emperor assumed the direct responsibility for the maintenance of the whole naval service. This was probably intended as an assurance for the better order of the ships, but, as might have been foreseen, it proved a disaster, as the money was repeatedly spent on wasteful civil-service projects, while the navy was starved of even necessary funds.

[1] Liutprand, *Legatio* (MGH), Hanover, 1877, 148.

The fleet often employed foreign mercenaries, and Russian or Varangians who entered the Imperial service often began their time in the navy, this being a form of service which would have suited the temper of the Norse seamen. From what is recorded of Haraldr Sigurðarson we may deduce that his first period of Varangian service will have been spent thus (see below, Ch. 4).

The strategos of each maritime theme commanded his section of the thematic fleet, while the supreme commander was the commander of the Imperial fleet, who was titled in the High Byzantine era the *Droungarios*, and was of the rank of patrician.[1] This official appears to have been known in the reign of Alexius I as the Grand Duke (*Megas Doux*), and his deputy as the *Thalassokrator*,[2] while later still Pseudo-Codinus refers to an Admiral of the (by then insignificant) Fleet.[3] These supreme commanders had other officers under them, and officers of the Hetairia were set to command the foreign naval mercenaries. In the tenth century 77 ships constituted the thematic fleet against 100 in the Imperial fleet, while the force manning the latter was 23,000–24,000 strong, against 17,500 in the former.[4]

The capital ships of the Byzantine fleet were the *dromoi*, which differed considerably in size, but were built on the same pattern, with a wooden castle (*xylokastron*) on the deck, and carrying various military engines. In the bows was a figurehead of gilt bronze,[5] usually the shape of the head of a wild beast, the lion being a popular motif, in which were housed the siphon and pumping mechanism to spray out the *Greek Fire*, the terrible Byzantine secret weapon which burned alike on land and water.[6] This substance was also carried in fragile bowls or spheres of glass, which could be hurled on to the enemy ships and which then set everything that the stuff touched ablaze. The rowers were arranged in two banks, with a normal complement of 25 to each row; there were also on average some 50 soldiers on each dromos. It is calculated that there will have been around 220 persons to the full complement on a capital ship, or even more, since the account of the Cretan expedition of 902 refers to 230 oarsmen and 70 others, or in all a crew of 300 on each dromos.[7] The *Chelandia* were smaller vessels, one class of which

---

[1] *Cedrenus Scylitzae Ope*, II, 289. There is also mention down to the time of Basil I of the στρατηγικὸς καραβισιανός as the commander-in-chief of the fleet, while the commanders of the thematic fleets bore the title of δρουγγάριος. [2] Stein, *Untersuchungen*, 57.
[3] *DO*, 138, 301 etc. [4] Neumann, *Byzantinische Marine*, 5.
[5] On the δρόμοι, see Leo VI, *Opera* (Migne, *P.G.*, XIX, 4–6); Vogt, *Basile I*, 371–2; Schlumberger, *Nicéphore*, 41, 52, 64.
[6] The most complete collection of earlier material on this subject is in J. R. Partington, *A History of Greek Fire and Gunpowder*, Cambridge, 1960, esp. 42–90; an article which opens a new aspect of the subject is J. Haldon and M. Byrne, 'A possible solution to the problem of Greek Fire', *BZ* 70 (1977), 91–9. [7] *DC* (CSHB), I, 653.

were named _Pamphyloi_; they were often manned by foreign mercenaries, and their complement would be 130–160 men. Finally there were the light supporting vessels, the so-called _ousiai_, on which Varangians were frequently employed; these were swift and easily manoeuvred ships, which were especially useful for coastguard duty or for chasing and overtaking pirate vessels. The Τακτικά speaks of 50–60 soldiers forming the complement of each of these ships, and their total crew will therefore have been _c._ 110 strong.[1] On formal expeditions two _ousiai_ generally accompanied each major vessel.

The commander of each dromos bore the title of _Kentarchos_, while over each division of 3–5 capital ships there was placed a _komes_,[2] though the titles _komes_ and _droungarios_ are later used without discrimination of the captains of single ships. The fleet had its banner, the sign being a cross surrounded by four fire-siphons.[3]

It appears that admission to the Imperial fleet, and especially appointment to one of the ships based on the capital, or in the personal service of the Emperor and his court, was very much sought after by personnel in the other divisions of the Byzantine navy. As the pay was higher, and the serving personnel could more easily obtain high court distinctions in these ships, this is understandable, and it is very likely that it was necessary to purchase such appointments in the same way as ones in the land Hetairia (see above, pp. 25ff.). It is, however, even more difficult to calculate the naval rates of pay than those of the land forces, though some inkling may be derived from the above mentioned narratives of the two naval expeditions to Crete. The pay of the Russians and Varangians in the sea-forces will certainly have been far smaller than that of those in the Hetairia. If it is true, however, that the commanders of the coastal protection vessels were entitled to keep a considerable proportion of the goods confiscated from pirate vessels, then this could obviously make a very sizeable difference to their emoluments. It is noted in _Haraldar saga Sigurðarsonar_ that he was to pay the Emperor 100 marks for every pirate vessel that he was able to capture, but could keep the rest for himself and his men. This could obviously be a very valuable source of income.[4]

---

[1] Leo VI, _Opera_, 1004.
[2] Stein, _Untersuchungen_, 57.
[3] _DO_, 167.
[4] On the Cretan expedition, cf. _DC_ (CSHB), I, 651ff.; _ERE_, 231; _CMH_, IV, pt 1, 130; Ostrogorskii, _History of the Byzantine State_, 258–9 and refs. there. For Haraldr III's activities in the Byzantine navy see Ch. 4 below.

Norse and Russian Forces in the Byzantine army to the death of Romanos III[1]

The earliest records that can be said to give a fairly certain clue as to the presence of soldiery from the Russian/Norse territories are from the reign of Theophilus (829–42). During his tenure of the throne bands of Norse warriors entered Southern Russia and penetrated as far as the Black Sea, becoming a threat to the city of Cherson, the capital of the Chersonese theme of the Empire. The city called for help from the Emperor, who sent a garrison and a force to raise and man a fortress at Sarkel on the lower Don, in the lands of his Khazar allies, the intention being to protect both them and the imperial frontier.

These activities by the Imperial authorities probably led to a desire on the part of the Viking chieftains to make closer contacts with Byzantium. One piece of evidence suggests that they were certainly at the court in 836–39 – this is the passage in the *Annales Bertiniani* composed by Bishop Prudentius of Troyes.[2] Prudentius tells of the arrival of an embassy from Theophilus at the court of Louis the Pious, who received them at Ingelheim on 18 May 839. The leader of the mission was Theodore Babutzikios, who had died *en route*, but among the Greek emissaries were men from a nation called *Rhos*, whose king, *Chacanos*,[3] had sent them on a mission of friendship to Byzantium. Theophilus asked Louis for leave for these persons to return home through his territories, as the road by which they had come was im-

---

[1] A shortened version of this chapter was read as a communication at the XIIIth International Byzantine Congress, Oxford, 1966, and was published in 1969 (see above, Ch. 2, p. 21, n. 4); see also A. Stender-Petersen, 'Das Problem der ältesten byzantinisch-russisch-nordischen Beziehungen', *Relazioni del X Congresso Internazionale di Scienze Storiche*, Rome, 1955, III, 174ff.

[2] *Annales Bertiniani*, ed. G. Waitz (MGH), Hanover, 1883, 20.

[3] *Annales Bertiniani*, 20; also Genesius, *Basileion*, ed. C. Lachmann (CSHB), Bonn, 1834, 71, who refers to Louis as ὁ ῥὲξ Φραγγίας.

passable because of the depredations of hostile tribes. Having had considerable trouble from Norsemen on his frontiers for a number of years, Louis was understandably reluctant to let them pass when he discovered that these men were *gentis Sueonum,* and the emissaries were detained until he had satisfied himself of their genuineness.[1]

It is a fair certainty that these men were the emissaries of a Swedish Russian prince who was attempting to make a trading deal with the Empire, and it is not unreasonable to assume that Theophilus, whose reign included a long series of military reverses against the Bagdad caliphate (the dynastic city, Amorium, was lost to them in 838) was seizing the opportunity to negotiate for mercenary troops from Russia, since he was sufficiently short of troops to send an embassy to the Frankish emperor. Moreover, only a few years later, in the reign of Michael III, 'Russian' soldiers had certainly entered the Byzantine service, and were even found in the Imperial guards. The most reliable source for this is the narrative of the murder of the regent Theoctistus in the chronicle of Genesius.[2] The act itself was committed by *Tauroskuthai*, which was at that time a synonym for 'Russian', and the greatest likelihood is that the reference is to Norsemen from Russia.[3]

Four years later, when Michael III was absent from the capital on an expedition against the Arabs, Constantinople was attacked by a fleet of *Rhosi,* under the leadership of two chieftains, named by Nestor the Annalist *Askold* and *Dir'* which are clearly corruptions of the Norse names *Höskuldr* and *Dýri.* These pirates harried the districts around the Bosphorus, but were repelled by the citizens of the capital under the leadership of the Patriarch Photius when they attempted to attack the suburbs. The Emperor turned back hastily from the East, and a great storm appears to have destroyed most of the Russian fleet, while the remnant was thoroughly defeated by the Imperial troops and made to return to Russia, after which they sent messengers to Michael to sue for peace. New treaties were drawn up subsequently (before 866), in which it was specifically contracted that the Russians should send troops into the Emperor's service.[4] We may therefore assume that more

---

[1] *Annales Bertiniani,* 20; the name Khagan (Gk. Χαγάνος) was a title of the King of the Khazars, but in the present context the O.N. name Hákon seems to both author and reviser a likelier candidate; for one thing, it is known that a Swedish monarch, Hákon son of Hrærekr, was ruling in 844 (see J. Jónsson, *Víkinga saga,* Reykjavík, 1915, 153n.).
[2] Genesius, *Basileion,* 89.
[3] Further details of the murder are in *ERE,* I, 156–9, and Greek sources cited there.
[4] *Повесть Временных Лет (Полное Собрание Русских Летописей),* ed. E. F. Karskii, Leningrad, 1926–9 (repr. 1962), I, col. 21 (under 866, the assault only); cf. also *Chronique byzantine de MS Brux. 11. 376,* ed. F. Cumont, Ghent, 1894, 33–4, and C. de Boor, 'Der Angriff der Rhos auf Byzanz', *BZ,* IV (1895), 445ff.

Map 1   The Empire of Basil II, *c.* 1025

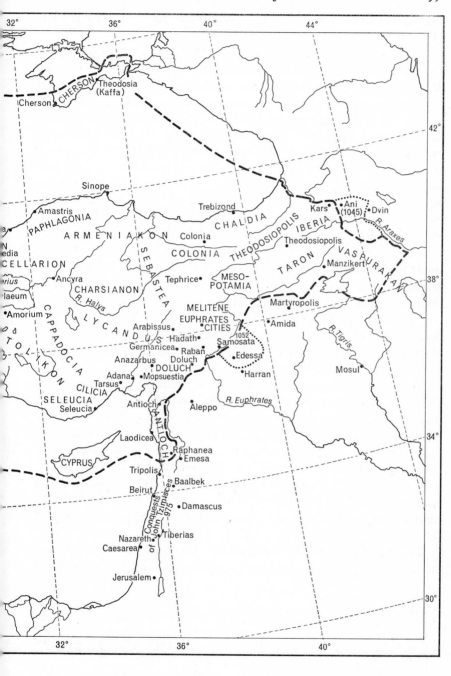

32° 36° 40° 44°

Cherson
CHERSON
Theodosia
(Kaffa)

42°

Sinope
Trebizond
Kars
Ani
(1045)
Dvin
R. Araxes

Amastris
PAPHLAGONIA
CHALIDIA
THEODOSIOPOLIS
IBERIA
VASPURAKAN

ARMENIAKON
Colonia
Theodosiopolis

COLONIA
TARON
Manzikert

edia
CELLARION
SEBASTEA
MESO-
POTAMIA

rius
Ancyra
Tephrice
38°

laeum
CHARSIANON
R. Halys
MELITENE
Martyropolis

Amorium
CAPPADOCIA
LYCANDUS
EUPHRATES
CITIES
Amida

Arabissus
Hadath
1052
Samosata
R. Tigris

TOLIKON
Germanicea
Raban
Edessa

Anazarbus
Doluch
Harran
Mosul

Adana
DOLUCH

Tarsus
Mopsuestia

CILICIA

SELEUCIA
Antioch
ANTIOCH
Aleppo
R. Euphrates

Seleucia
Laodicea

CYPRUS
Raphanea
Emesa
34°

Tripolis
Baalbek

Beirut
Conquests of John Tzimisces 975
Damascus

Nazareth
Tiberias

Caesarea

Jerusalem
30°

32° 36° 40°

Norsemen than before entered the Byzantine services during the last years of Michael III's reign.

Though there is no reason to believe that Basil I ceased to employ Russians of Norse origin, there is no direct reference to them in any Byzantine or other records of his military activities. The next actual note that we have of *Rhosi* is the already mentioned Cretan expedition of 902 (cf. above, p. 27), in which the 700 Russians received 7200 nomismata as their pay.[1] About the same time we have a reference by Nestor to an expedition by Prince Oleg (Helgi) of Kiev, which attacked the city of Constantinople by sea.[2] This attack (in 907) does not, however, appear to have been a great success, as there is no reference to it in comparable Byzantine records, even if Nestor makes much of it. Peace and a new trade pact were concluded in 911, in which conditions for the residence of the Russians in Constantinople were laid down, as well as for their part in the Imperial service; in this respect the Russians appear to have laid emphasis on being able to enter the army 'at whatsoever time they might come, and whatsoever their number.'[3] The names that are appended to this treaty are all of Norse origin, being Рурик (Hrœrekr), Карлы (Karl), Инегелд (Ingjaldr), Фарло (Farleifr), Веремоуд (Vermóðr), Рулав (Hralleifr), Гоуды (Gyði), Роуад (Hróaldr), Карн (Kári), Фрелав (Fréleifr) and Роал (Hróaldr, in another MS Pyap, 'Hróarr').

In the reign of Constantine VII we have quite a lot of evidence for 'Russian' contacts with the Empire. As has been mentioned earlier, they had made an expedition into the Black Sea as early as 830, when they also penetrated into the Caspian Sea.[4] Their largest raid came in 944, when they attacked the Southern Caucasus, captured the city of Berdaa in Azerbaizhan and used it as their base to harry the surrounding countries. The inhabitants defended themselves with vigour, however, and within the year the invaders had to retreat back to their own lands, though they are reported as taking with them a very great quantity of booty.

The other principal Russo-Byzantine event of the reign was the attack made by Igor (Ingvar) on Constantinople in 941. The principal

---

[1] See above, p. 27 and refs.

[2] *Повесть Временных Лет*, I, coll. 29–31 (under 907).

[3] *Повесть Временных Лет*, I, col. 33 (under 912). There has been considerable controversy as to whether this assault was real or imaginary; the arguments in favour of reality have been overwhelmingly presented by G. Ostrogorskii, 'L'expédition du Prince Oleg contre Constantinople en 907', *Annales de l'Institut Kondakov*, XI (1939), 47–62 and A. A. Vasilev, 'The Second Russian Attack on Constantinople', *Dumbarton Oaks Papers*, 6 (1961), 161–225.

[4] B. Dorn, *Каспи о походох древних Русских в Табаристан*, *Mémoires de l'Académie Impériale de S. Pétersbourg*, 7e série, 1ff.; cf. also V. G. Vasilevskii, *Русско-Византийская Исследованія (Труды, II)*, Saint Petersburg, 1908.

reason for this assault was probably that Constantine (or, rather, Romanos I, the reigning co-Emperor), had ceased to pay the retainers agreed in the treaty with Oleg, but whatever the pretext, this was naturally a pure act of piracy, as Igor probably knew that Romanos had sent the greater part of his fleet away on an expedition against the Arabs. There were, however, enough Greek ships left to do shattering damage to Igor's fleet with their armoury of Greek fire. He was forced to retreat after a heavy defeat, and after some desultory coastal raids he returned to Russia with, it is said, only 10 ships of all his original fleet. In 945 the original treaty with Oleg was renewed, with a few minor modifications, and the Empire and the Princedom of Kiev were declared allies in perpetuity against the depredations of other powers. Igor died shortly after this.[1]

It is possible to discern that some of the Kievan Russians were already Christians by this time, and that there was a church dedicated to St Elias in the town. When Igor's widow Olga (Helga) paid a state visit to Constantinople in 957 she was already a Christian convert, and in his detailed account of this visit[2] Constantine notes among other things that some Russians were baptized in the presence of the Court. In 949 we find Russian *ousiai* used as coastguard ships at Dyrrhachium and along the Dalmatian coast, while 629 'Russians' took part in the abortive expedition sent by Constantine VII to Crete in 949,[3] and one of Constantine's complaints to Olga was over his concern that the Russians had not kept their end of the bargain sufficiently well in respect of sending him troops when he needed their assistance. We find how-ever that a Russian troop was in the force led by Bardas Phocas in his Syrian campaign of 954–5. In the battle at Hadath, where Bardas was heavily defeated by Saif-ed-Dauleh (12 Nov. 955) we are told by Saif's poet Mutanabbi that with the Greeks there were on that occasion 'Russians',[4] and it is not unreasonable to surmise that other Russian units were with him on previous campaigns, such as the Syriac one of 947, in which he was also brought to a shattering defeat, caused, it was said, through his avarice, which was so great that he failed to give his mercenary troops their pay, and so they deserted him in mid-battle, from which he was narrowly rescued, sorely wounded, by his own servants and guards.[5]

[1] *Повесть Временныхъ Лѣтъ*, 1, 44 (under 941); the treaty is reported in coll. 46–54 (945).
[2] *DC* (CSHB), 1, 594ff.; see also *Повесть Временныхъ Лѣтъ*, 1, 60–4 (955).
[3] *DC* (CSHB), 1, 664.
[4] Mutanabbi, *Poem on Hadath*, tr. M. Canard (in A. A. Vasilev, *Byzance et les Arabes (867–959)*, Brussels, 1950, 331); cf. also Schlumberger, *Nicéphore*, 128–34.
[5] Rambaud, *L'Empire grec au Xe siècle: Constantin Porphyrogennète*, Paris, 1870, 425, assumes that these mercenaries were Russians and Bulgars.

After the dismissal of the incompetent Bardas, however, the Byzantines did better in their campaign against Saif-ed-Dauleh, especially after Basil the Chamberlain, Leo Phocas (brother of the Emperor Nicephorus) and John Tzimisces obtained commands and gained a number of serious victories. After Constantine's death, during the reign of his son and successor, Romanos II, a third Cretan expedition was sent off under the command of Nicephorus Phocas, which was finally successful. Leo the Deacon describes how at the first landing the Arabs had ranged themselves defensively along the shore, but that a Greek regiment (thought to have been a force of Russians by Schlumberger) led the assault on the defences, singing hymns to the Virgin (which would suggest that they must then have been Christian Russians) and broke through them. Thanks to their intrepidity, Nicephorus was able to land his troops, and gradually to conquer the whole island, the capital, Candace, falling in the following year.[1]

It is reasonable to believe that Nicephorus would have used some of the Russian troops from his Cretan expedition when he went to command the main army in the Taurus hills in a campaign against Saif-ed-Dauleh which ended in triumph with the capture of most of Saif's capital, Aleppo, on 23 December, 962 (though the Byzantines failed to capture the inner citadel).

At this point Nicephorus turned aside from the Syrian campaign, as a crisis in the government of the Empire occurred on the death of the dissolute Romanos II, who left only two small sons to share the imperial title. As a result of the subsequent intrigue and counter-intrigue he was eventually acclaimed and crowned as Emperor on 16 August 963. Prior to this, however, the eunuch Bringas, who had attempted to manoeuvre power into his own hands, attempted to raise an army against him, but this rebellion was put down by Basil the Chamberlain, who commanded the Grand Hetairia in the reign of Constantine, and so was very likely to have had Russians in his service (he was said to have had a private army of 3000 men).[2] Because of the frequent references to *Rhosi* in his various commands, some, including Schlumberger, have assumed that there was a separate Varangian regiment in the life-guards of Nicephorus Phocas, which was present at this coronation, but this cannot be right;[3] some Norsemen may have been members of the Hetairia, but they would only have been there as

---

[1] Nicephorus' Cretan expedition is described by Leo the Deacon, *Historiarum libri X*, ed. C. B. Hase (CSHB), Bonn, 1829, 24ff. and Theodosius Akroasis, *Ἅλωσις Κρήτης* (ed. by C. B. Hase in the same edition as Leo, 259ff.; modern studies are in *Nicéphore*, 25–79 and I. B. Papadopoulos: *Ἡ Κρήτη ὑπὸ τοὺς Σαρακηνούς (824–961)*, Athens, 1948, 90ff.
[2] *Nicéphore*, 295 (though Schlumberger does nothing more here than rehash Leo and other standard Byzantine writers).　　　　[3] *Nicéphore*, 307.

individuals, and not as a unit with the specific honorific responsibilities which were later given to Varangians.

In Nicephorus's reign we find *Rhosi* mentioned as part of the force sent to Sicily under the command of Manuel and Nicetas Phocas, sons of the Emperor's brother Leo, in 964–5, which was however resoundingly defeated at Rametta.[1] Ibn-el-Athir relates that among the booty sent back to the Caliph Muizz of Tunis by his victorious commander were 200 selected Greek mercenaries, who Schlumberger thinks may have been Russians and Armenians.[2] It is also possible that these entered the Caliph's service and were among the troops which he sent under his vizir Djauhar to conquer Egypt in 969.

As a consolation for his Sicilian mishaps, Nicephorus succeeded in conquering Cyprus back from the Arabs. The commander of this expedition was Nicetas Chalkutzes, and it may be regarded as certain that many of the naval troops which went were chosen from those who had accompanied the Emperor on his victorious campaign in Crete, and so will have included a number of Russians. In the capital, however, the Emperor was no longer as popular as of old, as his austere personal life, rigidly disciplinarian government, and heavy-handed methods of taxation for the financing of his expensive foreign wars all combined to turn the favour of the populace away from him. When the imperial practice of minting coinage of less metal-worth than its official value was added to these, rioting began. On Easter Day 967 sailors and dock-labourers fought against Armenian troops from the Hetairia, and on Ascension Day the same year the Emperor was stoned and assaulted by a crowd while in procession around the city. All this incited Nicephorus to improve the defences of the Imperial palaces. The Bukoleon was made into a particularly impregnable fortress, and from this time there are references to the *upper* and the *lower* palace. Schlumberger thinks that the upper is Nicephorus II's construction, while the lower was the older Bukoleon.[3] This point has some relevance for the history of the Varangians, in that it is likely that the guardroom of the life-guards, and hence of the Varangians, after they became the regular life-guards, was in the upper palace, while there are inscriptions on shield-decorations in the lower palace which may possibly have been scratched there by Varangians.[4] We are also told that the Emperor exercised these guards daily.[5]

In 967 Nicephorus went on a campaign against the Bulgars, but

---

[1] Leo the Deacon, *Historiarum*, 65–8; Ibn-el-Athir: *Kamil fit-ta ta'rih*, tr. M. Canard (in Vasilev, *Byzance et les Arabes*, 160–1 and by Birkelund, *Nordens Historie*, 92–3); cf. also *Nicéphore*, 447–9.   [2] *Nicéphore*, 459.   [3] *Nicéphore*, 546, n. 1.
[4] See below, p. 233 and refs. there.   [5] Leo the Deacon, *Historiarum*, 50–1.

found that he had other matters of greater moment to attend to at home, and so left Prince Svyatoslav of Kiev to harry them. Svyatoslav conquered a great part of the Bulgarian territories in a short while, but an attack on his own lands by the Pechenegs caused him to turn back. The upshot of this alliance was to be a rift in the next reign, however, creating a situation in which Russian was to fight Russian.

Otto I, the German Emperor, had, after their Italian rencontres, made various peace-overtures to Nicephorus, and in 968–9 he sent to Constantinople an envoy, Liutprand, Bishop of Cremona, through whose reports to his master we are indebted for many details of the Byzantine life of the time. He is, for instance, in no doubt as to the nationality of the *Rhos*, stating bluntly, 'the Russians whom we call by the other name of Norsemen'.[1] Though, thanks to his own silliness, Liutprand was a notably unsuccessful ambassador, and his reports are impregnated with his hostility towards Nicephorus, he is, nevertheless, a witness with an observant eye for detail, and the present book is not a little indebted to his record of his experiences. During his mission Nicephorus sent a fleet to assist his hard-pressed provincial governor in Italy, and Liutprand noted that among the ships were two 'Russian' and two 'Frankish' vessels along with 24 Greek *chelandia*.[2] It is not unreasonable therefore to deduce that the troops on those four vessels were respectively Norsemen and Normans.

The last incident of note in which Norse Russians are likely to have been involved in the reign of Nicephorus II is the Emperor's murder during the night between 10 and 11 December 969. Despite every gate being guarded, the Empress Theophano succeeded in bypassing her husband's security precautions, and the assassins entered the Emperor's bedroom without hindrance and murdered him without opposition. At this point, however, the guards of the inner rooms became aware of the intrusion, and rushed to the scene. It has been suggested that these were Varangians,[3] but there is no certain evidence in the available accounts that they were, and at best we can only surmise that if there were Varangians in the fight, they were there as individuals, as before.

There is no specific reference to Varangians by any of their synonyms in the reign of John Tzimisces, but there was one military occasion when Russians gave the Empire quite a lot of trouble, and the eventual Byzantine triumph is likely to have stimulated the entry of Norse Russians into the Imperial forces. This was a legacy from Nicephorus II's Bulgarian policy. After his intervention at Nicephorus's request in the quarrel over the non-payment of a peace-subsidy agreed with

[1] Liutprand, *Works*, tr. F. A. Wright, London, 1930, 8.
[2] Liutprand, *Works*, 418; cf. also *Nicéphore*, 634.   [3] *Nicéphore*, 736.

Tsar Simeon I by Romanos I, Svyatoslav had been obliged at first to go home to defend Kiev against a Pecheneg attack, but had returned to the Bulgarian field and conquered a large portion of the country from Tsar Peter's successor. He considered himself cheated by his Byzantine allies, however, and so invaded the Empire and burnt and plundered Philippopolis in 970. This brought John Tzimisces into the field in person, and in the next two years he not only recovered the losses caused by the Russian invaders, but also crushed Svyatoslav completely in battles at Arcadiopolis, Prslav, and, finally, at Silistria, where he besieged the Russians until they were obliged to sue for peace. A new treaty was made between the two parties and, from our knowledge of Byzantine conservatism and reliance on precedent, it is not unreasonable to assume that it included provisions for the employment of Norse Russians in the Byzantine armed forces. In view of the events of the next reign, this possibility acquires an even greater likelihood, but it must be stressed that no documentary evidence now survives to this effect.

John Tzimisces died of dysentery, caught while on a military expedition in Syria, on 10 January 976. The elder of the sons of Romanos II, Basil, now became the reigning Emperor, and the next half-century, which saw the apogee of High Byzantium, also saw the eventual emergence of the unit which forms the basis of our study as a separate military force.

It is necessary to pause for a moment here to view the character of the great Emperor who founded the Regiment. At the time of his emergence from the tutelary state to two great and able co-Emperors, Basil was twenty years old. He had seen one of these father-figures murdered in a particularly treacherous and callous manner by the other, and, Byzantine rumour being what it was, had been made more suspicious by the death of the Emperor John in a distant corner of the Empire from a disease which produced symptoms only too similar to those of some kinds of poisoning; furthermore he had discovered that his mother was involved up to her neck in the murder of Nicephorus. Moreover, such being the political temper of the Greeks, assassination as a means of advancement was only too popular a game – had not Basil's ancestor and namesake, the founder of his dynasty, made his way to the throne by that very means? It must have seemed very clear to the instinctively suspicious young man that if he was to survive he must have servants who had no natural axe to grind, and who would be unquestioningly loyal so long as their pay was large and regular, and whose military ability was well above the average of even the excellent

Byzantine army. From his observation of Nicephorus, who had used the big barbarians from the wastes of Russia with great success on the most diverse expeditions, and whose great military skill as well as many of his less endearing personal characteristics had rubbed off on to his stepson (whose career was to show how powerfully he had been impressed by him) Basil would have been induced to think favourably of the Norsemen from the steppes in this capacity. In time, when they were to prove the saviours of his throne in the hour of its greatest peril, their obvious suitability must have decided him once and for all. For it is by the end of his reign that we find them firmly installed in Byzantine records in such a way that there is no longer any doubt as to their function or status.

There is also an adventitious element in the growth of the Norse section of Basil's army. This can be seen from a note in the Russian records of the period, which speak of the influx of a large party of Norsemen into Russia in the 970s and 980s. Thus Nestor relates the story of how St Vladimir secured his throne against the rivalry of his brother Jaropolk by securing the services of a large army of Norsemen, with whose assistance he overcame Jaropolk's rebellion in the year 980. Soon, however, discord arose between Vladimir and his mercenaries, as they considered that they had conquered Kiev for their own use.

'This city is ours; we have conquered it, and we want a ransom from its inhabitants, two *grivny* for each person.' And Vladimir said to them 'Wait a month; by then enough foxskins will have been collected to pay you.' So they waited a month, but he gave them nothing, and then the Varangians said to him: 'You have cheated us! Now show us the way to Greece!' Then he said: 'Yes, you go.' And he chose out from among them good, wise and strong men and gave them cities (to rule) while the rest went to Constantinople to the Greeks, but he [Vladimir] sent messengers ahead of them and bade them tell the Emperor: 'See, Varangians are on their way to you. Do not keep them in the City, for then they will only give you trouble, as they have given me, but divide them up into many places, and do not let one man come back here again.'[1]

If this story is true, then the Emperor will have received quite a large number of Varangians into his service early on in his reign, and the greatest probability is that they will have been used for service in the Asian themes. It is in any case certain that they were not at first a regiment of guards, but, as we shall see presently, the story is a noteworthy one.

In 986 trouble broke out again between the Empire and the Bulgarians. Tsar Samuel II had invaded Greece had taken much booty

---

[1] *Повесть Временных Лет*, I, 78–9 (entry for 980).

there, and also transferred the inhabitants of Larissa to Prespa, where he was going to build himself a new capital. Basil II invaded Bulgaria in return, and besieged Serdica, but was forced to raise the siege and return to Philippopolis. On the return journey he was trapped in the pass known as the Gates of Trajan, and because of the incompetence of some of his generals was heavily defeated by the Bulgarians, who even captured the Emperor's personal baggage.[1] On top of this, when Basil got back, he was faced by a revolt by Bardas Skleros, and by another from Bardas Phocas. The latter soon dispossessed the former, and became the Emperor's chief and most formidable adversary; the more so as he was thought by many to have a right to the throne as the nephew of the great Nicephorus II. At this point Basil turned for aid to Prince Vladimir of Kiev, who sent him the contingent of Varangians which is exceptionally well documented in Byzantine history, being referred to in Greek, Armenian and Arabic sources.[2] This force of some 6000 men arrived in the winter 987–8.[3]

There can be virtually no doubt that this force is the Varangians to whom Nestor is referring in his story. The fact that he attaches the tale of their being sent to the Emperor to the end of their service with St Vladimir in his battle with his brother in 980 is no proof that they were sent off in that year, since an annalist tended often to combine matter because of its subject interest than because of strict chronology. Moreover, the continuation of Nestor's text demonstrates clearly that Vladimir was engaged in constant military troubles until 988, and would therefore have needed to keep this powerful force by him to serve his own ends until then, especially as he had gone to the trouble of summoning them from 'across the seas' (i.e. from Sweden). Morever, the Greek, Armenian and Arabic sources only speak of *one* contingent of Varangians, and that in 988, and Nestor's dates are not always as reliable as they should be, as his editors have pointed out; also, if Basil II had received such a reinforcement in 980 he could hardly have failed to use this army on his Bulgarian campaign and, in view of later events, there is little doubt that it would then have ended differently.

The despatch of the Varangians in 988 is not likely to have been solely as a result of Basil's request for help, however, and there is no

---

[1] Leo the Deacon, who was himself an eyewitness, describes the battle (*Historiarum*, 171–3).
[2] Cedrenus, *Cedrenus Scylitzae Ope*, II, 444; M. Psellus, *Chronographia*, ed. E. Renaud, Paris, 1926–8, I, 9; Zonaras, *Annales*, ed. M. Pinder and T. Büttner-Wobst (CSHB), Bonn, 1841–97, III, 553; S. Asochik, *Histoire universelle*, tr. E. Dulaurier and F. Macler, Paris, 1883–1917, II, 164–5; Elmacen, *Historia Saracenorum*, ed. T. Erpenius, Leiden, 1625, 313; Yahia ibn Said, *Histoire*, ed. and tr. I. Krachkovskii and A. A. Vasilev, Paris, 1925–32, II, 425–6 (this extract is also in V. P. Rozen, *Император Василий Болгаробоча*, Saint Petersburg, 1883, 24–5, see refs. there).   [3] Elmacen, *Historia Saracenorum*, as above.

reason to doubt the essential truthfulness of Nestor's report, and so deduce that Prince Vladimir used the opportunity to rid himself of an ally who was becoming too exorbitant in his demands. Moreover, diplomatic negotiations had been in progress in which Vladimir had indicated his willingness to accept Christianity, the price being the hand of the Imperial Princess Anna, a mature spinster by now. The Emperors agreed to this, but the characteristic Byzantine aversion to letting the princesses of the Imperial blood marry out of the Empire (the chief bone of contention between Otto I and Nicephorus II was just this point that the Byzantines considered it demeaning for a Roman princess to marry a barbarian), coupled with some doubt as to the genuineness of Vladimir's desire for conversion, caused a delay which led Vladimir to think that they were proposing to edge out of their side of the bargain, with the result that he attacked and sacked Cherson in 989, whereupon Basil and Constantine hastily fulfilled their side of the bargain. The Princess Anna brought with her a large company of clerics, among whom may well have been Þorvaldr the Far-Travelled, if there is any substance in the reports in his narrative.[1] It is certain, however, that various Russians and Varangians had accepted Christianity in Byzantium before the official Christianization of Russia, as we may see from the story of the Princess Olga and the Christian Russians at the court of Constantine VII; there is also a report of a Christian church in Kiev as early as 945.[2]

The most notable description of this Varangian reinforcement is in Psellus's *Chronographia*, where the historian sets out neatly the great Emperor's military wisdom and skill. 'The emperor Basil knew the folly of the Romans and, since a select force of Tauro-Scythians [i.e. Russians] had joined him recently, he trained them and put them in a division with other foreign troops, and so sent them against the enemy.'[3] It is by no means impossible that these 'other foreign troops' may have been Slavonic and Norse Russians who were already in the imperial service. One point to be borne in mind is that Italian writers who refer to the army sent by Basil to the aid of the catepan of Southern Italy appear to differentiate between Norsemen (Varangians) in the imperial service, and Russians.[4] The Emperor may also have received a later mercenary force of Slavonic Russians, though there is no mention of such a force in available sources, but the 6000 soldiers who came

[1] *Þorvalds þáttr viðförla* (Íslendinga þættir, ed. G. Jónsson), Reykjavík, 1935, 438.
[2] F. Braun, 'Das historische Russland im nordischen Schrifttum des 10. bis 14. Jahrhundert', *Festschrift Eugen Mogk*, Halle-am-Saale, 158.
[3] Psellus, *Chronographia*, I, 9; cf. also Vasilevskii, Труды, I, 196–210.
[4] P. Riant, *Skandinavernes Korstog*, Copenhagen, 1868, 141; cf. also G. Schlumberger, *L'épopée byzantine*, Paris, 1896–1905, II, 10 (hereafter referred to as *Épopée*).

to his aid in 988 are quite unlikely to have been any other than the Norsemen who had gone from Sweden to the aid of Vladimir of Kiev and had helped him on to his throne and secured it for him during the years after he attained it.

Basil II soon discovered what a treasure he had gained in these mighty men of the North. They first saw him through to victory in his battle with Delphinas, Bardas Phocas's lieutenant at Scutari in April 989, and their aid (coupled with a fortunate coincidence, whereby Bardas died from a heart-attack in mid-fight) brought him to victory in the last serious challenge to his power at home, in the battle of Abydos on 13 April 989.[1]

From this time onwards no hand was raised against Basil inside the Empire, nor could any hostile foreign power withstand him to the uttermost. There is no doubt that he revelled in his new-found domestic security, and that he ensured it through the creation of a life-guard which he knew to be exceptionally able, thoroughly disciplined, and (most valuable of all) totally reliable.[2] The new regiment relieved the Excubitores of the duties of personal guards to the Emperor, and from our available records of Basil's many campaigns there is no doubt that wherever he went, they accompanied him and were the spearhead of many of his most successful ventures. Gradually this Varangian regiment became the heart of the guards, and the same rule as to a high entrance-fee will certainly have obtained among them, as their regular pay and extra bonuses alike were way above the emoluments of the rest of the army. These select Varangians became known as the 'Varangians of the City' (οἱ ἐν τῇ πόλει Βάραγγοι) in distinction from the other Varangian units, who were known as 'Varangians outside the City' (οἱ ἔξω τῆς πόλεως Βάραγγοι); these were used in general military service (often as garrisons or on marine duty) as need called within the Empire, while the guardsmen never left the capital unless the Emperor himself was present. (As Basil II detested the atmosphere of his capital, and kept as much away from it as he could, they are not likely to have seen overmuch of it until he died.)

Our principal witness as to Basil's part in the setting up of a regular Varangian unit in the Grand Hetairia is the anonymous tract *De re militari*, from the end of the tenth century (sometimes attributed to

---

[1] Schlumberger cannot be right in his assumption (*Épopée*, 1, 723 n. 2) that French or Italian mercenaries under Hervé or Roussel de Baillou took part in the battle as Varangians: they may however have formed a part of the 'other foreign troops' referred to by Psellus (see above, p. 44, n. 3).

[2] Psellus's description of Basil's general opinion of the East Romans leaves precious little room for doubt on this point; see also R. J. H. Jenkins, *Byzantium: the imperial years*, London, 1966, 301ff., esp. 329–31.

Nicephorus Uranius).[1] In the present author's (and reviser's) opinion, J. Kulakovskii has proved conclusively that this tract demonstrates that Basil II took a special unit of *Rhos* (i.e. Varangians) with him on successive Bulgarian campaigns.[2] Three references in *De re militari* are of particular importance here; where we are told that this unit is in special attendance on the Emperor along with the archers and heavily-armed troops;[3] where we are told that this unit is sometimes used as infantry, and sometimes as cavalry;[4] and where the life-guards attending the Emperor on campaign are listed as the Grand Hetairia, the Scholae, the Immortals and 'the other units' (*ta loipa tagmata*), from which we may deduce that these *Rhosi* formed one of these last-named units if they were not a part of the Grand Hetairia.[5]

Let us now look at those of Basil II's campaigns in which it may be said with certainty that Varangians took part. The first one is the Syrian expedition of 999, in which the Emperor besieged and captured Emesa. Yahia relates that the inhabitants fled into the fortified monastery of St Constantine, but the Russians (i.e. Varangians) set fire to it, and so compelled the defenders to surrender,[6] after which the monastery was plundered, even the lead and copper being stripped from the roof.[7] From there Basil moved on to Baalbek, and was about to attack Damascus, but the city received military aid from Egypt, and he desisted from his intention, moved on to Caesarea Libani (mod. Arka), burned the town and captured a great many people whom he had sent to Constantinople to be sold into slavery. The Arabs made a great effort to resist his advance at Tripoli, but Basil shattered their force and then returned to Antioch.[8]

In the following year two Armenians refer to a campaign by the Emperor in Armenia, in the course of which an incident occurred which specifically draws attention to the presence of Varangians in the Imperial train.[9] The Emperor met Bagharat, King of the Abkhaz, his father, King Gurgen of the Iberians, and other Armenian rulers in the town of Havcic, and received them with great pomp, after which he let them return to their own dominions. Asochik then relates the following incident:

[1] *De re militari*, ed. R. Vári, Leipzig, 1901.
[2] J. Kulakovskii, review of the above, *BZ* XI (1902), 547–58.
[3] *De re militari*, 21 and 44.   [4] *De re militari*, 31 and 44.
[5] *De re militari*, 7.
[6] Yahia, *Histoire*, II, 458 (also in Rozen, *Император Василий*, 40); cf. also *Épopée*, II, 152–3.
[7] E. Honigmann, *Die Ostgrenze des byzantinischen Reiches*, Brussels, 1935, 107 and 157.
[8] *Épopée*, II, 155ff.
[9] Asochik, *Histoire universelle*, II, 164ff.; Aristakes of Lasciverd, *Histoire d'Arménie*, tr. E. Prudhomme, Paris, 1864, 19.

On the same day as the latter [i.e. King Gurgen] returned home a great quarrel arose in the Greek camp over a very trifling matter. The princes and nobles of the *curopalates* David [a tributary king who ruled a part of North-East Armenia] were camped not far from the Greek soldiery. A certain soldier from the Russian infantry was carrying hay for his horse, when one of the Iberians went up to him and took the hay away from him. At this another Russian came running up to help his fellow-countryman, and the Iberian now called for help from his compatriots. These came rushing up and slew the first Russian; whereupon the whole Russian force, some 6000 men, mobilized for a fight; they were infantrymen, armed with spears and shields. The Emperor Basil had asked for these men from the King of Russia when he married his sister to him. At this time all the Russians had become Christians. The princes and noblemen of the Taiskings now attacked them, but were defeated. The Grand Prince, by name Patriarchos[?][1] fell there, as did two sons of Ozhopenter, Gabriel and John by name, Zhorzhvand the grandson of Abu-Harba and many others, for the wrath of God lay heavy upon them because of their pride.[2]

This narrative is very important, and Vasilevskii has made some very pertinent comments upon it in his study of the text.[3] He points out that Aristaces of Lasciverd (writing about 100 years later) also refers to this incident in his continuation of Asochik, stating that the discord arose between the 'force of noblemen and the Western soldiers who are called Russians'; and that the nobles were justly repaid for their haughtiness, for 30 men of rank in the unit were killed. Vasilevskii also points out that there may have been old scores between the two that were settled in this encounter, as Bardas Phocas was strongly supported by Grusinians (Iberians) in his rebellion. Asochik states directly that there were 'Iberian soldiers' in his army against the Emperor, and that Basil II opposed him with a force including 'Western soldiers', who were, as Aristaces states, Russians. Basil will have replaced this Grusinian regiment, who had deserted him for the pretender, by his faithful *Rhosi*, and the recollection of this action will very likely have had its effect in starting the fight in 1000. The fact that Asochik speaks of an *infantryman* fetching hay for his horse is no evidence for whether the regiment as a whole was used as a cavalry or an infantry unit, since all infantry regiments would naturally have been accompanied by a considerable number of horses to carry baggage, booty, etc., and the Emperor was after all just returning from a successful expedition against the Arabs of Syria and Cilicia.[4]

---

[1] Asochik, *Histoire universelle*, II, 165; the name is doubtful, the MS being mutilated at this point (see Dulaurier's note). [2] *Histoire universelle*, II, 165.

[3] Vasilevskii, *Труды*, I, 200–3.

[4] Honigmann seems to think (*Ostgrenze*, 157) that this enmity towards the Varangians was perhaps caused by the fact that they had burned down Constantine's church in Emesa the previous year (see above, p. 46).

When Basil felt that he had pacified his eastern borders sufficiently, he turned his attention to his powerful Bulgarian neighbour and prepared to settle his scores with him. Since his successes in the 980s, Tsar Samuel II had continued to harass the Byzantine provinces next to him, but when the Emperor resumed hostilities in 996, and especially after 1001, when he himself returned from Asia Minor, the tide turned sharply. In a campaign in 1001 Basil reconquered the greater part of Macedonia, and from then on he gradually annexed Bulgarian territories in a series of annual campaigns, culminating in the great victory in the Cleidion pass (29 July 1014) with its barbarous aftermath, after which the last four campaigns were mere cleaning-up operations. There is no doubt that wherever he went during this long and arduous period, Basil was accompanied by the Varangians: it is not entirely out of place to suspect that there was as much racial sympathy as political trust here, bearing in mind, as Professor Romilly Jenkins has suggested, that Basil's ancestress, Basil I's second wife Ingerina, was in all probability herself a Norsewoman, probably named *Ingiríður*[1] – certainly Basil II's immense *practical* ability as a military leader, as distinct from the bookish temper of the other Macedonian emperors, came from this strain, and made him more than ready to favour the Norsemen whom fortune sent to his help when he most needed it, and to use them to the utmost. His partiality can be seen in the division of the spoils after the capture of Longon and the sacking of the Pelagonian fields in the campaign of 1016. In that handout the Emperor took one third of the booty, gave another *tois symmachousi...Rhos*, and the third to the rest of the army.[2] Moreover, the famous anecdote in Cedrenos, of the cry that went up as Basil charged into the battle at the head of his men 'Fly, the Emperor comes!' is more suggestive of the fiery Scandinavian than the calculating Greek.[3]

The Varangians were clearly used for other operations besides the Bulgarian campaign in 1016. In January of that year Basil II sent a fleet to assist his nephew Jaroslav against the Khazars of the Black Sea, and this fleet was commanded by the Byzantine admiral Mongos Andronikos, assisted by a Russian commander named *Sphengos* (? *Sveinki*), and its expedition succeeded in annexing the territories of Georgios Toulos, capturing the chief himself.[4]

When the Bulgarian wars ended with the submission of Samuel's

[1] R. J. H. Jenkins, *Byzantium – the imperial years*, 302; see also C. Mango, 'Eudocia – Ingerina', *Recueil des Travaux de l'Institut des Études Byzantines*, XIV/XV (1973), 17–27 and refs. there.　　　　[2] *Cedrenus Scylitzae Ope*, II, 465; cf. also *Épopée*, II, 316.

[3] *Cedrenus Scylitzae Ope*, II, 466; cf. also *Épopée*, II, 380.

[4] *Cedrenus Scylitzae Ope*, II, 464; Schlumberger thinks the Greek commander was Bardas Ducas.

successors in 1018, Basil turned south and held a great feast of thanks-
giving in Athens. Some scholars have surmised that he was then
accompanied by Varangians who carved the runes on the great marble
lion of Piraeus (cf. further below, pp. 230ff.),[1] but this can only remain
a surmise.

In 1021 Basil made an expedition against King Georgi of Georgia,
and his Varangians receive particular mention in this campaign for
their ferocity.[2] Thus when Basil had every man, woman and child in 12
(in other sources 24) districts killed,[3] Aristaces notes that it took three
months, and that the Varangians were particularly brutal in their execution of this task.[4] It is certain that they also took part in the final battle
at Aghpha near Erzerum, when King Georgi, having asked for peace,
attempted to surprise the imperial army.

King Georgi's men had begun the battle, and put to flight a part of the Greek
army. The Emperor then commanded that the letter which King Georgi had
written be raised up on an axe-hafted spear, and then he showed it thus to
God. 'Look, O Lord,' he said, 'on these men's letter, and then on what they
are now doing!' He was very angry, and had a splinter from the Holy Cross
brought to him, wrapped in a precious cloth, which he hurled to the ground
and said: 'If you give me into the hands of my enemies, I shall never again
honour or worship you.' And when he had done this and said this the battle
was joined and raged for a long time. King Georgi's men, and the army that
had first come from Georgia, were defeated and sent flying. The Russian
units in the Imperial army now attacked, and only a very small number of
the first assailants escaped from them, for neither the King nor the main
army had arrived. And on that day those fell who had most opposed the
making of peace.[5]

In 1024 an interesting incident occurred which shows how careful
Basil II was even towards the Russians. Cedrenos tells us that a kinsman
of Vladimir the Great, whom he names *Chrysocheir*, gathered a force of
800 men after the death of Vladimir and Anna. They took ships and
sailed to Constantinople, and pretended to want to join the Imperial
mercenaries. The Emperor thereon bade them lay down their weapons,
saying that they could apply to join when they had done so, but they
would not disarm, and went instead through the Propontis, thence to

[1] *Épopée*, II, 408ff.; see also F. Gregorovius, *Die Stadt Athen im Mittelalter*, Berlin, 1889, I, 62.

[2] Aristakes, *Histoire*, tr. M. Canard and H. Berberian, Brussels, 1973, 23–4; see also *Épopée*, II, 478ff.; Vasilevskii, *Труды* I, 211ff.; M. F. Brosset, *Histoire de la Géorgie*, Saint Peters-burg, 1849–51, I, 308ff.

[3] Aristakes, *Histoire*, 24, gives the former number; Samuel of Ani, *Summarii temporum* (Migne, *P.G.* XIX, 723–4), the latter.

[4] Aristakes, *Histoire*, 24.

[5] Brosset, *Histoire de la Géorgie*, I, 308–9 and refs. there; cf. also Vasilevskii, *Труды*, I, 212; *Épopée*, II, 527–9; *Cedrenus Scylitzae Ope*, II, 478.

Abydos, where they had trouble with the general in charge of coastal defences, whom they defeated easily, and moved on to Lemnos. There they were met by a fleet of Cibirriotes and by David of Achrida, the military governor of Samos and Nicephorus Cabasilas, the Duke of Thessalonica. These made a truce with Chrysocheir, betrayed him and killed him and all his men.[1]

It is clear that Basil II feared an attack on the capital, and even though he must have left an ample guard there, he obviously did not want anyone, not even the Russians, to get into the habit of demanding something from him; nor would he deal with Chrysocheir unless he and his men surrendered their weapons, and when the latter resisted this demand, he had his subordinates destroy him, though in the event they had to resort to treachery to succeed.

The name Chrysocheir is a curious one for a Rhos to bear. It was the name of a great Manichaean chieftain in the time of Basil I, and Zonaras refers to a Greek of that name (or nickname).[2] No relative of St Vladimir is now known with this name, and there is probably some confusion here. It is possible that he was a Slavonic Russian, but so far all attempts to explain the name as a Greek translation from the Norse have been none too likely, as Vasilevskii has pointed out.[3] On the other hand, if we read it as *Auðmundr*, then Chrysocheir need cause no further trouble; this is a Norse name for which there are both literary and archaeological evidences: *Snorra-Edda* refers to Auðmundr the sea-king,[4] and the name is found engraved (as *Aumutaer*) on a sword found at Korsödegaard by Stange in Norway.[5] It is, of course, equally possible that the Greek may be a version of O.E. *Eadmund*; if so, it will refer most likely to some English princeling who may have been related to the Norse ruling family in Kiev. This is not an impossible hypothesis when one remembers that when Canute dispossessed Ethelred II and his sons various English noblemen left the country also and went wandering, but obviously there is no proof either way – on the slender evidences available *Auðmundr* would appear to have a slightly better probability. What is certain is that whoever Chrysocheir was, he was taking no small risk, since the Russians of Kiev normally took a long way round rather than offend Basil II, as both Psellus and Manasses point out, and so he paid the penalty of the great Emperor's watchfulness.[6]

[1] *Cedrenus Scylitzae Ope*, II, 478; cf. also *Épopée*, I, 611ff. and Vasilevskii, *Труды*, I, 207.
[2] Zonaras, *Annales*, III, 244.   [3] Vasilevskii, *Труды*, I, 207ff.
   Snorra-Edda, ed. S. Egilsson *et al.*, Copenhagen, 1848–87, I, 546 II, 468, 546, 614.
[5] E. H. Lind, *Norsk-islandske dopnamn*, Oslo, 1920–4, I, 99–100.
[6] Psellus, *Chronographia*, II, 8; Manasses, *Breviarium historiae metricum*, ed. I. Bekker (CSHB), Bonn, 1836–7, 253.

In the catepanate of Italy we have references to the passage of Varangians on an errand of pacification in 1009.[1] In that year a nobleman of Bari by the name of Meles attempted to raise a rebellion and create an independent republic of Bari.[2] Basil II sent a force to quell the rising, in which Leo of Ostia noted that there were *Dani, Rossi et Gualani.*[3] This army captured Bari again in June 1011, and, from their known ability in siege-warfare elsewhere, we may safely assume that the Varangians played their part in this victory. After this reversal Meles sought assistance from the Normans, and the revolt simmered on until 1017, when Leo Tornicius became catepan of Italy.[4] His general Leo Passianos fought a drawn battle against the rebels at Arenula,[5] and Tornicius himself defeated them with great difficulty at Civita, near Ripalto,[6] but was defeated at Vaccarizza and was recalled and replaced by Basil Boioannes, one of Basil II's best generals, who began his first Italian campaign in 1018.[7] He recovered Trani,[8] and fought the decisive battle against Meles at Ofanto, where he crushed the rebellion completely. Leo of Ostia describes this victory:

When the Emperor heard that brave knights had invaded his land he sent his finest soldiers against them: in the first three battles they fought the Normans won, but when they were matched against the Russians (*cum gente Russorum congressi*) they were totally defeated, and their army was utterly destroyed; a great number of them were transported to Byzantium, and they were tormented there in prison until they died: from this episode we have the proverb 'The Greek on the cart catches the hare.'[9]

Meles fled from Italy after this defeat, was taken under his protection by the Western Emperor Henry II, and died at Bamberg in 1020.

The Normans now made peace with the Emperor, and a company of them entered Boioannes's army.[10] Basil II, trusting his efficient namesake, made him catepan for a further period to clear up the last embers of rebellion, and then sent him on an expedition to Croatia to pacify the

---

[1] See J. Gay, *L'Italie méridionale et l'empire byzantin*, Paris, 1909, 183.
[2] Gay, *Italie méridionale*, 183; *Épopée*, II, 542ff.; Vasilevskii, *Труды*, I, 203ff.
[3] Leo of Ostia, *Chronicon Monasterii Cassinensis*, ed. W. Wattenbach (MGH Scriptores VII), Hanover, 1846, 555ff.   [4] *Cedrenus Scylitzae Ope*, II, 457.   [5] *Épopée*, II, 563ff.
[6] Some scholars think that Meles did in fact win this close-fought battle, cf. F. Chalandon, *Histoire de la domination normande en Italie et Sicilie*, Paris, 1907, I, 54–5.
[7] Adhemar, *Historiarum libri III*, ed. G. Waitz (MGH Scriptores IV), Hanover, 1841, 140; Lupus Protospatharios, *Chronicon*, ed. G. H. Pertz (MGH Scriptores V), Hanover, 1844, *ad* 1013; cf. also *Épopée*, II, 568.   [8] *Épopée*, II, 568.
[9] Leo of Ostia, *Chronicon Monasterii Cassinensis*, 652; Aimé, *Ystoire de li Normant*, ed. O. Delarc, Rouen, 1892, I, 21; Adhémar, *Historiarum*, 140; Vasilevskii, *Труды*, I, 205–6, commenting on this point refers to S. A. Gedeonov, *Отрывки из изследовании о Варяжском Вопросу*, Moscow, 1862–3, 165, as to a possible relationship with the Galician proverb 'one will not catch a hare with an ox'. It is possibly an exaggeration to say that very many Normans were kept in the dark until they died.   [10] *Épopée*, II, 514.

tiresome King Chresimir. Boioannes accomplished this successfully,[1] and it is likely that his useful Varangians went with him on this expedition, as well as the one when he crossed over to Sicily and captured Messina. While the Croatian campaign was in progress, however, Basil II decided to extend his Sicilian campaign, and placed the protospatharios Orestes in charge of the large force he had assembled for this purpose. Orestes was but an indifferent general, however, and his army of Russians, Vandals, Turks, Bulgars, Vlachs and Macedonians was beaten by the Arabs, who recaptured Messina.[2] The Emperor thereupon assembled a second army and prepared to command it in person, while Boioannes brought his forces southwards and waited for him in Reggio. Before the campaign could begin, however, the great Emperor died (15 December 1025) and it was abandoned.[3]

With Basil II's death we come to a watershed in the affairs of the Byzantine Empire. His two immediate successors, Constantine VIII and Romanos III had neither his genius as a ruler nor as a general, and the remaining evidences for Varangian activities before the arrival of Haraldr Sigurðarson are few and uncertain. That they would have continued to be used as one of the most valuable units of the Byzantine army, there can be little doubt, but where they were used is far from certain. It is reasonable to suppose that they were the life-guards who rescued Romanos III from the consequences of his own incompetence in the defeat at Azaz,[4] and slightly more probable that they were among the soldiers with whom Maniaces (later their commander) captured Edessa in 1032. Matthew of Edessa tells of a soldier serving under Maniaces during this campaign, who was sent by him on an errand to the Emir of Harran, and who lost his temper with the Emir and struck at him with his axe. The Jerusalem manuscript of this chronicle states here that this man was of the Russian people (*ouroz arnen*),[5] and it is likely enough that Maniaces was given charge of this force as a reward for his success in avenging the defeat of the Emperor.

---

[1] *Épopée*, II, 599ff.

[2] *Annales Barenses*, ed. G. H. Pertz (MGH Scriptores V), Hanover, 1844, 53 (entry for 1027, but this is the wrong year; cf. *Cedrenus Scylitzae Ope*, II, 479 and Vasilevskii, *Труды*, I, 208).

[3] *Épopée*, II, 574; Gay, *Italie méridionale*, 415ff.

[4] Cf. *Épopée*, III, 79–84; Vasilevskii, *Труды*, I, 213; Honigmann, *Ostgrenze*, 107. Zonaras, *Annales*, III, 577, describes the battle, and Cedrenus (II, 493) mentions especially the bravery of the guards, giving particular praise to a eunuch who saved his master's possessions when others fled headlong. Gregorius Bar-Hebraeus (Abulfaradh), *Chronicon Syriacum*, ed. P. J. Bruns, Leipzig, 1788, II, 230, refers to the Slavs in the Emperor's army, and Kemaleddin (*Chronicle*, cited by Rozen) states that it was the Armenians who saved the Emperor in his flight; cf. further, Rozen, *Император Василий*, 319.

[5] Matthew of Edessa, *Chronique*, tr. E. Dulaurier, Paris 1858, 49; cf. also Vasilevskii, *Труды*, I, 214.

The protospatharios Theoctistus was sent to Egypt in 1033 to help the Emir Ibn Zairah of Tripoli against the Caliph of Egypt, and we are told that in his expedition, which captured the castle of Menik, there were Russians.[1]

Another military use of the Varangians at this time was in the campaign fought in the eastern reaches of Asia Minor under the command of Nicholas Pegonites, who captured the fort of Berkri in Armenia after a long siege in 1035.[2] Also, when the cubicularius Ispo (?Hispo) was sent to Italy in 1032 he led an army which contained units that had served in Asia. As there were a fair number of Varangians in service there during the time of Basil II's successors, it is quite probable that some of these will have been in this expedition.[3]

With the death of Romanos III in 1034 and the arrival in the same year of Haraldr Sigurðarson and his company in Constantinople we come to a new and rather more extensively documented era in the history of the Varangians, and it is therefore more logical to make a break in the narrative here, rather than at the end of the reign of Basil II. There is no doubt, however, that the day of his death marked as great a milestone in their lesser history as it did in the history of the Empire, for the regiment can be seen clearly as his specific creation in the military system, born partly out of chance, the provision of a large body of these tough, unscrupulous, but utterly loyal men at a moment of great decisiveness in Basil's career, and partly out of his need for a permanent body of such men to surround him and give him that feeling of safety that his suspicious temper craved, and no Greeks could give him.

---

[1] *Cedrenus Scylitzae Ope*, II, 495–6.
[2] *Cedrenus Scylitzae Ope*, II, 502ff.; Michael Glycas, *Annales*, ed. I. Bekker (CSHB), Bonn, 1836, 586; Aristakes, *Histoire*, 36–7; cf. also Honigmann, *Ostgrenze*, 172 and Vasilevskii, *Труды*, I, 214–15 and 263ff.
[3] Lupus, *Chronicon*, 58 (entry for 1032); *Annales Barenses*, 53 (entry for 1027).

4

Haraldr Sigurðarson
and his period as a Varangian in Constantinople, 1034–1043

Haraldr Sigurðarson, later King Harald III (Hardrada) of Norway, is without question the best-known of the Norsemen who entered the Imperial service as a Varangian. As the younger half-brother of King Olaf II (St Olaf), Haraldr spent the years following his brother's dethronement and death in exile in various parts of the world. Immediately after the débâcle at Stiklestad, his wounds having been healed at a remote farm in East Norway, Haraldr made his way via Sweden to Kiev, where he clearly held some kind of military post. The statement in *Heimskringla* that he 'became commander over the King's [Jaroslav's] defence army',[1] is so obvious an exaggeration as to be nonsensical, but equally clearly Jaroslav would have been pleased enough to make use of this young warrior and, in view of his royal lineage, would give him some kind of subordinate officer's rank. It is also perfectly reasonable for him to have been employed on the arduous *pólútasvarf*, as well as border warfare such as Snorri Sturluson attributes to him from a verse by the poet Þjóðólfr Arnórsson about the other Norse commander in the service of Prince Jaroslav, Eilífr Rögnvaldsson.

Eitt höfðusk at
Eilífr þars sat,
Höfðingjar tveir;
Hamalt fylktu þeir;
Austrvindum ók
Í ǫngvan krók,
Vasa Læsum léttr
Liðsmanna réttr.

One thing two lords did (Eilífr was there); they set their men in a circle of shields; the East Wends were hard pressed; the soldiers made the rights of the *Læsir* hard to get.[2]

---

[1] *Heimskringla*, ed. B. Aðalbjarnarson (Íslenzk Fornrit XXVI–XXVIII), Reykjavík, 1941–51, III, 70. [2] *Heimskringla*, III, 70; see also FJ *Skjald*, A I 385, B I 355.

This verse is also quoted in *Fagrskinna*, and we deduce from it that Haraldr had spent an appreciable period in Jaroslav's service (*Fagrskinna* reads *langa ríð*; *Heimskringla*, *nokkura vetra, ok fór víða um Austrveg*), though one could bring against this a stanza which is attributed in some MSS of *Fagrskinna* (*loc. cit.*) to Valgarðr of Vellir, but in *Heimskringla* (*Har. saga harðr.* ch. 2) to Bölverkr Arnórsson; the two last lines read

Austr vastu ár et næsta
Orðiglyndr i Gǫrðum.

You were the next and the next after year, O warlike one, in Garðar.[1]

It is possible to interpret this as meaning that Haraldr only dwelt the year after the Stiklestad débâcle at Jaroslav's court, but neither Snorri Sturluson nor the author of the *Fagrskinna* biography has so read it. It is also conceivable that *ár et næsta* may refer to his stay with Earl Rögnvaldr and his son Eilífr in Novgorod, and so being in their (or Eilífr's) tax-gathering expedition to the Eastern Wends and the Liasi.[2] What is certain, however, is that Haraldr went to Kiev, and stayed with Jaroslav; Þjóðólfr Arnórsson refers to this, and that he (Jaroslav) thought that Haraldr took after his great brother:

Jarisleifr of sá
Hvert jöfri brá
Hofsk hlýri frams
Ens helga grams.

Jaroslav saw the way in which the king was developing. The fame grew of the holy king's brother.[3]

A Russian annal states that in this particular year (1031) Jaroslav went on a campaign against the Liasi and captured the city of Cervin.[4] *Haraldar saga* mentions that Haraldr thereupon asked for the hand of Jaroslav's daughter Elisaveta (O.N. *Ellisif*),[5] but P. A. Munch has shown that this cannot have happened so early in his career, but would rather have been later, after his return from Byzantium, as Elisaveta can hardly have been ten years old at this point.[6] We have to bear in mind here the primary difficulty in interpreting the Norse sources for this period, that in general, like *Haraldar saga*, they were written down anything up to 200 years or more after the events, and though the

---

[1] As above.
[2] The Liasi were the modern Poles, who were referred to in O.Russ. as Ляси (sing. Лях), which was corrupted in O.N. into *Læsir*.
[3] FJ *Skjald*, A I 368, B I 338–9.
[4] *Повесть Временных Лет*, 150 (under 1031; cf. Vasilevskii, *Труды*, I, 258.
[5] *Flateyjarbók*, ed. G. Vigfússon and C. R. Unger, Christiania, 1860–9, III, 290.
[6] P. A. Munch, *Samlede Afhandlinger*, Christiania, 1873, I, 534.

authors had the remembered poems of the court-poets of the kings involved to guide them, yet they were quite as likely to misunderstand their sources as any modern historian. Thus, when they found a verse by Illugi Bryndælaskald (cf. below, p. 70) which stated that Haraldr had often assailed *á frið Frakka* 'the peace of the Franks', and Þjóðólfr's verses in *Sexstefja*, *Sás við lund á lundi | Langbarða réð ganga*, 'he who walked through the groves in the land of the *Langbarðar* [Lombards]',[1] they did not realize that the *Langbarðaland* of the poem was the Southern Italian district which formed the Byzantine province of *Longobardia*, and that the *Frakkar* were the French Normans who were disputing this very *Langbarðaland* in *Southern* Italy. Instead they assumed that these verses meant that Haraldr had gone from Russia to Wendland, then on to Saxony and France, committed piracy in these countries and gone on to Lombardy in *northern* Italy, on to Rome, then southwards to Apulia, and so on to Constantinople. It is far more likely, however, that Haraldr went the usual Varangian way, down the Russian rivers and across the Black Sea. Bölverkr Arnórsson gives an impressive description of the approach up the Bosphorus, and has Haraldr watch the gleaming roofs of the City as the splendid fleet draws near to it.

> Hart kníði svöl svartan
> Snekkju brand, fyr landi,
> Skúr en skrautla báru
> Skeiðr brynjaðar reiði.
> Mætr hilmir sá malma
> Miklagarðs fyr barði;
> Mörg skriðu beit at borgar
> Barmfögr háum armi.

The cool wind drove swiftly the ship's black prow; the armoured (so!) vessels bore their yards splendidly. The excellent king saw the metal-covered roofs of Byzantium out ahead; many a beautiful ship drew near to the high end (? wall) of the City.[2]

Both Greek and Norse sources agree that thereafter Haraldr entered the service of the Emperor Michael IV Katallakos.

There is a large body of legend about Haraldr's stay in Byzantium and his mighty works in the service of the East Roman Emperors. The Sagas of the Kings, not least Snorri's *Heimskringla*, have a lot to say about him, and some of this material has the authority of Haraldr's

---

[1] See above, p. 55, n. 3.
[2] FJ *Skjald* A I 385, B I 355; see also *Heimskringla*, III, 71; Finnur Jónsson reads, rather less probably, that it is the *hilmir Miklagarðs*, the Emperor, who is watching the fleet draw near.

distinguished fellow Varangian, Halldór Snorrason (†1055), the son of Snorri the Chieftain of Helgafell, who would be in a position to give some truthful eyewitness accounts of these happenings.[1] As will be shown later in this chapter, however, this is but a small portion of the written evidence, which is very extensive indeed, for Haraldr's Byzantine venture is noted in Icelandic, Norwegian, Danish and English sources from the Middle Ages.[2] All these evidences have a common point which vitiates them as serious witnesses to the Byzantine episode in his career, in that they are full of tall tales, and contain a number of anecdotes which, though credited to Haraldr there, are credited to others in other works of the period. Nineteenth- and twentieth-century scholars have studied these points at considerable length, and we must now turn to examine some of the most important anecdotes.[3]

The most reliable sources for the life of this great Viking king are the works of authors contemporary with him, and such numismatic and other archaelogical evidences as have survived.[4] Of the literary evidences the poems and poetic fragments by his own court poets are naturally first in consideration, and next to them a chapter from a Greek treatise, now usually associated with Cecaumenos, the Λόγος νουθε-τητικός, 'Advice for the Emperor'; the Emperor involved is uncertain, but the probable dating (last quarter of the eleventh century) would suggest Michael VII, Nicephorus III or Alexius I. This chapter, which is of great importance in our study, reads as follows in English:

Araltes [i.e. Haraldr] was the son of the King of Varangia, the brother of Julavos [i.e. Ólafr] who had inherited the kingdom after his father, and had Araltes next him in dignity. But Araltes, who was young and admired the might of the Romans, left the country and desired to enter our service and show respect to the blessed Lord Emperor Michael the Paphlagonian, and see with his own eyes Roman customs and government. He brought with him

[1] *Heimskringla*, III, 79.

[2] Beside the Norse and Byzantine sources referred to continuously in this chapter, Haraldr and his ventures in the East are chronicled by Theodoric the Monk (*Monumenta Historiae Norwegiae*, ed. G. Storm, Christiania, 1880, 57), Saxo (*Gesta*, ed. J. Raeder, A. Olrik and F. Blatt, Copenhagen, 1931–57, I, 305ff.) and William of Malmesbury (*De Gestis Regum Anglorum*, ed. W. Stubbs (Rolls Series), London, 1887–9, II, 318).

[3] Beside the general works on Varangica already mentioned, reference may be made to P. A. Munch, 'Kritiske Undersögelser om vore Kongesagaers Fremstilling af Harald Sigurdssøns (Haardraades) Bedrifter i den græske Kejseres Tjeneste' (*Samlede Afhandlinger*, I, 505–54); Vasilevskii, *Труды*, I, esp. 40–88; G. Storm, 'Harald Haardraade og Væringerne i de græske Kejseres Tjeneste', *Norsk Historisk Tidsskrift*, 2 Række, IV, 354–86; J. de Vries, 'Normannisches Lehngut in der islandischen Königssaga', *Arkiv for Nordisk Filologi*, 47; A. Stender-Petersen, *Die Varägersage als Quelle der altrussischen Chronik*, Aarhus, 1934.

[4] See P. Grierson, 'Byzantine coinage as source material', *Acts of the XIIIth International Congress of Byzantine Studies*, Oxford, 1967, 317–35; for other archaeological evidences, see P. H. Sawyer, *The Age of the Vikings*, 2nd ed., London, 1971, and P. G. Foote and D. M. Wilson, *The Viking Achievement*, London, 1970, *passim*.

a company of 500 brave men, and entered the service of the Emperor, who received him in a seemly manner, and sent him to Sicily because the Roman army was there, making war in the island. Araltes went there and did many notable things, and when the war was over he returned to the Emperor, who gave him the title *Manglavites*. Some time later Delianos began a revolt in Bulgaria; Araltes was then with the Emperor's expedition and performed great deeds of valour against the enemy, as was fitting for one of his noble race and personal ability. When the Emperor had reduced the Bulgarians to submission he returned [to Constantinople]; I was there myself, and fought for the Emperor as best I could. So, when we came to Mosynupolis, the Emperor rewarded him for his valour and gave him the title of *Spatharo-kandidatos*. After the death of the Emperor Michael and the next Emperor, his sister's son, Araltes wanted, in the days of the Emperor Constantine Monomachos, to return to his own country, and asked for leave to depart, but was refused it, and he found it hard to get away. Nonetheless he escaped in secret, and became king in his own country in the place of his brother Julavos. Nor was he angry at being made only *Manglavites* or *Spatharo-kandidatos*, but rather, even after he had become king, he kept faith and friend-ship with the Romans.[1]

The author of *Advice* tells this story of Haraldr as an example to emphasize to the reigning Emperor how unnecessary, and indeed harmful, it is for the state to place foreign mercenaries in high positions, however excellent they may be as soldiers; he takes Haraldr as his example: here was a man of royal birth, a shining example to warriors, who received no higher title than *Manglavites* and then *Spatharokandida-tos*, but did not take offence at this, and remained a firm friend of the Empire afterwards. Of course, as with all such polemical treatises, written from the side of the Byzantine civil servant, that prototype of his modern European counterpart, we must remember that the aim was to reduce the importance of the military side of the Empire and so retain power and perquisites in the hands of the bureaucrats, but nonetheless we may be thankful for its evidence, as a corrective to the equally one-sided tale told by the royal poets, concerned with glorifying their master, and by Icelandic historiographers of a hundred and fifty years later, to whom romantic exaggeration was a constant temptation. With the aid of *Advice* and Haraldr's court poets, and by checking what Greek and Arab sources tell us of Byzantino-Arab warfare during this period, we can obtain a fairly clear picture of the main events in Haraldr's military service under the Emperors.

The separate *Haraldar saga* relates that he did not wish it to be known in Constantinople that he was of royal birth, because the Byzantines

[1] *Λόγος Νουθετητικός*, ed. V. G. Vasilevskii and P. Jernstedt, Saint Petersburg, 1896 (hereafter referred to as *Advice*).

did not take very kindly to men of such exalted rank becoming mercenaries (can one see a memory of the perennially suspicious mind of Basil II in this remark?), and so he took the name *Nordbrikt (-brigt)*, and Már Húnröðarson was the first to suspect his true identity.[1] There may be some factual foundation for this story, but there is more than a hint of the folk-motif of the 'Prince in Disguise' in it, and in any case such a Byzantine policy of exclusion of royalty did not last long, as *Advice* contains no hint of it, and its author knows his true name and family.[2]

Moreover, Snorri states in the *Heimskringla* biography, as does the separate *Haraldar saga*, that Haraldr, as soon as he arrived in Constantinople, entered the mercenaries and 'served on the galleys with the force that went into the Grecian Sea'.[3] It is inherently very likely that Haraldr and his seafaring companions would be used at once to rid the waters of the pirates that infested them after the death of Basil II, for though the conquest of Crete by Nicephorus Phocas had been a great blow to them, these gentry were by no means finished. The Emperors had to have a constant coastguard fleet in the Aegean to keep them at bay, and, as has been mentioned previously in this book, Varangians were repeatedly used on this service because of their familiarity with sea-warfare (cf. above, pp. 30–1). A verse by Bölverkr Arnórsson refers clearly to these early maritime experiences of Haraldr in the Imperial service.

> Snjallr rauð í styr stillir
> Stál, ok gekk a mála;
> Háðisk hvert ár síðan
> Hildr, sem sjalfir vilduð.

The war-brave lord reddened his sword in battle and entered the [Emperor's] service; then every year afterwards a fight began where [he] wanted to have one.[4]

We may interpret this verse as meaning that Haraldr and his company were used to pursue pirates as need arose, but of course they will not have done so according to their own whims, but in obedience to the orders of the Byzantine admiral – one must allow for poetic exaggeration without necessarily losing sight of the facts behind his statement. There is every likelihood, however, that as the young man gained a reputation within the service, the Admiral was more ready to listen to and appreciate his suggestions as to where these pirates were most likely

---

[1] *Flateyjarbók*, iii, 290–304. How easily such tales can get about and become tangled has been shown by Miss C. E. Fell (cf. *The Icelandic Saga of Edward the Confessor* (1974), 187 – see below, pp. 142–3).   [2] Munch, *Samlede Afhandlinger*, i, 508.
[3] *Heimskringla*, iii, 71; *Flateyjarbók*, iii, 291.   [4] FJ *Skjald* A I 385, B I 355.

to be found, and Bölverkr may be referring to this by his *sem sjalfir vilduð*. But since the author of *Advice* implies that he was sent at once to Sicily, it is also quite possible that his first naval campaign was as part of an auxiliary fleet which Michael IV kept around the Sicilian coast to clear the seas there of pirates, and was earlier under the command of John the Camerarius and the story in *Advice* has mixed this up with Haraldr's later campaign in Sicily under the command of Georgios Maniaces (cf. below, pp. 65ff.). Another verse by Bölverkr states that Haraldr sailed *Blálands á vit*, which could imply that the Byzantine navy had to fight Arab pirates in the passage between Sicily and Africa.[1] The separate *Haraldar saga* states that Haraldr was to pay the Emperor a hundred (i.e. 120, the Norse 'hundred' being computed as twelve tens) marks for each pirate vessel that he captured, and that he could keep any booty above that for himself and his men. One accusation levelled against him later on was that he had kept back more than his due, and retained monies rightly due to the Emperor; we will[2] examine this matter later.

There was trouble from Arab pirates in other parts of the Empire during the first years of Michael IV's reign, and it is likely that Haraldr and other Varangian soldiers were used in the bothersome naval operations necessary to clear them off the seas. Zonaras mentions that a great Arab fleet from Sicily and Africa made shore-raids on the Greek islands, and even raided the mainland of Greece and Asia Minor, where they captured the town of Myra.[3] Cedrenus repeats this, and adds that these Arabs concentrated their activities in the Cyclades and the shores of Thrace.[4] The Byzantines, under the command of the strategos of the Cibirriotes, won a great victory over these pirates, destroying many of their ships and capturing many of them to sell into slavery, while others were executed with the usual barbarities.

Heimskringla also states that Haraldr took his force *vestr i Affrika, er Væringjar kalla Serkland*, an assertion based on a verse by Þjóðólfr Arnórsson, which says of Haraldr before he went to Sicily,

> Tøgu má tekna segja
> (Tandrauðs) á Serklandi
> (Ungr hætti sér) átta
> (Ormtorgs hötuðr) borga,
> Áðr herskörðuðr harðan
> Hildar leik und skildi,

---

[1] FJ *Skjald* A I 386, B I 356.
[2] *Flateyjarbók*, III, 296; cf. also *Fornmannasögur*, ed. C. C. Rafn *et al.*, Copenhagen, 1825–37, VI, 148.   [3] Zonaras, *Annales*, III, 589.
[4] *Cedrenus Scylitzae Ope*, II, 511–13; cf. also *Épopée*, III, 192.

Serkjum hættr, í sléttri
Sikileyju gekk heyja.

We may say that eighty cities were taken in Arabia; the young generous man risked his life, before the warrior who was dangerous to the Arabs went to fight behind his shield a fierce battle against them in the flat [*sic!*] Sicily,

while in another verse he remarks that

Vasat Affríka jöfri
Ánars mey fyr hánum
Haglfaldinni at halda
Hlýðisamt né lýðum.

It was not easy for the King of Africa to keep the snow-covered earth or to guard his people against him.[1]

We may interpret these verses as follows: (1) It may be stated that eighty towns were taken in the land of the Moors; the young, generous man risked himself before the soldier who was dangerous to the Moors left the field to conduct a fierce fight in smooth Sicily. (2) It was not easy for the King of 'Affríka' nor for his people to hold their land against him.

We also have one of Haraldr's own verses, in which he refers to his fighting in Africa

Hitt vas fyrr, es fjarri
Fóstrlandi rauðk branda,
Sverð í Serkja garði
Söng, en þat vas löngu.

Another time it was that I reddened swords far from my fosterland; the sword sang in the town of the Arabs (but this was long ago).[2]

Now *Serkland* cannot in this context mean 'Africa', and the phrase *Affríka jöfur* must be interpreted in another way than that it refers to Haraldr's military activities in that part of the world (cf. below, p. 66). There are no references in Greek sources to any special expedition to Africa in the reign of Michael IV: the expedition by Techneas to Egypt was in the reign of his predecessor, and if, as is most likely from the available evidences, Haraldr did not enter the Imperial service until 1034, then he cannot have taken part in it (though there is nothing known which absolutely bars his having gone there a year earlier, even if the probabilities are none too strong). Since, however, *Serkir* is often used in O.N. as a synonym for Arabs and Arabic-speaking peoples generally, it is not too far-fetched to surmise that the verses refer to

---

[1] In *Sexstefja*; see FJ *Skjald* A I 369, B I 339–40; also *ibid.* A I 380, B I 350 in a separate stanza, and *Heimskringla*, III, 75.   [2] FJ *Skjald* A I 359, B I 331.

Byzantino-Arabic fights in Asia Minor, where there was much fighting during Michael IV's earlier years, and where the two principal Byzantine generals were men who enter Varangian history in other ways, the strategos of Antioch, Constantine (who was Michael IV's brother) and Georgios Maniaces.

Despite the bold assertions of his poets, it is out of the question that Haraldr can have commanded an independent force during this period, for the evidence of *Advice* on his Byzantine rank precludes this entirely. His highest rank, as we have seen, was that of *Spatharokandidatos*, and he did not attain to this until he had proved himself in the Sicilian and Bulgarian wars, while the lowest ranking officer to hold independent command in the normal way was a *Protospatharios*: the *Spatharokandidatos* might occasionally take such a command if he was also the governor of a theme or an isolated district,[1] but such a responsibility does not ever appear to have been given to him. There is admittedly no reason to doubt Þjóðólfr's veracity about the eighty *borgir*, but it is more reasonable to interpret the statement with some discount, as referring to the fact that the unit in which Haraldr served took part in the reduction of eighty towns or castles, nor is such a number incredible when we reflect that the territory in question was a vast one, and the war a long one covering several years. Nor is it beyond credibility that Constantine or Maniaces may have sent the Varangians on their own at times to capture a castle or a town that needed no larger force to reduce it – after all, *oikonomia* was a leading theme in Byzantine thinking – and as *Advice* makes it clear that Haraldr's company was a select one of highly skilled warriors, it is far from incredible that the commanding general will at times have sent it off in his charge to do such a job, and that Haraldr will have gained both fame and fortune in this way. Also, Greek and other sources show that the Russians and Varangians were to be found in various Asiatic expeditions during this period, and we shall now turn to examine these.

The first refers to the Varangians being in winter quarters in the Thracesion theme during 1034. Cedrenos tells a curious anecdote which is particularly important because it is the earliest Byzantine reference to the Varangians by that name (Βάραγγοι), as far as can be traced.

A man of the Varangians who were scattered in winter quarters in the Thracesion theme met a woman of the region in a private place and tempted her virtue; and when he could not get her to agree willingly he tried to rape her, but she got hold of the foreigner's sword and struck him with it through the

---

[1] Thus Staurachius the Governor (ἔπαρχος) of Crete was a σπαθαροκανδιδᾶτος in rank (see Photius, *Epistolae* [Migne, *P.G.*, CII, 984], as was the στρατηγός Leo of Nicopolis; cf. A. Vogt, *Basile I*, Paris, 1908, 188 and 191.

heart, so that he died at once. When this deed became known through the neighbourhood the Varangians gathered together and honoured the woman by giving her all the possessions of the man who had attempted to rape her, and they threw his body away without burial, according to the law about suicides.[1]

This anecdote demonstrates the severity of the military discipline within the regiment, and also the nobility and justice of the Varangians. Bearing in mind their general reputation at other times as ruffians of a not too moral kind, it also suggests that at this time they were commanded by a disciplinarian who could impose on them a very different ethos, and the suggestion that this was Haraldr need not be far out, though there are other candidates (e.g. Eilífr) who are just as likely.

It is also very likely that Varangians were used in the continuation of the war under the command of Nicholas Pegonites (cf. above, p. 53). In this context we may bear in mind the recapture of Edessa by Maniaces and its relief by Constantine Katallakos in 1036, and in particular we may note the expedition to put down the rebellion of King Adam of Sebaste in 1034, when we are told by Matthew of Edessa that the commander was of the rank of *Akoluthos* which is the rank of the Varangian commander of that period.[2] It is therefore no far-fetched deduction to associate Þjóðólfr's and Haraldr's verses (the sources of Snorri and any intermediate prose version of Haraldr's life) with fighting against Arabic pirates off Asia Minor, and subsequently with wars in the Arab sector of Asia and Syria.[3]

We also have an inkling that Haraldr will have served in expeditions against the Pechenegs during the first four years of Michael IV's reign. Here we have a statement by Adam of Bremen that he fought against the *Scythae*, by which he is probably referring to Pechenegs, with whom the Empire was constantly at loggerheads from 1033 to 1036.[4] This constant warfare on two fronts, Asia and the West, meant that Basil II's magnificent war-machine was still in good order, if the troops were sufficiently mobile to be whisked from one frontier to another in a short period, and two stanzas by Stúfr Kattarson the Blind, which relate to an expedition to Jerusalem which must have taken place during the earlier part of Haraldr's service, are not so incredible when this factor is borne in mind.

[1] *Cedrenus Scylitzae Ope*, II, 508–9.
[2] Matthew of Edessa, *Chronique*, 352; cf. also *Épopée*, III, 200.
[3] *Cedrenus Scylitzae Ope*, II, 511–12; *Épopée*, III, 184ff.
[4] Adam of Bremen, *Gesta Hammaburgensis Ecclesiae*, 3rd ed., ed. B. Schmeidler (MGH, Scriptores Rerum Germanicarum), Hanover, 1917, 103ff.; *Cedrenus Scylitzae Ope*, II, 515; see also *Épopée*, III, 202–3.

Fór ofrhugi enn øfri
Eggdjarfr und sik leggja
(Fold vas víga valdi
Virk) Jórsali ór Girkjum
Ok með ærnu ríki
Óbrunnin kom gunnar
Heimil jörð und herði.
Hafi ríks þar vel líkar.

Stóðusk ráð ok reiði
(Rann þat svikum manna)
Egða grams á ýmsum
Orð Jórdánar borðum
Enn fyr afgørð sanna
(Illa gát frá stilli)
Þjóð fekk vísan váða
Vist of aldr med Kristi.[1]

These verses, which are used as a source by the separate *Haraldar saga*,[2] may be interpreted as follows:

The brave mighty warrior went from the Greek lands to conquer Jerusalem; the land was submissive to the wielder of battle, and with his mighty power the land came unburned into submission to the hand of the warrior. The counsel and the angry words of the Lord of Agder [Haraldr] stood on both sides of the Jordan; they made an end of men's treacheries; the people received sure trouble for proved crime; the King punished them severely.

In turn, the last two lines of each stanza make up together a refrain 'May [Haraldr] have a royal dwelling with Christ for ever, where [he] will like it well'.

Haraldar saga states:

'wherever he went through the land of Jerusalem, all cities and castles were opened for him, and surrendered without a struggle into his hand; this is proved by Stúfr the poet, who heard King Haraldr himself tell of this... King Haraldr made an offering at the grave of Our Lord, and to the Holy Cross, and to other holy relics in Jerusalem, of so much money in gold and jewels that it is hard to compute the amount; he also made the entire way to Jerusalem peaceable, slaying robbers and other evil folk... Thereafter he went to the Jordan and bathed himself in it, as is the custom of pilgrims, and thereafter he returned to Constantinople.'[3]

This narrative has numerous mistellings and exaggerations; Stúfr has understood Haraldr to say that he conquered Palestine for the

---

[1] The present author considers that the readings of some of the principal MSS, *ór Girkjum* (i.e. 'from Greece'), is more correct than Finnur Jónsson's *ok Grikkjum* (i.e. 'with the Greeks'), especially as *und sik* demonstrates that an accusative is called for, else the reading would be *ok Grikki*.

[2] *Heimskringla*, III, 83–4; see FJ *Skjald* A I 404, B I 373–4, and E. A. Kock, *Notationes norroenae*, Lund, 1923–44, § 880 and 3396s.   [3] *Fornmanna sögur*, VI, 101–2.

Emperor, but this was not so. In 1027 the Caliph of Egypt had agreed with Constantine VIII that he would allow the church of the Holy Sepulchre to be rebuilt, though nothing had been done about this for the next few years. In 1035, however, Moustansir-Billah (1035–94) succeeded to the caliphate and action began to be taken, as the Caliph was the son of a Byzantine mother and was averse to all bigotry and religious persecution; among other acts of clemency he set free 50,000 Christian captives on his accession, and in 1036 he made a thirty-year peace treaty with Michael IV in which the permission to renew this church was repeated. Michael sent masons to Jerusalem to begin the rebuilding, and also provided a guard of soldiers to protect pilgrims who might be attracted to the site in the renewed time of peace;[1] what seems most likely from comparison of sources is that Haraldr commanded a company of Varangians who were sent on escort duty to Jerusalem. From the very fact that Varangians were used for this expedition, we may reasonably surmise that a pilgrim party of high-ranking people, possibly even members of the Imperial family (the Empress Zoe's two sisters, Eudoxia and Theodora, were both of a distinctly pious disposition, for instance) were taking this opportunity to make their devotions in the holy places. Since this journey was made in peace, with the express agreement of the Caliph, what could be more natural than that all towns on the route should open their gates to the travellers; nor need we doubt that Stúfr's words about the punishment of wrongdoers are also true, that Haraldr and his detachment were obliged to fight various forms of brigands, such as Bedouins who infested a route as rich in potential spoil as this one, and whom it would be a service to the Caliph as well as the Emperor to clear out of the way.

The most notorious of Haraldr's military expeditions was, however, the campaign in Sicily and Southern Italy between 1038 and 1041, under the command of Georgios Maniaces. This campaign is recorded in Greek and Latin sources, as well as French chronicles that deal with the history of the Norman kingdom of Sicily and Southern Italy, and Arab sources note the Sicilian aspects of it as well.

Georgios Maniaces, the Byzantine commander of this war, or Gyrgir, as he is known in the Norse sources, may be said to have been the most notable Byzantine general between Basil II and Alexius Comnenus. By 1038 he had behind him a very distinguished career of military service in Asia Minor, and when Michael IV and his counsellors decided to resume activities in Italy in order to fulfil Basil II's plans

[1] Cf. *Épopée*, III, 204.

for the reconquest of Sicily from the Arabs, he was the obvious choice
for the command of the expeditionary force. His description by Psellos,
who knew him personally, brings vividly before us this giant with the
voice of thunder whose personality overawed even the most undisciplined of soldiers,[1] and there can be little doubt that once Maniaces
had made a reputation for himself, Basil II's less forceful successors
hastened to put him in charge of the regiment whose personnel needed
the most immediately effective direction. That this Turkish-born
former camp-waiter[2] had all the qualities of a great general is not only
shown by the surviving records of his campaigns, from the heroic
exploits at Dolukh onwards, but also by the peculiar character he bears
in the Norse narratives, where the tone is particularly that of the smart
reply that occurred to the speaker after the event. There is little doubt
in the present reviser's mind that Haraldr, as a somewhat undisciplined
junior, was rather frequently carpeted by the Chief, and that the smart
repartee and spectacular actions contained in *Haraldar saga* and *Heimskringla* alike are much-expanded self-justifications, originally told by
Haraldr and blown up by his flatterers.

The Italo-Sicilian situation at this juncture was that after Basil II's
death two Arab chiefs battled over Sicily for a while, and one of them,
Akhal Aboulaphar, sought the Emperor's help. Michael IV received
him kindly, gave him the title of *magister* and offered him help. The
catepan of Italy, Constantine Opos, crossed over to Sicily in 1037 to
assist Akhal, but in the meanwhile his brother and opponent, Abou
Hafs, had sought the assistance of Caliph Muizz-ibn-Badis of Tunis
and Kairwan, who had sent a force to his aid under the command of
his son, Abdallah-ibn-Muizz, and the Arabs of Sicily had gradually
gone over to his party. Þjóðólfr's verse (see above, p. 61) refers almost
certainly either to Muizz or Abdallah when speaking of *Affríka jöfr*,
probably the latter, who certainly had to do battle with the Varangians
later.

After Constantine Opos had to withdraw from Sicily as a result of
the superior generalship of Abdallah-ibn-Muizz (though Constantine
must not be blamed unduly, for he seems to have succeeded in retiring
in good order, and even in bringing back to Italy no less than 15,000
Christians whom he had rescued from slavery in the earlier days of his
campaign),[3] Michael IV decided to send the best general at his disposal
to attempt to reverse this misfortune Accordingly Maniaces was

---

[1] Psellus, *Chronographia*, II, 1ff.
[2] *Cedrenus Scylitzae Ope*, II, 500; cf. *Épopée*, III, 88. On Maniaces himself, see also L. Bréhier,
  'Hommes de guerre byzantins: Georges Maniacès', *Province* (Tours), November 1902
  (cf. *BZ*, 12 (1903), 411).   [3] *Cedrenus Scylitzae Ope*, II, 517; *Épopée*, III, 227.

created *strategos* of Longobardia, and sent to Sicily with the choicest forces available in the Empire.[1] Among his troops were certainly the Varangians under Haraldr Sigurðarson's immediate command, and it may well be that Haraldr was in charge of all the Varangian units sent on this campaign (though one must remember that this would have been an unusually swift promotion in a slow-moving system, as he was only 23 at the time). Besides the Varangians, Maniaces had with him a company of 300 Normans from Salerno, commanded by two sons of Tancred de Hauteville, William 'Ironarm' (*bracca ferrea*) and Drogo, and the Longobard Ardouin, a former vassal of the Archbishop of Milan.[2] From Greece came Katakalon Cecaumenos with a force of stalwart Armenians, and a great fleet was sent by the Emperor under the command of his brother-in-law, the patrician Stephen.

The wars of Maniaces in Sicily have been described in general in the larger histories of the Empire, and the present study will be limited to trying to discover what part the Varangians played in them.[3] That they must have had plenty to do needs no further emphasis, for in such battles as Rametta and Traina (later Fondaco di Maniace), the Byzantines cannot have had a single man to spare. We are consequently thrown back upon the not too reliable evidence of the verses of Haraldr and his poets, supported generally by the evidence of *Advice* as to the value of their services there.

Haraldr composed a number of verses to his queen, Elisaveta Jaroslavovna: in one of them he stated

> Sneið fyr Sikiley víða
> Súð, várum þá prúðir,
> Brýnt skreið, vel til vánar
> Vengis hjörtr und drengjum;
> Vættik miðr at motti
> Myni enn þinig nenna,
> þó lætr Gerðr í Görðum
> Goll-hrings við mér skolla[4]

'The ship passed in many places by Sicily; it moved swiftly at the men's instigation; then were we fine and hopeful. I do not think that the lazy man would bother to go that way, yet the Goddess of Garðar [i.e. Elisaveta] will not look at me.'

---

[1] Zonaras, *Annales*, III, 591.

[2] Geoffrey of Maleterre, *Historia Sicula* (Muratori, *Scriptores rerum Italicarum*, Milan, 1724–51, V, 552); cf. *Épopée*, III, 235.

[3] Cf. *Épopée*, III, 235 ff.; Ostrogorskii, *History of the Byzantine Empire*, tr. J. M. Hussey, 2nd ed., London, 1968, 332–3; *CMH*, 197 ff.; the Latin historians who handle Maniaces' Sicilian war are to be found in Muratori, *Scriptores*, vol. V.

[4] FJ *Skjald* A I 390, B I 329.

There is also a mention of a battle at sea off Sicily by Bölverkr Arnórsson, though it is not easy to decide whether he is referring to Haraldr's first period of service, when he was on a pirate-destroying expedition, or to this later one:

> Súð varð, þars blés blóði
> Börð rendusk at jörðu
> (Vátt drengliga dróttinn)
> Dreyra fullr við eyri;
> Vann und sik fyr sunnan
> Sikiley, liði miklu,
> Sand, þars sveita skyndu
> Sokkin lík of skokka.[1]

'The ship was filled with blood by the cape where [lit.] blood blew; the ships ran to the shore, the Lord fought nobly, [he] won sand under him to the South of Sicily for a great force, where the bodies of the dead let the blood pour on to the planks in the bottom of the ship.'

This description suggests that the fight was very close to land – perhaps the Arabs were trying to prevent the Byzantines from landing, and it was thought a great act of courage for Haraldr and his men to capture the foreshore, *vinna sand*, so as to enable the rest of the army, *liði miklu*, to get ashore.

Valgarðr of Vellir, probably a son or a near relative of Mörðr Valgarðsson (of *Njáls saga*), who appears to have been in Haraldr's company during his last years in Byzantine service, also refers to the Sicilian campaign, and uses strong words about the depopulation caused by the war:

> Skíifingr helt, þars skulfu
> Skeiðr, fyr lönd en breiðu
> Auð varð suðr of síðir
> Sikiley, liði miklu.[2]

The prince took a great force south of the broad lands where the ships quivered; Sicily was at length depopulated.

Clearly, in view of the disparity of numbers between the two forces, Maniaces must have used his Varangians as much on land as on sea, and we may assume without undue strain that the numerous stories in the two lives of King Haraldr have a base of sorts in events, even if, as we have already suggested, there is a certain amount of 'after the

---

[1] FJ *Skjald* A I 386, B I 355. On the word *skokka*, cf. I. Lindqvist, 'En fornisländsk sjöterm "skokkr"', *Festskrift til Finnur Jónsson*, Copenhagen, 1928, 385ff. The present author would read *sveita skyndu sokkin lík* for *sveita skyndi sokkit lík*; nor is Finnur Jónsson justified, in his opinion, in conjecturing *stokka* for *skokka*.

[2] FJ *Skjald* A I 390, B I 360. There is no good reason for preferring the reading *eydd* for the *auð* of the best MSS, as the verse is easy to understand without the alteration.

event' distortion in them. Also, it can hardly be overlooked that there would have been ample cause for friction between the two men in any case. Maniaces, a self-made man with all the virtues and defects of this class, would be highly unlikely to get on with the highly-born and equally self-conscious prince from the far North. Moreover, a general who made so much of the punctilio of military discipline was unlikely to take kindly to the free-and-easy Viking attitude to camp life. A tale in *Heimskringla* has clearly got its roots in this fact. Snorri relates that Haraldr and his Varangians wanted to pitch their tents on one occasion on high ground rather than down in marshy lands lower down, and how Haraldr was supposed to have tricked Maniaces into agreeing that 'the Varangians should have their choice in all that they specially desired'.[1] This is clearly exaggeration, but there is nothing to debar us from surmising that Maniaces was willing to let his select troop have better camping ground rather than let them risk an infection of malaria in the unpleasant damp of a marsh.[2]

Other reasonably buttressed activities by the Varangians during this campaign are those which will have been given to them because of their known abilities in past service, such as being used to capture small fortresses where a large army would have been an uneconomic proposition, and, of course, service in the navy under the admiral Stephen. In this connection the quarrel between Stephen and Maniaces would explain why the Varangians were to turn on the latter on a later occasion. Maniaces, it seems, held Stephen responsible for Abdallah's escape to Tunis after the battle of Traina, and not only reproved him for his inefficiency, but beat him over the head with a whip in his anger.[3] As Maniaces, for all his military brilliance, was unpopular with both officers and men because of his arrogance, it could be no surprise that soldiers of an independent turn of mind, such as the Varangians, would take the side of the naval commander in this quarrel. Moreover, it was Maniaces himself who was directly responsible for the quick recapture from the Empire of all except Messina, since after this very battle of Traina he offended Ardouin the Longobard by having a choice battle-horse taken away from him,[4] and also alienated the Normans by failing in generous division of the booty.[5] In consequence, when the Normans were most needed in Sicily, they defected from their alliance,

[1] *Heimskringla*, II, 73.
[2] Schlumberger draws attention to Delarc's observation on this point (O. Delarc, *Les Normands en Italie*, Paris, 1895, 94, n. 1; cf. *Épopée*, III, 247).
[3] *Cedrenus Scylitzae Ope*, II, 522–3.
[4] Aimé, *Ystoire de li Normant*, ed. O. Delarc, Rouen, 1892, 341, n. 2.
[5] William of Apulia, *Gesta Roberti Wiscardi*, ed. D. R. Wilmans (MGH Scriptores IX), Hanover, 1851, 250; cf. also *Épopée*, III, 243 (esp. n. 3) and 250, n. 1; see also *Cedrenus Scylitzae Ope*, II, 545 and 720.

and joined in a new rebellion in Italy which was to cause the Empire untold trouble.

There had been a rebellion in Bari in 1038, and another in Mottola in 1040, when the catepan of Italy, Nicephorus Doukianos, was killed with many other Imperial officials. In the latter year the Imperial troops recaptured Bari, and Argyros, son of the former rebel Meles, made peace and recognized the suzerainty of the Emperor, while a new catepan, Michael Dokeianos, arrived late in the year. He obtained the assistance of Varangian troops and is said to have had *Rhos* among his men. That these included Haraldr and his troop may be seen from the verse of Haraldr's poets: thus Þjóðólfr states

> Sás við lund á landi
> Langbarða réð ganga

He who led the march at the grove in the land of the Longobardians,[1]

and Illugi Bryndaelaskáld speaks directly of fights with *Frakkar*, i.e., Normans:

> Opt gekk á frið Frakka
> (Fljótreitt, at bý snótar
> Var a(t) döglingi duglum)
> Drottinn minn fyr óttu.

My Lord went often early to disturb the peace of the Franks; 'not swiftly did the vigorous king ride to the lady's bower'.[2]

(The verses in brackets are a quotation by Illugi from the story of Sigurðr Fáfnisbani, as he rides through the flames to Brynhildr.)

Two great battles were fought in this struggle, and *Rhos* are mentioned in both of them. The first was at Olivento near Venusia on 17 March 1041, and the second at Montemaggiore on 4 May the same year. The Normans won both battles despite a considerable disparity of number in favour of the Byzantines, and there is special mention of a great number of *Rhos* having fallen, especially in the battle of Montemaggiore, where we are told that much of Dokeianos' army was drowned in the river Ofanto, which was in full flood.[3] In the same way mention is made of Varangians in the army commanded by the exaugustus [i.e. viceroy, a title preserved in the *Chronicon Barense*] Boioannes, son of Basil II's great admiral, who fought against the

---

[1] FJ *Skjald* A I 370, B I 340; see also *Heimskringla*, III, 82, note.

[2] FJ *Skjald* A I 384, B I 354; see also *Heimskringla*, III, 82, note.

[3] Cf. Gay, *L'Italie méridionale et l'empire byzantin*, Paris, 1909, 457; also Geoffrey of Maleterre, *Historia Sicula*, V, 552 and Aimé, *Ystoire*, II, 25; *Annales Barenses*, ed. G. H. Pertz (MGH Scriptores V), Hanover, 1844, entry for 1042; F. Chalandon, *Histoire de la domination normande en Italie et Sicile*, Paris, 1907, I, 98, and *Cedrenus Scylitzae Ope*, II, 546.

Widener University

WOLFGRAM MEMORIAL LIBRARY

The Pennsylvania Campus
Chester, Pennsylvania 19013
(215) 499-4066

POLICY FOR OVERDUE BOOKS

It is the borrower's responsibility to check the book's date due slip and to return library materials on time. One week after the book is due, a notice is sent to the borrower. If this notice is ignored, a charge is sent for the book. Unpaid fines and charges are registered at the Business Office, and grades may be withheld until all bills are paid.

The fine structure is as follows per book:
    $1.50 - up to 2 weeks overdue
    $3.00 - up to 3 weeks overdue
    $5.00 - after 3 weeks overdue

If a book is lost the following charge is made per book:
    $23.00 to pay for the lost book
    $ 7.00 to pay for the processing

HELPFUL HINTS:
    *To avoid fines and charges, return materials promptly.

    *Items may be renewed in person or by phone (499-4066).

    *Items may be returned after hours by using the book drop outside the library.

    *Fines and charges may be paid by check, payable to Widener University.

1/83

Normans at Monte Siricolo near Montepeloso,[1] but this must have been a different troop to the one commanded by Haraldr, as he and his men had reached Bulgaria by then. In this battle Boioannes was entirely routed and captured, to be released for a huge ransom, and from then on Synodianos, his successor, was cooped up in Otranto, and unable to oppose the Normans seriously.[2]

Before we move on to deal with Haraldr's last Byzantine exploits it is convenient to pause and examine some of the anecdotes related of him in this period by Snorri and the other historians of the Norwegian kings. The greater number of them are easily demonstrable folktales fathered at various times on to various generals, and are most unlikely to be even *au fond* truthful tales about him. Admittedly both Snorri and the other authors intimate that these castles and towns are in Sicily, but since they also place the Sicilian episode before the pilgrimage to Jerusalem, it is not impossible that some of those that might have some factual foundation could relate to his service in Asia Minor (cf. above, pp. 63–5). Let us now examine these narratives individually.

The first is the story of how Haraldr captured a city by collecting small birds which made their nests under the eaves of the houses in the town, where the roof-coverings were made of reeds and straw. Shavings coated with wax and sulphur were then attached to these birds, and set alight, whereon the birds flew to their nests and set them on fire, and the fire then spread throughout the town and the townsfolk were obliged to surrender.[3] This tale is also told of the Russian queen Olga, as the method by which she captured Iskorot',[4] and Saxo tells it of Haddingr in almost identical words to Snorri's version.[5] Vasilevskii also points out that the tale occurs in a similar form in Asochik's chronicle, told of the Emir Ibn Khosrau of Bagdad.[6] The Emir has bundles of reeds made up, soaked in naphtha, and tied to dogs which were sent to him as payment of a tax, and these then set the town on fire; on another occasion he used doves anointed with naphtha on their wings, set on fire and let fly into the air: this he was to have done on Advent Sunday

[1] Besides the references in the previous note, see Leo of Ostia, *Chronicon Monasterii Casinensis*, 676; Aimé, *Ystoire*, II, 23; *Épopée*, III, 258ff.

[2] William of Apulia, *Gesta Roberti Wiscardi*, 250; Gay, *Italie méridionale*, 459.

[3] *Heimskringla*, III, 76–7; *Flateyjarbók*, III, 288–9; cf. also J. de Vries, 'Die Wikingersaga', *Germanisch-Romanische Monatsschrift*, n.s. XV, 90ff. and R. Zenker, *Das Epos von Isembard und Gormund*, Halle am Saale, 1896, 104ff.

[4] *Повесть Временныхъ Лет*, I, 59 (entry for 946).

[5] Saxo, *Gesta Danorum*, ed. J. Olrik, H. Raeder and F. Blatt (Copenhagen, 1931–57), I, 24; he also tells a similar tale of Friðleifr the Rash (I, 102–3), and there is an English version told of Gorm the Viking and how he captured Cirencester, cf. Stender-Petersen, *Die Varägersage*, 138–9.

[6] Vasilevskii, *Труды*, I, 232ff.

in honour of the Advent of Christ, as he liked Christians so much (!),
while Alexander the Great was said to have captured a castle set on a
high rock 'through the medium of birds'.[1] On the other hand, the
tales of Ibn Khosrau were supposed to have taken place in Armenia,
and Vasilevskii surmises that the tales of Olga and Haraldr originate
from them, having been picked up by Varangians who had winter
quarters there. The basic tale appears in any case later fathered on to
Genghis Khan.[2]

Similarly the tale of the ruse whereby Haraldr captures a town by
pretending to be sick and then dead must also be regarded as a version
of an itinerant folktale.[3] The *Heimskringla* version is, in essence, as
follows: Haraldr pretends sickness and death; the Varangians ask the
town authorities for leave to bury him in a church inside the town, and
imply that they will pay a large sum for the privilege to this church.
The permission is given, and the coffin is carried in through the opened
gate, where the bearers halt; they are Varangians who carry weapons
under their cloaks, and now hold the gate open until Haraldr and their
comrades come to their assistance, and they can capture the town. In
the independent *Haraldar saga* Halldór Snorrason's angry recrimina-
tions with Haraldr are placed here, and his wounds are mentioned, but
Heimskringla places that incident in connection with the Varangians'
games, a more likely place, since the story of these is unlikely to be an
itinerant tale, but rather a direct family legend among the descendants
of Snorri the Priest, and originally told by Halldór himself, and so has
a fair chance of being true history (cf. further pp. 211–12 below). The
story of the false death of the commander is an ancient itinerant;[4] thus
Saxo tells it of Froda I of Denmark when he captured Palteskja and
(later) London.[5] It is also told of Hasting the Viking when he besieged
Luna,[6] William of Apulia tells a similar tale of Robert Guiscard and
an Italian monastery,[7] and Matthew Paris has such an anecdote about
Guiscard, Frederic II and the expulsion of the monks of Monte
Cassino.[8] The opinion of Jan de Vries, that the story originated in

[1] Asochik, *Histoire universelle*, tr. E. Dulaurier and F. Macler, Paris, 1883–1917, II, 64.
[2] This is likely to have been a borrowing from a lost Armenian translation of Pseudo-
Callisthenes, see Stender-Petersen, *Die Varägersage*, 147–55 and J. Zecher, *Pseudo-
Callisthenes*, Halle am Saale, 1867, 87.
[3] *Heimskringla*, III, 80–1; see also *Flateyjarbók*, III, 300–2.
[4] Cf. Vasilevskii, *Труды*, I, esp. 40–88, and de Vries, 'Normannisches Lehngut', *Arkiv for
Nordisk Filologi*, 47.
[5] Saxo, *Gesta Danorum*, I, 38 and 46.
[6] Dudo, *Historia Normannorum*, ed. J. Lair, Caen, 1865, 132ff.; Wace, *Roman de Rou*, ed.
H. Andersen, Heilbronn, 1877–9, 643ff.
[7] William of Apulia, *Gesta Roberti Wiscardi*, 260 (he does not mention any name for the
place, but see Chalandon, *La domination normande*, I, 120.
[8] Matthew Paris, *Chronica Majora*, ed. H. Richards (Rolls Series), London, 1872–83, III, 538.

southern Italy and was originally told of Guiscard, being subsequently fathered on to other warriors, is the most probable one;[1] less likely is the explanation of Otto von Freisingen, who makes the original actor Robert II of Sicily, and the original venue in Greece.[2] Apart from mediaeval sources, however, we should recollect that there is also a classical tale by Polyaenus of a similar trick used by Kallikratides of Cyrene to capture Magnesia,[3] and the tale of how St Demetrius saved Thessalonica in 1041 has a suspicious family resemblance to this theme.

The story in *Heimskringla*, where Haraldr has his men tunnel under the walls of a besieged town, to emerge in a banqueting hall and capture the town, is of a somewhat different calibre.[4] It is true that there are numerous stories of such a military stratagem among the tales of ancient generals; thus Darius I is said to have captured Chalcedon by this means,[5] and Livy has a record of the capture of Veii by Furius Camillus through such a trick;[6] but this is so commonplace an incident of ancient and mediaeval siege warfare that there is no need for the incident in its basic form to be a folktale, and the author agrees with Vasilevskii that the anecdote could well be based on truth.[7]

The result of our investigation becomes, then, that we must distinguish carefully and sharply between the bulk of the stories and the two classes that are (1) tales of such commonplace practices of warfare as any experienced military commander would know about and regard as self-evident ways of operation (such as the tunnelling), and (2) tales which contain so large a number of personal characteristics, such as the narrative of Halldór's wounds and the games, and which are nowhere else to be found. These two classes are such in character as to make it unlikely that it is possible to prove them to be fictitious, and in default of proof of untruthfulness, we may take them as most probably containing a basic element of truth.

The rest of the anecdotes are quite another matter, since they all bear the unmistakable signs of the itinerant folktale. These are entirely untrustworthy, and highly unlikely to have happened to Haraldr and his troop, or to have originated from them after their return to Scandi-

---

[1] de Vries, 'Normannisches Lehngut', *Arkiv for Nordisk Filologi*, 47, 68.
[2] Otto von Freisingen, *Gesta Friderici I*, ed. G. Waitz, rev. B. de Simson (MGH Scriptores xv), Hanover, 1912, 53.
[3] Polyaenus, Στρατηγήματα, ed. J. Vulteius *et al.*, Leiden, 1690, 194; see also D. Obolensky, 'The cult of St Demetrius in Thessalonica', *Balkan Studies*, 15 (1974), 3–20, and A. Stender-Petersen, 'A Varangian Stratagem', *Varangica*, Aarhus, 1953, 189–98.
[4] *Heimskringla*, III, 77–8; see also *Flateyjarbók*, III, 296–7.
[5] Polyaenus, Στρατηγήματα, 624–5.
[6] Livy, *Ab urbe condita*, ed. B. O. Foster, London, 1924, III, 69.
[7] Vasilevskii, Труды, I, 236.

navia. As previously mentioned, the most likely explanation of their origin seems to the author to be that of Jan de Vries, namely that these stories originated in southern Italy, and Varangians who heard them there, or picked them up in the East from other Varangians, brought them back along with various other juicy stories all the way to Iceland.[1] We will examine this point better later on.

Peter Delianos raised a rebellion in Bulgaria in the summer of 1040. He was a runaway slave from Constantinople who claimed to be a grandson of Tsar Samuel, and he obtained a great following in the Epirote and Macedonian themes, including the support of Alousian, the younger brother of Ladislas, the last Tsar of the old Bulgarian empire. This army invaded Greece, and inflicted a heavy defeat on the garrison of Thebes, which attempted to oppose them. When the rebellion began Michael IV was in Thessalonica, but he hurried back to the capital at once to raise troops.[2] Among other forces he recalled Haraldr and his Varangians from Sicily, as we can see from *Advice*, and this is confirmed by a reference in a verse by Þjóðólfr, who refers to his master as *Bolgara brennir*.[3] It is not likely, however, that this company reached their new sphere of activities until early in 1041. The Emperor's brother Constantine defended Thessalonica from a siege by the Bulgarians during the winter 1040–1, and it is doubtful whether the Varangians from Sicily were there. Alousian besieged the city with a force of 40,000 men, but the garrison made a sortie on 26 October 1040, in which they inflicted heavy losses on the besiegers, 15,000 Bulgars being killed and the rest put to rout. A regiment by the name of *Tagma ton megathymon*, 'the troop of the great-hearted (brave)', won considerable renown by their conduct during the siege and the sortie,[4] and some, including Vasilevskii, have assumed that this title referred to Varangians, especially as Greek sources credited the relief to St Demetrius, the patron saint of the city, who was supposed to have been in the forefront of the battle on a white charger. The argument is that Snorri's story of St Olaf's miraculous assistance to Haraldr, and to the Varangians *á Pezinavollum*, applied here.[5] This cannot be so, however, and the author agrees entirely with Storm that St Olaf's miracle at Thessalonica cannot be in question here, since there are convincing reasons to believe that the battle of 'Pezina Fields' took place in the reign of John II.

[1] de Vries, 'Normannisches Lehngut', 78.
[2] Attaleiates, *Historiae*, ed. I. Bekker (CSHB), Bonn, 1853, 9.
[3] *Sexstefja* 1 (FJ *Skjald* A I 369, B I 339) *En Bolgara brennir | Bræðrum sínum vel tæði.*
[4] Obolensky, 'The cult of St. Demetrius'; *Cedrenus Scylitzae Ope*, II, 532 refers to his uncle Constantine, but this is probably a mistake.
[5] *Heimskringla*, III, 371–2; cf. Storm, 'Harald Haardraade'.

Moreover, the Varangians, though given many titles in Greek sources, are never given this one, which is almost certainly the name of a Greek unit. Furthermore, as we have seen, it is most unlikely that Haraldr and his unit could have returned to Greece so quickly from their Sicilian and Serbian duties, but there is nothing to prevent another detachment of Varangians from taking part in the defence, or the tale from becoming attached to the wrong lot in the recording.

What is certain is that Haraldr and his men returned in time to take part in the latter part of this war and helped to bring it to a victorious conclusion. We are told by the author of *Advice* that the Emperor rewarded Haraldr for his Italian services with the title of *Manglavites*,[1] and we may assume that this led to his transfer from the provincial Varangians to the life-guard proper, the 'Varangians of the City', and that probably most of his own men followed him in the change. By this time they had probably been able to make enough money to pay the entrance fee, if this was still being demanded. In that case they will have accompanied the Emperor, as the *Advice* implies, when he left the capital with a fresh army and succeeded in destroying the rebellion completely inside a year. Michael was helped in his efforts by the internal dissension among the Bulgars; thus Alousian had Delianos blinded and then deserted his countrymen and surrendered to the Emperor, who gave him a full pardon. Delianos and the other Bulgarian chiefs continued nevertheless with their resistance, until Michael crushed them completely at Prilep, whereon they surrendered. As we have seen from *Advice*, Michael then rewarded Haraldr further for good service by promoting him to the rank of *Spatharokandidatos*,[2] and we may deduce with good reason that if he held no higher rank in the Imperial service up to then he is unlikely ever to have held independent command of an army larger than the small force needed to reduce a small fortress or a minor township. Nonetheless, as we have seen, *Advice* represents him as perfectly content with this rank. Þjóðólfr refers to eighteen battles fought before he went back to Norway, and we may assume that these would have been the major engagements in which he took part as a mercenary of Michael IV.

> Þjóð veit, at hefr háðar
> Hvargrimmlegar rimmur
> (Rofizk hafa oft fyr jöfri)
> Átján Haraldr (sáttir);
> Höss arnar rautt hvassar,
> Hróðigr konungr, blóði

---

[1] *Advice*, 93; on the duties of the μαγγλαβίτης, see above, p. 22.
[2] *Advice*, 93.

(Ímr gat krás hvars kómuð
Klær, áðr hingat færir).

The people know that Haraldr has fought eighteen very fierce battles; peace has often been disturbed for the Ruler; the triumphant King reddened the sharp claws of the brown eagle with blood before he came here; the wolf gained a feast where you came.[1]

The Bulgarian battles were probably the last military actions in which Haraldr was engaged in the Imperial service. In the autumn, when he had restored order in Bulgaria and the other districts upset by the rebels, Michael IV made a triumphal entry into his capital, bringing with him the blinded Delianos and the other captured Bulgarian chiefs. Psellus, who was an eyewitness of the procession, described the toll that the strain of warfare had exacted from the Emperor's never very robust body, and it must have been clear to all, including himself, that he was a dying man.[2] In consequence he made an effort to set his own house in order, and with the consent of his wife (as the representative of the legitimate Macedonian dynasty) named his nephew Michael, son of his sister Maria and the Admiral (former shipwright) Stephen as his successor on the throne. Having done so, Michael IV died on 10 December 1041, and Michael V Calaphates succeeded him.

Michael V had been commander of the life-guards in his uncle's last days, and there is no doubt that he was well aware of the general unpopularity of his family (except for his predecessor, who alone of the clan appears to have preserved a good reputation because of his ability and personal virtues); in particular his uncles John the Orphanotrophos and Constantine the governor of Thessalonica were looked on with disfavour because of their avaricious tendencies. In consequence, when Michael became Emperor, he attempted to make changes such as would placate popular opinion, and began by stripping his Uncle John of his offices and banishing him from the capital. He also released Georgios Maniaces from the prison into which Michael IV had cast him after the uproar with Admiral Stephen and restored him to favour and power, put him in charge of a fresh fleet and a new army, and despatched him to Italy to put down the Normans and then to reconquer Sicily from the Arabs. This was hardly before due time, as the Byzantines had by this time lost all Italy except Bari, Taranto, Brindisi and Otranto.[3]

Not surprisingly, some of the members of the Imperial family objected to these actions, though Michael's uncle Constantine supported him, and received in return both the Imperial confidence and the

---

[1] *Sexstefja* 7 (FJ *Skjald* A I 370, B I 340–1).
[2] Psellus, *Chronographia*, I, 82–3.   [3] *Cedrenus Scylitzae Ope*, II, 547.

title of *nobilissimus*, while the men of the house who objected were arrested by the guards (probably, as so often in the past and in the future, Varangians were selected for this unsavoury task) and castrated. Even by the standards of the horror-sated generation of 1978 this may seem an unduly savage act of authoritarianism, but it is well attested by Psellus, who records his conversation with Constantine the *nobilissimus* about it, and makes it clear that the latter had at least tried, though he had failed, to dissuade the Emperor from carrying it out.[1]

From what has gone before, we may assume that at least one unit of the Varangians (the one under Haraldr's command) were hostile to Maniaces as the result of friction during the previous Italo-Sicilian campaign, and it can have been no joy to Haraldr that his unpleasant former superior was not only free, but once again in a situation of high authority. The Emperor cannot have been unaware of their disaffection either, the more so as he had been commander of the guards during the previous years, and this is likely to be the explanation for the alteration in the constitution of the Emperor's personal guards which Psellus records. 'He started to use young Scythians as his own guards; he had purchased these men himself as slaves before he ascended the throne, and they were all eunuchs, knew his temper well and were well adapted for the services that he demanded from them.'[2] These *Skuthai* were in all probability Pechenegs; nonetheless, Michael V does not seem to have abolished the Varangian regiment, nor do the Varangians or the other older Greek guards' regiments appear to have made any fuss about it; these units appear to have continued in use in the garrison of the capital, even though the *Skuthai* were given charge of the Emperor's personal safety and comfort. It is not impossible, however, that the Emperor had other more powerful reasons for suspecting Haraldr; the evidences appear to the author to point in this direction, and to suggest that this is what lies at the back of the narratives of Snorri and the Kings' Sagas as to the accusations levelled against Haraldr, and the imprisonment inflicted on him and two of his closest subordinates.

According to *Heimskringla*, Haraldr was accused of withholding money that rightly belonged to the Emperor, but for which he had been responsible, and he was incarcerated on this and other charges. We are then told how he was released from jail, which is said to have happened shortly before he and his Varangians attacked the Emperor's palace and blinded him; the sagas imply that this was done to revenge themselves for the arrest. Soon thereafter Haraldr left for Russia and thence for Scandinavia with his principal followers.[3]

[1] Psellus, *Chronographia*, I, 111. [2] Psellus, *Chronographia*, I, 95. [3] *Heimskringla*, III, 85-6.

Another chapter in the same tale describes how he sent gold and
jewels that he acquired in Byzantium to Jaroslav for safe keeping:

this was so great a sum that no man in the North had seen so great a treasure
in one man's possession. Haraldr had thrice been involved in *pólútasvarf*
while he was in Byzantium. There the law is that every time the Emperor
dies, the Varangians have a *pólútasvarf*, they then go round all the Emperor's
pólútir, where his treasure-chambers are, and each shall take free possession
of anything that he can get his hands on.[1]

There is no doubt that Haraldr will have gained enormous wealth
during his service under the Emperors. As we have seen in the case of
the battle of Longon, where Basil II gave his Varangians a third of the
booty,[2] the custom was to give the foreign mercenaries a large share
of the plunder of each campaign as a recompense for the fact that their
pay (except for the life-guards) was very low.[3]

Snorri and *Fagrskinna* agree that it was the Empress Zoe who accused
Haraldr of misappropriating funds of which he was supposed to render
an account, and her third and last husband, Constantine IX, who had
him arrested. This cannot, however, be correct; to take only one point,
the Emperor who was blinded by Haraldr was Michael V, nor is it very
likely that Constantine IX had him arrested, as the author of *Advice*
does not mention this, but merely refers to the fact that the Emperor
refused him leave to go home.[4] On the other hand *Haraldar saga* states
that it was 'Gyrgir', i.e. Maniaces, who slandered Haraldr to the
Emperor and Empress, and accused him of misappropriation of funds.[5]
We have already mentioned that Haraldr was to pay the Emperor
100 marks for every captured pirate vessel, and could keep the rest
of the booty for himself and his men, and the accusation seems,
therefore, to refer to some activity of Haraldr's company during
the first period in the Imperial service, when Haraldr was used on
naval service, and since Maniaces was nowhere near, holding as he
did a land command in Asia at that time, he is unlikely to have laid an
accusation concerning an incident in which he had no legal standing[6]
– though there is of course nothing to prevent him from having
encouraged another person more legitimately involved, such as an
appropriate Imperial fiscal official, in making the accusation. His own
misfortunes as a result of his political tactlessness in Sicily cannot have
made him think over kindly of the junior officer who basked in Michael
IV's favour while he himself lay in prison, and when he found himself

---

[1] *Heimskringla*, III, 90.   [2] See above, p. 48.   [3] See above, p. 28.
[4] *Advice*, 93.   [5] *Flateyjarbók*, III, 302–3.
[6] See above, p. 31; for Maniaces' service at the time, see above, p. 52.

back in a position of power and influence, it is very understandable that he would attempt to get some of his own back on all his enemies and, as Schlumberger observes in connection with the marriage of Theophano and Romanos II, venal officials are to be found in all periods of history.[1]

It is true that the surviving fragments of verse by his court poets do not mention the charge or the imprisonment, but this is clearly no disproof of them, nor is the silence of *Advice* on this point either proof or disproof; an accusation of financial malversation is after all not something that a monarch wishes to be flaunted about him, even from his past, and so we cannot draw any conclusions from their silence. At the same time, the Icelandic prose versions (being in all likelihood descended from the companions of his misfortune, particularly Halldór Snorrason, who had a personal axe to grind with King Haraldr), had no reason to indulge in courtly discretion, and may therefore be considered as likely to have passed on material with (at least) a substratum of fact, the more so as Halldór was so closely involved in most of King Haraldr's escapades as to be of all men the most likely to know what happened to him in his Byzantine days. Making the necessary allowances for the amount of distortion likely to occur in over a century of oral transmission, it is not unreasonable to assume that much of Halldór's own recollection has survived, particularly that the two comparatively sober accounts which we have in Icelandic have a reasonable chance of being correct.

Perhaps, however, it is the word *pólútasvarf* which takes us furthest in our investigation of this point. Snorri has read the first part of the word as a corruption of Lat. *palatia*, and so interpreted it as 'the Emperor's palaces', and there is some evidence that Norse speakers used *pólútir* in the meaning 'palaces'; thus some manuscripts of *Heimskringla* read *pollitta* or *polota*,[2] and the word is used precisely in this meaning in the *Itinerary* of Abbot Nikulás Bergsson (1159), where we read *Í Miklagardi i pollutum enum fornum er rit þat er drottinn varr reit sjalfr sinum hondum*, 'In Constantinople, in the old palaces, is that letter that Our Lord wrote with his own hands' (i.e. the celebrated apocryphal letter to King Abgar).[3] The *pollutir enar fornu* are in this context the old Imperial palaces, so named to differentiate them from the Blachernae group, where the Comnenian Emperor lived in the time of Abbot Nikulás. The *svarf* of these palaces ought therefore to mean by Snorri's

---

[1] G. Schlumberger, *Un empereur de Byzance: Nicéphore Phocas*, Paris, 1890, 7.

[2] For textual variation in MSS of *Heimskringla*, see the Introduction to Finnur Jónsson's edition (Copenhagen, 1893–1901).

[3] *Alfræði íslenzk*, ed. K. Kålund, Copenhagen, 1908–18, I, 25; cf. also F. L. Cross and E. M. Livingstone, *A Dictionary of the Christian Church*, 2nd ed., Oxford, 1975, 5.

definition that the Varangians simply went round them and helped themselves to anything they wanted. By any standard of knowledge of Byzantine affairs this is inconceivable, though it is not beyond the bounds of possibility that the Varangians who were on guard duty when the Emperor died were allowed to take certain precious objects as mementos of the occasion away with them when all was over – but these would certainly have been pre-specified under such circumstances.

There is, however, a much more probable explanation of this term, one which rests on the fact that the original Varangian regiment came to Byzantium from Russia, and was certain to include a substantial number of Russian-speaking soldiers in its ranks, and consequently to bring with it a number of Russian words for various regimental tasks, which are very likely, in the way that slang terms cling to objects and actions in an enclosed, self-perpetuating society, to have been commonplaces of Varangian speech in the time of Haraldr, and probably even later.

In Russian полота or палата can mean both 'palace' and 'chambers', and we find it used in this precise meaning in the narrative of *Fagrskinna* of the Emperor's bedchamber, *giengo sidan til konongs palata, þar en hann svaf*, 'the then went to the King's [i.e. Emperor's] chambers, where he slept'. The second half could then be a corruption of O.Russ. сбор, субору, 'collection', 'gathering'; accordingly the whole word should mean 'collection' (of treasures), or 'the gathering of treasures' in the palace (or chambers); accordingly, the Russian phrase would have been палатный сбор.

We must, however, doubt very strongly whether such a custom ever existed, if only for the above-mentioned dissuasive reason. The two comprehensive descriptions of Byzantine court ceremonial, Constantine VII's *De Ceremoniis* and Pseudo-Codinus, do not mention any such custom; granted that in 950 the Varangians were not yet established as a regiment with its own customs and privileges, and so this was unlikely to be found in Constantine's otherwise meticulous catalogue of court ceremonial, and Pseudo-Codinus was describing the life of a much impoverished Imperial household, whose finances could not have stood the strain of such a ravage. J. Hallenberg has, however, attempted to deduce from a reference in Pseudo-Codinus, where the custom of the Varangians tearing down the wreaths of flowers and green-leafed branches used to decorate the colonnade from Hagia Sophia to the old Imperial Palace, that this was an action connected with *pólútasvarf*, but the present author finds it

---

¹ *Fagrskinna*, ed. F. Jónsson, Copenhagen, 1902–3, 229.

difficult to see any connection between this duty and what Snorri describes.[1]

It must be admitted that there were certain similar activities in *Western* European lands. Thus it was the custom for a while in Rome that when the reigning Pope died his palace was sacked, and this was also the custom on the death of a bishop, both in Rome and elsewhere in Italy, but the custom was abolished (at least publicly) by a decree of the Synod of Rome in 904.[2] Also, when the Caliph of Bagdad died or was deposed, his residence was pillaged, sometimes extremely thoroughly, and the same was sometimes done to the homes of the ministers.[3] The author is inclined to believe, therefore, that some limited form of pillage was permitted to the Varangians in Byzantium during Haraldr's time there, though this custom can hardly have been allowed to go on for long.[4] On the other hand, the guards are bound to have received large disbursements of Imperial bounty on the death of any Emperor, if only to secure their loyalty to the new incumbent of the Throne.

If, as is very likely, there are some who cannot accept this explanation of the term, then there is another one which has been strenuously advocated by scholars, for which the prior assumption is a Russian interpretation of the word. We will first take an interpretation postulated by the present author, based upon this possibility.[5] The first half of the word could then be some corrupt form of the O.Russ. получать or получить, 'to receive', and сбор in the second half would still mean 'tax'.[6] It is quite conceivable that the Varangians' military *lingua franca* could have corrupted this into a Norse verb *at polúta*, and so *polúta-svarf(it)* came to mean either the receipt or the acceptance of these treasures (taking сбор in the sense of 'collection'), at the death of an Emperor. If, however, сбор is taken as meaning 'tax', then it could mean that the Varangians, or especially Haraldr and his company,

[1] *DO*, 226. This was first suggested by J. Hallenberg, *Anmärkningar öfver 1 Delen af Lagerbrings Svea rikes historia*, Stockholm, 1819–22, II, 207; cf. also Cronholm, *Wäringarna*, Lund, 1832, 216 and 227; S. Blöndal, 'Quelques notes sur le mot pólútasvarf', *Classica et Mediaevalia*, II, 9, n. 1; A. Stender-Petersen, *Varangica*, 151ff.

[2] F. Gregorovius, *Geschichte der Stadt Rom in Mittelalter*, 4th ed., Stuttgart, 1886–96, III, 203; cf. also C. Ducange, *Glossarium mediae et infimae latinitatis*, under 'spolium'.

[3] A. Mez, *Die Renaissance des Islams*, Heidelberg, 1922, 143 and refs. there.

[4] The spoliation of Blachernae on the deposition of Michael V was a very exceptional case and, apart from the depredations of the Fourth 'Crusade', no evidence is known of the deliberate pillaging of Imperial residences on the demise or dethronement of an Emperor. Of course, the story of such an event as the deposition of 1042 could, when being related in the far North, easily assume the character of a regular and permitted activity instead of being recognized for what it was, an individual act of licence.

[5] See above, n. 1.

[6] O.N. *skattr* is also found as an O.Russ. loanword 'скот', principally used in that period to denote taxes paid in cattle or other kind (furs etc.).

were used to collect taxes in districts where the ordinary tax-collectors found it difficult to gather it without military assistance, though the author would not want to assert outright that Haraldr or the Varangians were made actual tax-collectors, but rather suggest that they went with the normal officials and were available in case a forcible form of persuasion was necessary.

It may also be pointed out that there were ordinances concerning a specific tax, or rather, an obligation on landowners (even on monastic houses) to supply the Imperial troops with quarters and all their residential necessities. This was a heavy obligation in a country as militarized as the Eastern Empire, and naturally householders did their best to escape it, preferring to pay even large sums in ready cash rather than have a mob of barbarian soldiers quartered on them. It may help to refer here to a number of Imperial chrysobulls which grant exceptions from this obligation, and which particularly refer to Varangians. Thus the Great Lavra monastery on Mt Athos was exempted in 1060 from this obligation to house Varangians by Constantine X Ducas, who also gave the same monastery further privileges in 1068, mentioning in the document of exception especially that the house is free from 'payments to Varangians, Russians, Arabs or Franks'.[1] A third document is an exemption granted by Michael VII Ducas to the historian Michael Attaleiates from all kinds of taxes and obligations on his estates in Thrace and Macedonia, given by Attaleiates to found a monastery and hospice for the poor in Rodosto; there a specific exemption is granted from the obligation to accommodate soldiers, and among the foreign troops are especially mentioned 'Russians and Varangians'. This exemption is confirmed by Nicephorus III in 1079.[2] A fourth such document is a grant of exemption by Alexius I to the monastery of Patmos from all kinds of duties and taxes, and once more exemption from billeting of troops, including specifically Russians and Varangians, expressly named in the document.[3]

---

[1] Chrysobull from Lavra, *Actes de Lavra*, ed. G. Rouillard and P. Collomp, Paris, 1937, I 28, 80; cf. also review by F. Dölger in *BZ* 39 (1939), 235 and 41 (1941), 251.

[2] The additional privilege is printed in C. Sathas, *Bibliotheca graeca medii aevi*, Venice, 1872, I, 55; Nicephorus II's confirmation is in *ibid.*, III, 64.

[3] Printed in MM Acta, VI, 44ff., also in E. Zachariae von Lingenthal, *Jus graeco-romanum*, Leipzig, 1856–84, III, 373. In it are enumerated the peoples who formed the Byzantine mercenaries, and Russians, Varangians, Kylfings and Englishmen are clearly differentiated (cf. also Vasilevskii, *Труды*, I, 348ff.). Another document, dated 1068, states Λογιαρικῆς εἰσπράξεως Βαράγγωνῇ 'Ρώς, Σαρακηνωνῇ Φράγγων, 'tax-gathering by Varangians, Russians, Saracens or Franks' (printed in *История Афона*, ed. S. Porfiryi, Saint Petersburg, 1877, I, 186). The third document omits the ἤ between 'Ρώς and Βαράγγων; Vasilevskii thinks that this points to a composite word, 'Ρώς-Βάραγγοι or 'Βάραγγοι-'Ρώς, but this is not very likely, and even if there were such a compound it would only intimate that the Byzantines differentiated between Russian-speaking Varangians and Norse-

There are, however, many possible criticisms of this interpretation of the term *pólútasvarf*, and A. Stender-Petersen has produced a particularly noteworthy alternative interpretation in his article in *Classica et Mediaevalia*.[1] This takes as its point of departure a comment by Constantine VII in *De Administrando Imperio*, where the Emperor describes the tax-collecting methods of the Princes of Kiev.

At the beginning of November they go εἰς τὰ πολύδια ἃ λέγεται Γίρα, or into the lands of the Slavinians, the Berbians, the Drugubites, the Kubitzes, the Serbs and other Slavs who pay tax to the Russians. There they stay all the winter, and in April, when the ice melts on the river Dnepr, they return to Kiev. There they get back their μονοξύλονοι [boats carved out of single trees], get them ready, and so go to the Romans [i.e. the Empire]'.[2]

The words εἰς τὰ πολύδια ἃ λέγεται Γίρα were previously interpreted as if πολύδια was a scribal error for πολείδια 'small cities', and so translated 'small cities known as Gyra'. S. M. Solovev has pointed out, however, that this is a question of the transliteration of the Old Russian word полуде, 'tax-gathering expedition'. The rulers of Russia made these journeys annually to gather their taxes, which were paid in various kinds of goods, after which the gathered goods were sent off to Constantinople to be sold for the produce of the Empire.[3] It is then clear that Γίρα cannot be a place-name. Another Russian scholar, N. Popov, has suggested that it is simply the Greek word γύρα, 'circular', and this is very likely true in the author's opinion. Hence Constantine was using a Russian term, and following it up with its Greek interpretation, and the line should therefore be translated 'in a tax-collecting expedition, which is called [by them] a circular [round] journey'. This is supported by a reference in the *Epanagoge* of Basil I and Leo VI where γύρα is used in this meaning of tax-gathering expedition in the Imperial service: 'We command that no official shall be permitted to go on far

---

speaking Varangians, calling the latter simply Βάραγγοι. Franz Dölger *BZ*, 38 (1938), 235) points to other occasions where Βάραγγοι, 'Ρώς or 'Ρώς, Βάραγγοι, are mentioned separately (cf. also his *Regesten der Kaiserurkunden des altrömischen Reiches*, Munich, 1924–32, nos. 946 (June 1060), 97 (February 1073, where 'Ρωσσοβάραγγοι is surely a copyist's error for 'Ρώς, Βάραγγοι), 1042 (April 1079), 1147 (April 1088)). It is, however, possible to doubt whether Κύλπιγγοι mentioned in these documents came from Russia for, as Waldemar Nissen has pointed out (W. Nissen, *Die Diataxis des Michael Attaleiates von 1077*, Jena, 1894, 68–9) it is possible that the word refers to a German tribe (the Guduscani) who had been allowed to settle near the river *Kulpa* in southern Slavia, where that river runs into the Sava. Nevertheless the present author considers it most likely that Κύλπιγγοι there refers to the Russian *Kylfingar* (though the reviser lacks his certainty).

[1] Stender-Petersen, *Varangica*, 151–64.
[2] *DAI*, 62/63.
[3] S. M. Solovev, *Исторія Россіи*, Moscow, 1855–68, 1, 221ff. For a description see V. M. Klyuchevskii, *History of Russia*, London, 1911–31, 1, 78ff., also Stender-Petersen, *Varangica*, 151–64.

journeys, or on so-called round journeys (ἀποδημίας ποιεῖσθαι ἢ τὰς λεγομένας γυράς) without express permission'.[1]

Stender-Petersen argues that γύρα, 'round journey' is *svarf*, the second element of *pólútasvarf*, so that the word contains therefore a Russian and a Norse element which mean the same thing, i.e. полуде 'round journey' (to gather tax), and *svarf*, 'round journey (perhaps with forcible intention)'; in support of this theory he points to the mixed word *taparöx(i)*, where the first element, *tapar*, is clearly O.Russ. топор, 'axe'. This is not a very strong parallel, however; admittedly топор means 'axe', but *taparöx(i)* will certainly have been used of a particular kind of small axe of Russian origin, and that will have been why the Russian element remained in its name.[2]

Stender-Petersen considers that Haraldr, dwelling as he did with Prince Jaroslav both before (1031–3) and after (1043–5) his period of service in Constantinople, will have been sent by him on such tax-gathering expeditions, the more so as 'he was the commander of the King's defence forces' according to the saga. In return for his services he would then have been given a specific proportion of the amount brought back, and have sent it to Constantinople for sale, and so laid the foundations of his wealth. In so far as it affects the explanation of the text of *DAI*, there can be little doubt that the arguments of Solovev, Popov and Stender-Petersen are correct, but it is more doubtful whether it is possible to translate γύρα (or полуде) by the O.N. word *svarf*. The author has not been able to find any O.N. use of the substantive which will bear this interpretation in the written records, though the verb *svarfa* has been used in a meaning which could have given rise to a similar meaning of the noun,[3] and there is clearly no strong objection to *svarf* having been used of journeys in this way, as much force must have been used by the tax-gatherers on their expeditions to extort the revenue desired.

If, however, we read *pólútasvarf* as an old Varangian slang word for such tax-gathering expeditions in Russia, it is of course reasonable to think at first sight, as Stender-Petersen has done, that Haraldr had been on them, and that his wealth originated from them. Nevertheless, if we examine the matter a little further, we realize that there is a strong element of doubt in this argument because of the time involved. During

---

[1] *Epanagoge*, ed. C. E. Zachariae von Lingenthal, Tit. VII, par. η (reprinted in *Jus Graeco-Romanum*, ed. J. and P. Zepos, Aalen, 1962, II, 250). The attribution by Stender-Petersen (*Varangica*, 163) is wrong.

[2] H. Falk, *Altnordische Waffenkunde*, Christiania, 1914, 110.

[3] Cf. *Fornmanna sögur* XI, 40, *Hákon svarfaðisk þar um á Gautlandi*. The word *svarf* is used in the precise meaning of gaining money by force; so in the *Flateyjarbók*, I, 412 *þat er víkinga háttr at afla sér fjár með ránum eðr svörfum*.

his first stay in Russia, Haraldr was a young, unproven boy in his teens, and even if he went on an expedition with either Jaroslav himself or Eilífr,[1] he would only have gone as a very junior person, and not been likely to receive any great share of the takings. After his return, of course, it was another matter, as by then he had become an experienced senior officer of the Imperial forces, and, moreover, became Jaroslav's son-in-law during this period; nevertheless, there are weighty chronological objections again. It is extremely doubtful whether he could have left Constantinople and reached Kiev much before the middle of 1043, and as he had arrived back in Norway by 1045 (most probably, in view of subsequent events, in the Spring), it would not have been possible for him to have taken part in more than two of these expeditions at most, and this contradicts the direct statement of our Norse sources that he thrice took part in *pólútasvarf*.

There is a verse by Valgarðr of Vellir which Snorri quotes as evidence of the wealth brought back by Haraldr from the East.[2] Stender-Petersen argues that this refers to the remuneration for his tax-collecting activities in Russia and the sale of the goods in Byzantium, but the words are only: *farðir goll ór Görðum (grunlaust) Haraldr austan*, 'Haraldr brought gold from Garðar in the East without suspicion', and the verse canot be used as a proof of how or where the gold was obtained.

There is of course one other possibility still: the word *pólútasvarf* could easily have become Varangian slang for tax-gathering expeditions in the *Imperial* service. If Snorri's explanation, with the limitations pointed out by the present author, cannot be accepted, then this becomes the most likely meaning, and though there is no direct statement in either Byzantine or Norse sources that Haraldr and his company were so employed, there is yet no evidence in them to preclude this, and it can be regarded as certain that they will frequently have taken advantage of the provisions of the Imperial enactments concerning the obligations of housing, feeding and sustaining mercenaries mentioned earlier in this chapter to their own profit. The words $\lambda o\gamma\iota\alpha\rho\iota\kappa\hat{\eta}s$ $\epsilon\dot{\iota}\sigma\pi\rho\dot{\alpha}\xi\epsilon\omega s$ (cf. p. 82, n. 3) point directly to tax-gathering by Varangians. Nor is there any good reason to regard Snorri's statement that Haraldr's riches came from his military experiences in many countries

---

[1] Finnur Jónsson's explanation of (*liðsmanna*)*réttr* as an *attack* (by soldiers) can hardly be right; it would be most natural to interpret the word as it is used today in the meaning 'rights', especially if the journey was a tax-gathering expedition; it then refers to the *right* of the tax-collectors to claim the tax in the name of the sovereign who despatched them, and also to the *right* to claim privileges accorded to tax-collectors, such as billeting, food etc.

[2] *Heimskringla*, III, 91; FJ *Skjald* A I 391, B I 361.

in the Imperial service as basically untrue and, if the word *pólútasvarf* is to be read as meaning tax-gathering accompanied by forcible extortion, then these expeditions will have been undertaken by Haraldr in the service of the Emperor, and in all probability under the direction of an Imperial governor or tax official who accompanied the military contingent.

It is certain that the Imperial tax-collections did not always take place in peace and quiet, and also that they roused a great deal of resentment at times, as may be seen from a number of official complaints about the army's conduct on such occasions as have survived.[1] The general name for these obligations was also indicative of their status, as they were named ἐπήρεια, lit. 'threats' or 'force', to separate them from the δημόσια, or regular taxes. Franz Dölger has referred to a number of these complaints in his study of Byzantine extraordinary taxation, most notably to a letter from Michael Choniates, Archbishop of Athens, who particularly stresses that while he is willing to submit to ordinary taxation, he must beg to be freed from the additional mulcts, the oppression of the Governor and the assaults of his minions; 'the Governor of Greece assails the land as a herd of kids, and demands all he wants as if we were in an occupied enemy territory'.[2]

The present author regards it as most natural that what happened was: Haraldr was accused of abusing his position in the Imperial service by taking money unlawfully through keeping back more of the booty from a victorious fight than he was entitled to do, and perhaps also of extorting more than the lawful tax money from people that he and his troop visited on a tax-gathering expedition, i.e. of indulging in περισσοπρακτορία 'over-collection', as it was somewhat euphemistically known.[3] Stender-Petersen's interpretation of *pólútasvarf* supports this theory provided that one extends it to include a use of it to denote tax-collection in the Empire as well as in Kievan Russia. Whether Haraldr was guilty of undue *svarf*, or whether he was in fact innocently accused, it is no longer possible to determine, but to the reviser it is not unreasonable, bearing in mind certain student practices in the 1960s of invading academic administrative offices, that if there were any documents on the case in the files of the Imperial secretariat in Michael V's palace, one can understand the motivation of the Varangians and other soldiers who forced their way in,

[1] Cf. F. Dölger, 'Beiträge zur Geschichte der byzantinischen Finanzverwaltung,' *Byzant. Archiv*, 9 (1927), 60–1, esp. nn. 10–11.

[2] Michael Acominatos, Μιχαὴλ Ἀκομινάτου...τὰ σωζόμενα, ed. S. Lampros, Athens, 1879, I, 308.

[3] Cf. F. Dölger, 'Zum Gebührenwesen der Byzantiner', *Études dédiées à la mémoire de A. d' Andréadès*, Athens, 1939, 46ff.

when they made it their first task to destroy the entire Imperial filing system.

It is said that two Icelanders in the Varangian regiment were imprisoned with their commander, Halldór Snorrason and Úlfr Óspaksson son of Óspakr the brother of Guðrún Ósvífrsdóttir (cf. further p. 209 below). It is likely that both were at that time officers in the regiment; we are told of Halldór that he had carried Haraldr's standard.

One reason for the arrest, besides the presumed official charge of misappropriation of funds, which is given both in the Kings' Sagas and by William of Malmesbury, is the old canard about a love affair with a lady of high lineage.[1] We will glance at this later on, but it is sufficient here to point out that the fact that these two officers were imprisoned with the commander seems to dispose of this point right away – Haraldr would hardly need two officers to hold his hand in his private amours; also, *affaires du cœur* between young officers and court ladies will hardly have been rarer in Byzantine times than nowadays, and with no yellow press to make mountains out of molehills, the authorities were unlikely to take undue notice of such matters.

We do not know in which prison Haraldr was placed; according to *Haraldar saga* it was the one in the same street as the church of the Varangians, and the tower in which he and his companions were incarcerated was given the name of Harald's Tower by the Norsemen and pointed out for a long time afterwards by that name.[2] The place of the oldest Varangian church is known; it was the church of St Mary near the Hagia Sophia, and the tale is quite likely to be true. It is possible to see that a tower stood in this street which was possibly used as a prison.[3] It could also be true, however, that the prisoners were kept in cells in the palace itself. It may be shown that there was just below the quarters of the Excubitae a prison which had originally belonged to the Numeri division,[4] and was named the Numera after them. This place was near the Chalke gate.

The tales of Haraldr's battle with a lion and a snake[5] are so obviously

[1] William of Malmesbury, *De Gestis Regum Anglorum*, II, 318, 'pro stupro illustris feminae'. Saxo, *Gesta Danorum*, I, 305, states that Haraldr was 'homicidi crimine damnatus', a remark that might be connected with some act of violence during a tax-gathering expedition.

[2] Cf. *Flateyjarbók*, III, 304–5.

[3] On churches used by the Varangians see further below, pp. 185ff. and refs. there.

[4] A. G. Paspatis, *The Great Palace of Constantinople*, London, 1893, 155.

[5] *Fornmanna sögur*, VI, 165–6; Saxo, *Gesta Danorum*, I, 305; William of Malmesbury, *De Gestis Regum Anglorum*, II, 318, n. 116.

works of the imagination as to be barely worth mention. It is, however, possible that some slight foundation of truth may have lain behind the latter, as Saxo relates that King Valdemar the Great of Denmark had possessed the knife with which Haraldr killed the worm, and used to show it to his guests. Moreover, the Balkans abound in all manner of creeping things, both poisonous and innocuous, and one such could quite easily have crawled into a prison cell and been killed there, but there is no need to believe too literally a tale told in the land of Horrebow's snakes.

Most of the Varangians will have regarded Haraldr's imprisonment as an act of injustice, and Michael V must have known this when he acted as he did in replacing them as his personal guards with 'Scythian slaves'. Certainly the anger of the regiment appears clearly in their behaviour in the subsequent rising, on behalf of the two Porphyrogennetes, that felled him from his throne.

We have good and clear evidence as to the rising and its prehistory from Greek and Arabic sources as well as from Snorri and the other royal biographers of Norway. The principal Greek authorities are Psellus, eyewitness and contemporary recorder of most of what happened, and Scylitzes, another contemporary chronicler. Besides their work we have a good secondary source in the chronicle of Ibn-el-Athir, who has drawn on yet another contemporary Greek chronicle which is now lost. Finally, of course, there are also *Heimskringla* and *Haraldar saga*, of which the verse fragments are reasonably close in time to events, and either composed by eyewitnesses or after the narratives of eyewitnesses.

After dismissing the *orphanotrophos* John from the capital and stripping him of his offices, and returning Maniaces to Sicily with a greatly increased authority, Michael V turned to dispose of the only two other persons whom he felt to be dangerous to his safety, the Dowager Empress Zoe and the Patriarch Alexius. It would appear that in this his principal counsellor was his uncle Constantine, who was on bad terms with the Empress Zoe (it appears that he suspected her of emulating her grandmother and arranging for Michael IV's murder). In the spring of 1042 the issue was brought to a head, when the Emperor attended the Liturgy in the Hagia Sophia and was afterwards cheered enthusiastically by the crowds as he processed back to the palace. This enthusiasm was also shown on his attendance at the church of the Holy Apostles on Low Sunday, and appears to have determined him to chance his luck. Accordingly the Patriarch was informed that he was to depart to the Stenon monastery, where the Emperor announced that he would visit him the next day.[1] A present of four pounds of gold accompanied the order to disarm any possible suspicion, and Alexius duly departed without being alarmed.

On his return from church, Michael had the Empress arrested, her hair shorn, divested her of her Imperial robes, and forcibly removed her to the Prinkipo Islands in a nun's habit. According to Ibn-el-Athir, the Emperor now commanded the Varangians to surround the Stenon.[2] This would suggest that not all the regiment was disaffected, and that there were units whom he still trusted, and, secondly, that the usual Imperial practice of using Varangians or other foreign mercenaries for the nastier kinds of political or military operation was still being followed. It may be that the company used were Russians and not Norsemen, Ibn-el-Athir's phrase being 'Bulgarians and Russians', but the awkward double meaning of *Russian* in the writings of the time makes it impossible to state anything as certain. In view of the fact that the commander of the Scandinavians was in prison, and with him two of the senior officers, the probability is that these Varangians will have been of Slavonic Russian origin, since the loyalty of the rest of the Scandinavian contingent must have been very suspect just then. This unit surrounded the monastery that same evening, and the Patriarch must have realized very soon what kind of fate was likely to be in store for him. What is noteworthy is that he succeeded in bribing them to let him go, and Schlumberger is probably right in saying that the incident shows that the loyalty of even the non-Scandinavian Varangians to the Emperor was beginning to fade.[3] At any rate they allowed Alexius to get away from the Stenon, whereon he hurried into the city, took refuge in the Hagia Sophia, and summoned the highest officials of the State and the Army to him there.

While this was happening the Emperor had summoned the Senate and informed them that the Empress Zoe had attempted to get rid of him by poison, and that he had therefore deposed her as a ruling Empress and sent her into secure custody in the Prinkipo Islands. The Senate, venal as always (having been made the obedient tool of the Emperors several centuries before), accepted this decision, and Michael, reckoning that he was now master of the situation, ordered Anastasius, the sebastocrator of Constantinople, to proclaim the new order in the Square of Constantine. He was, however, too slow, for the

---

[1] *Cedrenus Scylitzae Ope*, II, 536 calls the monastery ἐν τῷ Στενῷ μονὴν αὐτοῦ, and hence most historians refer to it as the monastery of Stenon, but this is also the name of the waterway, and the author does not think it is at all certain which monastery is meant.

[2] Ibn-el-Athir, *Kamil fit-ta ta'rih*, ed. C. J. Tornberg, Uppsala and Paris, 1851–75, 9, 342; cf. Vasilevskii, *Труды*, I, 282ff.

[3] *Épopée*, III, 344.

Patriarch had discovered his intentions, and had taken steps to prevent them. He had the bells of the churches of the city rung, and the people called to arms to oppose the Emperor's treachery against his bene-factress, the true Augusta. The loyalty of the people to the old and tried Macedonian dynasty held firm, and when Anastasius appeared in the Forum to make the Emperor's proclamation at noon he was faced by a furious crowd who were clearly in no mood to listen to him, and from whom he barely escaped with his life. The crowd, intoxicated with its success over the Imperial emissary, now seized what arms they could and attacked the Imperial residence itself. Psellus, who was an eyewitness in the palace, as the Emperor's secretary, has left an excellent and vivid account of the subsequent events, and is indeed our chief witness as to the part played by the Varangians in the revolution.[1]

The vast majority of the Varangians appear to have joined the attackers at once. Psellus speaks of a state of great discontent among the Palace Guards, especially the *Tauroskuthai* (i.e. Varangians), towards the Emperor, and states that most of the men in the Guards left the Palace, from which we may deduce with some reason that they left to join the Emperor's opponents. He also mentions that many of those who attacked the Palace carried axes as their weapons and, as the Varangians' particular distinctive weapon was the axe, it is not un-reasonable to surmise that some of them were already involved in this first battle of the revolution, possibly even involved in the instigation of the crowd, but there does not appear to have been any struggle between the Varangians inside the palace and their comrades.

The party raised by Alexius the Patriarch now attempted to attack the residences of several of the Emperor's kinsfolk, especially the palace of the *nobilissimus* Constantine, near the church of the Holy Apostles. Constantine had an armed guard of his own, among whom there are likely to have been a number of Varangians, probably in his service since his time as governor in Asia Minor.[2] He now assembled his men and led a sortie which fought all the way through to the Em-peror's palace. Michael, hard pressed by the crowd outside, and gradually deserted by his own soldiery, was greatly relieved at their coming, and handed over the defence of the Palace to his uncle, who succeeded, with the aid of archers and ballistae on the rooftops, in driving back the mob from the doors. He also organized a boat to fetch Zoe back from her nunnery prison; meanwhile, however, the Patriarch and the other leaders of the revolution had been active. Under their direction the crowd broke into the prisons in the city and

---

[1] Psellus, *Chronographia*, I, 101ff.
[2] See above, p. 62; see also M. Dendias, Οἱ Βάραγγοι καὶ τὸ Βυζάντιον, Athens, 1925, 78.

released the prisoners. The story of how a noblewoman released Haraldr and his companions may perhaps be a little likelier through the statement of Psellus that women were involved in this activity, though we may reject out of hand the hagiographical addition that she was induced to do so by the intervention of St Olaf, who appeared to her and commanded her to set his brother free. This is a clear fiction, obviously copied from an ancient hagiographical motif and, as Vasilevskii has pointed out in another context, it is unlikely that St Olaf's sanctity would have been heard of in Constantinople at such an early date.[1] It is much more likely that the leaders of the revolution ordered the release of important prisoners, especially those whom the Emperor had put in prison and who were likely to be his enemies. Also, the way to ensure the support of the great majority of the Varangians was to release Haraldr and his companions, to whom the regiment was personally much attached, as events were to show.

Later in the day the boat sent to bring the Empress Zoe back returned, and she was immediately vested anew in her Imperial dress and brought out on to the balcony facing the Hippodrome to calm the mob. It was too late, however, for many refused to believe that she had returned, and the leaders of the insurrection were understandably afraid that, even though she was back, Zoe would remain only a helpless cipher in her stepson's hands. Moreover, they had also discovered an additional legitimate weapon against the upstart Emperor's encroachments in the remaining female survivor of the old Imperial house, Zoe's sister Theodora, whom they now persuaded to come reluctantly out of the convent where she had settled, and brought to the Hagia Sophia to be crowned as co-Empress with her sister. At the same time a declaration was made in the name of the two old legitimate Empresses that Michael V was deposed from the Imperial throne. The formalities of the situation were regularized through the experienced leadership of Alexius and his principal military assistant, the general Constantine Cabasilas.

In the meanwhile the siege of the Emperor's palace went on with undiminished vigour, being made the more difficult by the arrival from Sicily of the successful general Katakalon Cecaumenos, who brought with him a shipload of soldiers who joined Michael V's side. As Katakalon had fought and won a great battle against the Arabs of Sicily (see above, p. 67), in which he had with him a company of Varangians, it is likely that he brought some of these adaptable troopers back on his ship, and thus added to the division in which Varangian fought Varangian. The newcomers did not, however, succeeed in

---

[1] Vasilevskii, *Труды*, I, 276.

turning the tables once more, for the siege grew fiercer all the while, and the main attack on the palace was made on 20 April 1042 from three points, the Hippodrome, the Tzykanisterion and the Augusteum, near the Excubita. The main reason for the attack being made there was probably that the great *Chalke*, the Bronze Gates, led out into the Augusteum, but it is quite likely also that this point was chosen because most of the Varangians had joined the insurrectionist side by now, and it may well have occurred to the leaders that the Varangians who were on guard in their quarters in the Excubita might hesitate over fighting their own comrades; there is also the point that if any Varangians, such as Haraldr and his two companions, were imprisoned in the cells of the Numera, it would be easier and quicker to reach them and release them by that route.

The battle was a fierce one, and 3000 men are supposed to have been killed in the struggle.[1] Finally, however, Michael's supporters realized that the defence was hopeless; some surrendered, some succeeded in escaping by flight; among these was Katakalon Cecaumenos. The Emperor and his uncle the *nobilissimus* fled by boat in the dark to take sanctuary in the Studite monastery, where they assumed the monastic habit, entered the convent chapel and clung to the altar.

The insurrectionists now broke into the palace, and proceeded to strip it of its treasures. They made an especial point of breaking into the Treasury, where they also destroyed the taxation records, which could be thought of as being done in order to destroy evidence unfavourable to Haraldr in his case. One must not overlook, however, the equally probable desire by very many people to wreck a system that was generally detested in the Empire, which would lead to this act of vandalism as an effort to make tax-gathering more difficult in the future.

There is a half-stanza by Valgarðr of Vellir which may be referring to this particular destruction:

> Snarla skaut ór sóti,
> Sveyk of hús ok reykir
> Stóðu stopðir síðan,
> Steinóðr logi glóðum.[2]

The stone-licking flame shot crackling embers out of the soot, and smoke-columns rose vertical up from the falling houses.

---

[1] George Finlay (*The History of the Byzantine Empire*, London, 1906, 389, n. 3) thinks that the number 3000 is an exaggeration and stands simply for 'a large number'.

[2] *Snorra Edda*, ed. S. Egilsson *et al.*, Copenhagen, 1848–87, I, 506; cf. also FJ *Skjald* A I 390, B I 360; and *Corpus Poeticum Boreale*, ed. G. Vigfússon and F. Y. Powell, Oxford, 1883, II, 216.

If the lines really refer to the destruction of the Treasury, we may infer from them that the insurrectionists set the Treasury archives on fire. Our Byzantine sources, Scylitzes and Glycas, do not mention a fire, but state that the Imperial Treasury was ransacked, and Scylitzes also mentions the destruction of the Archives.[1] Schlumberger points out that as the final assault on the Palace was made at night, torches will have been in use to light the assailants,[2] though Psellus does not mention this point at all.

It soon became clear to the victors that Michael V and his uncle had escaped them, and it was not long before they discovered where they were. A crowd thereupon gathered round the Studite monastery, but its sacredness inhibited them from attacking it. Theodora's ministers thereupon sent a detachment of guards in to bring them out. For this event we have the eyewitness account of Psellus, who appears to have gone with the refugees to the Studion, and who records his conversation with them there. The guards forced their way into the chapel, dragged the Emperor and his uncle from the altar and set off with them to the Palace. On the way there they met another detachment, this time of Varangians under the command of Haraldr, who brought new orders from the new sebastocrator, Nicephorus Campanaras, to the effect that they were both to be blinded. Psellus states of this last detachment that they were 'brave men who did not shrink from anything',[3] and from our Norse sources we may regard it as proven that they were Varangians, commanded by Haraldr, to whom fell this unpleasant task. The court poets are so well agreed, and their testimony is so unambiguous, that they cannot be ignored. Thus Þjóðólfr states in his *Sexstefja*:

> Stólþengils lét stinga
> (Styrjöld vas þá byrjuð)
> Eyðir augu bæði
> Út heiðingja sútar;
> Lagði allvaldr Egða
> Austr á bragning hraustan
> Gráligt mark, en Girkja
> Götu illa fór stillir.[4]

The destroyer of the wolf's grief [i.e. 'soldier'] had out both the eyes of the Great King [i.e. 'Emperor']; then was the war begun; the ruler of Agðir [i.e. Haraldr] placed a grim mark on the brave man, and the king of the Greeks travelled an evil road.

---

[1] *Cedrenus Scylitzae Ope*, II, 539; Glycas, *Annales*, ed. I. Bekker (CSHB), Bonn, 1836, 592.
[2] *Épopée*, III, 369–70.
[3] Psellus, *Chronographia*, I, 113.
[4] FJ *Skjald* A I 370, B I 340.

Þórarinn Skeggjason also refers to this event in a half-stanza that he composed about Haraldr:

> Náði görr en glóðum
> Grikklands jöfurr handa,
> Stólþengill gekk ströngu
> Steinblindr aðalmeini.[1]

Finnur Jónsson wishes to read this 'The King of Greece went stone-blind by main illness, and the vigorous King gained the embers of the hands [i.e. gold]'. The present author feels, however, that a more accurate reading is 'The vigorous man gained again the gold of the hands of the King of Greece', as referring to Haraldr, and 'the King of the Greeks was made stone-blind as his chief suffering'. E. A. Kock has understood rightly that the reading should be *enn*, and not *en*, but the author cannot accept his explanation, as it is nonsense to talk of the Emperor gaining gold before he was blinded; it is on the contrary much more meaningful to refer the line to Haraldr and his men, who are very likely to have been very well paid for their unpleasant duty.[2] It is also obvious exaggeration by the Norse authors to suggest that Haraldr did this unprompted and as an act of revenge; in this instance he can only have acted as an army officer under orders.

The Emperor and the *nobilissimus* were next taken to the open space near the Studion known as Sigma,[3] where they were publicly blinded. Psellus, observing the execution, contrasts the bravery of Constantine, who underwent the brutal torment without a cry or resistance, and the Emperor, who 'howled pitifully'.[4] After the blinding, both were taken off to a monastery to end their days.

From all this evidence we may see that Haraldr had escaped from prison, and was in considerable favour with the new rulers; it seems very likely that he and his men were selected for this savage act of reprisal because of their foreign extraction, as Basil II had used his Varangians for some of his most ferocious acts of war. Moreover, out of the entire Varangian guard, this company would be regarded as peculiarly suitable because of their grudge against the ruler who had had their leaders arrested and shamed by imprisonment.

Besides carrying out the sentence upon Michael and Constantine, Haraldr appears to have acted as the judge and executioner of those

---

[1] FJ *Skjald*, A I 400, B I 368.
[2] E. A. Kock, *Notationes norroenae*, Lund, 1923–44, § 879.
[3] There was more than one palace so named because of the resemblance to the letter C (one such was a part of the old Blachernae Palace). The present reference is to a place near the Studion, especially noted by M. I. Nomidis, 'Η Ζωοδόχος Πηγή, Istanbul, 1937, 68ff.
[4] Psellus, *Chronographia*, I, 105.

Varangians who took the side of the upstart in the civil upheaval. Our authority for this is a half-stanza by Valgarðr of Vellir preserved in *Fagrskinna*:

> Helmingi bautt hanga,
> Hilmiskundr, af stundu,
> Skipt hafit ér, svát eftir
> Eru Væringjar færi.[1]

You commanded, son of the Prince, the half of them to hang there and then; you have so done that there are fewer Varangians left.

The present author cannot agree with Gustav Storm that this half-stanza is distorted; it is true that it cannot possibly refer to those Varangians who had fallen in the Emperor's defence, but Storm has not realized that those who stayed by Michael V and survived his fall would be tried for treason against Zoe and Theodora, convicted and executed.[2] Vigfússon and Powell have also misunderstood it,[3] nor is its absence from *Heimskringla* any proof of its being wrongly attributed or distorted. The interpretation is simplicity itself: *helmingr* is sometimes used in the connotation 'company', 'party', 'part'. *Hilmis kundr*, 'king's son', shows that the verses were composed before Haraldr himself became king; in all probability just after the event. *Ér* may be interpreted in two ways here; it is either used directly of Haraldr himself as a great lord, or else it may be understood as meaning 'you and your followers', and could then mean that Valgarðr himself was not a participant in the action, though there is yet one other way to interpret it. As will be seen in the narrative concerning the Varangians' assault on Nicephorus III, the regiment appears to have possessed the privilege of trying and judging its own members when they were found guilty of some offence, even when it was as grave a one as attempted murder of an Emperor.[4] It is not unlikely that this privilege was already in existence in 1042 (indeed, it is not unreasonable to surmise that it was one conferred on them by Basil II when he regularized the position of the Varangians in the army), and those of the regiment who had taken arms against their companions and not kept their oaths to defend the Empress of the legitimate line against the Emperor's treachery, were then clearly guilty of treason, and as such would be judged by their commander, Haraldr, who would without question condemn them to be hanged as traitors; nor is it unreasonable to suspect that Haraldr will have used the opportunity to settle scores

---

[1] FJ *Skjald*, A I 391, B I 361.
[2] G. Storm, 'Harald Haardraade og Væringerne', *Norsk Historisk Tidsskrift*, 2 Rekke, IV, 354–86.
[3] *Corpus Poeticum Boreale*, II, 216.   [4] See below, pp. 118–19.

with some of his rivals in the regiment (if there were any). In this case, therefore, *ér* would mean *þit*, 'you and your judges', and would imply that while Valgarðr acknowledged the justice of the sentence, he felt that it was distinctly severe, and wished inwardly that some of the condemned men had been reprieved. The final outcome of this upheaval, however, must have been that Haraldr was reinstated in all his former dignities, all accusations against him were withdrawn, and we may be certain that he will not have been the poorer for the ransacking of the Emperor's palace (if he managed to take part in it).

How Haraldr escaped from Constantinople in flat defiance of the Emperor's ban on his departure is somewhat obscure. Our best source here is *Advice*, where it is stated clearly that he had asked Constantine IX Monomachos for leave to depart, been refused it, and then left in secret, though with some difficulty. There are some noteworthy points in this statement.[1]

We may be reasonably certain that what prompted Haraldr to wish to return to Norway was news that his brother's son, Magnus (the Good) had been recalled to the country and had been made King; this is clearly implied both in *Heimskringla* and the other biographies. Haraldr must have considered himself much more capable than his nephew, and must have felt that it would be much more profitable for the Norwegian people, as well as for himself, if he were to go home and rule there with a king's authority, rather than to stay as a subordinate officer in the force of another ruler, however attractive the court life in Constantinople may have been. As long as the sons of the great Canute lived, Magnus was unlikely to hold much power or authority, since, even though he succeeded Sveinn Alfífuson in name as King of Norway, he was still a minor under tutelage, and it was only the discord between Harald Harefoot and his brother Harthacanute that enabled him to keep the northern kingdom in peace. On Harthacanute's death, however, Magnus was acclaimed King of Denmark as well by a large faction, and this must have stirred Haraldr into feeling that it would be profitable for him to become the co-King with his nephew, or else the governor of whichever country Magnus decided not to settle in. This is indicated in our sources by his contact with Svend Estridsson shortly after his return, but when the cleavage between Svend and Magnus became open, the ties of blood would appear to have been the strongest, and he turned away from Svend to support his nephew and succeeded him in 1047 as sole King of Norway.

In Byzantium the Empress Zoe had married Constantine Mono-

[1] *Advice*, 93; cf. also above, pp. 57ff., also *Advice*, ed. Litavrin, Moscow, 1972, 590–8.

machos on 11 June 1042, seven weeks after her recovery of the throne, and her husband was duly crowned as Emperor on the same day. Shortly afterwards, when George Maniaces heard the news in Italy, he raised a rebellion, but was defeated and killed in a battle against an army commanded by Stephen the sebastophorus at Ostrovo in February/March 1043, as will be noted later. It may be regarded as practically certain that Haraldr had already left Byzantium by then, for if he and his company had accomplished such a noteworthy act as to defeat 'Gyrgir' and kill him, his poets would certainly not have been silent on the subject, and there can be virtually no doubt that the writers of the prose biographies would have made a particular point of including such a spectacular deed in their narratives. Accordingly, Haraldr must have petitioned the Emperor for leave to depart in the autumn of 1042, and gone either late in the same year or very early in 1043. It is possible to conjecture that the reason why Constantine IX refused to let him go was his need for him and his company in the battle with Maniaces; but there is an even more likely reason in the approach of a Russo-Byzantine war which broke out in the end in 1043, and which will be examined in the next chapter.

Unfortunately, the Norse sources have interpolated into the story of Haraldr's departure a rather silly romantic fable about his love-affair with a noble Greek lady, a relation of the Empress Zoe, by the name of Maria. The nonsensicality of this tale can be seen from the fact that Snorri describes the lady as the daughter of Zoe's *brother*.[1] As Constantine VIII had no son, this is clear nonsense, made the more so by the fact that both Zoe's sisters were unmarried. The only woman of the families of Zoe's three husbands who is known to have been called Maria was Maria the wife of the Admiral Stephen, and mother of Michael V, and as she was a woman of mature years by this time, she is clearly not the right person for this story. It is of course quite possible that Haraldr had some affair in his Byzantine period with a noblewoman called Maria, but the obvious elements of fiction in the surviving tale make it a most unlikely one. Thus Maria lets Haraldr escape through an escape hatch in the floor when he is being sought (readers of *Grettis saga* will not need much of a reminder of how this is told of Þorsteinn drómondr and his lady-love Spes)[2] and this and other motifs suggest that the whole narrative is one that has been fathered on to several Varangians before it stopped as a story of Haraldr Hardrada. Haraldr is

---

[1] *Heimskringla*, III, 85; cf. also Vasilevskii, *Трудьі*, I, 234–6. Vasilevskii refers to the O.H.G. poem *Rother*, whose action is also set in Constantinople, and which bears many resemblances to this episode.

[2] *Grettis saga*, ed. G. Jónsson (Íslenzk Fornrit VII), Reykjavík, 1937, 297–81.

supposed to have asked for Maria's hand, and been refused by Zoe, whereupon he took her with him when he fled, only to send her back with a dignified escort, simply to spite the Empress and to demonstrate to her that he could have done as he pleased with her kinswoman. The sagas intimate that Zoe herself had wanted to marry Haraldr but this must be fiction, since even though Zoe was noted for her lasciviousness, her instinct for survival would not have led her so far from the Byzantine path of decorum. The same applies to the anecdote of how she had asked Haraldr for a lock of his hair, and he replied with a coarse epithet; such a conversation was out of the question between the Empress of the East and her military subordinate.

Snorri describes the actual departure as follows:

Thereafter they went to the galleys of the Varangians and took two of them, and rowed in along the Bosphorus. When they came to where the iron chains were strung right across the water way, Haraldr ordered that men should take to the oars on both galleys, and everyone who was not needed for rowing should pick up his bedding and go aft to the stern of the galley; the two boats then slid up on to the iron chains, and as they stuck and lost their impetus of motion, Haraldr ordered all men to run forward into the bows. Thereupon Haraldr's own galley tipped forward, and slid off the chains into the water on the other side, while the other stuck fast on the chains and broke open, and much gear and many men were lost, while some of the men were picked up in the water. In this way Haraldr got out of Constantinople and so went into the Black Sea.[1]

In all probability this story is correct in its essentials. As is shown on Map III, there was a great iron chain across the Golden Horn, and, at least from the time of Manuel I Comnenus, across the Bosphorus, as a defence for the harbour. These chains rested on rafts placed at appropriate distances, which were drawn into the shore in the daytime, and refloated across the waterways at night. There is however a good deal to criticize in this account. The galleys of the Varangians were right by the Tower of St Eugenius, into which one end of the chain across the Golden Horn was fastened, alongside the Neorion, the great harbour of the Byzantine fleet, where the naval arsenals and stores were situated. P. A. Munch has surmised that *Sæviðarsund* is here a mistake for *Stólpasund*, and that the name was given to it because the wooden rafts, *viðir*, were used to support the chains.[2] This can hardly be right, but we may be fairly sure that the chains across the Golden Horn are meant, since the chains across the Bosphorus had not been

---

[1] *Heimskringla*, III, 85.
[2] P. A. Munch, *Samlede Afhandlinger*, I, 548–9.

put up then[1] (but see below, p. 100). Stender-Petersen has contended that the story of Haraldr's escape across the chains is an international vagrant, descended from an old Roman story about Caius Duilius,[2] who used this method to escape from the harbour in Syracuse. The answer to his contention is, however, that this ruse must have been the commonest of commonplaces in military tactics, and any competent commander would have known it; since Haraldr had spent a long time as an officer in Byzantine naval circles, he could hardly have failed to have heard it and noted it. Moreover, individual details in Snorri's account make it more likely to be correct, such as the business of the bedding and the loss of one of the galleys; as we have suggested earlier, it is unsafe to regard common tricks as necessarily only happening in commonplaces of fiction. In this connection we need only glance at another story which Stender-Petersen adduces from the chronicle of Nestor, of how Oleg attacked Constantinople by having wheels put under his ships, and as a favourable wind filled the sails, he crossed the peninsula by land and entered the harbour.[3] Stender-Petersen also refers to another tale from Frontinus, that of Lysander and his capture of Athens in 404 B.C., and to Karamzin's description of how Mohammed II had his warships dragged across the neck of land between Beshiktash and Galata and so captured the harbour of Constantinople in 1453.[4] Since this is a well-attested event, why should it, and Haraldr's trick to get out, be treated together as itinerant folktales, just because Lysander won Athens by a naval trick?

Saxo connects Haraldr's departure with his imprisonment, stating that Haraldr and his companion killed a dragon in their prison, which so impressed the Emperor that he pardoned them, gave Haraldr a ship and money, and let them go in peace. This is of course contradicted by our much better witness, the author of *Advice*, and so it can be disregarded.[5]

There remains one other possibility. It may be that Haraldr and his company were given orders by the Emperor to leave the City and go to do a tour of garrison duty in a provincial town, as was done with the Russian Varangians, and that they prepared to leave and set off out of the harbour, but altered course as soon as they were clear of the harbour

---

[1] The O.N. name for the Bosphorus, *Sæviðarsund*, is sometimes found as *Sjáviðarsund*, and is then interpreted as 'channel between two seas, with a wide view on emerging'; see especially the notes by G. Schönning and S. Thorlacius to the earliest edition of *Heimskringla* (Copenhagen, 1777–1826, III, 170).

[2] A. Stender-Petersen, *Die Varägersage*, 97ff. and refs. there.

[3] *Повесть Временных Лет*, I, 29–31.

[4] Frontinus, *Strategemata*, ed. G. Gundermann, Leipzig, 1888, 17; cf. N. M. Karamzin, *История Государства Российскаго*, Saint Petersburg, 1830–1, V, 222–3.

[5] Saxo, *Gesta Danorum*, I, 305.

defences and sailed northwards through the Bosphorus instead. It is
not impossible that, in view of the impending war with the Russians,
the Emperor had had a chain placed across the channel also, and Haraldr
then used the tactic described by Snorri – in this way the tale of the
passage through *Sjáviðarsund* would be correct, and as its author was
quite likely to have his source for his statement from some scaldic
poem now lost, this is not as unlikely as it might seem at first glance.
It should be borne in mind, however, that all this must only be conjecture based on possibilities raised by the unreliable Norse sources, by
virtue of the absence of appropriate documents from the Byzantine
record offices (for which we may thank the Western 'Crusaders' of the
destruction of 1204).

It is not intended to trace Haraldr's career after he left Constantinople
here, as he does not enter Varangian history again; but it should be
noted that on his return to Kiev he married Jaroslav's daughter
Elisaveta and stayed for a while with his father-in-law before returning
to Scandinavia to join his nephew and succeed him as King of Norway.
There is however one point to be noted before we leave his part of
Varangian history. The author of *Advice* states specifically that after
he had become king, Haraldr kept up his friendship with the Emperors,
and this is a worthwhile point to pause on. The trade between Scandinavia and the Empire could be mutually profitable, as a wise man such
as King Haraldr would know only too well, and he would therefore
attempt to foster it. There is also a subsidiary point to be noted, in
respect of one of the minor puzzles of early Icelandic history, the
curious episode of the so-called 'Armenian' bishops. Though it has
been shown by Professor Magnús Már Lárusson that these gentry were
not Armenian, but from Slavonic Europe,[1] they may still be noted in
this context as representatives of a larger quarrel that was taking place
in the 1050s, between the highest authorities of the Western and Eastern
churches on the one hand in the persons of the pompous and self-
important Humbert and the peppery and equally self-important Michael
Cerularius, and also in the Northern part of Europe, where Haraldr of
Norway, with his Byzantine training and sympathy, was engaged in a
long and acrimonious battle with Archbishop Adalbert of Bremen over
that prelate's encroachment on what Haraldr clearly regarded as his
rights by the Byzantine model, of the appointment of bishops. The

[1] M. M. Lárusson, 'On the so-called "Armenian" bishops', *Studia Islandica*, XVIII, Reykjavík,
1960, 23–38. This view has been violently contested by Ya. Dashkeevich, 'Les Arméniens
à Kiev jusqu'à 1240', *Revue des études arméniennes*, X (1974), 336–40, but it will not do to
make unsubstantiated allegations as he does of the place-name *Ermland* without giving
chapter and verse for them.

difficulties encountered by Bishop Ísleifr as a result of the activities of Messrs Petrus, Abraham and Stephanus are a clear echo of the ructions at a higher level, and are reflected in the persuasion by which the *Alþingi* passed an enactment forbidding all missionization not authorized by Western ecclesiastical superiors.[1] The lack of interest felt by King Olaf Kyrre in things ecclesiastical made a peaceable solution of the quarrel with the Archbishop possible, and we hear no more of Eastern bishops intervening in the religious affairs of Scandinavia, but this small episode of the 1050s reveals the extent to which Byzantium could stretch out an arm in that period as far as Iceland and find not only sympathy, but knowledgeable men there, since at that time there would be such highly-descended men as Halldór Snorrason and Bolli Bollason in places of eminence in the land, who would welcome emissaries from the great Empire where they had spent what they were likely to regard as their golden years.

King Haraldr III is unquestionably the most notable of all the known Varangians, and Icelandic sources bear him a generally friendly witness, praising his wits and his physical courage and ability, even though many of his actions were not judged with any great friendliness. As an example of the generally friendly tone of the Icelandic recollection we may take the vow made by the men of Þórðr kakali Sighvatsson before the battle of Flói on 25 June 1244, 'to have masses said for a twelvemonth for the soul of King Haraldr Sigurðarson. This vow was made fast by handclasps.'[2] Snorri, in his clear-eyed character summary has probably come very close to a correct evaluation of him:

King Haraldr was a vigorous and strong ruler in his country, a man so wise that it was common opinion that no ruler existed in the North who was his like in wisdom and profound counsel. He was a great fighter in battle, brave in the clash of weapons; he was strong of body and skilful in the management of arms (as we have stated earlier); yet there is much more unwritten of his famous acts; this is because of our ignorance and also that we do not wish to put down in writing unattested tales; even though we have heard speech of him, and many other things mentioned, yet we feel it to be better that our witness will be supplemented in the future rather than that it should become necessary to withdraw some of it. There is a great story of King Haraldr in the verses which Icelanders made for him and his sons; in return he was a great friend to them all. He was also a great friend to Icelanders generally; thus when there was a great famine in Iceland, King Haraldr gave permission for four ships to take grain thither, and ordained that the hundredweight should not be sold dearer than for a hundred [i.e. 120 ells] of cloth; he also allowed poor men to go across to Norway so long as they could obtain the food needed for their journey, and in this way the

[1] *Grágás*, ed. V. Finsen, Copenhagen, 1852, I, 22.
[2] *Sturlunga saga*, ed. K. Kålund, Copenhagen, 1906–11, II, 65–6.

land survived until the times improved. King Haraldr sent the bell out for the church that the blessed Olaf had sent the timber out to build, and was raised [at Þingvellir] for the Alþingi. Such are the memories that men have of King Haraldr and many others of princely gifts that he gave to men who visited him.[1]

This interesting description also explains why the Icelandic oral memories of Haraldr are generally in his favour, and also Snorri's caution as a historian. He must have known a great mass of tales about the King, some written, such as the tale of Erlendr from *Morkinskinna*,[2] and other oral ones, but he did not want to include any in his own narrative which were not credible, and so he preferred to follow the scaldic poems; we have noted, however, that Snorri has included some tales which cannot stand up to the criticism of our own time, but it may be said that in general he exhibits an admirable restraint and critical acumen. Let us end this chapter, therefore, with his description of Haraldr which shows his care in his selection of sources and his ability to catch a vivid portrait-glimpse of this greatest Varangian.

Halldór, the son of Brynjólfr Camel, the Old, was a wise man and a great lord; he spoke thus when he heard men talking and making a great contrast between the temperament of the brothers [King Olaf and King Haraldr]. 'I was with both the brothers, and close to both of them, and knew the tempers of both; never have I met two men so alike in temper; both were the wisest and bravest of men, desirous of riches and power, high-tempered and not of common humour, forceful rulers and fierce to punish. King Olaf forced the people to accept the Christian faith and right conduct, and punished those who refused them savagely; therefore the lords of the land could not bear with his justice and raised up an army against him and so slew him on his own land; therefore was he made a saint. King Haraldr went out as a viking to gain fame and wealth, and then took rule over all people whom he could conquer; therefore he fell on another king's soil. Both brothers were noble and well-conducted in everyday life; they had both travelled far and wide, and became famous and excellent for their long and successful travels.'[3]

To this we may add:

King Haraldr was a handsome, well-looking man, fair of hair and beard, with long sideburns, one eyebrow rather higher than the other, big hands and feet, but both in good proportion; he was five ells tall.

He was fierce to his enemies and punished all opposition heavily... King Haraldr was most avaricious of power, and of all things that went well; he was generous in his gifts to his friends and those whom he liked...he never fled in a battle, but sought often a way out when he was obliged to tackle an overwhelming force. All men who served under him in battle and warfare said that when he was in great danger which was approaching swiftly, he would find a counsel that all saw was the best to follow.[4]

---

[1] *Heimskringla*, III, 119.
[2] See below, p. 214.
[3] *Heimskringla*, III, 200.
[4] *Heimskringla*, III, 198–200.

5

The Varangians between 1042 and 1081

When Zoe and Theodora had settled once more on the throne as reigning Empresses, they continued to show favour to the regiment that had served them so well in their need. Psellus gives a description of their state receptions at which the Varangians were prominent among the guards on duty: 'near them [the Empresses] were the staff-bearers and the sword-bearers, and the men who carry axes on their right shoulders [i.e. Varangians]'.[1]

Zoe's third husband, Constantine IX Monomachos, was in no way the equal in abilities to his predecessor Michael IV, and the Empire was greatly weakened in his day through his reliance on civil servants. He was not, however, entirely destitute of military skill, and was obliged to defend his throne early in his reign against a formidable enemy. In April 1042 Maniaces had returned to Italy and began a ferocious campaign of reconquest for the Byzantines.[2] On the fall of Michael V, however, his enemies regained power in Constantinople, and through the machinations of the Emperor's mistress's brother, Romanos Skleros, Maniaces was recalled to the City. His reaction was to have himself acclaimed Emperor and raise a revolt in the catepanate of Italy, but he did not have the success he had hoped for, as neither the Langobards under Argyros, son of Meles, nor the Normans of Calabria were willing to rally to his cause. On the arrival of Basil Theodorocanus as the new catepan of Italy with a large army, which is very likely to have included a Varangian contingent, Maniaces therefore retreated across the Adriatic and harried the province around Dyrrhachium, hoping to get assistance from the Serbs, who had revolted at the same time. With

---

[1] Psellus, *Chronographia*, ed. E. Renaud, Paris, 1926–8, 1, 118.
[2] *Annales Barenses*, ed. G. H. Pertz (MGH Scriptores v), Hanover, 1844, entry for 1042.

their help he then turned to face an Imperial force under the command of the sebastophorus Stephen, who had under his command several companies of Varangians. The armies met at Ostrovo, and the rebels came near to having the victory, but Maniaces was severely wounded in the side at a critical point in the battle and fell dead off his horse, whereupon his men lost courage and surrendered. The triumphant Imperial commander had Maniaces' head cut off and borne in his triumphal procession through Constantinople, the Varangians marching behind it with their axes on their shoulders. Another detachment of Varangians preceded the victorious general, who was followed by the Emperor on a white steed, and by other detachments of the life-guards.[1]

In the same year, 1043, a quarrel arose in the Russian quarter near the church of St Mamas, in which a merchant of high rank was killed. Prince Jaroslav of Kiev took up his cause on behalf of the relatives, but the demand he made for weregild was so inflated as to be obviously a pretext for a quarrel.[2] Constantine refused to accept the conditions demanded, and prepared to defend the City. He also showed commendable prudence in disposing his doubtful forces: Russian Varangians were sent off to serve in distant frontier provinces, and all Russians in Constantinople were put under guard. In June, when a large fleet under the command of Vladimir (Monomakh), son of Jaroslav, assailed the City, the Byzantines met it in the Bosphorus and defeated the combined force of Russians and Scandinavians, largely thanks to the use of Greek fire.[3] The scale of the victory is indicated by the statement of Cedrenus that 15,000 bodies were found on the shores of the Black Sea, and this is corroborated by the statements of Ibn-el Athir and Abul-Faradh on the reprisals taken on the prisoners.[4] The remnants of Vladimir's force were able to escape in good order, but were caught on the way back by Katakalon Cecaumenos as they tried to get back by the land route and completely shattered; this victory put an end for ever to Russian attempts at aggression on Byzantium, and secured Constantine's throne for him from outside attacks.

In the next year, however, there was an uproar in Constantinople when a rumour was let loose that the Emperor was proposing to set aside (or even murder) the two aged Basilissae in favour of his mistress Skleraina, on whom he had conferred the title of Augusta, and to

---

[1] Psellus, *Chronographia*, II, 6–7; Gregorius Bar-Hebraeus (Abulfaradh), *Chronicon Syriacum*, ed. P. J. Bruns, Leipzig, 1788, II, 240.

[2] *Повесть Временных Лет*, ed. E. F. Karskii, Leningrad 1926 (reprinted, 1962), 154–5, entry for 1043; *Cedrenus Scylitzae Ope*, II, 551.

[3] *Cedrenus Scylitzae Ope*, II, 551. For an eyewitness account see Psellus, *Chronographia*, II, 8–12.

[4] Ibn-el-Athir, *Kamil fit-ta-ta'rih*, ed. C. J. Tornberg, Uppsala and Paris, 1851–75, 9, 356; Bar-Hebraeus (Abulfaradh), *Chronicon Syriacum*, II, 241.

whom he had assigned quarters in the Blachernae. Constantine was attacked by the mob as he was returning in procession from church on the feast of the Forty Martyrs of Sebaste, but was saved by his Varangians, who got him back safely to the Palace, where Zoe and Theodora promptly appeared on the balcony and spoke to the crowd to calm them and dispel the rumour.[1]

In 1045 Constantine was engaged in the final subjugation of the last Armenian independent district under the Empire, and a Grusinian source states that he used a force of 3000 Varangians to assist King Liparit in his revolt against King Bagrat IV of Carthelia and Abkhasia.[2] Late in the year we find between 700 and 800 of them engaged in battle in the valley of Sasir, where Liparit defeated Bagrat completely.[3]

In the autumn of 1047 we are told that the Emperor had despatched all his available troops to frontier duties, and only had his mercenary guards by him in the capital. A general of noble family, Leo Tornicius, thereon attempted to seize the opportunity to revolt, and laid siege to the City. Constantine succeeded in overcoming the rebels by setting a great many prisoners free in return for their services against the besiegers and, though the sortie made by the garrison failed to penetrate the ring, Tornicius soon realized that the vast majority of the citizens of Constantinople had no intention of betraying their loyalty to the Empresses and their consort. Moreover, after he had been obliged to raise the siege his men began to desert him, and in the end he was forced to surrender and petition for mercy, whereupon he was blinded. In view of the composition of the guards during the previous years, it is certain that there were Varangians serving on the Emperor's side and, in view of the tendency of the government to leave the less delicate jobs to them, we may regard it as not unlikely that the execution of the punishment of the chief rebel was also entrusted to them.[4]

In 1048 the struggle against the Seljuk Turks was renewed in Asia Minor, and the Pechenegs reinvaded Bulgaria. They defeated the Grand Hetairarch Constantine Arianites at Adrianople, but the timely arrival of Nicetas Glavas with the Schools turned defeat into a conditional victory. As members of the Hetairia, it is certain that Varangians would have been in a force under the command of the Chief of the division, and they would also have been among the force of guards that caught a band of marauding Pechenegs a little later at Calasyrta near Constantinople – certainly the barbaric gesture of cutting off the

[1] *Cedrenus Scylitzae Ope*, II, 555–6; cf. also *Épopée*, III, 424–5.
[2] *Cedrenus Scylitzae Ope*, II, 572–3.
[3] Vasilevskii, *Труды*, I, 315. Brosset (*Histoire de la Géorgie*, Saint Petersburg, 1849–51, I, 225) has unfortunately followed this erroneous version.
[4] See above, pp. 93–4.

heads of all the slain robbers and laying them at the Emperor's feet in triumph has a Varangian air about it.[1]

Constantine IX assembled a fresh force to settle the Pechenegs, and included in it the cream of his mercenaries, including the Varangians under their commander, the *Akoluthos* Michael, and sent it off under the command of Nicephorus Bryennius. Michael fought two engagements against them on his own responsibility, at Goloe and at Toplitzon, being victorious on both occasions, and together with Bryennius beat them heavily at Chariopolis. The Pechenegs now retreated to Perieslavetz, where Michael and Basil the syncellus were sent against them, though with a force that was badly under-equipped through bureaucratic mismanagement in the capital.[2] Not surprisingly, this ragamuffin band was resoundingly defeated, and Michael was barely able to rescue the remnants, largely, according to Attaleiates, who is with Cecaumenos our chief witness for this campaign, because of the gallantry of the future Emperor Nicephorus Botaneiates.[3] Constantine thereupon gathered a mercenary force of Russians and Normans, but the Pechenegs were now prepared to make peace, and a thirty-year treaty was concluded under which they returned across the Danube.[4]

In an interval in his Bulgarian campaign, Michael the *akoluthos* was sent with a contingent of Varangians across to Asia Minor, where he assembled an army of Varangians and Normans to restrain Sultan Toghrul of the Seljuks from raiding the frontier themes.[5] When he was in turn recalled to cope with the Pechenegs he was replaced by the patrician Basil Apocapis, who defended Manzikert with great skill against the Seljuk besiegers with the aid of a force that certainly included Normans, one of whom invented a way of destroying the Turkish siege engines, and most probably Varangians as well.[6] Equally, Varangians and Normans are stated by Cedrenus to have been in the force with which Michael defeated Toghrul at Baiberd in 1055.[7]

The Norman war in Italy continued all through the reign of Con-

---

[1] *Épopée*, III, 586 and refs. there.

[2] Cecaumenos, *Strategicon*, ed. B. Vasilevskii and P. Jernstedt, Saint Petersburg, 1896, §67.

[3] Attaleiates, *Historiae*, ed. I. Bekker (CSHB) Bonn, 1853, 39–43.

[4] On this war see *CMH*, Pt 1, 203; Ostrogorskii, *A History of the Byzantine State*, 2nd English ed., tr. J. M. Hussey, Oxford, 1968, 334; *Épopée*, III, 595; on the Pecheneg encounter the same and Vasilevskii, *Труды*, I, 171–5.

[5] *Épopée*, III, 598 and refs. there.

[6] Our principal authority is Matthew of Edessa, *Chronique*, tr. E. Dulaurier, Paris, 1858, 99–102.

[7] Aristakes of Lasciverd, *Histoire*, tr. M. Canard and H. Berberian, Brussels, 1973, 23–4; cf. also *Cedrenus Scylitzae Ope*, II, 606; A. F. Gfrörer, *Byzantische Geschichten*, Graz, 1872–7, III, 510; E. Honigmann, *Die Ostgrenze des byzantinischen Reiches*, Brussels, 1935, 181, n. 8.

stantine IX, and some Varangian units are sure to have been in the
Byzantine forces that attempted to cope with the growing power of
their enemy. They are certainly listed as being with the catepan John
Raphael in Bari in 1046; after the defeat and capture of the catepan
Eustathius Palatinus at Taranto in 1048[1] a Varangian force captured
Stira and Lecce,[2] and after the inhabitants of Bari had revolted and put
Palatinus in chains, a naval force of Varangians and Russians was sent
to reduce the town under John Raphael, but failed to hold it, and only
succeeded in freeing Palatinus by agreeing to let the town remain
free.

Constantine IX died on 11 January 1055, and Theodora, the only
survivor of the legitimate Imperial family, reigned alone in name for the
next eighteen months. She appears to have esteemed her Varangians
greatly, and when she died the guards, including the Varangians, took
oaths of fealty to her successors, Michael VI Stratioticus, and in consequence the attempted *coup d'état* by Theodosius, a kinsman of Constantine IX, failed, and he was obliged to surrender and beg for mercy.
Cedrenus refers to the activities of the Varangians in this episode, and
calls them 'a Celtic people who were mercenaries with the Romans'.[3]
Michael contented himself with exiling the pretender to Pergamum, but
he himself had been gradually losing the favour of the senior generals,
particularly that of Katakalon Cecaumenos, who was at this time in
the theme of Colonia, on the Armenian border; he was said to have had
under his command a detachment of Varangians and two of Normans;
Cedrenus refers to these as δύο τάγματα Φραγγικὰ καὶ 'Ρωσικόν,[4]
but from what Psellus says about the guards of Isaac Comnenus (see
below), it is clear that they were Varangians.

Katakalon now conspired with a number of his colleagues, and they
gathered on 8 June 1057 and acclaimed Isaac Comnenus as Emperor.
Katakalon secured the loyalty of the Asiatic Varangians and Normans
by forging a letter from Michael VI in which he himself was appointed
the commander in chief of the army against the Turks, after which he
led this army to Nicopolis. There he summoned the commanders of
the individual units to him and received them one by one, seated on
horseback in full armour, telling them the truth and giving them a
choice of acknowledging Isaac Comnenus as Emperor or death. All of

---

[1] Lupus Protospatharios, *Chronicon*, ed. G. Waitz (MGH Scriptores v), Hanover, 1844, 58,
entry for 1046; also Anonymus, *Chronicon Barense* (Muratori, *Scriptores*, v, 151), ed. G. H.
Pertz, Hanover, 1844, entry for 1047; also G. Musca, 'L'espansione urbana di Bari nel
Secolo XI', *Quaderni Medievali*, 2 (1976), 66.

[2] Lupus, *Chronicon*, 59 (1047); cf. also F. Chalandon, *Histoire de la domination Normande en
Italie et Sicile*, Paris, 1907, I, 115.

[3] *Cedrenus Scylitzae Ope*, II, 613.   [4] *Cedrenus Scylitzae Ope*, II, 624.

them chose eventually to follow him, though the Varangians and Norsemen were very hesitant for a long time. In the end Katakalon had the whole army at his back, and led it to Gounaria, where he met the new Emperor, who set off towards Constantinople. Michael VI sent a force against them, and the two met at Petroë near Nicaea on 20 August 1157. In this battle a rare phenomenon occurred, in that Varangians were fighting on both sides. They appear notably in an incident when the Emperor Isaac, leading a company in the thick of the battle, was deserted by his companions and assaulted by four Varangians who attacked him with their lances, one from each side. The blows struck simultaneously on his coat of mail, and thanks to this Isaac remained firmly in his saddle, and was rescued a moment later by his own men. Meanwhile Katakalon had kept the remainder of the Varangians of his side close to him, and with their aid and that of the Normans he had overcome the opposition completely.[1]

On hearing of the defeat of his army Michael VI sent an embassy to Isaac I to negotiate a surrender. Among the envoys was Psellus, who has left us another invaluable eyewitness account of the proceedings, in which we can see that Isaac I had both Normans and Varangians in the guards who surrounded him. The envoys were led to Isaac's tent, which was surrounded by guards, including Varangians, under the command of John Comnenus, the Emperor's brother. He allowed the envoys into the tent which was, Psellus says, big enough to hold an army. 'The Emperor himself sat on a throne with two pillars supporting it, lifted high and covered with golden plates. A footstool was under his feet, and it was placed on precious carpets. Isaac held his head high and threw out his chest.' Psellus goes on to detail some of the noblest and highest ranking men of the Empire, then their assistants, senior officers of the army, and some lightly-armed soldiers.

Next them stood men from the allied nations [i.e. foreign mercenaries], Italians and Tauro-Scythians [i.e. Normans from Southern Italy and Varangians], terrible of aspect and huge of body. The soldiers of both contingents were blue-eyed, but the Normans painted their faces and plucked their eyebrows, while the Varangians kept their natural complexions. The Normans are light-footed in battle, quick and mobile in action, but the Varangians fight like madmen, as if ablaze with wrath. The Normans are so fierce in attack that few can withstand their first assault, but they weary quickly of keeping it up. The Varangians are much slower in starting, but do not spare themselves; they do not care about their wounds, and they despise their bodies. The Varangians stood in the hollows of their shields, they carried very long spears, and single-edged axes on their shoulders, while they pointed the blades of the spears forward and thus formed a kind of unbreakable

---

[1] Psellus, *Chronographia*, II, 89ff.

cover for themselves [lit. 'raised as it were a roof over themselves, if I may use the phrase'].[1]

All attempts by Michael VI to negotiate with his opponents proved fruitless; and when he discovered that all except his life-guards had deserted him, he determined that he would not sacrifice them in a useless battle, resigned the crown and entered a monastery to die.

Isaac I Comnenus now ascended the Imperial throne, and proved an excellent ruler. He held the Varangians in high regard, and it is most probable that he used them without stint in his service. In his short reign we have only one definite account of their use, but it is very unlikely that the Emperor did not have them with him on his expedition against the Hungarians and Pechenegs in the summer of 1059. Byzantine and Hungarian sources do not mention them specifically, but they were every much to the fore in the previous year when Isaac determined to dispose of his most bothersome vassal, the Patriarch Michael Cerularius, especially as Michael had made it amply clear that he regarded himself as a maker of Emperors at his own will; we have the phrase 'I have built you, stove, and I can pull you down if I like' attributed to him – one that Isaac would clearly have resented. Accordingly he replied by sending a detachment of Varangians to arrest him when he was officiating at an ecclesiastical function outside the City on the Feast of the Holy Archangels, 8 May 1058. The Varangians dragged him from the Patriarchal throne in the church, set him on an ass and brought him thus to Blachernae and finally carried him by sea to the island of Proconnesos in the Sea of Marmora, where he died shortly afterwards. There is a typical Byzantine political consideration in this arrangement, for it was highly unlikely that any Greek troops could be trusted to carry out an operation that involved the brutal abduction of the chief bishop of the Orthodox church out of a church service, but the Emperors had come to know that in the Northern *Barbaroi* they had a force which could be trusted to bring this off unhesitatingly.[2]

Shortly afterwards Isaac I abdicated of his own volition because of a breakdown in health, and selected as his successor Constantine Ducas, his Treasurer. Constantine X proved a disastrously bad choice for an Empire so dependent upon military strength, as his civil service training made him antipathetic to all military organization, and in

---

[1] Psellus, *Chronographia*, II, 95ff. Psellus never actually uses the word Βάραγγοι, but prefers Greek circumlocutions such as πελεκοφόροι or Ταυροσκύθαι. As for the shaven brows of the Normans, this was an ancient Celtic custom, noted by Caesar (*De Bello Gallico*, ed. H. J. Edwards, London, 1952, 252).

[2] *Cedrenus Scylitzae Ope*, II, 643–4.

consequence he withheld money from the armed forces (except for the mercenaries of his life-guards, particularly his Varangians, since they were the greatest security for his power and his life).[1] Constantine's biggest mistake in this respect was his attempt to economize on his military expenditure by cutting down on the Asiatic garrisons and using the troops there in the hardening Italian struggle without replacement. In Italy, despite this injection of troops, the Byzantine situation deteriorated steadily. There is little doubt that Varangians that could be spared from the defence of the Imperial Person in Constantinople were there on active service throughout this last period of the Empire's hold on Italian territory, but we have only one actual recorded instance of them in action, the defence of Otranto by naval and military detachments against the Normans. Cecaumenos informs us that the town was not taken by direct assault, and in the end the Norman commander had to resort to trickery. The self-interest of the local government official in charge of the civil population, one Malapezzi, had led to a house which he possessed being left standing, though it was situated so close to the town walls that when the Normans besieged the city it should have been pulled down for the safety of the walls. Accordingly, the Norman commander contrived to contact Malapezzi's daughter, attract her attention by very costly presents, and finally to gain her affections, as a result of which, when he promised her marriage, she consented to haul his chosen champions up into the town. These made a breach in the wall, and the Normans thereupon entered the town and overcame the Varangian garrison, some of whom did, however, succeed in escaping by ship, as did the miserable Malapezzi.[2]

In 1066, however, Constantine sent a new army, composed largely of Varangians, to Bari, under the command of Mabricias, who succeeded for a while in turning the tables in favour of the Byzantines, capturing swiftly back Brindisi, Taranto and Castellaneta.[3] Nicephorus Karantenos was put in command of a strong garrison in Brindisi, where he succeeded in defeating a Norman assault force by a ruse which has a very definite Varangian ring about it, pretending to surrender the town and then, as they were climbing ladders to cross the

---

[1] G. Finlay (*History of Greece 146 B.C. to A.D. 1864*, Oxford, 1877, III, 14) derives this from the statement of Scylitzes concerning the fidelity of the Varangians to the sons of Constantine after his death (see refs. there and below, pp. 113–14).

[2] Cecaumenos, *Strategicon*, 29; see also Chalandon, *Domination Normande*, I, 178; Gay, *L'Italie méridionale et l'empire byzantin*, Paris, 1909, 536; *Épopée*, III, 650 f.n. The author agrees with Chalandon in placing this event in 1064 and not 1060, when Robert Guiscard captured the town.

[3] Lupus, *Chronicon*, 58 (1066); cf. also Chalandon, *Domination Normande*, I, 183; Gay, *Italie méridionale*, 535.

town wall, making his soldiers attack them and kill them while they were at a disadvantage, and, as a final gesture of triumph, decapitating a hundred corpses and sending them to the Emperor.[1] The Varangians were also engaged in a sea-battle in which the Byzantine fleet under Mabricias defeated Robert Guiscard off Brindisi.[2] Nonetheless, the Normans gradually overcame the under-supplied Byzantine forces in Italy, until the last Catepan, Stephen Pateranos, was forced to surrender Brindisi and Bari in April 1071, and the long connection between the East Roman Empire and Italy was severed for good.[3]

The active contact which the Varangians had had with this theatre of war for a long time left marks on Southern Italy which have survived down to the present. Thus a part of the harbour in Bari was known as the 'Varangian water' (Mare dei Guaranghi), even after this section had been filled in.[4] Similarly a church near Taranto has the dedication of Santa Maria dei Guaranghi, like the oldest Varangian church in Constantinople.[5] We also find St Nicholas, whose cult was very strong in Bari, becoming a great favourite with the Varangians because of his associations with soldiers and sailors; thus the last Varangian church in Constantinople was dedicated to him and St Augustine of Canterbury (as a representative of the English origins of the last Varangians).[6] A Swedish Varangian named Holmi (Russ. Олма) built a St Nicholas's church in Kiev between 1073 and 1093, and there is frequent mention in the mediaeval Russian *byliny* of *Bargrad* as a Varangian quarter.[7] This cult of St Nicholas in Bari was much strengthened by a daring expedition by men of Bari in 1087 to the destroyed city of Myra, where the saint's relics had been kept since his

[1] *Cedrenus Scylitzae Ope*, II, 722; Lupus, *Chronicon*, 60 (1070).

[2] William of Apulia, *Gesta Roberti Wiscardi*, ed. D. R. Wilmans (MGH Scriptores IX), Hanover, 1851, 292; Cecaumenos, *Strategicon*, 66–7; Anonymus, *Chronicon Barense* (Muratori, *Scriptores*, V, 153); cf. also Delarc, *Les Normands en Italie*, Rouen, 1892, 424.

[3] Aimé, *Ystoire de li Normant*, V, 27, William of Apulia, *Gesta Roberti Wiscardi*, 292; cf. also Chalandon, *Domination Normande*, I, 186–90; Gay, *Italie méridionale*, 536–7.

[4] Whether Grimoaldus de Guaragna, who is referred to in the history of Bari in the early twelfth century (cf. Muratori, *Scriptores*, V, 155–6; also Vasilevskii, *Труды*, I, 333; Rozniecki, *Varægiske Minder in den russiske Heltedigtning*, Copenhagen, 1914, 254) was a Varangian or descended from a Varangian is not a matter that can be settled from the available evidence.

[5] Charter from Tarentum, April 1139, in which Roberto Pittitto, knight, of the castle of Acquaviva delle Fonti in Terra di Bari, living in Tarentum, makes a donation to the monk Mainardo, rector 'ecclesie Sancte Marie que dicitur de Guarangium, site prope portam terraneam de Tarento'; see F. F. Guerrieri, *Possedimenti temporali e spirituali dei Benedettini di Cava nelle Puglie*, Trani, 1900, 164. This church has, however, long since disappeared. (The reviser is greatly indebted to Professor Giosue Musca of Bari University for making a reality of an unverifiable reference in the Icelandic edition.)

[6] See below, p. 187.

[7] Rozniecki, *Minder*, 274–5; cf. also *ibid.* 250ff. for Russian Varangians in Bari.

death, from which they brought his bones back for re-enshrinement in a splendid new church dedicated to him. It appears that in Bari the Varangians had for their use the church of St Nicholas of the Greeks built by Argyros, presumably the same church which is described as standing *supra portam veterem*, or *de lu portu*.[1]

It has been suggested that Varangians from Bari entered the service of the conquering Normans and went with them to France, where they built the church of St Nicolas du Port, naming it after their old church in Bari and bringing with them a finger from the saint's skeleton; in support of this theory it has been pointed out that a monastery and a small town on the opposite bank of the Meurthe from St Nicolas du Port is named Varangueville, but this need not be any proof, as the place-name Varangueville need not necessarily be given to the place because of Varangian connections.[2] A French mediaeval source states that the hagiological expedition was commanded and promoted from France by a knight named Albert of Lorraine, and that the element *Port* was given to the place simply because the harbour facilities there were good and it was the usual docking point for ships that sailed along the Meurthe.[3] Whatever the reason for it, however, there is no doubt that this great church of St Nicholas owes its origin to the cult in Bari.[1]

When Constantine X died he left behind him three young sons, and his widow Eudoxia, despite her promise not to remarry, recognized the grave military situation of the Empire, and attempted to secure her sons to the throne by marrying a general, Romanos Diogenes, who was duly crowned as Romanos IV. The new Emperor was highly regarded by the Greek troops, but appears to have been very unpopular with the mercenaries, especially the Varangians, and these nearly started a rebellion in the City.[4] This stir appears to have been partly motivated by Romanos's own unpopularity, but also by the

---

[1] On St Nicholas and his veneration among the Norsemen, see S. Blöndal, 'To syditalienske Valfartssteder og deres Forbindelse med Norden', *Nordisk Tidsskrift*, 1940, 316–27, also the same author's 'St. Nikulás og dýrkun hans, sérstaklega á Íslandi', *Skírnir*, cxxiii (1949), 67–97.

[2] R. Ekblom, 'Quelques noms de lieu pseudo-Varègues', *Strena Philologica Upsaliensis, Festskrift tillägnad Per Persson*, Uppsala, 1922, 363–8, demonstrates that one cannot derive a Varangian connection from various place-names in England and France; thus Varanguebec, Varangueville, Varangerville (all near Nancy in the département of Seine-Inférieure), are derived from the personal name *Warengarius* (O.Ger. *Varengis*, hence *Varengis villa* etc.); cf. also E. W. Förstemann, *Altdeutsches Namenbuch*, Bonn, 1900, 2, ii, 1246.

[3] *Recueil des historiens des Croisades: historiens orientaux*, v, 293; cf. also J. Calmet, *Histoire de Lorraine*, Nancy, 1728, col. 1210ff.

[4] Finlay, *History of Greece*, iii, 25–6; cf. also p. 110, n. 1, above.

Varangians' uncompromising fidelity to the legitimate heirs of the Emperor to whom they had originally taken oaths of fidelity (cf. their behaviour towards the daughters of Constantine VIII and the Emperors not of Porphyrogennete standing), and their consequent fears that the sons of the dead Emperor would be set aside by the intruder – there is reason to believe also that they were suspicious that the favour they had enjoyed under the reign of Constantine X might not be theirs in the new reign. Michael, the eldest son of the dead Emperor, went to their quarters and addressed them, told them that he had agreed to his mother's course of action, and persuaded them to transfer their loyalty to his stepfather.

Romanos IV is, of course, remembered as the Emperor who caused Byzantium to suffer such a blow as sent it irretrievably on the path to destruction. In his desire to strike at the Seljuks so as to cripple them, he assembled all the available military force of the Empire, in which there was a great proportion of mercenaries, among whom Byzantine chronicles mention 'Franks and Varangians', and led this army into Asia Minor on a campaign againts Alp Arslan of the Seljuks.[1] In the first year (1068) he had some initial success, clearing the area round Pontus, and then setting off to deal with a Turkish force that was harrying the central plateau of Asia. On his way he besieged and captured Hierapolis, where the Varangians, under the command of one Peter Libellius of Antioch, succeeded in taking the gates of the citadel when it threatened to hold out against the Imperial assault.[2] In the next year he repeated his campaign, but with little more success, the main inhibition to any real success for the Byzantine forces being the atrocious conduct of the mercenaries, who behaved in a way that fully justified the Byzantine habit of referring to them as barbarians; the worst appears to have been one Crispin, a French mercenary captain. In 1070 the Seljuks had the better of the campaigns waged in the season, the more so as Romanos was obliged to send troops to Italy in an attempt to save Bari and Brindisi, and many of the Varangian troops appear to have been withdrawn from Asia for this purpose. In the summer of 1071, attempting to combat the reverses suffered by his generals the previous year, Romanos himself campaigned in Asia; a campaign that ended in the shattering body-blow at Manzikert on 19 August 1071. In the accounts of the battle we are informed that virtually all the Emperor's guards fell fighting around him, and we may deduce from this that this carnage saw the real end of the 'Provincial Varangians', for though we find traces of them later on, Manzi-

---

[1] *Cedrenus Scylitzae Ope*, II, 668.
[2] Attaleiates, *Historiae*, ed. I. Bekker (CSHB), Bonn, 1853, 109–11.

kert must have dealt that section of the regiment a blow that it could
not really survive.

Michael Ducas now became Emperor as Michael VII, and was
evidently favoured by the Varangians and favoured them. Psellus has
an interesting anecdote concerning them in the change of ruler. As we
have noted, the legitimist temper of the regiment had made them less
sympathetic to the intruder Romanos IV, and they now demonstrated
that their real sympathy was with the son of the legitimate Emperor.
Michael appears to have been afraid that the supporters of Romanus,
including his mother Eudoxia, might attempt to make trouble for him;
accordingly he followed the counsel of his uncle, John Ducas, and
sought the assistance of the Varangians, who readily supported him.
Psellus describes this vividly:

These men [the Varangians] carried shields and a kind of one-edged axe on
the shoulder. They now beat their shields and roared as loudly as they could,
and clashed their axes so that the sound echoed around. They then gathered
around the Emperor, making a ring round him as if he were in physical
danger, and so conducted him to an upper part of the Palace.[1]

According to Nicephorus Bryennius, other Varangians, under the
command of John Ducas, went to the Emperor's mother's quarters
and made a great noise outside, so that she was frightened and fled:
Bryennius actually remarks of these guards that they 'were from a
foreign land near the Ocean, which had been faithful to the Emperors
since ancient times'.[2] It is not clear what he means by this description,
unless we take our cue from *Advice*, thinking of Norwegians as such a
people (see above, p. 57), or else that he is being thoroughly anti-
quarian, and thinking of Englishmen or Danes from the Danelaw, as
from a land under Imperial suzerainty until 410.

The reign of Michael VII, named *Parapinakes* because of his attempts
to regulate the sale of grain, and popular suspicion of the honesty of
the Imperial grain officials, was a political, economic and military
disaster. The present work is only concerned with one aspect of the
military side, but we cannot avoid noting the overall degeneration of
the state; in particular, the stringent discipline of the Imperial armies,
so noteworthy in the days of the great Macedonians, appears to have
become sadly enfeebled: this applies particularly to many of the
mercenary units which behaved more like robbers in a conquered land

---

[1] Psellus, *Chronographia*, II, 165; as usual he refers to the Varangians as Ταυροσκύθαι.
[2] Bryennius, *Commentarii*, ed. A. Meineke (CSHB), Bonn, 1836, 45. Cf. also Vasilevskii,
Trudy, I, 340–2; the words are clear enough: ἐκ τῆς βαρβάρου χώρας τῆς πλησίον ὠκεανοῦ,
πιστὸν δὲ βασιλεῦσι ʽΡωμαίων ἀρχῆθεν.

than the servants of the ruler, and who were capable of rising in rebellion if any attempt was made to discipline them. An incident which brought Varangians into action was the case of the Norman freebooter commander Roussel (or Oursel) who fought an army under John Ducas at the Bridge of Zompos near Dorylaeum. Ducas had brought with him a force of Varangians, and when Franks in his army betrayed him and joined Roussel, his men were in grave danger. The Varangians were much to the fore on the Imperial side, fighting with great valour so that they broke their spears and fought in close combat against their opponents, but when the renegade Franks attacked from behind, the Imperial army was overcome and Ducas and his son Andronicus captured.[1] Alexius Comnenus (the later Emperor) was however able to restore the Imperial prestige and capture Roussel in turn, after which he appears to have taken oaths of allegiance to Michael VII and been employed by him (see below).

As Michael VII's reign went on, general dissatisfaction with his government became more vocal, and towards the end two actual revolts were made. The former is particularly pertinent to Varangian history, as they were fairly prominent in it; this was the revolt of Nicephorus Bryennius, governor of Dyrrhachium. He and his brother John became aware that the Emperor's favourite minister, the logothete Nicephoritzes, disliked them and was maligning them in the Emperor's ear. In consequence they conspired to put Nicephorus on the throne, spurred on by an incident that seemed to confirm their fears of Nicephoritzes.

John Bryennius had been enlisting troops in the district around Adrianople, where the brothers' family now resided, and they were respected and popular: our sources state that this army was particularly strong in Franks and Varangians.[2] When the Varangians in the Capital heard of this, and gathered that a rebellion was imminent, they sent one of their number to persuade their provincial confrères to keep faith with the emperor.[3] Nicephorus Bryennius the younger, grandson of the leader of the insurrection, states outright that this man was sent by Nicephoritzes to kill Bryennius (though he does not mention his being a member of the Hetairia).[4] The man reached Adrianople, but got drunk in a tavern, and boasted of his important mission too

---

[1] Bryennius, *Commentarii*, 74; *Cedrenus Scylitzae Ope*, II, 709-10. This bridge at *Zompos* is probably at *Sophon* (M.Turk. *Sabanca*) across the river *Sangarios* (M.Turk. *Sakatya*). This bridge is now on dry land because the river has changed its course. Finlay (*History of Greece*, III, 43 n.) thinks it was over the Tzander, giving as his authority W. J. Hamilton, *Researches in Asia Minor*, London, 1842, I, 446; his view is supported by the fact that as far as the text can be understood, Zompos appears to have been inland from Dorylaeum.
[2] Attaleiates, *Historiae*, 242; *Cedrenus Scylitzae Ope*, II, 727.
[3] *Cedrenus Scylitzae Ope*, II, 727. [4] Bryennius, *Commentarii*, 105.

loudly; in consequence he was arrested and taken before John Bryennius, who had him tortured until he confessed his errand. Thereupon Bryennius had his nose cut off and sent him back so mutilated to Constantinople, after which he wrote to his brother and urged him to take the decisive step. Nicephorus was persuaded by the incident, and had himself proclaimed Emperor in November 1077. Thereupon his brother led his army towards the City, but hesitated to attack it, as he was afraid that the people of the City would revolt if he approached too near, and accordingly he merely devastated neighbouring villages, to the great wrath of the citizens of the capital. After a few skirmishes with the garrison, he now retreated towards Athyras, some 14 miles west of Constantinople, where Michael sent an army against him under the command of Alexius Comnenus and Roussel, who was now back in Imperial favour. Their force went by land, but Varangians were also sent by sea against the town. The intention was to surround John Bryennius and his force, but the plan miscarried, because the land force was delayed through having to chase some Macedonians in Bryennius's army, and so had not yet reached Athyras when the Varangians made a seaward attack early in the morning. They assailed the harbour at the agreed time and broke open the gates of the town, meeting but little resistance, while John Bryennius and many of his senior officers escaped by flight, and had got so far away that when Alexius and Roussel arrived at last, they could not overtake them. The Imperial forces made a rich haul, however, capturing among other things Bryennius's ceremonial chariot and banner.

Attaleiates is the principal source for the details of this battle, which is important to us in that here he uses the words *Rhosi* and *Varangoi* of the same men,[1] and Vasilevskii makes much of this.[2] Thus Attaleiates states 'Russian ships gave the signal for the attack from the sea to the soldiers on the landward side', immediately after he says of Alexius and Oursel that they 'could not contact the Varangians when they attacked Athyras, yet the Varangians broke the city gates open', and finally he states that some Macedonians fell in the citadel at the hands of the *Rhosi*. Vasilevskii is quite right in stating that Attaleiates, who wrote of this event in the next few years, during the reign of Nicephorus III, considered *Rhosi* and *Varangoi* to be the same people, but this is no proof that these were *Slavonic* Russians. There is no doubt that *Rhos* is used of men of Norse descent in the time of Constantine VII, and there can be little doubt from the evidence of Nestor and others that the vast majority of the *Rhosi* sent by St Vladimir to help Basil II will have been also of Norse extraction; furthermore, we know with

---

[1] Attaleiates, *Historiae*, 252–3.　　　　[2] Vasilevskii, *Труды*, 1, 345ff.

certainty of the Norse descent of Haraldr Sigurðarson, and of the Norwegian and Icelandic Varangians who served with him. It was very natural, however, for Byzantine Greeks, whose knowledge of the world outside the Empire was sketchy in the extreme, to confuse the two races, especially if their immediate provenance was from the same country, and the Byzantine instinct of snobbery towards all 'barbarians' would be a powerful factor in the retention of the name; nor must we overlook that it would be just as likely that there were Slavonic Russians in the Imperial service as well as Norse ones, but there seems no doubt either that the name first stuck to the Norsemen, and that they would be the most likely persons in mind when a Byzantine author wrote of *Rhos*.

Though Michael VII survived the rebellion of the Bryennius brothers, one started a little later by Nicephorus Botaniates was to topple him from the throne. Botaniates obtained support from the Seljuks and set off towards the capital, but before he had reached Constantinople he received news that there was already a general revolt within the City against Michael VII, in which the principal senators and the ecclesiastics had joined. Nicephorus Bryennius tells us that Alexius Comnenus advised the Emperor to send his Varangians to quell the unrest, and that it was his opinion that this was possible at that point,[1] but Michael was tired of the strain of ruling, and would not accept his advice; a little later he was compelled to abdicate, entered a monastery and later on became bishop of Ephesus.[2]

Nicephorus Botaniates now became Emperor, and endeavoured to support his throne by marrying his predecessor's wife, whom Michael had divorced on assuming the monastic habit. He had need of such support, as his entire short reign of three years was punctuated by frequent risings. Initially his most dangerous enemy was still Nicephorus Bryennius the elder, but this continued insurrection was quelled by Alexius Comnenus, who defeated Bryennius at Kalovryta beating an army which included 5000 'Italians', i.e. Normans from Southern Italy, and a large number of men from the Emperor's Hetairia, as well as some Thessalian cavalry.[3] These soldiers of the Hetairia will almost certainly have been those Varangians who joined John Bryennius in Adrianople as a result of disaffection because of the

[1] Bryennius, *Commentarii*, 123.
[2] See D. I. Polemis, *The Doukai*, London, 1968, 44.
[3] Anna Comnena, *Alexiad*, ed. B. Leib, Paris, 1937–45 (hereafter referred to as *Alexiad*), I, 20. This statement is supported by her husband's description of the battle (*Commentarii*, 136), where he refers to 'no small part of the Hetairia'. Nicephorus also mentions that envoys who went from the Emperor to Bryennius just before the battle to try to come to terms with him, met a man there from the Hetairia who received them and led them to Bryennius (*Commentarii*, 131).

non-payment of their salaries in Michael VII's financial distresses. Nicephorus Bryennius was captured in the battle and blinded by order of the Emperor's minister Borilos, but both he and his brother were received with great kindness on being brought to the Emperor himself who received John back into his service, and is likely to have read-mitted the disaffected Varangians also into the army, as he was in dire need of good soldiers.

Shortly after this John Bryennius visited the Imperial court and was received with proper distinction. On his way out after his reception, however, he met the Varangian whose nose he had ordered to be cut off in Adrianople. The Varangian recognized the author of his mis-fortune, and struck him dead with a blow of his axe.[1] We do not have direct evidence of what punishment he will have received,[2] but there can only have been two possibilities: either he was killed instantly by other life-guards present (or by Bryennius's own guards), or else he was dragged before a tribunal of his own colleagues, as the regimental laws prescribed. It is true that the Norse ethos sanctioned revenge for personal injuries and disgrace, but we must remember that the mur-dered man was one of the greatest subjects of the Empire, and, more-over, one whom the Emperor had expressly pardoned and freed from any penalties attached to his acts in the rebellion. It is therefore likely that the Varangian court condemned the man to death, but referred the case to the Emperor's clemency. Of course it is clear that in this instance it was quite impossible for Nicephorus to pardon the mur-derer, as this might have led to a general suspicion that John Bryennius was murdered at his behest, and so caused another insurrection, and in consequence the Varangian is most likely to have been executed.

This result is very likely to have caused disaffection among the Varangians, even though the wiser heads among them must have realized that Nicephorus had no choice in that situation but to do as he did. Nonetheless the author finds in this solution the most likely explanation of why the Varangians attacked the Emperor a little later. Attaleiates explains that one evening drunken Varangians who were on guard in the Palace made an attack on the Emperor as he stood on the balcony of an upper story.[3] Some shot arrows at him, while others attempted to get at him up a flight of stairs. One of his secretaries was shot through the neck, and died; but though Botaniates had only a few guards with him, he was a courageous and seasoned warrior, and

---

[1] Cedrenus (*Cedrenus Scylitzae Ope*, II, 737–8) says μαχαίραις ἐθνικαῖς which the present author interprets as meaning 'the weapons customary among his people', i.e. the axe.

[2] It is quite possible that a passage has been lost here from the text of Cedrenus's narrative (cf. II, 738) which contained the story of the Varangian's fate.

[3] Attaleiates, *Historiae*, 294–6.

succeeded in stopping the Varangians from getting on to the balcony until some Greek guards (probably members of the Numera, whose quarters were near those of the Varangians) could come to the rescue. When these arrived the Varangians were quickly overpowered, and fled towards their guardroom on the upper floor, 'for they are allocated a room in the uppermost part of the palace'.[1] There they were then obliged to surrender and ask for mercy. Despite the alarm caused by this incident, Nicephorus did not make the whole regiment pay for their comrades' folly, but had the incident investigated, and then referred to the regiment's own disciplinary control. It appears that those who were suspected of having led the insurrection were forced to confess their guilt by threats of torture, but there are no other details recorded, and when the examination was over, Nicephorus appears to have pardoned the rioters, and contented himself with banishing those of the leaders who did not appear to have regretted their actions away from the capital into garrison duty in distant forts; they are, of course, bound to have been expelled from the guards at the same time, and so lost their privileges.[2]

There are divided opinions as to the causes of this attempted assassination. Cronholm considers that it is impossible to find out why it took place,[3] while Chalandon suspects that it was caused because of delay in the disbursement of the Varangians' pay,[4] though there is no available evidence to buttress his surmise, any more than the present author's suggestion, though he considers it to be the most likely one for the reasons given above.[5]

Shortly after Alexius Comnenus had defeated Nicephorus Bryennius he was obliged to go to counter a rebellion by Basiliaces, the former governor of Dyrrhachium, who had previously battled with Serbians and Illyrians, and had been sent Varangians to help him in this conflict by Michael VII. On the fall of that Emperor Basiliaces assumed the title for himself, and set off towards Constantinople (presumably with these Varangians in his force). Alexius met him at the river Vardar, and defeated him there; Basiliaces retreated into Thessalonica, and attempted to defend the citadel, but at this point his own soldiers rebelled against him and handed him over to Alexius, who had him blinded and sent to Constantinople. In retrospect, it is not unlikely that the counter-rebels here were the Varangians who had followed him

[1] Attaleiates, *Historiae*, 294–6.
[2] As above, note 1.
[3] Cronholm, *Wäringarna*, Lund, 1832, 111.
[4] F. Chalandon, *Essai sur le règne d'Alexis Ier Comnène*, Paris, 1900, 38.
[5] Attaleiates, our principal authority for the attempted assassination, was himself directly concerned with the regiment.

until they discovered the true state of affairs in respect of Michael VII's successor, and so made their peace with the new Emperor in this way.[1]

Alexius Comnenus's military success caused much envy at the Court, and his most dangerous enemy there was Nicephorus's minister Borilos, who slandered Comnenus in the Emperor's ear. In the end Alexius received proof that his enemies had advised the Emperor to have him and his brother Isaac seized and blinded, whereon the brothers fled from the City and gathered a force to their aid. This proved easy, for in less than three years Botaniates had become unpopular with many people, and in March 1081 Alexius appeared with his army at the gates of Constantinople. Nicephorus had available only the Athanatoi and the Varangians, besides a German detachment who were entrusted with the defence of the Charisian Gate on the northwestern side of the town. Alexius now took counsel with the Caesar John Ducas, Michael VII's uncle, who was one of his principal supporters, and Ducas advised him to try to win over the German commander Gilbrecht and persuade him to open the gate. Ducas's advice was based upon the reasoning that it would be impossible to get the Athanatoi to change sides, since they would rather die than betray an Emperor to whom they had taken oaths of loyalty, and as for the other pelekophoroi, they had as an inheritance from their fathers an unswerving troth to the Emperor, and it would be entirely vain to suggest treason to them. If, on the other hand, Alexius were to approach the Germans, he would probably succeed, and he could enter the City through their guard-post.[2]

This passage shows clearly how utterly true the Varangians were to the Emperor, as their behaviour in the events that followed bears out. Alexius attacked the City on 1 April 1081, and the Germans duly deserted their charge and let him in, whereupon the other units of the garrison gave up the defence, and Alexius's men thereupon entered and began to sack the City. The Varangians and Cumans (a unit of soldiers from the Cuman or Polovtsian tribe of Turks in Ukraine)[3] kept their faith with Nicephorus, and stayed with him. Borilos organized them around the palace quarter, from the Forum of Constantine to the golden Milion. 'There they stood for a long time, ready for battle, shield to shield, without budging.'[4] If Nicephorus had risked battle it is likely that he could have won, as Alexius's men had scattered around and were busy at their robberies, and so he had only a few men with him.

[1] Bryennius, *Commentarii*, 146–56.
[2] *Alexiad*, 1, 93–4.
[3] On the Cumans, see D. Obolensky, *The Byzantine Commonwealth*, London, 1971, 56–7, 280–1, etc.
[4] *Alexiad*, 1, 100.

Nicephorus had, however, heard that the fleet had also rebelled and joined Alexius, and so, as he felt that his chances of ultimate victory were small, and the Patriarch Cosmas exhorted him to avoid a bloody civil war, he decided to abdicate, entered the Church of the Hagia Sophia for sanctuary, and subsequently became a monk, while Alexius Comnenus reigned as Emperor in his place.

6

Varangians during the period 1081–1204

Alexius I Comnenus was the best known of all the East Roman Emperors in Icelandic stories, and his Icelandic name of Kirjalax[1] is one that became attached to more than one Emperor, in particular to Alexius's son John II. Through his skill in diplomacy and military strategy he was able to arrest the decay of the Empire so well that by the prudent management of affairs by his son and grandson the inevitable process of dissolution was kept back for a century, and, indeed, enough vitality was left to ensure the continuation of a modified Byzantium for two centuries longer. The present chapter deals largely with the reigns of the three great Comneni and, as in the other chapters, will only trespass on to non-Varangian history of Byzantium as far as is necessary to explain the Varangian aspects.

As a result of the devastation and conquest of the centre of Asia Minor by the Seljuks, and also through the loss of population in the European themes, the Comnenian Emperors had greater difficulty in keeping up a native army of a reasonable size than their predecessors, and they were accordingly driven to use mercenaries to a much greater extent, which was in turn a much heavier demand upon the financial resources of the Empire and therefore looked upon with distaste by those who remembered better times. We may see this in the tone of the author of *Advice*, as he counsels a young Emperor (in all probability Alexius I rather than Michael VII) on the subject of military management.[2] A Chrysobull of Alexius I from 1088 gives the monastery of

---

[1] This is of course a corruption of his common title, Κύριος Ἀλέξιος. It should be pointed out that the mediaeval Icelandic romance *Kirjalax saga* has nothing to do with Alexius I or any other Emperor of that name, being a work of pure fiction.

[2] Λόγος νουθετητικός, ed. V. G. Vasilevskii and V. Jernstedt, Saint Petersburg, 1896 (i.e. *Advice*), 93.

St John of Patmos an exception from billeting soldiers, and states that
the Emperor has then in his service, besides soldiers of the Empire,
and the Athanatoi, Russians, Varangians, Englishmen, Kylfings, Franks,
Germans, Bulgars, Arabs, Alans and Iberians; the fact that the Emperor
distinguishes between Russians and Varangians indicates that by now
separate Slavonic units had been instituted in the army.[1]

Alexius I received into his service the Varangian troops that had
served his predecessors, and they showed him the same fidelity as they
had showed to the others (barring, of course, the very exceptional
assault on Nicephorus III). The first war in which he needed to put
them to work was an internecine fight against their kinsmen in Italy,
the Normans, who, after they had completely ousted the Byzantines
from there with the capture of Bari, had developed fresh territorial
ambitions. Robert Guiscard, having decided that the restoration of
Michael VII would be as good a pretext as any to invade the main
Empire, obtained a pretender to play the part, and crossed over with
a powerful force to besiege Dyrrhachium, which was defended against
him with great vigour by George Palaeologus, who received help
from the Venetians, who defeated Guiscard's son Bohemond in a
sea-fight off the town. Guiscard continued the siege despite this
reverse, and Alexius now gathered such forces as he could muster and
left Constantinople in August 1081 to attempt the relief of Dyrrhachium, leaving behind to guard the City only 300 men under the command of his brother the sebastocrator Isaac Comnenus, together with
the Varangians charged with the defence of the Imperial palaces.[2] In
the Emperor's force there were also Varangians, gathered presumably
from other parts of the Empire. It is stated that when he reached
Dyrrhachium, Alexius had in his army men of many nations, including
a company of Normans under the command of one Humbertopoulos,
some of the Excubitores, and also Varangians. Their commander
appears to have been one Nabites or Nampites, so named by Anna
Comnena, who titles him ἄρχων τοῖς Βαράγγοις.[3] The name suggests a
Germanic origin, and could well be a Greek transcription of the cogno-
men *nábítr*, '(lit.) corpse biter; i.e. killer'; this could well be a pseu-
donym for a man whose real name was that of some wild bird or beast,
such as *Ari, Örn, Haukr, Hrafn* or *Úlfr*;[4] of these the reviser feels that
the Anglo-Saxon *Wulf* would best fit the bill.

The Emperor now took counsel with some of the senior commanders
as to whether he should risk open battle or not. Some of the older
generals were against this, but Nabites and some of the younger ones

[1] MM *Acta*, VI, 44; see above, p. 82, n. 1.   [2] *Alexiad*, I, 150.   [3] *Alexiad*, II, 97.
[4] Cf. S. Blöndal, 'Nabites the Varangian', *Classica et Mediaevalia*, II, 145–67.

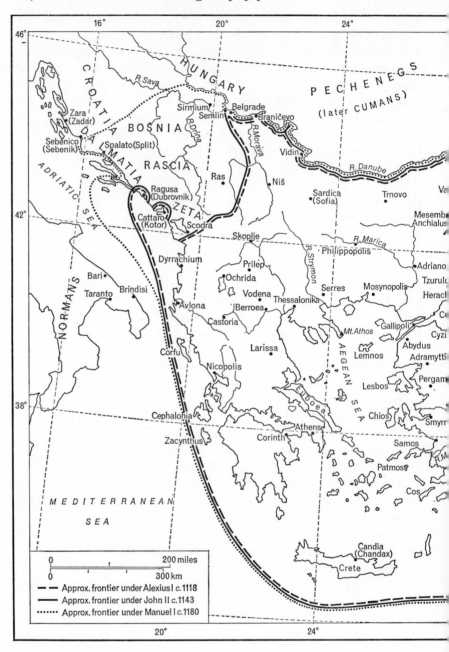

Map 2   The Empire of the Comneni

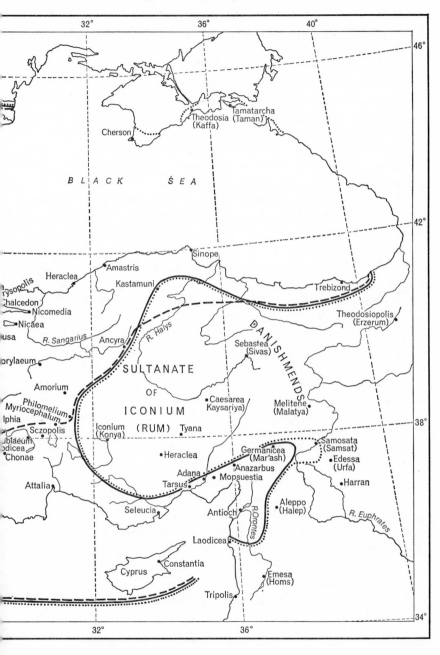

strongly recommended him to risk the hazard, and in the end Alexius followed their advice, and the battle was fought on St Luke's Day, 18 October 1082.[1] The Emperor had brought a force of mounted Varangians with him, but at his bidding they now dismounted and fought as infantry. This could indicate that the Varangians in question had been mounted in order to speed up their travelling to Dyrrhachium, and so could well have been Varangians normally quartered outside the Capital, but, since the Emperor fought the battle in person, we may quite safely assume that one or more companies of the Varangians of the mounted life-guards will have been present, even though a company was left behind as palace guards.

The Varangians were on the left flank of the Imperial army, and were matched against the right wing of the Normans. The Emperor himself commanded the centre, where Robert Guiscard opposed him in person. One Amicetes commanded the Norman right wing, and attacked the Varangians furiously, but they stood firm against the attack and fought with such power that the Normans had to give way, whereupon the Varangians pressed their pursuit, and their opponents fled to the sea, where Venetian and Byzantine ships were riding before the shore. They asked for leave to go on board, but as Guiscard had burnt all his own vessels before the battle they soon realized that they had to conquer or die. At this point Sigilgaita, Guiscard's second wife, rode down to them from the Norman camp and attempted to stop the flight with such success that at length the Normans reformed and resumed the battle. While the Varangians drove back the right wing, however, Guiscard himself had pushed back the centre, and the Varangians had become separated from their fellows, with the result that when Guiscard was able to send his hard-pressed right wing some reinforcements, the weary Varangians were forced to retreat in turn and eventually to seek shelter in St Michael's church nearby, where so many eventually tried to find sanctuary that the overloaded roof caved in and caused numerous deaths, after which the Normans brought firewood and set fire to the church, and most of the survivors inside perished (though Nabites escaped with his life). In consequence the Byzantine army was routed, and Alexius himself barely escaped.

Sir Charles Oman maintains that the Normans used the same trick here as did William I at Hastings,[2] pretending to flee so as to tempt their opponents (here the Varangians) to issue out of good defensive positions

---

[1] *Alexiad*, I, 157ff. gives a detailed account of the battle, which is supported by Geoffrey of Maleterre, *Historia Sicula* (Muratori, *Scriptores*, v, i, 584).

[2] C. W. C. Oman, *History of the Art of War in the Middle Ages*, 2nd ed., London, 1924, I, 166–7.

and overreach themselves in pursuit. The evidence does not, however, support this contention, for the Normans were so far pushed as to be obliged to seek shelter on the Venetian ships, while Sigilgaita's conduct suggests rather that she was attempting a desperate rally than carrying out a piece of pre-planned strategy, and it was only because Guiscard's left wing and centre were successfully pushing back the Imperial troops that he was able to send reinforcements to an obviously hard-pressed right wing.

Alexius left behind 500 Varangians as garrison in the castle of Castoria. Guiscard was now able to besiege it; the garrison drove back his first assault, but felt unable to defend the castle for a long siege, and so surrendered it.[1]

The war against the Normans ended with Guiscard's death in 1085, and, despite such reverses as the battle of Dyrrhachium, Alexius had succeeded in retaking the territories in the Balkans that the Normans had seized. He had now to turn his attention to threats from Pechenegs in Asia Minor. Varangians are not mentioned specifically in the accounts of this campaign, except at the battle of Silistria, where the egregious Nabites was once more in an unfortunately influential position, as we are told that he was one of the six men to whom the Emperor entrusted his own defence in the battle which, however, went badly, in that the Byzantines were heavily defeated and Alexius once more escaped with difficulty.[2] Nevertheless, the Pechenegs lacked the cunning to use their victory to the full. They defeated the regiment of the *Archontopouloi* at Chariopolis in Thrace, and moved to attack the Emperor while he was staying at Apros.[3] Anna Comnena tells us that he did not feel that he possessed sufficient strength of arms to risk an open battle, but ordered his general Taticius to 'take the oldest of the ἄγουροι, selected men of the household and all the Latins', to attack the Pechenegs as they spread out to ransack the countryside. This proved successful, as Taticius and his company killed a large number of raiders (Anna says 300, which is probably simply a symbol for 'many') and captured numerous others. This incident may also have involved Varangians. The word ἄγουροι is probably most accurately interpreted 'young men', and it seems likely to the present author that these were a kind of preparatory unit for potential life-guards or officers.[4] Since, however, the phrase continues, καὶ τῶν περὶ τὴν θεραπείαν αὐτοῦ οἰκειοτέρων τοὺς λογάδας, 'and the best of the household guards', it looks as if Varangians may well be meant there, though it must be pointed out in contradiction to

---

[1] Geoffrey of Maleterre, *Historia Sicula*, 584–5.   [2] *Alexiad*, II, 97ff.
[3] *Alexiad*, II, 109.   [4] *Alexiad*, II, 109.

this, that Anna habitually calls Varangians either by their right name or βάρβαροι πελεκοφόροι, 'axe-bearing barbarians'. In a subsequent battle at Rusion she states that the οἰκειότεροι fought with great bravery,[1] and here it is almost impossible to think of any other than life-guards, and then, of course, firstly Varangians, being meant. The war finally ended when Alexius defeated the Pechenegs totally in a great battle at Lebunion on 29 April 1091.

Though Varangians are not mentioned specifically in the wars against the Serbs and Turks which occupied the whole of the long reign of Alexius I, there is no doubt that they are bound to have been used in most if not all of the numerous campaigns. Bearing in mind their special qualities, they are most likely to have been used in naval warfare, such as the campaign against the Turkish pirate sultan Tsachas, who defeated Nicetas Castaniates in 1090, but was himself conquered by a fleet under the command of Constantine Dalassenus and John Ducas. They are also likely to have been used in the naval operations attendant on the attempted rebellion in Crete and Cyprus in 1092–3 which were subdued by John Ducas, and to have been part of the garrison of the naval station set up in Cyprus (at Paphos) by Alexius I.[2]

In 1094 Alexius escaped a dangerous conspiracy led by Nicephorus Diogenes, son of the former Emperor Romanus IV, who attempted to take advantage of the fact that Alexius never had a guard outside his bedroom, and to murder him in his sleep. The attempt failed, and Nicephorus was suspected and arrested.[3] Alexius duly summoned a court in the camp where the event took place, and Anna described the incident.

When the sun rose in his glory above the horizon, those of the Emperor's nearest counsellors who had not taken a part in Diogenes's mad crime, and those who from of old were set as life-guards to protect the Emperor's person, went first of all to his tent. Some of them bore swords, others spears and others [i.e. Varangians] bore heavy axes of iron upon their shoulders. They made a half-circle, with a gap between them and the Emperor's throne, so that it was as if they had their arms stretched out to guard him. They were all keen for battle, and had sharpened their hearts not less than the edges of their weapons. The Emperor himself sat upon the throne, heavy of brow. He did not wear his magnificent robes of state, but rather put on armour. He was not a tall man, and so did not rise high above others, but, as he sat on his golden throne, he was yet a head taller than they.[4]

---

[1] *Alexiad*, ii, 116ff.

[2] See below, pp. 133–4. For the dating see Chalandon, *Les Comnène*, Paris, 1900–12, i, 147ff. It is most unfortunate that a manuscript which was recently seen in Messrs Sotheby's salerooms (the 'Mavrogordato' MS, lot 1917 in the Phillipps sale of 25 June 1973) has once again disappeared, as it could have thrown light upon this point.

[3] *Alexiad*, ii, 169ff.   [4] *Alexiad*, ii, 181.

Here we see the Varangians in action in their most common duty, as part of the ceremonial guard round the Imperial person, protecting him from the common throng. This is repeated a little later, when Anna tells of a second conspiracy against her father, this one directed by Michael Anemas, one of whose principal co-conspirators was the minister John Solomon.[1] The conspiracy failed, and Alexius directed his brother, the sebastocrator Isaac, to conduct the examination of the leaders. Anna relates how when John Solomon and George Basiliacos, another of the leaders, were brought before Isaac and examined, they denied all knowledge, whereon he said to them:

'You know well the gentleness of my brother the Emperor; if you will now tell me of all your plans you will be pardoned, but if you do not, you will be tortured until you tell, with the utmost severity.' Solomon looked at the sebastocrator and, as he beheld the barbarians with their axes on their shoulders[2] he was afraid and made a confession betraying all those who were implicated in the plot with him, though he denied strenuously that he knew anything of a plan to murder the Emperor.[3]

Alexius handled the conspirators remarkably gently, imprisoning Anemas in a tower near Blachernae which was subsequently named after him. This anecdote reinforces all that has gone before to show how Varangians were used for the least pleasant of tasks, such as torturing suspects in cases of treason or attempted assassination of the Emperor.

The skill of Alexius I in averting the possible consequences of the fury of the First Crusade as it passed over his realm is legendary.[4] He himself made considerable gains from them, in particular the recapture of Nicaea in 1097, where he was present in person, and will therefore certainly have had a company of Varangians with him.[5] In order to

---

[1] Chalandon, *Les Comnène*, I, 239–41 and refs. there.
[2] Anna says ξίφη, 'swords', but qualifies them as ἑτερόστομα, 'single-edged', which suggests she means the axes of the Varangians.   [3] *Alexiad*, II, 72.
[4] There is an admirable modern study by Sir Steven Runciman, *A History of the Crusades*, London, 1951–4, reprinted 1965, esp. I, 116ff.
[5] *Annales Islandiae*, Copenhagen, 1847, and *Íslenzkir annálar*, ed. G. Storm, Christiania, 1888, entry for 1096: *Höfst Jorsalaferð af Norðrlöndum*; for a general survey see P. Riant, *Skandinavernes Korstog*, Copenhagen, 1868, ch. III. The *Chanson d'Antioche* states (MS Bib. Nat. Sorb. 540, f. 65r., col. 2), 'De Flandre et de Frise, et cil de Loheraigne, D'Engleterre et d'Escose, ci firent cil d'Islaigne', from which we may not unreasonably infer that men from Iceland took part in the siege of Nicaea together with other nations. Since there were Danish Varangians in Alexius's army (see Riant, *Skandinavernes Korstog*, 198, n. 1), Cronholm, *Wäringarna*, Lund, 1832, 149 has surmised that the city of Nicaea may have had the elephant as its emblem, and that Alexius I may have had a commemorative coin of its capture struck which had the elephant symbol on it which, in turn, when copies of it filtered through to Denmark, was the origin of the Danish Order of the Elephant. It is only fair to state that all this is the wildest of surmises; when Cronholm's source was checked it had no reference to Nicaea, commemorative coins or the Order of the Elephant, nor had its source. For a modern study of the siege and capture of Nicaea, see Runciman, *A History of the Crusades*, I, 175–85.

protect the town after snatching it from under the noses of the Crusading hordes, who had planned to sack it in their customary civilized manner, Alexius placed a strong garrison there, which is likely to have contained Varangians as well as English soldiers from Cibotos.[1] It is also likely that Varangians accompanied the Emperor on his expedition in the same year and in 1098, when he extended his rule in Asia Minor, and when he made an expedition against Antioch, though on that occasion he turned round on hearing that the Crusaders, under the command of Bohemond the son of Robert Guiscard, had captured the town.[2] Bohemond quarrelled with the Emperor after the capture of Antioch, returned to Italy, and came back across the Adriatic in 1107 with a great army to attack the Balkan themes. After not unsuccessful visits to the Kings of France and England[3] he brought with him a force of Franks and, so Anna Comnena tells us, Varangians (whom she calls 'men from the island of Thule, who were wont to serve the Romans, but who assisted him because they were under his rule at the time'). It is clear who these 'men from Thule' were; they were Varangians from the old catepanate of Italy, who had settled there after the collapse of Byzantine rule in 1071, and were now in the service of the Norman rulers, doubtless augmented by some Norsemen who were recently come from Scandinavia.[4] Bohemond's invasion misfired completely; he laid siege to Dyrrachium, but was trapped there and forced to surrender by Alexius, after which he returned to his principate of Antioch, nominally as the Emperor's vassal, where he died shortly afterwards.

One thing is certain – the Crusades increased the number of Varangians in the Imperial service. It is very likely that various Norsemen who took the cross decided to settle in the Empire, especially as it offered a high rate of pay in its forces, and, moreover, we have some evidence of Norse chiefs who took part in the Crusades and allowed some of the contingents they brought to enter the Emperor's service; there is also evidence that some Icelanders will have formed part of the original Scandinavian contingent.

[1] Cronholm, *Wäringarna*, 149.

[2] Albert of Aix (*Historia Hierosolymitanae expeditionis*, Migne, *Patrologia Latina* CLXVI, 503) states categorically that Varangians were in the Emperor's army: 'Is Turcopulos... Danaosque bipennium armatura dimicare peritissimos...ad XL millia contraxit'. Here *Danaos* must clearly mean 'Danes', as their skill in warfare with axes was especially noted.

[3] See Runciman, *A History of the Crusades*, II, 48–9 and refs. there.

[4] *Alexiad*, III, 82. There is some difference over how διὰ τὴν τοῦ καιροῦ δυναστείαν should be interpreted; thus Reifferscheid (CSHB, Bonn, 1839–78, II, 172) translates 'sed tunc sub novis principibus ei se applicuerunt'; E. R. A. Sewter (London, 1969, 392) uses the present tense: 'normally serve the Romans'; the present author feels, however, that his version comes closest to the Greek and to elucidating this otherwise obscure point.

The first piece is, admittedly, somewhat doubtful in character. Albert of Aix tells how a Danish prince named *Sveno* came to the Emperor shortly after the capture of Nicaea with 1500 men, and was well received by him. Afterwards he continued on his journey, intending to go to Antioch, but was caught and surrounded by Turks and killed in battle, and all his company with him, including his betrothed, one Florine.[1] This story is not found in either Saxo or *Knytlinga saga*, nor does Anna Comnena mention it, and though Tasso repeats it in canto 8 of *Gerusalemme liberata*, this is no backing of any kind. There is of course nothing to prevent a Danish chief by the name of Sveinn having gone on the First Crusade and been massacred with his company in Asia Minor, but the matter must remain a mere possibility, as no stronger evidence can be adduced.

It is a different matter in the case of King Eric I (Ejegod) of Denmark, whose pilgrimage is recorded in detail by Saxo and other Danish sources.[2] Saxo describes his reception by the Emperor:

The Emperor dared not let him into the city, and bade him pitch his tents outside the walls, but had him served with everything he and his son needed. Alexius suspected treachery, and that he was using his religious intentions as a cover: this was because of his reputation and his greatness, and so the Emperor wished rather to spend money on his keep in a camp than to let him into the City. He also began to suspect those Danes who had hitherto been in high esteem with him, as he was afraid that they might value their own King and country more highly than their duty to the sovereign who paid them their wage, for those who speak the Danish tongue are foremost in the mercenary force of Constantinople, and the Emperor uses them as his life-guards. King Eric was not blind to the Emperor's intentions, however, and pretended that he feared nothing, asking merely for leave to enter the City to show his reverence and make his prayers in the churches, because he was primarily visiting the City in order to pray there. The Emperor praised his piety, and promised to answer him the next day.

The Danes who were in the service of the Greeks [i.e. of the Emperor] sought an audience of the Emperor and asked earnestly for leave to go and greet their King. The Emperor allowed them to do so, but commanded them that they should not go all together, but a few at a time (*segregatim*) so that the King could not affect them all at once with his words. In secret, however, the Emperor had sent men who knew both languages [i.e. Norse and Greek] with them, and they were to tell the Emperor what was said between King

[1] Albert of Aix, *Historia Hierosolymitanae expeditionis*, 470. William of Tyre and other chroniclers also tell this tale, but alter its details somewhat; it is worth noting that in one, the *Estoire des Eracles*, Sveno is simply called 'uns hom nobles et puissanz de Danemarche' (*Recueil des historiens des Croisades: historiens occidentaux*, 1, 185).

[2] Eric's pilgrimage has been studied in detail by A. Fellman, *Voyage en Orient du roi Erik Ejegod*, Helsinki, 1938, but this large and elaborately produced volume is unfortunately so crammed with irrelevant or, at best, peripheral matter as to be much reduced in usefulness.

Eric and the Varangians. They now entered and greeted the King, who bade them be seated. He then addressed them, and said that the Danes who were in the mercenary service of the Greeks had for a long time earned the greatest honour by their valour and their qualities; even though they were foreigners they ruled over the natives of the land, and had a much better life than in their homeland; moreover, the Emperor had made them his own life-guards, and they could rather thank the abilities of those who had served before them for possessing this high position of trust than their own abilities. Therefore they were above all things to take care to prize moderation rather than drunkenness, for they would be better able to fulfil their duties as soldiers if they neither became drunk with wine nor caused the Emperor unnecessary worry. On the other hand, if they drank more than moderately, they would become slovenly soldiers and quarrelsome to boot. He also reminded them that when they fought the enemy they must take care rather to show valour than to care for their lives, rather prefer to fall than to flee or save their lives by cowardice. He promised them that if they returned to their fatherland he would reward their good service with kindnesses, while if they lost their lives in battle after brave conduct against the enemy, their near relatives should be cherished by him. Thus he spoke to all the Varangians, and specially emphasized to them to be faithful to the Emperor.

The Emperor heard about this from the men whom he had sent to act as spies, and said thereupon that it was wrong to overvalue the caution of the Greeks, as they had doubted the lord of the people who were known from their own experience to be averse to all treachery, and that from the re-iterated experience of his countrymen he should have known that no treachery lurked in their King. So, when the Emperor saw that only piety and no treachery motivated the King, he commanded the City to be decorated, and had carpets laid in the streets, after which he led the King by the hand with great ceremony and the great joy of the beholders, up to the Town Hall and to his own palace, and showed this man whom he had suspected when innocent, so great an honour that no man could show more to another. He gave him quarters in [one of] the Imperial palaces to show the greatest honour to his guests, and none of the Emperors has since lived in that palace, as if to show that none presumes to match himself against such a great man by living in the same quarters, and so that respect for his visit would be the everlasting memory of the guest. The Emperor also sent for a man who measured the King, and painted excellent likenesses of him in full size, both sitting and standing; so much did he admire the King's greatness that he wished to have his figure always before him.

The Emperor did not wish to let such a guest leave him empty-handed, and asked him what he most desired; and when he heard that the King despised wealth and desired most to have holy relics, then he gave him some excellent presents of these. The King was very glad to receive these holy gifts, and had them sent to Lund and Roskilde, sealed by the Emperor's seal. And also, so that his birthplace should not miss gaining a holy relic, which might be venerated, he sent some of the bones of St Nicholas and a splinter from the Holy Cross to Slangerup, as he had had a church erected there, and it is said that he was born on the spot where you may see the altar in the church.

The Emperor offered him a great deal of gold, but the King refused it, so that men should not think that he had turned away from his self-denial and desired the riches of the Greeks. The Emperor then pretended that he offended him by refusing the gift, and said that if Eric despised the gift he considered that he despised himself; so, by pretending to take offence, he forced the King to receive this gift also with thanks. The King, however, preferred to be a giver rather than a receiver, and repaid the Emperor's generosity by his own. His presents were all the more precious because of their rarity and their novelty, and so all the dearer to the Emperor because of their rarity in Greece.

The Emperor gave him pirate vessels and supplies, and so he went on to Cyprus. Now the property of the soil there was that it would not bear that bodies be buried in it, and therefore corpses were hurled out of the ground the next night after their interment. Here the King fell ill of a fever, and when he felt that he had not long to go, he asked that his body should be buried by a very famous city in Cyprus, saying that the earth that rejected the dust of other men would allow his dust to rest there in peace. He was then buried according to his desire, and to his body was given such grace that the earth gave up her ancient anger and she who had previously rejected the bodies of men now became patient and let his body lie still, and thereafter also the bodies of others. Eric's queen also died upon this weary pilgrimage.[1]

This narrative of Saxo's is most noteworthy. Its former part, about King Eric's stay in Constantinople, seems to be derived from a man who had been there, possibly even in the King's retinue or in the Varangians there. As Eric I died in 1103, and Saxo was born around 1150, this is not by any means impossible; he could well have known in his youth a man who had been a witness to what happened on that occasion in Constantinople. What is said about Eric's residence is, however, a misunderstanding. What probably happened was that he was quartered in one of the palaces in the old complex in Blachernae, set aside for the use of foreign sovereigns who visited the Emperor; as Cronholm observes, it would be out of the question for it to be the Emperor's own quarters there.[2] The second part, about the journey to Cyprus, is very different in quality; here Saxo has clearly got hold of an old-wives' tale about the bodies buried there, and he also did not know the facts about Queen Bothilda's death, as he seems to think that she also died in Cyprus, whereas she died on the Mount of Olives near Jerusalem.[3] Saxo also does not mention the Cypriote town in which

[1] Saxo, *Gesta Danorum*, ed. J. Olrik, H. Raeder and F. Blatt, Copenhagen, 1931–57, I, 338ff.
[2] Cronholm, *Wäringarna*, 144.
[3] Robert of Elgin, *Historia Canuti minoris regis* (in Langebek, *Scriptores Rerum Danicarum*, Copenhagen, 1772–92, IV, 257) gives her death as on the Mount of Olives; cf. also Saxo, *Gesta Danorum*, ed. P. E. Müller, Copenhagen, 1839, I, 164 n.

King Eric died. This was Paphos, where there was a Varangian garrison, and the King was buried in the then Cathedral, near the present Chrysopolitine church.[1]

There is also an Icelandic source which in date of composition is much nearer to the events than Saxo: this is the *Eiríksdrápa* by the Icelandic law-speaker Markús Skeggjason, composed by him upon hearing the news of Eric I, and sent by him to Eric's successor, King Nicholas. Markús says of the reception in Constantinople:

> Hildingr þá við hæzt lof aldar
> Höfgan auð í gulli rauðu
> Halfa lest, af harra sjölfum
> Harða ríkr, í Miklagarði;
> Áðan tók við alvalds skrúði
> (Eiríki þó vas gefit fleira)
> Reynir veitti herskip hánum
> Hersa máttar sex ok átta.

The King received, with the highest praise of the men of the time, half a ton from the Lord [i.e. the Emperor] himself, and before that royal robes (yet more was given to Eric); the King gave to him [Alexius] eight and six warships.[2]

Knytlinga saga has drawn heavily on this poem, from which its author has the story that Alexius gave Eric 'half a ton of gold' and his robes and fourteen warships, which he interprets by saying that the King received this great gift in a way 'which was costly for King Eric, as he kept a large court and his cash ran short',[3] and states that the Emperor gave him the choice of seeing games in the Hippodrome instead, which would have cost Alexius as much to hold as the gold he donated. The number of the ships, however, may be regarded with very high probability as correct, however much one allows for story-tellers' exaggeration in other things in the sources, as this is neither an unduly large number nor out of character with the size of the retinue that King Eric took with him as a royal crusader in a dangerous age; it is also not wise to discredit near-contemporary evidence too far. Granted that

---

[1] Cf. Abbot Nikulás Bergsson's *Leiðarvísir* (*Alfræði Íslenzk*, ed. K. Kålund, Copenhagen, 1908–18, I, 21); also L. Philippou, *Guide to Paphos*, Paphos, 1936, 12ff.; G. F. Hill, *History of Cyprus*, Cambridge, 1940–52, I, 266 and 304; Riant, *Skandinavernes Korstog*, 161.

[2] FJ *Skjald* A I 451, B I 419; in both versions this is stanza 30.

[3] *Sögur Danakonunga*, ed. C. af Petersens and E. Olson, Copenhagen, 1919–25, 192–3. A. Fellman, *Voyage en Orient*, 146 and 190, thinks this unlikely, and refers to a letter from a Professor C. Amantos of Athens who says that he does not believe it, as Alexius could not have given Eric any ships. There is every evidence, however, to judge from the most recent studies of the Comnenian period in Byzantium, that by *c.* 1100 the Emperor was once more in possession of a respectable navy as well as of a very well-equipped army; cf. Ostrogorskii, *A History of the Byzantine State*, 2nd English edition, tr. J. M. Hussey, Oxford, 1968, 367 as well as references given at the beginning of the notes to Ch. 2 above.

the Byzantine fleet was nowhere near as large or as powerful as in the heyday of Basil II, Saxo's *piratica navigia* gives us a pointer which may be usefully followed up here, for it is very likely that Alexius had at his disposal a number of pirate vessels which his sailors had captured, and which he could dispose of without undue strain on his naval budget. The most likely solution seems to be Turkish vessels captured by John Ducas in his final, victorious campaign against Tsachas.[1] This raises another, related question: is it not likely that many of King Eric's retinue entered the Imperial service as Varangians and were sent to join the Varangian garrison at Paphos? The story of the *hálfa lest gulls* points strongly in this direction; this sum is the equivalent of 40 talents, which Riant calculated in 1868 to be the equivalent of 1,850,000 gold francs (in to-day's eviscerated currencies there is probably no exact equivalent, but clearly this was an enormous sum at any time).[2] It is hard to believe that Alexius, whose prudence and financial acumen were of the same order as his political and military ability, would have made an unknown ruler of a far distant country a present of such magnitude on an impulse – great honour could have been shown for far less in a straitened Empire. On the other hand, it could well have been that King Eric permitted a number of the men in his entourage to enter the Emperor's service. His retinue must have been a large and well-selected one for such a hazardous enterprise, but as he was travelling as a pilgrim, and not bringing a crusading army, and had travelled most of the way by the land-route over Russia, we may doubt the statements of some authors that he went with an army of several thousands.[3] We may, however, deduce with some certainty from Saxo's number of ships the size of the force that set out for Cyprus. If they were dromons, as is most likely, since Saxo names them *piratica*, they would each hold between 230 and 300 men (see above, pp. 30–1), and this would give us a total of 3220–4200 passengers, soldiers and crew. From this we may deduce another activity; that Alexius used the opportunity to send a company of Varangians to Paphos, in which it is quite likely that there were a number of King Eric's former retinue. Their pay,

---

[1] See above, p. 128.

[2] Riant, *Skandinavernes Korstog*, 160, n. 3; cf. also C. C. Rafn, *Antiquités Russes*, Copenhagen, 1850–2, II, 132, who calculates (*ibid.*, n. 17) according to the system set out by Páll Vídalín, 'Glósur yfer forn-yrdi lögbókar Islendinga', *Rit his Íslenzka Lærdómslistafélags*, IV, (1782), 263, counting 1 *lest* = 4152 *pund*; a more usual Icelandic reckoning is 1 *lest* = 12 *skippund* (1 *skippund* = 320 *pund*) = 3,840 *pund*; hence the half *lest* would be 1920 *pund*.

[3] E. Wall, *Illustrerad wärldshistoria*, Stockholm, 1877, 341, states that Eric was accompanied by 6000 men, while F. Münter, *Kirchengeschichte*, Copenhagen, 1831, II, 2, plumps for 3000, in which he is supported by Fellman, *Voyage en Orient*, 45. The relevant volume of the most recent general history of Denmark (H. Koch, *Kongemagt og Kirke, 1060–1241*, Copenhagen, 1963, 94ff.) wisely avoids any opinion as to the size of Eric's retinue, as the sources are not such as to give any reliable indication of it.

the cost of the fitting of the fleet, and doubtless some disbursement for King Eric, some undoubtedly as an honorific present, and possibly some simply as a gift of gratitude for his granting permission to his men to join the Varangians (and possibly for a promise of more to come from Denmark later); these will have totalled no small sum, and the 40 talents need not then seem such a ludicrously large amount. The present author doubts gravely whether Eric I's actual retinue was more than a thousand men, while the rest were probably Varangians on their way to duty in Cyprus; one could also surmise that there may have been some Russian princes in the company, who joined the King as he passed on his way southwards, and then took service with Alexius. All things considered, however, and allowing for every conceivable discount on the grounds of embellishment by the narrators, Eric I's visit must have given a great boost to the Varangian force at the turn of the eleventh and twelfth centuries.

Shortly before Eric I made his visit to the Emperor (*c.* 1102–3), a number of Norsemen had set out on a Jerusalem pilgrimage under the leadership of Skofti Ögmundarson, a Norwegian chieftain, and his sons. The leaders died *en voyage*, but one of the ships of their expedition reached the Holy Land, and some of the pilgrims returned via Constantinople. Snorri mentions that the stories told by these returned travellers of their Jerusalem experiences, not least that 'in Miklagard the Norsemen received all the treasure they could desire, [that is] those who wished to enter the Emperor's service',[1] greatly stimulated the two young Kings of Norway, Eysteinn and Sigurðr (I), the recently enthroned sons of Magnus (III) Barefoot, into preparing a crusade. King Sigurðr became the leader of the Crusaders, while King Eysteinn stayed behind to guard the state.

According to the most recent research, King Sigurðr is not likely to have set out from Norway before 1108.[2] Most of the highly-coloured anecdotes of his travels are of no consequence here, but some of the incidents of his return journey do come under our purview, as he went back via Cyprus (when he will in all probability have visited Paphos and the Varangians there) and Constantinople. According to Snorri, who is backed in this assertion by Arabic historians, Sigurðr had with him a fleet of sixty vessels when he left Norway;[3] allowing for a variety

[1] *Heimskringla*, III, 238.
[2] So Albert of Aix (Migne, *PL*, CLXVI, 687). This point has been examined by H. Koht, 'Sigurd på Jorsalferd', *Norsk Historisk Tidsskrift*, V Rekke, 5, 153–68, and his conclusions support Albert's statement.
[3] *Heimskringla*, III, 239; Ibn-el-Athir, *Kamil fit-ta-ta'rih* (*Recueil des historiens des Croisades: historiens orientaux* I, 275); Ibn Khaldun, *Narratio de expeditione Francorum in terras Islami subjectas*, ed. C. J. Tornberg, Uppsala, 1840, 71.

in the size of vessel and of crew, this would suggest that he travelled with an entourage of not less than 6000–8000 men. Munch and Riant have suggested 10,000, but this is more than doubtful if one bears in mind the approximate population of Norway at the time,[1] and the needs of the state at home, coupled with the fact that Magnus III's last disastrous Irish expedition had been a costly drain on Norwegian manpower.

Both Snorri and the Kings' Sagas give detailed descriptions of King Sigurðr's arrival in Constantinople and his stay there, but these narratives are very obviously encrusted with anecdotes that have been fathered on to him and are quite clearly about older personages – a point that was noted as early as 1700 by Þormóður Torfason.[2] Snorri states that he waited for a fortnight at *Engilsnes* for a favourable wind 'and each day there was a sharp wind northwards along the sea, but he wanted to wait for a wind that blew across his course, so that the sails could be set to run along the entire length of the ships, because all his sails were trimmed with satin, both fore and aft'. At length he got the wind he sought, 'and sailed in towards Constantinople; he sailed near to land; all the way along the shore there are cities and castles and villages without a break, a continuous line along the bows so that there was no gap, as if it were one wall. All the people who could stood outside to watch King Sigurðr's sailing in.'[3]

This *Engilsnes* is undoubtedly the Gallipoli peninsula.[4] It is interesting that the Russian annal that describes Oleg's expedition of 907 mentions that the Russians (i.e. Norse Russian) had sails trimmed with satin, while the 'Slovenes' in his fleet had sails of thin cloth which tore when the wind freshened.[5] It is not at all unlikely, of course, that King Sigurðr waited for a convenient wind to enable his sailing in the Marmora to be as splendid as he could make it; the 'Crusaders' of 1204 did this, according to Robert of Clari.[6] The Norse sources go on to say that the Emperor allowed him to ride right from the Golden Gate up to the Blachernae, and that the way had been covered with precious cloth, King Sigurðr and his lords had ridden mounts shod with gold, and that one shoe was loose and fell off, but no one thought it

---

[1] P. A. Munch, *Samlede Avhandlinger*, Christiania, 1873, II, 50; Riant, *Skandinavernes Korstog*, 245, n. 1, presumably based on Albert's 'in decem millibus virorum pugnatorum'.

[2] T. Torfaeus, *Historia rerum Norwegicarum*, Copenhagen, 1711, III, 438; cf. also H. Koht, 'Kong Sigurd', *Norsk Historisk Tidsskrift*, v Rekke, 5, 153–68 and J. de Vries, 'Normannisches Lehngut in der islandischen Königssaga', *Arkiv for Nordisk Filologi*, 47, 51–79.

[3] *Heimskringla*, III, 252.

[4] So explained in the notes to *Heimskringla*, ed. G. Schönning and S. Thorlacius, Copenhagen, 1777–1826, III, 243.

[5] *Повесть Временных Лет*, 30–2; cf. also Stender-Petersen, *Die Varägersage*, 92.

[6] Robert de Clari, *La conquête de Constantinople*, ed. P. Lauer, Paris, 1924, 40.

worth his while to pick it up[1] (though Snorri could not bring himself to swallow that one).

The whole story reeks of exaggeration. First of all, it is highly unlikely that a barbarian monarch would have been allowed to ride *through* the Golden Gate, the gateway used in this way only by the Emperors when making a triumphal entry into the City. It is, of course, possible that Alexius, wishing to make friendly gestures to a king who brought a large and warlike following that might be valuable to him, might have had some of the roads to Blachernae decorated for his state entry, and he will certainly have received Sigurðr there. As to where he let him stay there can be no certainty – in all probability in the same palace in which he accommodated Eric of Denmark, the *pólútir enar fornu*. But the story of the gold horseshoe is pure fiction, a folktale told of Fortunatus and a commonplace in folk literature; thus similar tales are told of Duke Robert I of Normandy and of Count Boniface of Tuscany, as well as one from about 1120 of Mangold von Werden.[2]

The Kings' Sagas go on to tell of Sigurðr despising the Emperor's gifts, giving a bag full of gold over to his men to divide among them, an action repeated twice, and finally, when a great chest of gold with two gold rings on top is sent to him, he accepts it, gives his men the gold, draws the rings on to his arms, and then makes a speech in Greek to thank the Emperor! This anecdote is so obviously an invention that no further comment is necessary – it is enough to observe that Snorri ignores it.

The story already told of Eric I (the choice between games in the Hippodrome and the equivalent of their cost in cash) is repeated here, and we need make no further observation about it either, except to note that it is clear from Markús Skeggjason's verses that Eric received 40 talents, but we have seen what is a much more likely explanation of this sum. Of course there is no need to deny that if spectacular games were being held in the Hippodrome while Sigurðr was in Constantinople, then Alexius would of course, as a normal act of politeness, have invited his royal visitor to see them. Equally unlikely is the story that King Sigurðr invited the Emperor and Empress to dine, and the Empress had bought up all the firewood in the City in order to test the King's ingenuity; he rises to the occasion, by obtaining walnuts to be used as fuel for cooking, the feast is a success, and the Empress admires his resourcefulness. There is a similar tale of his grandfather, Haraldr III,

---

[1] Cf. *Fornmannasögur*, ed. C. Rafn *et al.*, Copenhagen, 1825–37, VII, 94–9.

[2] Wace, *Roman de Rou*, ed. H. Andersen, Heilbronn, 1877–9, III, 3067–102; Bertold of Reichenau, *Quomodo portio Vivifice Crucis Werdeam pervenerit*, ed. O. Holder-Egger (MHG Scriptores, XV, 2, 769–70); cf. also P. A. Munch, *Samlede Avhandlinger*, II, 587.

in *Morkinskinna*,[1] and it is also told of Mangold von Werden and Robert I of Normandy, ignored by Snorri, and a very obvious itinerant folktale.[2]

Finally we have the tale of how, when King Sigurðr left for home, he gave all his ships to the Emperor, and included with the gift the gold-covered dragon's head from his own vessel, which was set up in St Peter's church in Constantinople. There were several churches dedicated to St Peter in Constantinople, but if there is any fact behind this anecdote, the most likely ones were either St Peter's in the Bukoleon or the old monastery of St Peter near to Blachernae, where the dragon's head could be seen from the sea (which makes this a slightly more likely location). Frederik Schiern has maintained that this dragon's head was one which was removed from this church in the days of the Latin emperors, taken to Bruges and then finally put up on the Town Hall of Ghent,[3] but there is good evidence that this cannot be so.[4] *Morkinskinna* adds a point that Sigurðr's ships remained for a long time on show in Constantinople;[5] this may well have been so, but it is hardly likely to have been true of any but the most useless ones, for the Byzantine fleet was by this time not so well off for usable vessels as to scorn any additional ships that could be put to practical use. The most likely response by Alexius to this gesture would be to put every tub that could still float into active service and man them with Varangians. Here all our sources agree: that King Sigurðr returned home from Constantinople by the land route over Russia, and that a great part of his retinue stayed behind in the Empire *ok gekk þar a mála*, i.e. became Varangians. This is a very important point in the history of the regiment: there is no reasonable doubt that King Sigurðr set out from Norway with sixty ships; one is mentioned as lost in a gale, but in counterbalance he is stated to have won eight others from pirates in Spain. We may be sure that a number of vessels had become so battered

---

[1] *Morkinskinna*, ed. F. Jónsson, Copenhagen, 1900, 65–6; also *Flateyjarbók*, III, 295, where Haraldr gives a feast for the Emperor and the bishop who is to consecrate St Olaf's church; on that occasion he has kindling, peat and nuts burned.

[2] Wace, *Roman de Rou*, 352ff.; see also G. Paris, 'Sur un épisode d'Aimeri de Narbonne', *Romania*, IX, 515–46; E. Wilken, *Geschichte der Kreuzzüge*, Leipzig, 1807–32, I, 38; Riant, *Skandinavernes Korstog*, 278. The entire anecdote may have descended from *Aimery de Narbonne* (ed. L. Demaison, Paris, 1887). J. de Vries ('Normannisches Lehngut') considers that the root of the episode may be in some nine-days'-wonder in Constantinople which occurred during the period 1025–75.

[3] F. Schiern, 'Bemærkninger angaaende de af Sigurd Jorsalfarer...opsatte Dragehoveder',
[4] *Overskuelse over Videnskabelige Selskabets Forhandlinger*, 1859, 145–62.
I. Undset, 'Sigurd Jorsalfars Dragehoved', *Norsk Historisk Tidsskrift*, 3 Raekke, 3, 377–8; the dragon's head in Ghent was carved there in the city in 1377. Undset refers to a letter from the Danish archaeologist Henry Petersen (to I. Undset, 12 November 1888).

[5] *Morkinskinna*, 351.

by sea-damage or battle-damage that they had to be abandoned, so that it is probably most sensible to reckon on not more than 40–50 ships under his command when he arrived at Constantinople. If we reckon on at least 50 men in the crew of each vessel, this brings him there with a retinue of at most around 3000 men; making a maximum allowance for losses in battle or subsequently from wounds, there would have been a force of 4000 Norwegians with him when he set out; if some 2500 entered the Imperial mercenaries, then Alexius was doing well; in any case, as we can best gauge from our sources it is unlikely that Sigurðr had more than a quarter with him on the return journey, and the story that Alexius supplied him with horses and guides for himself and his company has the ring of truth about it in this context.

William of Malmesbury tells of how King Sigurðr exhorted his men to be moderate in drinking wine as a necessity; this reads like a rehash of the story of King Eric's instructions to his men, and even with the corroborative detail of a demonstration of the deteriorative effects of alcohol on the liver (which reads nowadays more like the contents of a temperance oration by Mr Chadband than a tale in a mediaeval Norse story) it is a fairly unlikely event, though once more we must not overlook the possibility of a basis in fact, namely that the Varangians had a besetting fault of drunkenness and that this was recognized and commented upon by one or both kings.

William of Malmesbury has another fairy-tale about how Alexius did not wish Sigurðr to leave (we recognize the motif straightaway here from the story of Haraldr III and Constantine IX), and how the King said that he was only going to be away a short while, and left behind chests said to be full of precious gems – when he did not return they were opened and found to be empty. The commonness of this theme needs no elaboration.[1]

All in all, we may take it as reasonably certain that the Norse contingent in the Varangians increased sharply as a result of the visit of these two Scandinavian kings, in that it is quite possible that as many as 4000–5000 fresh men entered the Byzantine army as mercenaries, though, obviously, only a choice few will have entered the actual life-guards, while the rest will have been used for the multifarious service needs of an Empire constantly in military straits. In every way it is clear from our sources that Alexius I had a great regard for his Varangians – not least from the evidence of his daughter, for whom these tall, fair, exotic Barbarians had an evident fascination – and Varangians who stayed on in his service could expect promotion to

[1] Wiliam of Malmesbury, *De Gestis Regum Anglorum*, ed. W. Stubbs (Rolls Series), London, 1887–9, II, 486.

high dignities, as we can see, for instance, in the *Basilica*, where there is a note that a Varangian of the rank of *syncleticus* (i.e. member of the Senate) slew another Varangian of the same rank. From similar sources we can also see that the Varangians were attached to the Emperor – if we had no other evidence, the very fact that his name became the generic one for the *stólkonungr* in Norwegian and Icelandic tales would indicate his popularity.[1]

Down to just before the reign of Alexius I the Varangians had been overwhelmingly composed of Norsemen, either of Scandinavian or Russian extraction, until the time that separate troops of Slavonic Russians were formed. In this period, however, a new element enters the regiment's composition, Englishmen.[2] The exodus of Anglo-Saxons after the Battle of Hastings, as their properties were gradually taken over by the Norman nobility of William I, can be seen to have eventually flowed around the Mediterranean and reached the Eastern Empire. We have evidence of varying quality for this, but some is irrefutable; in particular the chrysobull of Nicephorus III of January 1080, which refers to *Inglinoi* besides *Rhos* and *Varangoi*.[3] This is supported by the narrative of Normans concerning the siege and battle of Dyrrhachium, where Geoffrey of Maleterre says outright that on the Byzantine side there fought *Angli quos Waringos appellant*, on whom Alexius's *maxima spes victoriae fuerat*;[4] he is supported by Ordericus Vitalis in his *Historia ecclesiastica*, who states equally clearly that the Emperor entrusted the Varangians with the custody of his principal palace and his treasures;[5] he also states a little earlier that these English expatriates in Constantinople attempted to get King Svend (II) Estridsson of Denmark to reconquer England from the Normans,[6] which suggests that these were Englishmen from the Danelaw of Scandinavian parentage. This passage does not, of course, prove that these Englishmen

---

[1] *Basilica*, ed. C. G. E. Heimbach, Leipzig, 1833–97, V, 746–65; see also *De Ceremoniis*, ed. J. J. Reiske (CHSB), Bonn, 1828, *Commentarii*, II, 476.

[2] Up to the present the attitude towards the principal Norse source for the English emigration to Byzantium has been typified by Finnur Jónsson's contemptuous dismissal 'det er alt kun Fabler' (*Den oldnordiske og oldislandske Litteraturs Historie*, 2nd ed., Copenhagen, 1920–4, II, 846), as may be seen from A. A. Vasilev, 'The opening stage of the Anglo-Saxon immigration to Byzantium', *Annales de l'Institut Kondakov*, IX (1937), 37–70, and the passages on pp. 218 and 392 (n. 58) in the Icelandic edition of this book. All these minimize the reliability, and hence the importance, of the appendix to *Játvarðar saga*; it may be seen in what follows in this chapter, however, that the situation is now greatly changed.

[3] The text is in 'Επετηρὶς 'Εταιρίας Βυζαντινῶν Σπουδῶν, III (1926), 120–4; see especially 122.

[4] Geoffrey of Maleterre, *Historia Sicula* (Muratori, *Scriptores rerum Italicarum*, Milan, 1724–51, V, 584).

[5] Ordericus Vitalis, *Historia ecclesiastica*, ed. M. Chibnall, Oxford, 1969–, II, 202.

[6] Ordericus, *Historia ecclesiastica*, II, 202.

were admitted to the Varangians, but we must also note another passage in which Ordericus remarks that these Englishmen *per Pontum in Thraciam navigaverunt*;[1] Vasilev, commenting on this, suggests that one may interpret *per Pontum* as *per mare*, meaning the Black Sea (Pontus Euxinus), and that this implies that these refugees made their way at first to Norse chiefs in Russia, from whom, and on whose advice, they then made their way to Constantinople.[2] If we read the passage in this way, it becomes very understandable that they were able to enter the Varangian units; also, the heavy loss in this regiment at Dyrrhachium will have encouraged Alexius to accept these Northerners into his service in a unit where their language was easily understood. We may accordingly take it as certain that he took Englishmen into his service as Varangians, but it is equally certain that the regiment was by no means Anglicized in his reign, especially not the section in the life-guards, as the chrysobull of 1088 to St John's Patmos shows, by its distinction between Varangians and Englishmen.[3] Moreover, the addition to the force that was acquired as a result of the visit of Eric I and Sigurðr I will have strengthened the Norse element very considerably again.

In this connection we must now notice one of the earlier anecdotes concerning English Varangians, the story in *Játvarðar saga* of Earl Sigurðr 'of Gloucester' and the émigré Saxons who made their way to Byzantium by an adventurous journey via Spain and Sicily. The trouble with this story is, of course, in the first instance, its strong resemblance to the adventures of King Sigurðr on *his* voyage to the East. Nonetheless, there is no reason to disbelieve the basic event, that a party of Saxons reached Byzantium. The last passage, referring to the dislike of these Saxons to *Pálsbók* (presumably a misapprehension by either the author of the Latin note from which Gizur Hallsson worked, or a direct one by Gizur or his follower in the construction of the story, through thinking that Paulicianism, *against* which Alexius I fought strenuously all his reign, was the religion of his Empire), can then be surmised to contain a kernel of fact, in that these earlier Englishmen (if the author's original suggestion that they arrived in Byzantium as early as 1070 is tenable, which the reviser doubts) passed on and set up homes in Russia, and were possibly instrumental in causing their compatriots to turn back and enter the Emperor's forces. This must, however, remain a hypothesis, and its foundation is admittedly none too strong, but the task of disentangling fact from accreted fiction in the

---

[1] Ordericus, *Historia ecclesiastica*, III, 16.
[2] Vasilev, 'Opening Stage', *Annales de l'Institut Kondakov*, IX, 53.
[3] See above, p. 123, n. 1.

Western sources for our subject is one which often leaves only such a tenuous surmise as the remaining possibility.[1]

There is also the evidence here of Anna Comnena, which is tiresomely ambiguous in this respect. She states that the Varangians came from *Thule*; by this she is clearly referring to the place she describes in the *Alexiad* when she refers to the extent of the old empire of the Romans, stretching from the pillars of Hercules in the West to the pillars of Dionysus in the East, and from Egypt and the hot countries in the South 'up to the famous Thule and the peoples who inhabit the lands of the North and have the North Pole [i.e. the Pole Star] over their heads'.[2] It has been argued, notably by the present author in the original version of this book, that Anna, being as well versed in the classical writings as she was, would be unlikely to ignore or avoid using the ancient name of *Britannia* or *Brettanike* for the old Roman province, and to refer to it as Thule, but Anna has been convicted on numerous occasions of an over-extensive and far from reliable literary knowledge, and it is quite likely that she confused several sources, because her emphasis on the point that these Thuleans had been servants of the Emperors in distant past years suggests that she must have meant Britain (and then, of course, in particular, England), since Scandinavians, however friendly, were never *subjects* of Rome. Moreover, as Tacitus makes clear, the climatic conditions she notes can apply to the northernmost British islands as well as places further north.[3] Nor does the passage in Procopius's history of the Gothic wars, which Anna is quite likely to have read, give any help either way, except to confirm the opinion held by her that Thule is an island, and his observations that the neighbours of the Thuleans were *Skridfinni*, which could conceivably be read as either a debased muddle of *Skrælingjar* or some corruption of *Finnar*, is of no real help in elucidating the question, which has to be decided on more empirical grounds. From our other evidence we know that Englishmen were in the service of the Empire at the *latest* by 1080, and from Anna's liking for the Varangians, visible throughout the *Alexiad*, we can have little hesitation in surmising that her search for information would lead her to enquire directly of the soldiers (or at least of their officers!): Scandinavian Varangians would certainly not have told her that their country was a former Roman province, but well-informed Saxons would have had no hesitation in doing so. To settle the question, the combination of the careful division in Imperial chrysobulls between *Inglinoi* and *Varangoi*, coupled with the

---

[1] See above, p. 141, n. 2; cf. also C. E. Fell, 'A Note on Pálsbók', *Mediaeval Scandinavia*, 6 (1973), 102–8.   [2] *Alexiad*, II, 73.
[3] Tacitus, *Agricola*, ed. H. Furneaux and J. G. C. Anderson, Oxford, 1949, 9.

name of *Varangeia* given by the author of *Advice* to Norway, makes it most unlikely that *Thule* in this context refers to either Iceland or Scandinavia, but every pointer that shows signs of bearing some weight of criticism indicates the likelihood of England and, therefore, of Englishmen in the Varangian regiment as well as in units apart. The reference in Nicephorus Gregoras to a Thule in the neighbourhood of Russia merely confuses the issue,[1] and confirms the reviser in his opinion that in Byzantium *Thule* was a term of convenience to cover any northern island with suitable vagueness.

The last sentence represents the state of opinion on the subject at the point where the author left off his work, and the reviser feels it right to allow his view to be noted. In the years after 1950, however, the question of the veracity of *Játvarðar saga* as a whole, and the 'emigration epilogue' in particular, has come in for very drastic re-examination, which must be looked at in some detail. In 1956 Mr H. L. Rogers read a paper to the Viking Society on the general pattern of the saga and its sources.[2] In the discussion afterwards a very strong case was found for the saga being, not a mere rehash of the official Latin *Vita* by Ailred of Rievaulx on the basis of which St Edward was canonized, but drawing also on the older Latin life by Osbert of Clare, which was the basic source of information on him until *c.* 1160; from what is known of Gizur Hallsson's foreign travels he was in England in the mid-1150s, and with the greater certainty of the sources of the Icelandic compilation being of twelfth-century origin rather than of the fourteenth century as guessed at by Finnur Jónsson, whose contemptuous 'det er alt kun Fabler' typifies older opinions, it therefore became a fruitful question to examine the probable truthfulness of its record.

In 1959 the reviser examined the English sources relating to the Norman Conquest and its aftermath, and was particularly attracted to the accounts by Simeon of Durham and Ordericus Vitalis and their description of the principal opponents to William I. Among these he found Simeon's description of the career of Siward Barn presented points which suggested a similarity to the mysterious Earl Sigurðr 'af Glócestr', of *Játvarðar saga*. Further, a lengthy search having disposed of any other possible claimants, the chances of the saga epilogue recording the facts of an emigration seemed to him to be high, the more so as Greek sources which were checked in 1960–1 in the opening stages of the revision of the present book showed a definite change in

---

[1] Nicephorus Gregoras, *Byzantina historia*, ed. L. Schopen and I. Bekker (CHSB), Bonn, 1829–55, III, 517.

[2] H. L. Rogers, 'An Icelandic Life of St Edward the Confessor', *Saga Book of the Viking Society*, XIV (1953–9), 249–72.

the nomenclature of the Guards about this time (see below). By 1962, therefore, the reviser had come to the conclusion that, bearing in mind the comparatively short period elapsing between the events involved (*c.* 1070–85) and the probable date at which Gizur obtained the materials for the history of the countries that he was to use in his *Flos Peregrinationis* (*c.* 1150–5), Dr Blöndal's opinion of the general untrustworthiness of *Játvarðar saga*, based as it was on the sledgehammer opinion of Finnur Jónsson, was not tenable. As it happened, however, a great deal of work on the other problems of the book caused the examination of the matter to be put aside, and it has been left to three younger scholars to produce the evidence and arguments which seem to the reviser to be the most likely solution to the questions posed by the saga and its evidence.

In 1974 Miss Christine Fell published a paper to follow up her examination of the hagiographical sources of *Játvarðar saga*[1] in which, basing her argument upon the discovery by Dr Krijnie Ciggaar of a hitherto undiscovered Latin chronicle, the *Chronicon Universale Anonymi Laudunensis*,[2] and the work of Dr Jonathan Shepard on the evidences relating to Englishmen in Byzantium, she came down heavily in favour of the essential truthfulness of the *Játvarðar saga* appendix, having previously completely overthrown Mr Rogers's conclusions by showing that the compiler of *Játvarðar saga* does not draw only on Ailred and Osbert, but also on William of Malmesbury and Vincent of Beauvais. In a paper published in 1973 in *Mediaeval Scandinavia*, she also advanced strong arguments for the thesis that the *Pálsbók* of the appendix, regarded by older commentators as Paulicianism, was in fact simply an Icelandic name for Greek Orthodoxy.[3] Dr Ciggaar, in her article in the *Revue des Études Byzantines*,[4] in which she published portions of the Laudun chronicle which bear an astonishing direct resemblance to the *Játvarðar saga* appendix, has provided further support for this essential truthfulness, and advances powerful arguments for a weighty influx of Englishmen into the Empire in the period 1080–5.

[1] C. E. Fell, 'The Icelandic Saga of Edward the Confessor: hagiographical sources', *Anglo-Saxon England*, 1 (1972), 247–58; see also the same author's 'The Icelandic Saga of Edward the Confessor: the version of the Anglo-Saxon emigration to Byzantium', *Anglo-Saxon England*, 3 (1974), 179–96.

[2] MS Phillipps 1880 (see below, n. 4).

[3] C. E. Fell, 'A Note on Pálsbók', *Mediaeval Scandinavia*, 6.

[4] K. N. Ciggaar, 'L'émigration anglaise à Byzance après 1066', *Revue des Études Byzantines*, 32 (1974), 301–42. It is unfortunate that Dr Ciggaar has weakened the case put in her article by showing in her more recently published doctoral dissertation *Byzance et l'Angleterre* (Leiden, 1976) that she has merely used Dasent's translation of *Játvarðar saga* instead of checking the original text. Her edition of, and commentary on what turns out to be only a part of the *Chronicon Laudunense* (see pp. 20–71 of her thesis) have also left the present reviser uneasy about the value of the *Chronicon*, as it cannot be evaluated in its entirety, and so we cannot see how Dr Ciggaar's passage fits into the work as a whole. Her attack on Miss Fell (pp. 67–8) loses much of its force for this reason.

It should be borne in mind, of course, that the Laudun *Chronicon*, though preserved in a manuscript a century older than the version of *Játvarðar saga* which is left to us, is, as Miss Fell has shown, by no means without blemish itself in its record but, coming as it does to buttress the appendix, and to demonstrate the accuracy of the hagiographical main part of the saga with evidence of a possible common archetype from which both have drawn their information, it gives very powerful support to the conscientiousness and care of the saga's fourteenth-century compiler. Dr Jonathan Shepard, approaching the problem from another angle in two recent articles,[1] has adduced interesting evidence from Black Sea place-names to suggest further that the eventual home of these migrants to the north of Constantinople, as described by the saga, was between Cherson and Sugdaea, which agrees well with the *sex dægra haf í ætt austrs ok landnorðr frá Miklagarði.*[2]

As a result of the work of these scholars it may be inferred with some certainty (1) that an emigration of some substance took place from Northern England in the 1070s, in which a large number of Englishmen, unwilling to acknowledge William I as their sovereign, but powerless to overthrow him, set off on a migratory journey in the course of which, passing through the Balearic Islands and Sardinia, they arrived in Byzantium in time to assist either Nicephorus III or (more likely) Alexius I at an awkward moment, and so were well received and tempted to stay in the Empire and enter the Imperial service, and (2) that they were not willing to accept Orthodoxy, and so were subjected to some trouble by a section of the ultra-Orthodox, as a result of which they migrated further north to settle in the Crimea, but (3) enough of them did stay on and enter the Varangian contingent to bring into it an element which changed its composition substantially there and then, and came in time to dominate the regiment. Dr Ciggaar's suggestion that the English were a welcome means to Alexius I to dilute a Scandinavian force which had become suspect to the Emperor after the attempt on Nicephorus III's life has much to commend it, as it is in line with the political and administrative actions of that shrewdest of Emperors.[3]

From our evidences we may see that Alexius I thought highly of the English, and used them extensively in other work besides that of the Varangian regiment. He had had the city of Cibotos fortified, and he now placed a garrison there to keep back the Turks who had settled

[1] J. Shepard, 'The English and Byzantium', *Traditio*, XXIX (1973), 53–92.
[2] J. Shepard, 'Another New England?', *Byzantine Studies*, I (1974), 18–39; see *Saga Játvarðar konúngs hins helga*, ed. J. Sigurðsson, Copenhagen, 1852, 42.
[3] Ciggaar, 'Émigration anglaise à Byzance', *Revue des Études Byzantines*, 32, 338.

in Nicaea.[1] Both these facts are mentioned in *Alexiad*[2] and by Orderic, who calls the town *Chevetot*,[3] and states that the Normans had pressed so hard on the Englishmen there that the Emperor moved them to Byzantium and made them into his life-guards; he also states that French crusaders came in 1096 to Chevetot 'which had been recently edified by the Emperor Alexius, who was going to give it to the Englishmen who fled from before William the Bastard, but because of the trouble the Turks gave him, he was not able to complete the refortification'. This is a much more credible story than the other one: before he recaptured Nicaea, Alexius was going to erect a great defensive fortress here, which was not, however, complete by 1096; on the other hand, if he wished to finish it after the recapture of Nicaea and the surrounding country, he could do so without further interruptions from the enemy. We shall see later how this core of English mercenaries attracted others to the service of the Comnenian Emperors, until in time they replaced the Norsemen in the Varangian guards, as it became impossible for these to make their way to Byzantium by the overland route. The English church in Constantinople, which was the work of these mercenaries, will be dealt with later in this book; it suffices here to make the point that by the time of Alexius's death, an English element was firmly installed in the Imperial services and English scholars, even, were to find their way to Athens by the thirteenth century.[4]

Alexius I died the night of the 15th and 16th August 1118 in his palace in the Mangana. He had chosen his son John as his successor, having called him to the purple in his lifetime, but the Empress Irene and her daughter Anna, who wanted an Emperor who would be more amenable to the wishes of the gynaeceum, had decided that they wanted Nicephorus Bryennius the historian (Anna's husband, and grandson of the Nicephorus who rebelled against Michael VII and Nicephorus III) on the throne, even though he himself had no wish to become Emperor. When Alexius felt himself dying, he slipped his ring into the hand of his son, and adjured him to hurry away and have himself proclaimed sole Emperor at once. Despite their vigilance and their constant

---

[1] There has been some dispute as to the whereabouts of Cibotos. The present author has followed W. Tomaschek, 'Zur Topographie Kleinasiens', *Sitzungsberichte der Akademie der Wissenschaften in Wien*, 124 (1918), 9, but P. Kierkegaard, in his translation of Ordericus Vitalis (Copenhagen, 1899, II, 220) maintains that it was the present Ghemlik.

[2] *Alexiad*, III, 7.

[3] Ordericus, *Historia ecclesiastica*, II, 202.

[4] On this see P. Kalligas, Μελέται Βυζαντινῆς ἱστορίας, Athens, 1894, 151; also F. Gregorovius, 'Die Legende vom Studium der Wissenschaften in Athen im 12en Jahrhundert', *Zeitschrift für Geschichte und Politik*, 5 (1888), and his *Die Stadt Athen im Mittelalter*, Stuttgart, 1889, I, 229–32.

pressure upon the sick Emperor, the Empress and Anna failed to notice this, and so father and son were finally able to outwit them. With the ring in his hand John hurried to the Hagia Sophia and was crowned by the Patriarch, after which he returned to the old Emperor's palace. Here the Varangians denied him admittance, until he declared the death of his father to them, and showed them his ring, whereon they accepted him as the new Emperor and let him in, and he was able to take over the control of the army and navy,[1] and duly to put down an attempt at revolution by his mother and sister.

John II Comnenus is one of the few mediaeval sovereigns to earn praise from all sides of opinion. He was much engaged in warfare all his reign, generally with success, and appears to have commanded his forces with skill, courage, steadiness and economy of effort on every occasion. There can be little doubt that, heavily engaged as he was in securing the borders on both sides, as well as keeping order within them, John must have used a regiment whose military ability he knew so well from his father's reign with frequency and decision, even though we have only one direct piece of evidence of them in action. This is the battle of Beroë in 1122, in which he finally crushed a Pecheneg assault on the Bulgarian frontiers.[2] We have both Greek and Norse sources for this battle, in which the constancy and bravery of the Varangians was clearly a powerful factor in the Byzantine victory.

Thus Snorri, using a curious place-name probably derived from the name of the warring tribe rather than from any real field-name nearby, describes the battle:

It so happened in Greece when King Kirjalax reigned, that the King went on an expedition against the Blökumenn. Now when he came to Pézínavellir a heathen king met him with an overwhelming force. This army had with it cavalry and great wains with castellations on top; when they camped for the night they arranged these wains side by side round the outside of their camp, and dug a great ditch around them; in this way they had a great fort like a castle. The heathen king was blind. Now when the King of the Greeks came, the heathens ordered their line of battle in front of the fortress of wains, and the Greeks arranged their battle-line opposite them; both parties then rode forward and fought, and the battle went badly for the Greeks; they fled with great loss of men, while the heathen had the victory. At this the King [i.e. John II] sent forward Franks and Flemings, and they rode forward against the heathen and fought with them, but the same thing happened; many of them were killed, and the rest fled as best they could. At this the

---

[1] Zonaras, *Annales*, ed. M. Pinder and T. Büttner-Wobst (CSHB), Bonn, 1841–97, III, 763–4; Nicetas Choniates, *Historiae*, ed. I. Bekker (CSHB), Bonn, 1835, 9–12.

[2] There is a party of historians who maintain that the battle of Beroë was fought in 1123, but John II was certainly in the town in 1121–2, preparing for the conflict, cf. F. Chalandon, *Les Comnène*, Paris, 1900, II, 48–51; also R. M. Dawkins, 'An echo in the Norse sagas of the Patzinak war of John II Comnenos', *Mélanges Boisacq*, Brussels, 1937, 243–9.

King of the Greeks was very angry with his soldiers, but they answered him that he should make use of his wineskins, the Varangians. The King replied that he would not waste his treasures by sending few men, however brave, against so great a force. At this Þórir helsingr, who commanded the Varangians, replied: 'Though a blazing fire were opposed to us, yet would I and my men leap into it if I knew that by it I could purchase peace for you afterwards, O King.' The King answered: 'Make a vow to the blessed Olaf the King, for your support and victory.' The Varangian unit consisted of four and a half hundred men; they now made a vow by clasping of hands and promised to build a church in Constantinople at their own expense and with the help of good men, and have this church consecrated to the honour and glory of the blessed King Olaf. After this the Varangians ran forward on to the battlefield; when the heathen saw this they said to their king that there came yet again a force from the army of the King of the Greeks 'and this', they said, 'is but a handful of men'. The King answered 'Who is the noble-looking man who rides a white horse in front of their ranks?' 'We cannot see him' they answered. The odds were not less than sixty heathen to every Christian, nevertheless the Varangians went very bravely forward into the battle. But when the armies met such a fear and terror came over the heathen army that they began to flee at once, while the Varangians followed them up and slew a great many of them. Now when the Greeks and Franks who had previously fled before the heathen saw this, they came forward and assisted the Varangians in pressing home the victory; by then they had reached the fortress of wains, where a great slaughter took place. As the heathen fled their blind king was captured, and the Varangians had him with them. The Christians now captured the camp and the fortress of the heathens.[1]

Snorri explains in the previous chapter how the Emperor knew of the sanctity of King Olaf.

It so happened in the battle of Stiklestad, as we have stated earlier, that King Olaf threw away his sword Hneitir when he was wounded. Some man of Swedish birth who had broken his own sword picked Hneitir up and fought with it; this man escaped from the battle and went with other refugees; he got away to Sweden and returned to his own home. He kept this sword all his life, and his son after him, and so one kinsman after another, and it went with the possession of the sword that the last owner told its name to the next. Then, much later, in the days of the Emperor Kirjalax of Constantinople, there were large forces of Varangians in the City. One summer, when the Emperor was on a military expedition, the army was in camp, and the Varangians kept guard around the King; they lay on the ground around the camp. They had divided the night into watches among them, so that those who had kept the previous watch could lie down and sleep. All the Varangians bore full armour and arms; it was their custom when they lay down to sleep that each had his helmet on his head, his shield to cover him, and his sword under his head, keeping his right hand upon the hilt. One of the company, whose turn to watch came towards the end of the night, woke up near

---

[1] *Heimskringla*, III, 371–2.

dawn, and found that his sword was gone. He searched, and found it some distance away from him. Accordingly he rose up and took it, thinking that his companions had been playing a trick on him to tease him, but they denied this. This happened three nights in a row; by this time he himself had begun to wonder at it, as did others who saw and heard this, and they asked him why this could be. He then told them that the sword was called Hneitir, and had been borne by St Olaf in the battle of Stiklestad, and explained to them the subsequent history of the sword. This was then told to King Kirjalax; he sent for the man who bore the sword and gave him in gold three times the value of the sword, after which the King had the sword taken to the church of St Olaf that is attended by the Varangians; where it has stayed above the altar. Eindriði the Young was in Constantinople when this happened; he told this tale in Norway, as Einar Skúlason testifies in the poem that he composed about St Olaf, where this event is noted.

In other words, Snorri's source for his narrative is Einar Skúlason's poem *Geisli*, which we know to have been composed in 1152 or, at latest, 1153, some 30 years after this battle.[1] There the poet himself cites his source: *slöng Eindriði ungi...brag ræðu* (st. 45). Eindriði could easily have been present in the battle, or have spoken to men who were in it, and in this way the evidence is no worse than any other well-attested historical narrative not relying entirely on public records.

Let us now see what the Byzantine sources tell us of the battle. The nearest in chronological terms is Cinnamus, who describes an invasion by the Pechenegs (whom he calls *Skuthai*), against whom John II led an army and encamped near Beroë over the winter, setting out against them in earnest in the spring.

When the armies met it was doubtful for a while which of the two would win. The Emperor himself was wounded in one foot. The Romans fought with great valour, and at length the Scythians were completely defeated; some fell and others were captured. One unit, however, brave men, returned to their camp and would not think of flight, but rather risk their lives along with their wives and children, and fight in their fort of wains; they had covered their wains with the hides of oxen and fastened them firmly together, after which they placed their wives and children inside the fort. A fierce fight now ensued, and many men fell on both sides. The Scythians used their wains as a defensive palisade, and the Roman army lost many men. Now when the Emperor saw this, he wanted to get off his horse and fight with his soldiers, but when the Romans refused to let him, he commanded the axe-bearers who stood around him (they are a Britannic people who of old served the Roman Emperors) to attack them with their axes and to break the fort of wains. They did this at once, and the Emperor thus captured also the Scythian camp; at this most of those who escaped by flight surrendered

---

[1] Cf. F. Jónsson, *Litteraturs Historie*, II, 66. *Geisli* is edited in *Flateyjarbók*, I, 1ff., and in FJ *Skjald* A I 467–9, B I 437–41.

to the Emperor of their own accord, and for love of those who had been captured: they were then transported to the Roman Empire and taken into the army, and so dwelt there for a long time.[1]

Besides Cinnamus, we have the evidence of the Chronicle of Nicetas Choniates, who describes the battle in very similar terms. He does not mention the Emperor's wound, but describes the fort of the Scythians in more detail. He states that when John saw how difficult it was to capture it, he knelt in tears to pray before the icon of the Blessed Virgin. After this he continues:

He [John] took his life-guards, who had as weapons very long shields and one-edged axes, and were like an unbreakable wall of stone, and sent them against the Scythians. They broke the fort open, and put them to disgraceful flight, while the Romans followed them after energetically. The men of the itinerant folk [lit. wain-dwellers] fell in thousands, and their camp was plundered.

He also goes on to state that many of the fugitives surrendered, and some of them were made to settle in a western theme of the Empire, where they entered the army, while many others were sold into slavery.[2]

Nicetas completed his work around 1206 at the earliest.[3] He is an impartial and reliable historian, who held several important posts in the Empire, both in Constantinople and Nicaea, and had good access to records and histories there. He does not appear to have known Cinnamus's book on the Comneni, and in consequence the two accounts provide valuable corroboration of one another, as well as of Snorri's narrative, in that they enable us to make the necessary adjustment to his claims. It is necessary to note the battle of Beroë carefully, as Cinnamus's statement has been interpreted by some as meaning that the English had entirely replaced the Norsemen in the regiment by this time. The author is, however, not at all certain that this is so, since we must take certain points about Cinnamus and his history into consideration when trying to assess the situation. In the first instance, the surviving text is at best only an abstract of Cinnamus's much longer work; secondly, he was writing principally about Manuel I, and his observations on earlier Emperors are much less detailed than his statements about that prince; thirdly, he was writing late in the day, *c.* 1180–3, and though there is every sign that he was a conscientious chronicler, he could hardly have had access to many eyewitness accounts by then as to the actual nationality of the Varangians involved at

---

[1] Cinnamus, *Epitome…historiarum*, ed. A. Meineke (CSHB), Bonn, 1836, 1, 7–8.
[2] Nicetas, *Historiae*, 20–3.
[3] Cf. K. Krumbacher, *Geschichte der byzantinischen Litteratur*, 2nd ed., Munich, 1897, 282.

Beroë;[1] in the present author's view (with which the reviser agrees with some reservation), the observation about the British is as likely to be an interpolation by the abstracter, who was obviously writing at a somewhat later date, and only knew English Varangians. Einar, and through him Snorri, drawing on a man whose Norse descent is indisputable, and who was an almost certain contemporary in Byzantium of the fighters in the battle,[2] provide, together with our knowledge of the large influx of Scandinavians into the Varangians in the previous reign, fairly conclusive evidence that if there were Englishmen in the unit that fought at Beroë, then they were not by any means an overwhelming majority.

The evidence obtained from Eindriði is worth a closer look. *Geisli*, st. 55 states clearly

> Halft fimmta vann heimtan
> Hundrað, brimis sunda
> Nýztan, tír, þats næra,
> Norðmanna, val þorði.

Four and a half hundred [i.e. 480+60] Norsemen, who dared to feed the ravens, won great renown,

and this statement of one so close to the battle weighs very heavily in favour of a Scandinavian composition. We may add to it a characteristic of John II as described by Nicetas; his strong preference for placing men of the same nation in the same regiments,[3] and as we know that there were extant separate units of Englishmen in the Byzantine army at this time, as well as separate units of Norsemen and Russians, there can be little doubt on that score alone that John continued the practice formulated by his father, and kept them separate.

The tale of Hneitir has also originated from Eindriði; we find it in *Geisli*, and the cautious Snorri accepts it for *Heimskringla*; it is true that Eindriði is not described as an actual eyewitness of this incident, but he has clearly believed it, and so brought it back to Norway. Naturally, a young man is likely to be told tales by old sweats on the lines on which modern old sweats play pranks on their junior recruits, but one of his intelligence is not likely to have been easily taken in (see later about his career in the regiment), and it is highly probable that there was in Constantinople a church consecrated which was built by the Varan-

---

[1] On the text of Cinnamus, see C. Neumann, *Griechische Geschichtsschreiber*, Leipzig, 1888, 78–103, and Krumbacher, *Geschichte der byzantinischen Litteratur*, 279–81.

[2] See below, Ch. 10. As to Eindriði's presence in Norway in 1150–2, see *Orkneyinga saga*, ed. S. Nordal, Copenhagen, 1915: 'þat sumar [1150 or 1152] kom útan af Miklagarði Eindriði ungi; hann hafði þar verit lengi á mála'.

[3] Nicetas, *Historiae*, 39; cf. also Chalandon, *Les Comnène*, II, 22.

gians to the glory of 'the Holy Virgin Mary and the Blessed King Olaf';[1] moreover, with their respective theological backgrounds, it would be natural fo the Greeks to attribute the victory to the Blessed Virgin and for the Norsemen to ascribe it to the action of their patron saint; we must also remember that the oldest church used by the Varangians was dedicated to the B.V.M.,[2] and it is more than likely that it contained a chapel dedicated to St Olaf, over whose altar the sword was placed, where there can be no doubt that Eindriði saw it, and so was strengthened in his belief in it.

There now remains the matter of the place names *Pézínavellir* and *Blökumannaland*. The former, as we have pointed out, points clearly to a confusion of the name of the tribe, *Pechenegi* and *Vallaka*: *Blaka* is a very likely phonetic confusion also, pointing towards Wallachia, where the battle took place, as the main Pecheneg country was north of the Danube, in the Wallachian district: both points suggest a good tradition behind the story, which is more than the anecdote of the blind king who suddenly sees – this miracle of St Olaf is also told of Haraldr III in *Morkinskinna*,[3] and has clearly ended up here despite its fairly obvious folktale tone because of the strong veneration of the saint all through the Middle Ages in Scandinavia.

Though this is the only direct reference to the Varangians in the reign of John II, there can be little doubt that they must have accompanied him at such times as the siege of Antioch in 1137, where the Emperor was conspicuous for his personal bravery and the disciplined skill of his army as distinct from the typical sluggishness and incompetence of the Western lords involved.[4]

John II died as the result of an injury in the hunting field on 8 April 1143 and was succeeded by his fourth son, who reigned as Manuel I. Like his father, Manuel was much involved in military activities, both in the West and the East, and there can be no doubt that wherever he went – and his military adventures were very many during his long reign – he will have taken his Varangians with him as well as used them in border policing and military garrison work generally.[5] In the present

---

[1] So in *Bergsbók* (Cod. Stockh. Kungl. Bibl. Perg. 1, fol.); cf. *Den store saga om Olaf den Hellige*, ed. O. A. Johnson and J. Helgason, Oslo, 1941, 834.   [2] See below, p. 186.
[3] *Morkinskinna*, 65–6.   [4] Runciman, *A History of the Crusades*, II, 211ff.
[5] A panegyric on the Patriarch Michael II Oxeites, apparently written in 1143, preserves an account of the succession of Manuel I: this stresses the support given to him at the critical time of his father's death by all manner of men, especially by the Varangians, who are described there in the unusual phrase Τοὺς ἑτεροστόμους πελέκεις αἴροντες, οἳ ἐκεῖθεν ἡμῖν ἥκουσιν ᾧ ὁ βόρειος πόλος ὀρθὸς ἐφέστηκε – 'those bearing one-edged axes who come from their homes at the North Pole'; see R. Browning, 'The death of John II Comnenus', *Byzantion*, 31 (1961), 234.

study, however, we propose to confine ourselves to such occasions as give concrete evidence of their actual or very highly probable presence in an action.

The first incident dates from the war caused by the assault on Greece by Roger II of Sicily in 1147. Choosing a time when Manuel was heavily occupied with ridding himself of the wearisome guests who crossed the Empire on their way to participate in the Second Crusade, Roger attacked via Corfù, which he occupied and garrisoned, and made his way with much damage from destruction and plunder across the country to Thebes, which he also plundered and occupied. Manuel had first to dislodge a force of Cumans, who had crossed the Danube into Bulgaria, but he sent to the relief of the province an army containing some Varangian units under the command of Stephen Contostephanus, his brother-in-law, and John Axuchos. This force besieged Thebes early in 1149, but Contostephanus was mortally injured by a stone from a mangonel. Cinnamus tells us that he was laid down between the decks of the ship on which he flew his flag, but ordered his youngest son Andronicus and 'the commander of the axe-bearers' to direct it.[1] For the moment the Byzantines had to beat a retreat, but when Manuel himself brought reinforcements (including, no doubt, his personal unit of Varangians) the Normans were obliged to surrender the town.

The next point at which we can note Varangian increases as the result of a large-scale expedition by a Northern prince comes in the same period. The Second Crusade, involving as it did the Western Emperor (Conrad II) and the French King (Louis VII) personally, caused quite a stir in Europe, and no doubt numerous Scandinavians and Englishmen joined it individually,[2] as well as the one Northern ruler known to do so with a considerable following, Rögnvaldr kali, Earl of Orkney. It is not clear when he set out, but the indications are that he missed the main action of the Crusade, and did not leave until between 1151 and 1153.[3] What is certain, however, is that the principal

---

[1] Cinnamus, *Epitome...historiarum*, 97–8. From the words Καὶ τῶν πελεκοφόρων προσκαλεσάμενος τὸν ἐξάρχοντα we may gather that the soldiers involved were Varangians, and Chalandon's surmise about heavy Greek infantry being armed with axes cannot be maintained, as this affair was clearly happening at sea.

[2] It is not possible to rely on the very happy-go-lucky surmises of F. Münter (*Kirchengeschichte*, II, 715) that since 149 of the 500 ancient Norwegian families had the French lily in their coats of arms, they must have acquired this heraldic symbol on the Second Crusade; there is certainly no French evidence to support this, nor yet does any mediaeval Norwegian record even remotely suggest it; also, highly aristocratic symbols are apt to be added to heraldic scutcheons without any shred of real right to do so, if it adds to the wearer's consequence.

[3] Guðbrandur Vigfússon (*Orkneyinga saga* (Rolls Series), London, 1887, 159ff.) and Finnur Jónsson (*Litteraturs Historie*, II, 33) opt for 1152; E. Bull (*Det norske folks historie*, Oslo, 1931–8, II, 138) for 1152, and P. A. Munch (*Det norske folks historie*, Christiania, 1852–63, II, 833) for 1153.

influence that pushed him into making the journey was the suggestion of the Varangian Eindriði the Young, whom we met earlier in this chapter. Eindriði was in Norway a little earlier, on an errand which is fairly certain to have been recruiting for the regiment in which he had risen to a senior rank; various points in *Orkneyinga saga*[1] hint fairly strongly that his was a recruiting visit rather than a mere furlough. The saga does not give Eindriði a very good character in general, but there is a good and evident reason for this, as is revealed; when the two had passed through the Straits of Gibraltar, with a retinue of fifteen ships, of which Eindriði had hitherto commanded only one, he 'parted from the Earl with six ships', made for Marseilles, and in all probability made straight from there to Constantinople after revictualling. As the saga was written from a standpoint sympathetic to the swashbuckling Earl Rögnvaldr it is not surprising that the cautious action of Eindriði, whose job was to bring reinforcements safely to his master the Emperor and not to go gallivanting with them all over the Mediterranean Sea and risk their lives against Arab, Norman or Moorish pirates before they could be of service to the Empire, would be seen with a jaundiced eye. The Earl continued the long way to Crete, Acre and overland to Jerusalem, and then, after a short stay in the Holy Land, to Constantinople. A curious incident is recorded on the way. The Orkneymen had stopped at a port called in the saga *Imbólum*, which was in all probability Neochori, the harbour of the city of Amphipolis in Macedonia, which was known by this name down to the seventeenth century.[2] It is possible that there was a Varangian garrison there, and that the travellers had a hospitable reception from the following incident:

One evening, as they walked out of the town, Erlingr the Halt went out on to the jetty where the ship lay, when men of the town met them and said '*Miðhæfi*! *Miðhæfi*!' Erlingr was very drunk, and pretended not to hear them. As they met Erlingr jumped from the quay and landed in the mud that was underneath, and his men had to run to drag him out, and they were obliged to strip every garment off him.[3]

Earl Rögnvaldr composed a humorous verse on this incident, recorded in the saga, where he makes this word rhyme with *úgæfa*, but its meaning is uncertain; the most likely interpretation is that by R. M. Dawkins, that it is a Norseman's mishearing of the Greek $\mu\grave{\eta}$ $\delta\iota\acute{\alpha}\beta\epsilon$, 'don't cross', called as a warning to Erlingr because these men had seen a weak spot in the planking of the jetty just where Erlingr was

[1] *Orkneyinga saga*, ed. Nordal, Copenhagen, 1915, 214–62.
[2] Riant, *Skandinavernes Korstog*, 362.
[3] *Orkeyinga saga*, ed. Nordal, 256–7.

going to leap down to the ship.[1] On the other hand, Dawkins's conjecture that *Imbólum* was the island of Imbros is far from likely in view of his other conjecture that *Engilsnes* was Capo di Sant' Angelo on the southern point of the Peloponnese; this is way out of the route for Constantinople, and there seems no viable reason why the ship should make this long loop on its way southwards on a journey to the City. On the other hand, if we interpret *Engilsnes* as the Gallipoli peninsula, then the narrative of *Orkneyinga saga* is both logical and correct.[2] We are told that when Earl Rögnvaldr and his fleet neared Constantinople 'they took much trouble with their manner of sailing, and sailed with great dignity, for they knew King Sigurðr the Crusader had done so'. A verse attributed to the Earl assumes that they will take service with the Emperor:

> Ríðum Ræfils Vakri
> Rekum ei plóg af akri,
> Erjum úrgu barði
> Út at Miklagarði.
> Þiggjum þengils mála,
> Þokum fram í gný stála,
> Rjóðum gildis góma,
> Gerum ríks konungs sóma.

Let us ride the sea-king's steed [ship] to Byzantium; let us not drive the plough through the field, let us plough with the watery bow. Let us receive the Emperor's pay, let us press forward in the clash of weapons, let us redden the wolf's fangs, let us do honour to the great king,[3]

but the saga adds a corrective to this hope; the Emperor Manuel received them well:

he gave the Earl much money and offered them places as mercenaries if they wished to stay there. They stayed for a while over the winter and fared well enough. Eindriði the Young was there; he was high in the Emperor's service; he would have little to do with Earl Rögnvaldr and his men, but rather spoilt things for them with others.[4]

From this we can deduce the end of the story. Eindriði had clearly reached high command among the life-guard section of the Varangians, and had duly brought those men who had left Earl Rögnvaldr at Gibraltar to the City, and into the mercenaries, and was also able to persuade many of the Earl's remaining companions to become Varangians; but the Earl and his principal followers, such as Erlingr the Halt,

---

[1] R. M. Dawkins, 'Greeks and Northmen', in *Essays presented to R. R. Marett*, London, 1936, 35–7.
[2] See above, p. 137.
[3] *Orkneyinga saga*, ed. Nordal, 258; cf. FJ *Skjald* A I 511, B I 486 (*idem*).
[4] *Orkneyinga saga*, ed. Nordal, 258–9.

were none too keen to do so once they discovered that they would have to serve as subordinates to Eindriði, with whom they had parted on very cool terms. It is very likely, on the other hand, that Rögnvaldr handed over his ships to the Emperor, as he was not going to need them any further; he returned the land way by Dyrrhachium and over Italy. Manuel will of course have reimbursed Rögnvaldr generously for them, and doubtless given him a present in return for the force of men that he brought with him, and this will have served the Earl as his passage-money back along the long land-road from Rome to Denmark and Norway. The saga mentions that Rögnvaldr had no ships in Norway, which is another proof of the fact that he left them all with the Emperor, as is the point that he made his way back to Orkney on an Icelandic merchantman owned by Þórhallr Ásgrímsson – almost certainly a descendant of Ásgrímr Elliðagrímsson of *Njáls saga*.[1]

The reinforcement to the Varangians that this pilgrimage brought is not easily computed, but six full crews of men of war, plus a large proportion of the crews of the other nine can hardly have been fewer than 800–1000 in all.

The next certain incident in Manuel I's reign which involves the Varangians is the abortive attempt on the Emperor's life made by his cousin Andronicus in 1154. Cinnamus relates how Andronicus was foiled in his attempt, made when Manuel was sleeping in a tent, because the guards noticed him and drew their swords; and again when he set a troop of Isaurians loyal to him to lie in wait for the Emperor and murder him, because the Empress discovered the plot and sent 'one Isaac, a man of foreign descent, but a great friend of the Basileus' after him with 300 men.[2] This Isaac was the Varangian commander, a man of strict discipline, who later became a monk under the name of Michael and took part in the Synod of Blachernae of 1166.[3] Manuel found out in time, went home by another route, and had Andronicus arrested.

In 1155–6 Renault de Châtillon, Prince of Antioch, attacked Cyprus, where there was a Varangian garrison in Paphos. Despite an early success, in which he captured both the governor, John Comnenus, and the garrison general, Michael Branas, de Châtillon was eventually totally defeated by Manuel, and brought by the Varangians to grovel at the Emperor's feet in his triumph.[4] The guards were also much in

---

[1] F. Jónsson, 'Røgnvald Jarls Jorsalfaerd', *Historisk Tidsskrift*, 8 Række, IV (1913), 151–65.

[2] Cinnamus, *Epitome...historiarum*, 129–30.

[3] Cinnamus, *Epitome...historiarum*, 298; see also Chalandon, *Les Comnène*, II, 285, 648, 650; Nicetas, *Thesaurus orthodoxae fidei* (Migne, *PG*, CXL, 232).

[4] William of Tyre, *Belli Sacri historia* (*Recueil des historiens des croisades: historiens occidentaux*, I, Paris, 1841), 280; Cinnamus, *Epitome...historiarum*, 182–3; Chalandon, *Les Comnène*, II, 444–5.

evidence a little later, when Manuel received Baldwin III of Jerusalem,[1] and when he made his state entry into Antioch as a conqueror, and took over the city in a way in which even his father had not succeeded in doing.[2]

In the naval war against the Venetians in 1172 the *akoluthos* Aaron was sent with a fleet against them which must have contained a Varangian element. This expedition failed, largely because (or so it was said) of the treachery of the commander, who let the Venetian marauders know of the place where he was to ambush them, which angered the Emperor sufficiently to depose him from his post and have him blinded.[3]

In 1176 Manuel I was obliged to conduct an expedition against the Turks in Asia Minor, and directed it in person, taking with him his guard of Varangians as well as detachments of the regiment from the Asiatic themes. Through the incompetence of his scouts, Manuel's army was shattered at Myriocephalum on 17 September 1176; a blow from which he never really recovered, and which may be said to have ended the days of Byzantium as a major power for good.[4] The massacre of the Byzantine troops was, as both Cinnamus and Nicetas make clear, overwhelming, and Manuel, severely wounded, only just got away to join the advance troops who had been allowed to pass. Most of his guards were killed in the engagement, and this appears to have included the vast majority of the Varangians in immediate attendance on the Emperor, though some clearly got away, as a letter from Manuel himself to Henry II of England attests; in it he states that those *Inglinoi* who had been in the battle and were now returning home could give the King further details of it beyond the description in the letter.[5]

Manuel made one more effort to do battle with the Turks late in 1179, when he personally led the forces that went to the relief of Claudiopolis, where he was successful enough to drive the Turkish forces back, and conclude peace with them.[6] As he was there in person there are bound to have been Varangians present, and no doubt these took their share of the fighting, but the success of Claudiopolis can

[1] Cinnamus, *Epitome...historiarum*, 185; William of Tyre, *Belli Sacri historia*, 861; Chalandon, *Les Comnène*, II, 447ff.

[2] Cinnamus, *Epitome...historiarum*, 186; William of Tyre, *Belli Sacri historia*, 864; Chalandon, *Les Comnène*, II, 451ff.; there is also a poem on this event by Prodromos (*Recueil des historiens des croisades: historiens grecs*, II, 319).

[3] Cinnamus, *Epitome...historiarum*, 280ff.

[4] The main study of this battle and its consequences and sources is A. A. Vasilev, 'Myriokephalon', *BZ* 27 (1927), 288ff.; source references are given there.

[5] Roger of Hoveden, *Chronica*, ed. W. Stubbs (Rolls Series), London, 1868–71, II, 101ff.; see also more generally Nicetas, *Historiae*, 321ff.; Cinnamus, *Epitome...historiarum*, 299ff.; Chalandon, *Les Comnène*, II, 507–15.

[6] Nicetas, *Historiae*, 257; Chalandon, *Les Comnène*, II, 515.

have been only a very slight recompense to him for the disaster of Myriocephalum; certainly, Manuel's reputation in Western Euope as a mighty ruler was irretrievably ruined by this defeat, as was his health, for though he was able to save the worst of the immediate situation, Byzantine prestige had suffered to an extent from which it was never to recover even as far as it had after the débâcle of Manzikert. He died on 24 September 1180, and with him died the Empire that shone in the eyes of Western contemporaries with a glow that was to produce the envy that led to the third and most terrible disaster of all.

Manuel I was succeeded in name by his son, Alexius II, a boy of twelve, who was under the tutelage of his mother, Marie of France, and his cousin Alexius, grandson of John II. Despite her general unpopularity with the people of the City, the Dowager Empress appears to have retained the loyalty of the mercenaries, which enabled her to put down one revolt, led by Maria, Manuel I's daughter of his first marriage.[1] The chauvinist element in the Empire was not, however, pleased at being under the rule of a princess of barbarian origin, and so turned for leadership to the one remaining member of the Comnenian house with some reputation, the notorious Andronicus, and with their support he succeeded in gaining control of the Capital. Then, when the Varangians came over to his side, he was able to seize the regent Alexius and have him blinded, after which Maria Comnena and her husband were disposed of by poison.[2]

The support which the Varangians gave to Andronicus at this point can only be explained by the surmise that they had come to believe that the young Emperor's mother and the Regent were contemplating treachery against him, and that Andronicus was more likely than they to be a loyal defender of the Imperial person to whom they were sworn. It was not long, however, before the new regent's real intentions became clear, as he embarked on a systematic removal of Manuel's family from his way. He began by having the Dowager Empress accused of treason, and when the judges were unwilling to comply and condemn her to death, he threatened them with the Varangians and had the mob assault them, after which new, more complaisant judges were appointed who passed sentence as he wanted, and the Dowager was duly executed.[3] Andronicus now had himself crowned as co-Emperor, and in time had the legitimate Emperor murdered and married his widow.

[1] Nicetas, *Historiae*, 303ff.
[2] Nicetas, *Historiae*, 323ff. Nicetas states that Alexius was arrested by Γερμανῶν, οἳ κατωμαδὸν τοὺς ἑτεροστόμους πελέκεις ἀνέχουσιν, which clearly refers to Varangians.
[3] Nicetas, *Historiae*, 344–5.

There is not much evidence of Varangians in action during the short reigns of these last inglorious representatives of the Comnenian house. In the case of Andronicus I, as the appointed candidate of the chauvinist mob in the City, he was by inclination and necessity anti-Latin in his actions, and there can be little doubt that this affected his relationship with the Varangian regiment as a whole, and contributed to their action at his fall. There is, however, some doubt about this, bearing in mind that the regiment is likely to have been divided in its allegiance, as at this time it will have been composed of a mixture of two nationalities, Englishmen and Scandinavians. From Manuel I's letter to Henry II we can note the presence of the former, and from a note in Saxo, writing here of contemporary events, we know that news of Bishop Absalon's great victory over King Przemyslav of the Wends in the Sound of Rügen on Whit Monday 1184 reached the Varangians in Byzantium and was received by them with great joy.[1] The Scandinavian Varangians were no lovers of the Franks, but there is less likelihood that the English members of the regiment were hostile to them, and this would clearly have caused a division of opinion in the ranks. Moreover, Andronicus's high-handed and crass method of civil government was rapidly causing a fragmentation of the Empire; thus Isaac Comnenus, a cousin of the Emperor, seized hold of Cyprus by a trick (Nicetas says that he forged a letter of authority from Andronicus, and so ensured the support of the garrison, which, if no serious changes had taken place in its composition, still contained a Varangian unit at Paphos)[2] and ruled over it until he made the miscalculation of capturing the wife of Richard I of England, who dispossessed him in favour of the ex-King of Jerusalem, Guy de Lusignan, and so brought to an end the island's connection with the Empire.[3] In the end even his own mob turned against Andronicus in 1185 and by this time his reputation was such that not even the Varangians made any attempt to defend him. His fate is described in detail by Nicetas, and those curious about such horrors may look there at the miserable end of a great dynasty.[4]

For the next nineteen years the family of Angelos ruled in Byzantium with increasing feebleness. Isaac II, cast on the throne by a series of

---

[1] Saxo, *Gesta Danorum*, I, 545: 'eandem victoriam suam Absalon apud Byzantium incredibili famae velocitate vulgatam postmodo ab equitibus suis, tunc tempore in ea urbe stipendia merentibus accepit'.

[2] Nicetas, *Historiae*, 320.

[3] Runciman, *A History of the Crusades*, III, 43–7, and refs. there. Nicetas (*Historiae*, 547) calls Richard πελεκοφόρων κατάρχων Βρεττανῶν, οὓς νῦν φασιν Ἰγκλινούς, 'lord of the axe-bearing Britons, whom men now name Englishmen', which demonstrates clearly the presence of Englishmen in the Varangian guards as an accepted fact.

[4] Nicetas, *Historiae*, 447.

accidents that read like a Victorian thriller, proved an incapable ruler and was deposed and blinded by his brother Alexius (III) in 1195. The Varangians are not mentioned in any source for this period as having accomplished any specific military feat, but it is hard to believe that Isaac, perennially pressed for troops to hold his fragmenting realm together, did not make use of them most of the time. In particular, in the fierce battle in the passes by Beroë, it is most likely to have been they who saved Isaac's life when he was hard pressed.[1] On the other hand, the two bits of documentary evidence we have from this reign show them in their customary role of doers of unpopular jobs, such as acting as escort for the Patriarch Dositheus into the church of Hagia Sophia when his unpopularity with the clergy and the mob made Isaac fear that they might assault him during the enthronement ceremony.[2] Nor did Isaac neglect an opportunity to recruit for the regiment, as we may see from his attempts to get Danes passing through on a pilgrimage to Jerusalem to join it.[3]

When Alexius III ascended the throne he made it one of his first duties to write to the three kings of Scandinavia, Sverre of Norway, Knud Karlsson of Sweden and Knud VI of Denmark to try to cajole them into sending reinforcements for the Varangians in order to support his precarious throne. The messengers were in all probability all Norsemen; we know the names of two of them, Hreiðarr of Vík, who brought King Sverre his letter, and Pétr illska who did the same for King Knud of Denmark, but not that of the envoy to Sweden.[4] The former, of whose activities we have a certain amount of evidence in *Sverris saga*, appears to have been a less effective recruiting agent than Eindriði ungi. Although a certain number of men were gathered in Norway (King Sverre was not willing to lose trained soldiers but did

---

[1] Nicetas, *Historiae*, 561–4; see also Ostrogorskii, *A History of the Byzantine State*, 405.

[2] Nicetas, *Historiae*, 533.

[3] *Historia de profectione Danorum in Terram Sanctam* (J. Langebek, *Scriptores Rerum Danicarum*, Copenhagen, 1772–92, V, 341ff.); see also J. Olrik, *Krøniker fra Valdemarstiden*, Copenhagen, 1900–1, 173.

[4] *Sverris saga*, ed. G. Indrebö, Oslo, 1920, 133–4; see also below, pp. 218–20. It is just possible that the sender of the three chrysobulls was Isaac II, just before his deposition, as Reiðarr had reached Norway in the summer, and even the fastest messenger from Byzantium to Scandinavia found the overland route slow. The saga, however, calls the Emperor *Kirjalax*. Though we have noted that this tends to be an omnibus name for the Eastern Emperors after Alexius I, we must remember that (*a*) *Sverris saga* was composed very close to the subject's own lifetime, and exists in manuscripts of very respectable antiquity; (*b*) much of its material was given directly to Abbot Karl Jónsson by King Sverre himself, who is likely to have got the name right, and (*c*) 'summer' is an elastic term in Norse historiography, so that there is no irrefutable reason why Alexius III could not have sent his messenger off hot-foot in the first days of his reign, especially as he, a usurper, was badly in need of such superior and loyal troops as Varangians were, and Reiðarr and his companions, travelling as they presumably did at their utmost speed at the Imperial behest, still reached Scandinavia before the autumn set in.

allow the sons of farmers and merchants who wanted to go to depart), through an agent named Þorgils Hreiðarr appears to have drawn a part of this force off into the army of the Böglungs which was being assembled to oppose Sverre by Bishop Nicholas. Nonetheless it is more than likely that some of those recruited made their way in the end to the City, for the Varangians appear to have been fairly strong again by the time of the fall of the City to Dandolo's robbers (see below).

There is no mention of Varangians being used on military expeditions during the reign of Alexius III any more than during the reign of Isaac II, but once more we find them at work in the City, coping with the civil unrest that blazed up with increasing frequency in these last years of Imperial disintegration. In the year 1200 a general by the name of John Lagos was found to have indulged in gross peculation of the stores under his charge. On being discovered, he tried to raise a riot in the City, and a part of his followers tried to break into the Hagia Sophia and acclaim him there as Emperor, but the Varangians were on guard at the doors and prevented them.[1] Similarly, when John Pachys, a member of the Comneni, attempted to seize the throne, Nicetas tells us that Alexius gathered together such of his relatives as were accustomed to bear arms, and went by night along the shore towards the Hodegon monastery, where they made contact with the *pelekophoroi*, with whose help they made a sudden attack on the insurrectionist mob around the Hippodrome and scattered them, capturing John and killing him in a brutal manner.[2]

This episode is of some importance to the present study, as it gives us some indirect evidence from which we can determine the whereabouts of the main headquarters of the Varangians. The Emperor was in Blachernae when the riot began. Clearly there were some Varangians with him, and these would have a guard-room in the palace, but equally, this cannot have been their main quarters, because of the expedition made to collect the main troop, which must have been at the Hodegon. The celebrated icon of the Blessed Virgin which was given a special veneration whenever the Emperors set off on a military expedition was kept in the church of the Hodegon, and the main arsenal of the Empire, the Mangana, was also nearby.[3] It would therefore be logical for the Emperor to station his most loyal soldiery at this strategic point, drawing only as many as were wanted for individual guard duty off to

[1] Nicetas, *Historiae*, 695.
[2] Nicetas, *Historiae*, 697ff.
[3] On the icon, see Nicetas, *Historiae*, 497; on the Mangana, see above, Ch. 2 also A. G. Paspatis, *The Great Palace of Constantinople*, London, 1895, 11 and 46, and Du Cange, *Constantinopolis Christiana*, Paris, 1680, III, 133–4.

Blachernae. On the other hand, in this crisis, Alexius III will have reckoned (with good reason) that it would be too hazardous to send the small troop of Varangians or other guards whom he had with him in Blachernae through the City in an endeavour to attack the rebels who had quartered around the Hippodrome or the old palace that John Pachys had seized, as they were certain to be overpowered by the mob if the uproar chanced to spread. In consequence he sent his officers by sea, together with as big a force as he dared to release without denuding Blachernae of its defences, down to the Hodegon, where they contacted the much larger main force of Varangians, and so made up a force large enough to set about the rebels. From all this we may assume that the total number involved will have been quite considerable, as there will have been not only enough soldiers there to man the guard-posts at the Mangana and the old palace, but also a constant pool to replace troops moved about, as in the headquarters of any regiment.

Unfortunately, not even the excavations under the aegis of Professor Talbot Rice have yielded any positive evidence as to the precise site, but it is to be hoped that when further archaeological work is undertaken in the district the foundations will be revealed.

We come now to the greatest of all the blows that destroyed Byzantium, the sack of the City by the French–Italian expedition of 1202–4. This had set out as a crusade to recapture the Kingdom of Jerusalem from the armies of Saladin, but had been diverted from its course by the advent of Alexius, son of the deposed Emperor Isaac II, who attempted to obtain help from the leaders to depose his uncle. The latter, with an incompetence that is unbelievable, had so far neglected the defences of his capital that the once-great navy of the Empire was reduced to a mere twenty half-rotten hulks that were no match for the fleet of the Venetians, the walls were in a state of appalling disrepair and even his large land army, estimated by the opposition as at least 60,000 men, was in a state of such disaffection as to make it doubtful whether he could rely on more than the small portion of it which was made up of the mercenaries;[1] this force was estimated by Byzantine and Western eyewitnesses as around a quarter of the whole army, not more, that is,

---

[1] *Annales Herbipolenses* (K. Hopf, *Chroniques gréco-romaines inédites*, Berlin, 1873, 91) state that in one skirmish Alexius III lined up his army outside one of the gates of the city, and that it was then some 100,000 men in 17 divisions. This is doubtless a gross exaggeration, as the text also states that the Latins opposed them with a mere 7 divisions of 700 men (650 infantry and 50 cavalry). Robert of Clari (*La conquête de Constantinople*, ed. P. Lauer, Paris, 1924, 65) states that Alexius V had 4000 men in his fight with Henry of Flanders; this is a much more likely number for the hard-pressed Byzantine force.

than 15,000 men in all,[1] of whom the English and Danes (i.e. the Varangians) and Pisans are referred to by the historians as those who fought most strenuously. Opposed to them was the land force of 33,500 men (at most) under the command of Enrico Dandolo.[2]

The general history of the events leading up to the sack of Constantinople has been covered with such thoroughness by all the major historians of the Eastern Empire that it would be superfluous to repeat them here, especially as they may be read in English in a convenient and easily accessible summary by Sir Steven Runciman.[3] We will therefore confine our present narrative to an examination of what may be found out about the part played by the Varangians in the last agony of the unbroken Empire.

The first attempt was made by the invaders at the sea-entrances through the Bosphorus. There Manuel I's great defensive chain appears to have been lost or removed, as the Venetians encountered no obstacle until they entered the Golden Horn, where the chain across the entrance barred their way. It was fastened to the Galata Tower, which then lay right on the waterline, and was defended on this occasion by Norse and English Varangians, who made a sortie and succeeded in driving off the invaders. In the end, however, the Venetians succeeded in sending a heavy draught vessel with shears attached to it on to the chain and cut it (a tactic not unknown in twentieth-century naval warfare), and on its collapse the defenders retreated from the tower, many being killed, though the remnant returned safely to the City.[4]

On 17 July 1203 the main assault was made both on sea and land. The assailants succeeded in breaking the walls near Blachernae, but were repulsed by Varangians and driven back with much slaughter. This success did not however avail them very much, as in the meanwhile the sea assault, directed by Dandolo, had succeeded in breaking through the walls on the harbour side, and Alexius hastened to withdraw men

---

[1] The number can be calculated from the narrative in *Annales Herbipolenses* (*loc. cit.*) of the sortie made by Alexius V at a later point, who is said there to have had a force of 15,000 men. As it is clear that he was brought to power by the Varangians, the present author suspects that this fact is the backing to Karl Hopf's untenable statement (*Geschichte Griechenlands*, Berlin, 1876–8, 196) that the Varangians alone numbered 15,000, though this is a quite impossible figure; cf. Vasilevskii, *Труды*, I, 369.

[2] The sources speak of 4500 cavalry, 9000 esquires and 20,000 infantry, and of a naval force of 50 galleys.

[3] Runciman, *A History of the Crusades*, III, 107–31; see also E. Bradford, *The Great Betrayal*, London, 1967, chs. I–III; *CMH*, pt I, 286ff.

[4] Count Hugo of St Pol states in a letter to his friend R. (? Robert) de Balves (*Revue de l'Orient Latin*, VII (1899), 11–14) that 'Angli, Pisani, Geneviani, Dani' defended the tower, fired across the Latins and made several assaults on them, and that the arrows were especially dangerous. As the English were especially noted as archers, the chances are that the bowmen here were English Varangians.

from the land walls to support the seaward defence, arraying his remaining force outside the walls.[1] The invasion on the seaward side was also halted, but to cover their retreat the Venetians set fire to the houses near the harbour, and so burned down a whole quarter of the City. At this point Dandolo also heard of the defeat of the landward assault, and decided to abandon the seaward attack and hasten to the relief of the others, though when he got there he found that this was not necessary, as the landward assailants had made an organized retreat, and the Byzantine force stood immobile on the outside of the walls.

The next night Alexius III, despairing of success, fled from the City with such treasure as he could gather at short notice. Thereupon the eunuch Constantine, the Imperial Treasurer, turned to the Varangians and suggested to them that Isaac II should now be brought out of prison and put back on the throne, promising them a large reward in return for their help. They agreed, and with their assistance the blind Emperor was proclaimed once more the Basileus, together with his son Alexius IV.[2] The latter made his entry into the City shortly afterwards, riding between Baldwin of Flanders and Enrico Dandolo.

It was not long before it became clear that the new Emperors had no means to fulfil their extravagant promises to their allies, and over the winter there were several rows between Greeks and Latins which further exacerbated the ancient enmity. In the end Alexius IV, despairing of controlling his own subjects, was about to ask the Franks and Venetians once more for help to quell a conspiracy to enthrone Nicholas Canavos in his place, when he entrusted his general Alexius Murzuphlus, a member of the Ducas family, with his plan. Murzuphlus despised this idea, and turned to the Varangians, telling them that if this plan went through, they would be replaced as guards by Latins. This appeal to their pockets succeeded, and the Varangians made such a riot outside Alexius's dwelling in the palace that he became frightened, and asked Murzuphlus to save him. Instead, the latter led him through a secret door and had him seized and imprisoned, after which he had himself proclaimed Emperor on 5 February 1204 with the support of the Varangians as Alexius V.[3] Alexius IV was quietly strangled in prison a few days later, while the miserable Isaac II died, probably of grief, shortly after that.

It now became impossible to avert an open war between the Latins and the Greeks. Alexius V did what he could to repair the neglected

---

[1] Geoffrey de Villehardouin, *La conquête de Constantinople*, ed. E. Faral, Paris, 1938–9, 1, 158; Robert of Clari, *La conquête de Constantinople*, 46–7; Nicetas, *Historiae*, 720ff.; see also P. d'Outremann, *Constantinopolis Belgica*, Tournai, 1643, 180.

[2] Nicetas, *Historiae*, 727.

[3] Nicetas, *Historiae*, 744–7.

defences, but he was too late, despite his most strenuous efforts, to do more than delay the final conflict. In the meanwhile, however, he endeavoured to dishearten the enemy by making sorties to weaken their power. He led these in person on several occasions, and so is bound to have had the guards on whom his throne depended with him; in one instance this was particularly noted by the chroniclers, when Henry of Flanders had taken 1000 men on a stores-replenishment raid up to Philea, where Alexius opposed him with a considerably larger force, but was disastrously beaten and lost both the Imperial standard and icon of St Mary the Wayfinder to the enemy.[1]

The full assault came on 9–12 April 1204. The Franco-Venetians broke in through three gates, and were opposed by Alexius V on an open space near the Pantepoptes monastery. The guards did not trust themselves to oppose the force that poured in against them, and so withdrew with the Emperor to the Bukoleon, while the Latins burned the centre of the City in order to hamper a possible attack northwards by the Greeks. At this point Alexius V gave up hope and fled by sea with his wife and mother-in-law. The surviving Greek nobles and leaders now gathered in Hagia Sophia, and tried to choose yet another Emperor. Dr B. Sinogowitz has argued that they succeeded in choosing Constantine Lascaris, the brother of Theodore, Alexius III's son-in-law, but Nicetas gives no indication of this, concentrating his narrative on Theodore's activities in the crisis.[2] He appears to have made a last-minute effort to rally the despairing Greeks, but morale had been broken too sharply by this time for him to succeed. He then turned to the Varangians, and pointed out to them that to submit to the Latins would be to lose their privileged position and to be at best ordinary troops in their army. No one was, however, willing to listen to him; even the Varangians were only willing to fight if they were given increased pay.[3] As the armed bands of the Latins appeared at this moment, no further resistance became possible, the last Greeks fled, and the Varangians surrendered tamely to the conquerors, thus ending the history of the regiment that was begun so gloriously with ignominy, as the Empire crashed in an orgy of Latin destruction and vandalism that horrified even Innocent III.[4]

---

[1] Villehardouin, *La conquête de Constantinople*, II, 26; Robert of Clari, *La conquête de Constantinople*, 750–1. There is also mention of it in correspondence from Baldwin of Flanders to Innocent III (*Epistolae Innocentii III*, ed. S. Baluze, Paris, 1682, I, 53).
[2] B. Sinogowitz, 'Über das byzantinische Kaisertum nach dem vierten Kreuzzuge', *BZ*, 45 (1952), 345–56; Nicetas, *Historiae*, 755; see also *CMH*, pt I, 286.
[3] Nicetas, *Historiae*, 756.
[4] *Epistolae Innocentii III*, I, 57.

7

The ghost of the regiment:
Varangian evidences 1204–1453

This chapter is both brief and fragmentary, for such few evidences as can be garnered about the service of Englishmen, Scandinavians or others in the Varangian guards of the Lascarides and Palaeologi, as well as serving the puppets of the shadowy Latin Empire in Constantinople, are far too uncertain and infrequent to give any sort of coherent picture.

Of Constantinople itself, after the Latins had ravaged their fill, we have a remark by Robert of Clari which merits some note, as it may refer to the eventual fate of the last Varangians of the old Empire. He states that on the day after Alexius V fled the City, 'priests and clerics in their habits – these were Englishmen, Danes and men of other nations', had come to the Latins in procession and begged for mercy, saying that the Greeks were fled and that only poor folk were left within the City.[1] This must be an error; of course there is no denying that English and Danish priests *may* have been in Byzantium, but in view of the religious chasm that had opened between the Latin and Greek churches, these can hardly have been numerous – at most one or two chaplains of each nationality for the troops in the Imperial mercenary force. On the other hand, the very fact that these nationalities are mentioned by Robert suggests that what arrived was a deputation of English and Danish officers of the former Varangians, together with the clergy in attendance on the regiment. If these were then taken on by the new Latin regime, it will have been as ordinary soldiers.

There are only two references which even suggest that some nominal Varangian unit was employed by the Latin Emperors. The first is very

---

[1] Robert of Clari, *La conquête de Constantinople*, ed. P. Lauer, Paris, 1924, 79.

dubious, the evidence being some scratched shields in the ruins of the Bukoleon, and will be dealt with later. The second, however, is more interesting, as it refers to a perfectly feasible, if somewhat improbable, incident.

When Henry of Flanders, the only effective Latin Emperor, died in 1216, his brother-in-law, Peter of Courtenay, was elected to succeed him, but he was captured by the Despot Theodore of Epirus and died there in captivity. His Empress-elect, Yolande, had travelled by sea, and reached Constantinople safely. She now directed the election of her son Philip of Namur who, however, refused the dignity, and let his brother Robert be chosen in his place. In connection with this there has survived a narrative in *Þorláks saga helga* which, if not an ingenious invention of the hagiographer, is our one real piece of evidence of Varangians in the service of the Latin rulers.

Shortly after the sanctity of the blessed Bishop Þorlákr was declared, Philip of Flemingland [Flanders] was chosen to be King in Byzantium. Thereupon Norwegians went thither from Norway to join the Varangians, and they were able to bring this joyous news to those who were already in service, about the holiness and power of miracles of the holy Bishop Þorlákr, after which they went to church and gave thanks to God for His glory. When men became aware of this news, they told the King, who sent for some of the Varangians and asked what was this news that he had been told. One of them explained as clearly as he could what was known of the life and habits of the blessed Bishop Þorlákr, where he was born, what had been his lot, how his sanctity had been declared, and those miracles that he knew of as true. The King received all this well and sympathetically. Now shortly afterwards the Varangians were to go into attack against pagans who were attacking the Empire. When the armies joined in battle the loss fell on the Varangians to begin with, and at length they fled to a certain castle, though this was but slight shelter, while the others pitched their camp around it and intended to make the final attack on them in the morning. That night the Varangians were in great distress, expecting their death very soon. Then one of them said: 'We may yet win a fair victory in the trust of the blessed Bishop Þorlákr, though the odds against us are overwhelming, if he will but strengthen and support us; let us make a vow with all our hearts, and our lot will become better.' They vowed to have a church built to the honour of the blessed Bishop Þorlákr if they should return. Then, when they had made their vow, all fear left their hearts, and they longed to encounter the heathen. When it was barely light enough to fight, they prepared to descend into action, but first they prayed with fervour and made the sign of the Cross with all reverence. After this they ran towards the enemy with trumpets blowing and great noise, saying: 'Forward now with courage in the trust of the blessed Bishop Þorlákr; let us win with speed or die as brave men.' And when the heathen heard the blessed Bishop Þorlákr named a fear fell on them, so that they did not know what they did; they fought one another, while most of them fled, and many were captured and their hands bound behind their backs and their weapons and clothes were taken and brought with the booty back to Constantinople, where the Varangians themselves told the King and his men of the happening, while the heathen bore witness as far as they were concerned. The King was pleased, and took the first stone himself and carried it to the church that was built to Bishop Þorlákr, himself provided masons and all materials for it and had it consecrated in honour of the blessed Bishop Þorlákr, and those who have come from there speak of many miracles performed in it.[1]

The exaggerations of this story are self-evident, but it is far from impossible that there is some foundation for it in actuality. The principal difficulty is, of course, that there is no other reference to a church dedicated to St Þorlákr in Constantinople. On the other hand, if there were Varangians in the service of the Latin rulers (especially in the slightly more prosperous days of Henry of Flanders and his immediate successors), then it is by no means impossible that if there were Icelanders among them, a chapel would be dedicated in their church to their national saint, especially while the Latin rite prevailed in the City. We must admit that the sanctity of Bishop Þorlákr was neither then nor since acknowledged by the central hagiographical bureaux of the Holy See in Rome, but it had been acknowledged by the Archbishops of Niðarós very early, and doubtless this would have sufficed on the fringe of Latin Christianity that was the Latin Empire of Constantinople. The main objection to any credibility for the story has come from Icelandic scholars, Jón Sigurðsson and Guðbrandur Vigfússon, who edited the sagas of St Þorlákr in the great edition of *Biskupa sögur*;[2] it was based on the point that they could find no Emperor named Philip in the regnal lists of the Eastern Emperors, and so speculated on its referring to Baldwin I or Henry. What is of interest to us, therefore, is that the obscure hagiographer in a distant island had heard of the election of Philip of Namur to the Latin Empire, and associated this anecdote with him, even though this election never came into effect because of Philip's refusal of the crown. The attribution of the incident to Varangians is in this context self-explanatory, but, unfortunately, no proof *per se* of any Varangian presence in the Latin armies – though common sense would suggest that the Latin rulers, whose desire was to appear in every way as Emperors of the East, would have endeavoured to recruit and maintain just such a prestige unit – the more so as they had had tangible experience of their fighting ability during the 1203–4 campaign. That there were Danes and Englishmen in Constantinople in some numbers

---

[1] *Biskupa sögur*, ed. J. Sigurðsson and G. Vigfússon, Copenhagen, 1858–78, I, 363–4.
[2] *Biskupa sögur*, I, 363 n.

in the early Latin period we know from a religious provision made
for them by the Latin Patriarch, but there is no sign that they were
any unified force.[1]

Even though the Varangians would not accede to Theodore Lascaris's
request to fight in the last moments of the Angelian dynasty, it is
highly probable that when the uncertain situation about the Greek
ruler had been resolved after the death of Constantine Lascaris in the
battle of Adramyttium on 18 March 1205, some of them would have
sought Theodore out in Nicaea, where he was setting up the Greek
Empire of the East.[2] If they were not a separate unit in the early days,
and they are not mentioned by George Acropolites in his account of
the battle of Antioch in which Theodore secured his title by defeating
and killing the Turkish Sultan Kaikhosru, and capturing his unpopular
father-in-law, the former Alexius III, and putting him out of harm's
way in a monastery,[3] they had certainly reappeared by the later years
of his reign.

In the days of the two great Nicene rulers, Theodore I and John III
Vatatzes, the Nicene court gradually took on the same form and ceremonial as the court of the unbroken Empire had had. The Imperial
guards were divided into five regiments: the Scholae, the *Keltai
Pelekophoroi* (i.e. Varangians), Vardariots, Tzusi and *Korynophoroi*
('Club-bearers'), who are quite unlikely, however, to have had any
connection with the *Kylfingar* of Russia of earlier times.[4] These Varangians are certain to have been for the most part Englishmen or Scots,
for after the ravage of Constantinople it is exceedingly doubtful whether
any Norseman served in the armies of the Greek Emperors again. The
command of the guards was placed under a Grand Hetairarch again
in the reign of John III, when Michael Libadarius is mentioned as
holding the post.[5]

John III's first military engagement as Emperor was against the
Latin Emperor Robert of Courtenay, who had taken under his wing
two of Theodore I's brothers, who had desired the throne in Nicaea.
In the battle of Poimanenon John commanded the Nicaean army per-

---

[1] L. Santifaller, *Beiträge zur Geschichte des Lateinischen Patriarchats von Konstantinopel (1204–
1261)*, Weimar, 1938, 175 (letter 58). C. Verlinden, *Les empereurs belges de Constantinople*,
Brussels, 1945, 145–7, delineates sharply the extreme seriousness of the Latin situation
in 1217–18, and makes Philip of Namur's decision to stay at home very understandable.
[2] For Varangians in Nicaea generally, see M. A. Andreeva, *Очерки по культуре
Византийского двора в XIII веке*, Prague, 1927, 19ff., and M. Angold, *A Byzantine
Government in Exile*, London, 1975, esp. chs. IX and X.
[3] Georgius Acropolita, *Annales*, ed. I. Bekker (CSHB), Bonn, 1837, 18.
[4] Andreeva, *Очерки*, 50–2.
[5] Acropolita, *Annales*, 72.

sonally, and won a great victory, in which such Varangians as he had in his service will have been well to the fore.[1]

In 1233 John of Brienne, regent for the infant Baldwin II of Constantinople, broke the truce of 1225, and once more Greek and Latin were at war, and once more Vatatzes's superior generalship and better troops proved the stronger, depriving the Latins of the greater part of their European territories as the first encounter had deprived them of their Asiatic lands bar a few square miles around Nicomedia, and also enabling him to incorporate into his realm the shadow Empire of Thessalonica. There can be little doubt that on this campaign, as on the other, John had his Varangians in action. He certainly used them, as George Pachymeres tells us, as the guardians of his treasure-house at Magnesia,[2] where he had assembled a considerable wealth by his frugal and sensible government, as did his son Theodore II in his treasury at Astyza.[3]

On the death of Theodore II in 1258, his infant son John IV succeeded him, but George Muzalon was appointed Regent. Muzalon was murdered in the following year, and his murder brought forward Michael Palaeologus, who succeeded in advancing from the Regency to a co-Emperorship, despite his difficulty in obtaining funds for the necessary bribery from the Imperial treasury which was permanently guarded by Varangians.[4] In the end, however, Michael succeeded in his design, and was crowned co-Emperor in Nicaea on 1 January 1259. In connection with this ceremony there was considerable trouble when Michael broke his promise to have John crowned, which caused some high officials, in particular Archbishop Manuel of Thessalonica, to object to the ceremony. Manuel finally gave way after threats had been freely used, and it was noted by Pachymeres that he feared in particular a company of Varangians who stood by fully armed, 'ready for attack or defence according to the pleasure of the rulers'.[5] Bearing in mind the reputation of the regiment in the Empire, it can hardly be surprising that Manuel gave way rather than be submitted to their attentions.

We find a fair number of Varangian references in the reign of Michael VIII, which is not surprising when we remember that it is the last time that Byzantium appeared on the international scene as a power of any formidability. With a rare mixture of ability, luck and cunning,

[1] Acropolita, *Annales*, 37–8; see also A. Gardner, *The Lascarides of Nicaea*, London, 1912, 118–19.
[2] Georgios Pachymeres, *De Michaele et Andronico Palaeologis libri XIII*, ed. I. Bekker (CSHB), Bonn, 1835, I, 71.
[3] Pachymeres, *De Michaele et Andronico Palaeologis*, I, 68.
[4] Pachymeres, *De Michaele et Andronico Palaeologis*, I, 71ff.
[5] Pachymeres, *De Michaele et Andronico Palaeologis*, I, 103.

Michael replaced Greek power in the City, defeated all attempts to unseat him by his numerous enemies, and reconquered enough territory to give the reasserted Empire a shadowy, precarious semblance of its Comnenian self. In the course of his active life he was constantly at war with great and small states in the Balkans and Asia Minor, and we find that his guards, of whom the Ἐγκλινοβάραγγοι of his letter of 1272 were clearly the most used unit, were employed very actively throughout his reign.[1]

The first definite reference after the initial coronation in Nicaea (although we may be sure that the tradition-conscious Emperor will have followed precedent and had his *pelekophoroi* around him at his second coronation in the Hagia Sophia in 1261) concerns Michael's difficulties with the Frankish states in Southern Greece in 1264, where mercenaries made up the bulk of the army. A Seljuk contingent deserted to the Franks because of the delay in the arrival of their pay, and the remaining Greek force, which included some of the Varangians, was heavily defeated at Makriplagi.[2] There is also a direct reference to them as guards of an important prisoner in the Greek narrative of William of Villehardouin's capture and imprisonment by Michael.[3]

In the following year Michael went in person to oppose an invasion by Bulgars and Tartars in Thrace. On this occasion he had with him Azz-ed-Din, former Sultan of the Seljuks, who had fled to Byzantium to escape the onslaught of the all-conquering Hulagu Khan, and had been stuck there since, as Michael found that he could oblige the Mongols by keeping him in polite captivity. Azz-ed-Din resented this, and plotted with King Constantine of Bulgaria to have Michael surprised and captured on the campaign. An ambush was made, which was very successful, though Michael himself escaped on to a ship and got back to the capital, and his Varangians, guarding the army's treasury and the Emperor's plate, as well as Azz-ed-Din, succeeded with a great effort in gaining the shelter of the small fortified town of Ainos, which was then besieged by Constantine. They withstood several fierce Bulgarian assaults on the town castle, but the fortifications were in a bad state of repair, and they doubted whether they would be able to hold out for a prolonged siege. When Constantine offered them their lives and the possession of the town if they handed

---

[1] Prostagma of Michael VIII, in A. Heisenberg, *Aus der Geschichte und Literatur der Paläologenzeit*, Munich, 1920, 39 and 61–2; line 30 refers to εἰς τὸ καβαλίκευμα ἵνα ἔχῃς Βαράγγους, while l. 49 refers to ἀκολουθῶσι κοινῶς οἱ τῶν ἀμφοτέρων Ἐγκλινοβάραγγοι καὶ προοδεύωσι καὶ Βαρδαριῶται. See also Vasilev, 'The opening stages of the Anglo-Saxon immigration to Byzantium', *Annales de l'Institut Kondakov*, IX (1937), 59.

[2] D. J. Geanakoplos, *The Emperor Michael VIII Palaeologos and the West*, Cambridge, Mass., 1962, 174 and refs. there.

[3] *Chronicle of the Morea*, ed. J. Schmidt, London, 1904, 286–7.

over Azz-ed-Din and his retinue, they eventually followed the advice of the Bishop of Ainos and gave in, surrendering the Sultan and his men, whereupon Constantine went away with his force. On the following day a galley sent by the Emperor came to their relief, whereupon they returned to the capital with the army treasury and the Imperial plate, to face a furious Emperor, who had the guards flogged, dressed in women's clothes and led on donkeys round the streets of the City, while he had the Bishop of Ainos charged before a court.[1]

In 1272, when Michael VIII had his son Andronicus crowned as co-Emperor, he took steps to deprive his brother John, the sebastocrator, of the marks of Imperial privilege that he had kept until then, taking especial care to remove his life-guards. It is unlikely that these will have included any Varangians, however, as their number is bound to have been small at best, and their especial task was to guard the Imperial person and, since John III's day, the Imperial treasury.[2]

In his long and tortuous negotiations with the Papacy Michael met with much opposition from both clergy and laity whenever he attempted to move towards any reunion, and from time to time he met such opposition with force. Thus he imprisoned the future Patriarch John Bekkos in the Tower of Anemas in 1273, putting him under the guard of Varangians (doubtless to frighten him into submission).[3]

In 1280 the Emperor suspected that John, the son of the Despot Michael, was attempting to conspire against him. He had him and the monk Theodore Cotys arrested, and accused them of conspiracy, which both denied strenuously. Michael refused, however, to believe that they had never discussed anything more than buying and selling property and other innocuous things, and ordered the Varangians to tie Cotys up for torture, which so frightened the monk that he fell down dead.[4]

After Michael VIII's death in 1282 Byzantium soon lost its last vestige of standing as a political power, and after only a few years of the sole reign of his son and successor, Andronicus II, the Varangian guards were to be found in such references as there are either as ceremonial troops standing around the throne on such very few occasions as the Byzantine Emperor was still able to keep up his full formality or, last vestige of their grimmest function, as prison guards and assistants to legal inquisition. Of this last duty there is an anecdote from the reign of Andronicus II which shows it in action.[5]

---

[1] Pachymeres, *De Michaele et Andronico Palaeologis*, I, 229–40.
[2] Pachymeres, *De Michaele et Andronico Palaeologis*, I, 321.
[3] Pachymeres, *De Michaele et Andronico Palaeologis*, I, 378; there he calls the Varangians Κελταί; cf. also A. van Millingen, *Byzantine Constantinople*, London, 1899, 159.
[4] Pachymeres, *De Michaele et Andronico Palaeologis*, I, 484–6; again the Varangians are called Κελταί.   [5] Pachymeres, *De Michaele et Andronico Palaeologis*, II, 73ff.

The sebastocrator of Neopatras, Michael, son of John Angelos Ducas, tried to gain power in Thessalonica, but was betrayed into the hands of the Emperor, who put him into the custody of a Varangian officer named Erris ("Ερρις; i.e. Harry). Michael's sister was also in custody, and it is said that she and Erris fell in love, which her brother discovered, whereupon he determined to use this fact to his own advantage. Finally he promised to marry her to Erris if he could get them out of their imprisonment, which the latter promised to do. Two Varangians were on duty in the prison as guards (the place appears to have been in some extension of the Emperor's palace), also a young lad who acted as the prisoners' servant. As he did not trust his guards to join with him in the escape plan, Erris called them in one by one and killed them, but the boy was suffered to live, as they felt that it was cowardly to kill such a young lad, and so he was merely tied up and gagged, and left behind as the three escaped. Since Erris was a high-ranking officer, the guards at the outer gates recognized him and thought that he was moving the prisoners from one place of confinement to another, and let them pass without hindrance through the gates. The fugitives reached a ship which Erris had got Michael's friends and relatives in the City to make ready, and set sail for Euboea, where they hoped to find safety with Michael's sister, who ruled the district under the protection of the Venetians. Almost as soon as they had weighed anchor, however, a furious storm blew up, and finally they had to seek shelter in the harbour of Rodosto by the Sea of Marmora. Unfortunately for them, there were in the town soldiers who knew of their escape, and the three fugitives were re-arrested and brought back to Constantinople, where Michael was put back in custody. We hear no more of the rogue Erris, but may assume with some certainty that he was executed for treason. Michael Ducas now remained in prison for another eight years, when he made another attempt to escape, this time by trying to set fire to the prison, which was near the Emperor's own quarters, but Andronicus himself noticed the fire, and sent for men to put it out. To do this they broke into the prison, only to find Ducas there with a drawn sword. He killed the first man who entered, whereupon the Emperor sent for the Varangians, who killed him with their axes.

On the death of his son and co-Emperor, Michael IX, Andronicus II was obliged by a strong faction of his supporters to accept his grandson, Andronicus (III) as co-Emperor in turn. At his coronation, John Cantacuzenos informs us, there was some of the old splendour still to be seen, as around the throne in the Hagia Sophia stood 'the so-called Varangians with their axes, and young men of noble blood, some splendidly armed, others unarmed'.[1] The peaceful coexistence of the two did not last long, however, and in 1328 Andronicus III forced his grandfather to abdicate (on which occasion, we are told by Gregoras, the old man was abandoned even by his guards), while in 1330, when the young Emperor was seriously ill and his partisans were afraid that his grandfather might attempt to resume the throne if the grandson should die, the Varangians were used as a threat to compel the old man to renounce all worldly interest by becoming a monk.[2]

On the death of Andronicus III his nine year old son was proclaimed Emperor as John V. The real ruler was, however, Andronicus's minister, John Cantacuzenos, who took charge of the safety of the young Emperor and his brother Manuel, setting five hundred men to guard them, and adding to this force 'axe-bearing Varangians, as many as were then in service'.[3]

From then on, however, the mention as such of the Varangians ceases for all practical purposes. Apart from the dissertation on court ceremonial attributed to Pseudo-Codinus, which will be examined in the next chapter, there are no references in the documents from the reigns of John V, Andronicus IV, Manuel II or his sons which indicate any Scandinavian or English military presence in the fading Byzantine army. On the other hand, there is a note by Ducas which suggests that their functions had been taken over by Cretans, who may thus have been the last to bear the responsibilities of the former Varangians. When Murad II overcame his brother Mustapha in the struggle for the Ottoman throne after the death of Mohammed I, he was not a little displeased with the co-Emperor John VIII for supporting the pretender. The Emperors sent the theologian Corax on an embassy in an attempt to placate the Sultan, but the embassy had no success, and Corax was duly accused of treason and of pocketing for himself the costly presents sent as emollients to the Sultan. Manuel II had him arrested during the investigation of the matter; the Cretans who guarded the palace doors now demanded to be allowed to torture him to obtain a confession, and were allowed to do so. Ducas describes them thus:

---

[1] John Cantacuzenos, *Opera*, ed. L. Schopen (CSHB), Bonn, 1828–32, I, 200.

[2] Gregoras, *Byzantina historia*, ed. L. Schopen (CSHB), Bonn, 1829–30, I, 298; cf. also A. E. Laiou, *Constantinople and the Latins*, Cambridge, Mass., 1972, 284ff.

[3] John Cantacuzenos, *Opera*, I, 560. This sentence has been misunderstood, as in Pontanus' translation in CSHB, to mean that the Varangians numbered 500, but the words ὅσοι ἦσαν show clearly that Cantacuzenos did not remember how many Varangians there were on that occasion; on the other hand the courtiers and the servants may well have numbered 500 *in all*; also, a little later (II, 14) Cantacuzenos noted that when he left the Imperial palace he had 500 men there as a defence force, but that he had taken most of them away and left just a few 'who were accustomed to be there'; these will have been the Varangians, and they were clearly much fewer in number.

'The Cretans are always most loyal and have a God-given enthusiasm for protecting churches and holy things, also the dignity of the Emperor and the glory of the City.' The examination ended in the purported discovery of Corax's guilt, and the gifts for the Sultan were also found, whereupon he was condemned to be blinded, and the sentence was carried out by the Cretans at the palace gate with such brutality that Corax died from it a few days later.[1]

After this event, if we accept the Cretans as the last successors of the Varangians, we have only one more definite reference, this time from the final fall of Constantinople. Phrantzes, describing the débâcle, speaks particularly of the excellent defence by the Cretans who defended the towers of Basil, Leo and Alexander near Blachernae. They repelled all attacks by the Turks and fought with such fervour and bravery as to excite the admiration of Mohammed II, who, when they were finally obliged to surrender after all was lost, gave them their lives and permitted them to sail away home unmolested and with all honour.[2] These men are described as sailors and, if the Cretans were the last functioning force of Varangians, they would then, as their predecessors habitually did, have served in the last Byzantine navy before being allocated the defence of these towers of the Emperor's palace in the final struggle. If this is so, then the end of the second regiment of Varangians was at least more glorious than that of the first, who surrendered so tamely to the robbers of 1204.

---

[1] Ducas, *Historia Byzantina*, ed. I. Bekker (CSHB), Bonn, 1834, 184–7.

[2] G. Phrantzes, *Chronicon*, ed. I. Bekker (CSHB), Bonn, 1838, 287–8. A valuable Cretan text corroborating Phrantzes is found in R. Browning, 'A note on the capture of Constantinople in 1453', *Byzantion*, 22 (1952), 379–87.

8

The Emperor, his Court, his guards and his city

In the eyes of his subjects the Emperor of the East was the visible symbol of Divine rule, and his Empire the visible image of the Heavenly Kingdom. This view is found among the Norse sources for Varangian history too, thus Þórarinn loftunga refers to God in a poem as *Grikklands gætir*, 'the Guardian of Greece'. There can be no doubt that the Westerners who came from far away, attracted by the report of the splendour of the Basileus and his enormous wealth, would be even more impressed when they saw the reality, especially in the golden age of the Macedonian dynasty. To them the *stólkonungr*, their corruption of the title they had picked up in Russia on their way (*stolnyi knyaz*), would indeed be the greatest of monarchs, and the wealth which he showered on them be amply sufficient to make them his loyal servants, alike in war and peace.

It is of course as warriors that these men came to settle in Byzantium, and the military aspect of the Empire was what concerned them most. During the greater part of the Varangian period, i.e. from the time of Constantine VII to the rape of the City in 1204, the Emperors were frequently generals of genius, such as Nicephorus Phocas, Basil II, Michael IV and the two first Comnenian Emperors, and even when less warlike sovereigns ruled there were commanders of distinction found in the Byzantine forces such as John Curcuas or George Maniaces, or the great Admiral Basil Boioannes. It is therefore entirely proper to take a look at the situation in which the Varangians performed their duties.

Except when the Emperor commanded a campaign in person, the Grand Domestic was Commander-in-Chief of the Byzantine forces; as a recognition of this, even when the Emperor commanded, he had

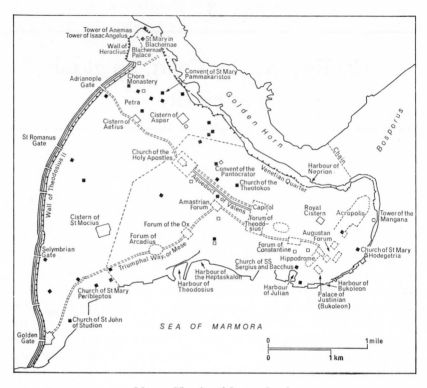

Map 3   The city of Constantinople

certain privileges in camp. Under him, the *Droungarios* of the *Vigla* was
responsible for order in the camp at night. He set up the guard-posts
round the camp, placing a hundred members of the Hetairia as an outer
ring round the Emperor's (or general's) tent, and another hundred as
the inner ring of guards; after they entered the Hetairia (and from the
reign of Basil II onwards) this was very likely the special duty of the
Varangians, whose own tents will have been near the Imperial one.
Whenever the Emperor stayed the night on a campaign in a provincial
town, its keys were handed to the Varangians each night for security;[1]
a curious modern reminder of this was the Danish custom in Copenhagen down to the death of Frederik VI (†1839) that when the King
was in residence, the keys of the city were delivered up to him personally each night. One point of interest in the Varangians' terms of
service was that if any mercenary soldier died childless while still in

---

[1] John Cantacuzenos, *Opera*, ed. L. Schopen (CSHB), Bonn, 1828–32), 1, 389.

service, the Grand Domestic inherited his arms and the horse assigned or belonging to him.

In the heavily-regulated daily life of the Emperor, of which we have two very detailed descriptions, the *De Ceremoniis* of Constantine VII and the *De Officiis* of Pseudo-Codinus, representing conveniently the state of the Court at the two ends of the time-span that we have investigated, the Varangians played a not inconsiderable part and are found in various places under various titles. Their principal duty was the guardianship of the Emperor's person; though in the case of certain exceptionally favoured persons, such as John Palaeologus, brother of Michael VIII (see above, p. 173) detachments of the life-guards might be granted to them as marks of their dignity and Imperial favour, the Varangians were very strictly reserved to the service of the Basileus himself; we may note in this context that in the last negotiations between Andronicus II and his grandson for peace between them, the young Emperor made the point as a mark of his restraint that he had not brought either his spear-carriers or his Varangians with him.[1]

According to Pseudo-Codinus, the Varangians were assigned guard-duty over the Emperor's *kellion* (his office, where he signed edicts or other important documents of state) and were also on duty in the *Triklinion*, which became by his day the chief ceremonial reception chamber in Blachernae.[2] On such occasions, when the Emperor received dignitaries in state, the Grand Domestic or the Protostrator would bear the Emperor's sword in the entrance and exit processions, and hold it during the ceremonies, while a high officer of the guards, after Basil II's time presumably a Varangian, bore his banner and shield, the Varangians processing around the *dibellion*, and standing around it during the reception. When the Emperor went to Divine Service in state he was accompanied by Varangians, and special regulations governed how far they were to march with him on each particular occasion in the year; thus on Candlemas Day he rode from the palace to the church of St Mary in Blachernae, when the Varangians, their axes on their shoulders, accompanied him up to the Hypsela gate and thence to the church where, however, they did not wait for him, but returned in order to the Hypsela and received the Emperor there when the service was over, accompanying him back to the place where he dismounted.[3] On the Nativity of St John the Baptist they accompanied him in similar style to the Petra monastery, and on the Decollation to

---

[1] Gregoras, *Byzantina historia*, ed. L. Schopen (CSHB), Bonn, 1829–30, I, 398.
[2] Pseudo-Codinus, *De Officiis* (i.e. *DO*), ed. J. Verpeaux (CSHB), Bonn, 1835, 179–80.
[3] *DO*, 243–4.

the Studion; on the Feast of Commemoration of the Deposition of the Blessed Virgin's robe in the church of St Mary Blachernae (2 July), they also accompanied him there for a service.

At the coronation of an Emperor the Varangians walked on either side of him, together with 100 young men chosen from the noblest families of the Empire.[1] When the Emperor was lifted up on a shield to be acclaimed before the coronation itself, which was done under the direction of the Patriarch and the high officials of the state by the guards, he was carried out by them to be shown to the people outside for their acclamation. After the service the Varangians then joined the courtiers and the youths who had formed the guard of honour with them in the palace, where the Emperor scattered gold and silver coins among them from his lap, for which the assembly duly scrambled like Westminster schoolboys for their Shrove Tuesday pancake.

On the greater feasts of the church the Emperor gave great banquets, during which the great personages of the state and the ambassadors of foreign powers came before him to bring him good wishes; on such occasions the Varangians also paid him their compliments in their own language – in English, we are told by Pseudo-Codinus,[2] as will have been the case after the disappearance of the Norse element, though the Scandinavians will clearly have used their own tongue in their day – and beat on their shields. On the next day a great dinner was held, when the Varangians were fed from the Emperor's own table; the food was handed to them by the Grand Domestic, while he was the only person who was served by the Emperor himself.

The Varangians got a special mention in the Palm Sunday festivities. During the previous week the passage from the palace in Blachernae to the church was decorated, and on the Feast of St Lazarus (the eve of Palm Sunday) the floor was strewn with branches of myrtle, laurel and olive. When the Emperor and his suite have passed through to the church and returned 'a boy pulls out one of the branches as a signal that the Emperor has given permission for all the decorations of the passage to be rifled: the Varangians do this, with the other soldiers on duty in the Palace'.[3] This will have been a valuable perquisite for the guards, as the branches may have been blessed, and so saleable in the City at a good price, while the hangings, cloths and other decorations will have been of considerable intrinsic value.

At Christmas the Varangians took part in the high festivities. One of the ceremonies of the day was a parade in Blachernae which is described by Pseudo-Codinus. He states that the life-guards paraded

---

[1] DO, 264; see also Cantacuzenos, *Opera*, I, 203 and 401; Gregoras, *Byzantina historia*, III, 189.
[2] DO, 209–10, 'ἤγουν ἐγκλινιστί'.   [3] DO, 226.

in the palace – presumably in one of the great halls or the courtyards – before the Imperial banner and twelve other banners bearing images of the saints, and that in the great days, when the guard consisted of 6000 men, 500 men paraded before each banner.[1] If he means only the Varangians, then this would suggest that he is referring to the period of the reign of Basil II, when the Varangians were made up of the 6000 men sent to him by St Vladimir, but this is not very likely, as we have seen that this force was divided up and used here and there according to the military needs of the state, as garrison or field troops. It may be that the total of all the guards' units at this time was 6000, made up of divisions of 500, as we are told of the Excubitores (see above, p. 19); we may also note in support of this the narrative of the battle of Beroë in 1122, when John II had with him 480 Varangians as life-guards. This suggests that unless he wanted a particularly strong force of his best fighters, the Emperor normally took only a limited number, probably usually one division of *c*. 500 men, with him on campaign.[2]

In church the Emperor sat on a high throne, behind which stood specially delegated Varangians, their axes in their hands until the Basileus had sat down, when they raised them on to their shoulders.[3]

At Christmas there was also the curious custom recorded by Constantine VII as the Dance of the Goths, which, it has been suggested, was performed by Russians. As the reviser has pointed out elsewhere, however, this is highly unlikely, being much more likely to be a relic of the days of Theodosius I, when Goths were common mercenaries in the Roman armies, and their barbaric dances a relish to the Romans.[4]

The Varangians appear to have had special guard-rooms in all parts of the Imperial palaces for the part of the regiment on guard-duty there. Thus we know that they took over the old quarters of the Excubitores, whom they replaced, and called them *skipt*: there is also the matter of the graffiti in the Bukoleon, which could indicate the work of a vandalistic Varangian, and there is no doubt, as we have seen, that they had guard-quarters in Blachernae after this became the chief residence of the Emperors; further, as we have discovered, they had quarters in the Mangana in the reign of Alexius I. Where the *regimental* HQ was,

---

[1] *DO*, 196.

[2] This is discussed at length by Vasilevskii (*Труды*, I, 373ff.), who maintains that the number 6000 refers to the original regiment of 'Ρῶσι in Basil II's service.　　[3] *DO*, 197–8.
'Constantine Porphyrogennetos, *De Ceremoniis*, ed. A. Vogt (Classiques Budé), Paris, 1935–40 (i.e. *DC* (Budé)), II, 182ff.; also 'Commentaire', 186ff.; see also B. S. Benedikz, 'The origin and development of the Varangian regiment in the Byzantine army', *BZ* 62 (1969), 23.

however, is far from being quite certain, though we get some indication of their location at the end of the story of Alexius III and the rebellion of John Pachys. While the Emperors lived in the old set of palaces, the *pólútir enar fornu* of Norse sources, as at least one scholar has suggested, the HQ was near the church of SS Sergius and Bacchus,[1] while others have considered that the place-name *Vlanga*, still used of a quarter of the City near the Sea of Marmora,[2] is derived from a Varangian presence there at one time; certainly there was a harbour there (the Harbour of Theodosius) at one time, and an arsenal near the waterfront, and the haven for the war-galleys, the Heptaskalon, is on the doorstep, but the present author considers that this is not very likely. Later on, it was suggested by B. G. Baker that the Varangians' headquarters were in the Tower of Isaac Angelus near Blachernae.[3] If this was so, then the Tower of Anemas belonged to this complex, for we know that political prisoners were often kept there, and as we have seen from the surviving evidence, it was one of the principal duties of the 'Varangians of the City' to look after such persons, as well as to undertake the less pleasant tasks of judicial interrogation or punishment such as torture, amputation of limbs or blinding. As we have seen (pp. 162–3) the most likely place – at any rate in the latter days of the Empire – was near to the Mangana and the Neorion; this is supported not only by the actions of Alexius III, but by the story of the departure of Haraldr Sigurðarson from the City; his galleys had to pass over the chain across the Golden Horn, which, if the regimental HQ had been by the Heptaskalon, on the Sea of Marmora, they would not have had to do. A further support of this is the point indirectly supported by the duties of the Varangians in Magnesia and Astyza, that because of their incorruptibility, the regiment would have been used to look after the Imperial treasury in Constantinople, and this was also near to the Mangana, though the point is not made for more than it is worth.

The regimental discipline appears to have been very strict, as we may see from the anecdote about the soldier who was killed by the woman whom he tried to rape. On the other hand it is quite clear that members of the regiment were not tried by ordinary military judges, but had themselves the right to try their companions for breaches of discipline; we see this from the story of the attempt on the life of Nicephorus III, though this story reveals that the final authority rested, as in all matters of the realm, with the Emperor himself.

[1] Dr A. M. Schneider in a letter to the author, dated 2 September 1937.
[2] See map in Nomides, 'Η ζοωδοχως Πηγή, Istanbul, 1937; also A. Bélin, *La Latinité de Constantinople*, Paris, 1894; also R. M. Dawkins, 'The later history of the Varangians', *Journal of Roman Studies*, XXXVII (1947), 44–5.
[3] B. G. Baker, *The Walls of Constantinople*, London, 1910, 246.

The main weapon of the Varangians was the one-edged axe, made in the form of a spear with an axe-blade below the point and a grip on the handle, as may be seen from the seals of the Grand Interpreter of the Regiment in the days of the Palaeologi.[1] As, however, there has been no such weapon discovered in any Norse, English or Byzantine weapon hoard, Dr A. Alföldi has maintained that this picture is not that of a real Varangian axe of the day, but the symbol of a lictor; this has been supported by Dr W. Holmqvist.[2] It is possible to surmise, and this is supported by the statement of *Advice*, on Haraldr Sigurðarson's rank, that when Varangians reached the dignity of *Manglavites* they also inherited the lictorial duties, preceding the Emperors in procession and clearing the way for them with their fasces, but the illustration itself provides a powerful objection to this argument in the shape of the spear-point on the end of the handle, and the curved handle which is never found on lictorial symbols. The present author feels therefore that it is most likely that the image on the seal is a correct representation of the Varangian axe, though the transverse lines on the handle may well be remnants of a lictorial symbol which was altered upon their replacement by the Varangians as the Imperial guards, and made to fit the shape of the axe-handle. On the other hand, axes with curved handles were known among Norse vikings; thus *The War of the Gaedhil and the Gall* refers to the fact that the viking Brodir (the slayer of King Brian Boru) fought at the Battle of Clontarf with an axe with a handle in the middle of the shaft.[3] It is also worth noting that similar axes, the glaives of Scottish mediaeval weaponry, are to be found in collections of mediaeval weapons in Scotland; in them the handle is on mid-shaft, with a hand-guard to protect the user's hands from glancing blows along the handle.

Besides their axes the Varangians will have carried spears and swords, the former when in service as cavalry. In this respect they appear to have had an ambivalent status, since at Dyrrhachium they arrived on horseback but fought as infantry, while at Petroë they fought as cavalry (see above, p. 108). For their defence they had coats of mail,

---

[1] The seal has been reproduced and discussed in G. Schlumberger, *Sigillographie de l'empire byzantin*, Paris, 1884, 350, and a description is added in the same author's *Un empereur au Xe siècle: Nicéphore Phocas*, Paris, 1890, 49.

[2] Dr Alföldi discussed the question with Dr Holmqvist in Stockholm shortly after 1945, and Dr Holmqvist relayed their conclusions to Dr Blöndal. (Information from Dr Holmqvist: the reviser is greatly obliged to Dr Olof von Feilitzen for his help in elucidating the source.) The reviser, having examined the seal, is inclined to support their conclusions.

[3] *War of the Gaedhil and the Gall*, ed. J. K. Todd, London, 1867, 203; cf. also B. Bjarnason, *Nordboernes legemlige Uddannelse i Oldtiden*, Copenhagen, 1905, 17; and H. Falk, *Altnordische Waffenkunde*, Christiania, 1914, 112.

greaves and steel helmets or caps and round shields. The mailed coats could be of very great strength and made with great skill, as in the case of Haraldr Sigurðarson, whose coat *Emma*, which protected him down to the calves, was made in Byzantium.[1]

Beating on their shields in honour of the Emperor was a gesture which the Varangians inherited from the Goths, and used on occasions of ceremony, as when Michael VII sought their help (see above, p. 114).

The Varangians kept their arms under strict control; the *vopnaþing* recorded in *Grettis saga* (an item which has a fair degree of probability) is most unlikely to have been an isolated incident, but rather a form of regular kit inspection at which the men's arms and armour were examined and any worn or defective items put right.[2]

The commander of the regiment was by title *Akoluthos*, or in Latin *proximus*, being so named as he walked next to the Emperor himself on occasions of ceremony. This post existed long before the Varangians became a part of the life-guards; previously it will have been borne by the commander of the *Vigla*. This officer is mentioned in various places in Constantine VII's *De Ceremoniis*; among his duties is the ordering of the court processions on certain days;[3] on those occasions we are told that he bore on his shoulder a *manglavion* and an axe, and he is then named *Droungarios*, which was the title of the commander of the *Vigla*.

From such names of these commanders as have survived, we can see that this post was normally given only to exceptionally trustworthy or able officers, sometimes even to members of the Imperial family, as in the case of John Comnenus, brother of Isaac I. They were used by the Emperors for important embassies; thus Manuel I sent the *Akoluthos* Basil Cumatenus to inspect the daughters of Prince Raymond of Antioch, of whose beauty he had had a report, and so had a mind to ask for one in marriage,[4] and another holder of the post, the *Akoluthos* Aaron, had a seat at a General Synod of the Church. There may have been times, of course, when there may have been a foreign commander in this post, as in the case of the egregious Nabites, whose military bungling may well have been the cause of the composition of *Advice* (or at any rate of the strong remonstrance against the granting of high military or civil offices to barbarians). It must be admitted, however, that the

---

[1] *Flateyjarbók*, III, 418, *niðr á skó*; *Ljósvetninga saga*, ed. B. Sigfússon (Íslenzk Fornrit x), Reykjavík, 1940, 104, *á mitt bein*.

[2] *Grettis saga*, ed. G. Jónsson (Íslenzk Fornrit VII), Reykjavík, 1937, 272.

[3] Constantine Porphyrogennetos, *De Ceremoniis*, ed. J. J. Reiske (CSHB), Bonn, 1828, I, 522; see also Reiske's commentary, *ibid.*, II, 606. In the register of the Court Officials (*ibid.*, I, 718, the ἀκόλουθος is regarded as one of the subordinates of the δρουγγάριος τῶν ἀριθμῶν (cf. *ibid.*, II, 846). From this Reiske deduces that the Hetairia was at that time part of the 'Αριθμός.

[4] Cinnamus, *Epitome…historiarum*, ed. A. Meineke (CSHB), Bonn, 1836, 210.

wording of our source is not such as to enable us to state categorically that Nabites *was* an *Akoluthos* in rank. The words ὁ τῶν Βαραγγίων ἡγεμών and ἄρχων τῆς Βαραγγίας[1] can equally well suggest that he was merely the commander of the detachment of Varangians from outside the City who accompanied Alexius on these expeditions. In view of his influence, however, it seems far more likely both to the author and the reviser of the present work that he was in fact commander of the actual life-guards and these will at least have been with Alexius on the expedition against the Pechenegs. Later on, however, as the Varangians declined from being a crack regiment to the less spectacular state of palace guards, keepers of political suspects and police thugs, the *Akoluthos* also lost position in the Byzantine hierarchy; in Pseudo-Codinus we find him as the fiftieth man in the order of precedence, a great fall from his former importance.[2]

As in the case of all the mercenaries, the Varangians needed interpreters, both for daily events and for negotiations. These were in the charge of the Grand Interpreter (*Megalodihermeneutes*) of the Varangians, a personage of considerable standing, the seal of one of whom is mentioned earlier in this chapter. This official bore a magnificent uniform, a mantle embroidered in gold, and carried a staff as the symbol of his office. The *Akoluthos* bore at court a similar uniform, but no staff, and so was in all probability armed. The *Spatharokandidatoi* wore a splendid chain of their rank, the *maniakeion*, round their necks. Other officers assigned to the Varangians in Byzantine sources were *Primikerioi*, probably so named because their names were the first in the army lists.[3]

The Varangian regiment had a church where the soldiers worshipped. Norse sources state that it was dedicated to St Olaf, and, as we have seen, it was supposed to have been erected as a result of the vow made by the regiment in the battle *á Pézínavöllum*. We must note, however, that Cinnamus, who describes the fight most fully on the Byzantine side, does not mention St Olaf, but attributes the victory to the prayer made by John II to the Blessed Virgin Mary. If this is so, then we may surmise that since the Emperor himself took a part in the building of this church for the Varangians, the Theotokos would not have been omitted; moreover, one version of the text of the saga of St Olaf (in *Bergsbók*) says outright 'he [the Emperor] had a church made and dedicated to

---

[1] Anna Comnena, *L'Alexiade* (hereafter *Alexiad*), ed. B. Leib, Paris, 1937–76, I, 155 and II, 97.
[2] *DO*, 184.
[3] *DO*, 179, 301, 305, 309.

the Blessed Virgin Mary and to the Blessed King Olaf'.¹ Certainly, the oldest Varangian church that we know of from Byzantine sources was dedicated to the *Panhagia Varangiotissa*; it was probably this one that was built after John II's victory at Beroë. Nor can we entirely ignore the Norse tradition about King Olaf's sword, Hneitir, being kept there above the altar as a relic, as we have the direct testimony of Eindriði the Young for this, as recorded by Einar Skúlason in *Geisli* (st. 50);

> Yfirskjöldungr lét jöfra
> Oddhríðar þar síðan
> Garðs of golli vörðu
> Grand altári standa.

The Lord of Kings [the Emperor] let the maker of danger in the storm of points [the sword] stand above the gold-encrusted altar.²

We find this church mentioned in a synodical document of the Oecumenical Patriarchate in February 1361,³ when it was no longer being used as a Guards' Chapel, but had been attached to a nunnery. It would appear that the nave had been destroyed by this time (the most probable occasion being during the destruction wrought by the Franco-Italian wreckers in 1204). This house of nuns is spoken of as a small house, 'behind the choir of the Hagia Sophia', i.e. to the north-east of the Cathedral. Both nunnery and church have long since vanished, probably in the alterations made at the behest of Mohammed II and his successors when the cathedral was turned into a mosque.⁴

The special connection between the Blessed Virgin and the Varangians may be seen from two other documentary points. In Byzantine Italy there was the church of Santa Maria dei Guaranghi near Taranto (see above, p. 111) and from a deed of gift by Doge Giacomo Tiepoli of Venice, who donated it to the monastery of St Thomas in Torcello, we find *ecclesiam et claustrum Stae Mariae Varangorum positum in insula Creta* in 1230.⁵ Precisely what the Varangians' connection with this church and monastery was is no longer clear; the most probable explanation seems to the reviser to be that a garrison of Varangians founded them as the result of a pious vow which brought them success in an expedi-

---

¹ *Den store saga om Olaf den Hellige*, ed. O. A. Johnsen and J. Helgason, Oslo, 1941, 834.
² FJ *Skjald* A I 468, B I 439.
³ *Acta et diplomata graeca medii aevi*, ed. F. Miklosich and J. Müller (hereafter MM, *Acta*), Vienna, 1860–90, I, 423ff. In this the supervision of the house is given to one Alexius Sophianus: it refers to a μονύδριον behind the choir of Hagia Sophia 'honoured with the name of the Most Holy Mother of God', ἐπικεκλημένον τῆς Βαραγγιωτίσσης; see also Vasilevskii, *Труды*, I, 277 and 397.   ⁴ See also *Échos de l'Orient*, 1924, 448ff.
⁵ Printed in F. Cornelius, *Ecclesiae Torcellanae*, Venice, 1749, I, 234; see also *ibid.*, I, 192 and L. Santifaller, *Beiträge zur Geschichte des Lateinischen Patriarchats von Konstantinopel (1204–1261)*, Weimar, 1938, 97 and 99.

tion, or, alternatively, that the church had been the chapel of a Varangian garrison and kept the connection in its name after it became part of the monastic foundation.

It is worth noting also that there is no mention at all in the *Leiðarvísir* of Abbot Nikulás Bergsson, composed in 1154–9, nor yet in the continuation of this work, which was certainly written before 1204, of any church dedicated to King Olaf, nor of his sword as a relic, though we must also bear in mind that there appears to be a section missing where we would expect these descriptions to be, and so this evidence does not possess any real weight either way.[1]

In respect of the English Varangians who began to pour into Byzantium after the Norman conquest of England in 1066, we have some evidence for a church set apart for them as a chapel. In the first instance, Goscelin has a story of a noble Englishman who had a church built in Constantinople and dedicated to SS Nicholas and Augustine of Canterbury; this Englishman was said to have obtained the Emperor's favour and so married a rich woman of high family, after which he had the church built and dedicated to these two saints, alongside his house; on the southern side was an icon of St Augustine, and on the northern one of St Nicholas. This church became popular with the English in Byzantium, and after the Varangian regiment had become entirely English in composition, this church became their chapel.[2]

By chance, we have some suggestion of the whereabouts of this church. To the south of Blachernae were the ruins of the Bogdan Serai, the former palace of the Governors of Moldavia, which was burned down in a disastrous fire in 1784, and was never rebuilt. This church has been held by Canon C. G. Curtis to have been dedicated to SS Nicholas and Augustine of Canterbury, by Paspatis to St Nicholas alone, and by Mordtmann to St John the Baptist. Mordtmann's reason is that the rocks nearby prove that this is the church of St John *in Petra*.[3] Van Millingen examined it in 1912, and found the ruins being used for a cowshed, the author looked at them in 1937, and found them empty. It is difficult to make up one's mind as to the probabilities, but one additional factor should be remembered here. One of the towers of the land wall of the City, between the Adrianople gate and the Topkapi, had built into it a number of gravestones with inscriptions com-

[1] *Alfræði íslenzk*, ed. K. Kålund, Copenhagen, 1908–18, I, 25–6; see also *Hauksbók*, ed. F. Jónsson and F. Jónsson, Copenhagen, 1892–6, 177.

[2] Goscelin in *Liber Miraculorum (Acta Sanctorum*, Majus VI, 410 (26 Maii); cf. also Ducange, *Constantinopolis Christiana*, Paris, 1680, IV, 130, and references to St Nicholas in G. Anrich, *Ἅγιος Νικόλαος*, Leipzig, 1913–17.

[3] A. van Millingen, *Byzantine Churches in Constantinople*, London, 1912, 280–6; A. G. Paspatis *The Great Palace of Constantinople*, London, 1895, 360; A. D. Mordtmann, *Esquisse topographique de Constantinople*, Lille, 1892, 75.

memorating Varangians and (probably) members of other units of the guards.[1] These stones were there until 1865, when the then British envoy asked the Porte to allow them to be moved into the British cemetery in Scutari. A Turkish official who had his knife into the envoy forestalled this by having the stones taken away and used for building materials, and the copies of the inscriptions which had been made were destroyed in a fire in 1870. Robert Byron, who followed this story up in his book *The Byzantine Achievement*, then added a further mystery by stating that the documentation on the case was to be found 'in a prison in Cambridge'. A lengthy search by the reviser in all imaginable corners of the city and University of Cambridge has however failed to bring any sort of documentation on these mysterious gravestones to light, and he is seriously inclined to regard this statement of Byron's as a will-o'-the-wisp.[2] Worse, a trek made on his behalf by Dr Jonathan Shepard in 1974 showed that the modern vandals, the 'site rede-velopers', had entirely destroyed whatever archaeological relics there may have been there.

A little east of Bogdan Serai stands the church of St Mary Pamma-karistos, in a vault by which was found a stone with the inscription ΙΝΓ BARF. This inscription, noted and published by C. G. Curtis and S. Aristarkes in 1885, was interpreted by them as an abbreviation for ΙΝΓ[ΛΙΝΟΥ] ΒΑΡ [ΑΓΓΟΥ] Ε [ ], 'English Varangians',[3] but the pre-sent author finds this too laborious an explanation, when a much simpler one would be the Norse name *Ingvar E*..., the rest having either been lost or worn off by the time that the decipherment was made. This stone was reported by Bélin as having been transferred to a museum in Stuttgart, but so far no Stuttgart museum has admitted the possession of such a stone, and as so much damage was done in the town in two world wars, the likelihood is that it, too, has been irretrievably lost.[4]

It is very natural for mercenary troops to be unpopular in the country in which they do their service. The Varangians were, admittedly, notable for their fidelity to the reigning Emperor, and the occasions

---

[1] A. Bélin, *La Latinité de Constantinople*, 20; he considers that these had come from some-where in the Bogdan Serai; see also E. Pears, *The Fall of Constantinople*, London, 1903, 154 n.

[2] R. Byron, *The Byzantine Achievement*, London, 1929, 147 f.n. The reviser is greatly obliged to Professor Bruce Dickins for his help in searching for the mythical 'prison Archive'. R. M. Dawkins ('The later history of the Varangians'), is also sceptical of Byron.

[3] C. G. Curtis and S. Aristarkes, Ἀνέκδοτοι ἐπιγραφαὶ Βυζαντίου, Ἑλληνικὸς Φιλολογικὸς Σύλλογος (Ἰστανβούλι), XVI (1885), παράρτημα, 3–39, esp. 36 n.

[4] Bélin, *La Latinité de Constantinople*, 20; cf. also Dawkins, 'The later history of the Varan-gians', n. 13.

when they failed so rare as to be notorious, such as the division of the
loyalty of the regiment during the revolt that deposed Michael V, the
drunken assault on Nicephorus III or the amorous dereliction of his
duty by Harry the Englishman under Andronicus II. On the other
hand, the high social position, high salary and high perquisites that
went with the post were sure to make a Varangian the object of envy
to plain citizens of the Empire. Moreover, it will hardly have increased
their popularity that they were habitually used for the most unpleasant
military and police duties, the sort that scarcely any Greek soldier would
touch, such as the dragging of a Patriarch in full vestments out of
church during service, as Isaac I had them do with Michael Cerularius,
the torture of suspects such as Corax the Theologian, or the more
brutal forms of executions such as the blinding of Michael V and his
uncle. There is a survival of the popular Greek attitude to these barbarians in a children's rhyme noted by Poqueville:[1]

$$\Phi\rho\acute{a}\gamma\gamma o, \ M\acute{a}\rho\alpha\gamma\gamma o,$$
$$\pi\acute{\iota}\tau\zeta\iota, \ \kappa\alpha\kappa\acute{a}\rho\alpha\gamma\gamma o$$

(Frank, Marangian, filth and dirt),

where Μάραγγο is assumed by some (e.g. Vasilevskii) to be a corruption
of Βάραγγος. The present author feels, however, that a more likely
explanation of the rhyme lies in interpreting the second word literally
as the Mod. Gr. word for carpenter, μαραγγός, with the emphasis on
the third syllable, rather than an attempt to take a cue from the
children's dislocation of emphasis to get a rhyme with Φράγγος, by
placing it on the first syllable; in that case the rhyme is merely a
scatological insult to some French carpenter.

Another sign of their unpopularity, and this time a more valuable
one, is in the great twelfth-century poem *Digenes Akritas*, where the
hero rescues his beloved from a band of 300 Varangians. The Akrites
being an independent and bold race, who often had scant respect for
the Emperors whom they officially protected on the eastern borders,
there is little doubt in the author's mind that the frequent presence of
Varangians there on garrison duty was because the Emperors felt it
necessary to have a garrison of exceptional ability to keep the Akrites
themselves in check, and there can hardly have been any very warm
feeling between the two warlike nations.[2]

Finally there is evidence to this effect in a satire regarded as from
the eleventh century, the Διήγησις τοῦ Πωρικολόγου. This mock trial of
the grape in a pseudo-Aesopian quarrel among the fruits is conducted

---

[1] Cf. Vasilevskii, *Τργδυ*, I, 220ff.
[2] Cf. *Digenis Akritas*, ed. and tr. J. Mavrogordato, Oxford, 1956, lxi ff. and lines 61–4.

by the officials appropriate to the case, the ἄρχοντες καὶ ἡγεμόνες, in the chair being old Judge Melon, assisted by such dignitaries as Treasurer Cucumber and the Varangians, whose decision falls against Grape, whereupon he is sentenced to be hung on a vine, cut down with knives and trodden under men's feet, while his blood is to be drunk by men so that they can lose their senses.[1] This short, but entertaining piece is largely a temperance tract as well as a gentle satire on the pomposity and formality of the Court, and it may well be that the presence of the Varangians among the judges is a hit at their reputation as heavy drinkers, as Snorri's remark in the tale of the battle of Beroë (see above, pp. 148ff.) suggests. This work was clearly popular in the Balkans, as there are translations of it into Serbian and Turkish.[2]

A search in the folk tales and folk poetry of the Balkan nations may well yield some Varangian motifs, though so far neither the author nor the reviser of the present study has been able to find any, while place-names may also, when better studied, yield signs of the Varangian occupation of certain areas, as in the cases of Crete and Southern Italy that we have already noted. This is of course less likely as a result of the long Turkish occupation, which had an obliterating effect on many instances of local nomenclature, but one place-name has come to the author's notice from Greece, the name *Arachova*. Rozniecki has pointed out that a Russian *bylina* speaks of a town with this name, which was probably originally called *Varachov* or *Varyagov* 'Town of the Varangians'.[3] It is common in vulgar Russian to elide an initial *v* in front of a vowel, and the poem is not at all clear as to the whereabouts of this town; it may even be referring to a place in Варяггия, i.e. Sweden, but in Greece there are four small townships known to the author with the name *Arachova*, the most famous being Arachova near Mt Parnassus, some 10 km from Delphi, noted for brave men and fair women, folk-dances, good wine and beautiful woven tapestries; Karaiskakis won an outstanding victory over the Turks there in 1826. Next comes Arachova in Laconia, between Argos and Sparta, in a mountain pass which was a fine strategic position; in the Middle Ages a castle stood there which was fiercely fought over when the Frankish knights gained control of this part of the Peloponnese, as is stated in the *Chronicle of Morea*,[4] where the town is sometimes called *Arachova la grande* to differentiate

[1] Cf. K. Krumbacher, *Geschichte der byzantinischer Litteratur*, 2nd ed., Munich, 1897, 883; A. Heisenberg, *Dialekte und Umgangssprache des Neugriechischen*, Munich, 1918, 44; Dawkins, 'Later Varangians', 44.

[2] The Greek text is edited by W. Wagner, *Carmina graeca*, Leipzig, 1874, 199–202; a German translation (from the Turkish) is in *Archiv für slavische Philologie*, 2 (1877), 192ff.

[3] S. Rosniecki, *Væringiske minder i den russiske Heltedigtning*, Copenhagen, 1914, 191ff.

[4] *Chronique de la Morée*, ed. and tr. J. A. Buchon, Paris, 1825, 228ff., 350, 414, 416.

it from the other places of the same name. In the same chronicle it is however also known as *Arachovos* or *Araklivon*, which might point to an older name of purely Greek origin (? Heraclion). Thirdly there is Arachova in Arcadia, between Tripolis and Olympia; near it is another place-name, *Vlankova*, which might also point to a Varangian origin. The fourth place is Arachova in Epiros, on an eponymous mountain. This name has sometimes been derived from O.Slav. *Orechova* from ореч, 'nut', hence as meaning 'Nut-town', but this explanation can hardly apply to all four, and the position of two of them suggests that they were places where the Emperors felt it worth their while to keep good garrisons, and so installed Varangians. The whole area in which these towns are found was largely populated by Slavonic-speaking people, as a horde of Slavonic place-names testifies, supported by a statement by Constantine VII in *De Thematibus* to the effect that a great number of Slavs moved in to the Peloponnese after a great plague in the days of Constantine V, so that the countryside lost its Greek charac-teristics and became Slavonic in temper.[1] The Emperors tried steadily to hellenize these people, as they were a quarrelsome lot and con-stantly giving trouble to their Greek neighbours, and in the end they succeeded. An additional argument for Varangians being in the garri-sons there at this time was also that the early Varangians were them-selves of Russian origin, spoke Russian, and so would have found it easier to maintain communications with the people under their care and to keep order in times of stress than Greek soldiers would have done.

There are a number of Varangian relics in present-day Romania, which have been investigated by A. Philippide, whose principal con-clusions may be noted here.[2]

The word *Baranga* is found in the connotation 'old wolf who howls first of all when the wolves begin to howl', and also in the meaning 'the strongest and bravest bull who leads the way when the herd moves, and is furnished with a bell'. When a countrywoman speaks to a bellowing child she says 'Baranga, why do you howl so?', and when a man curses his wife and bawls after her she says to him 'Why do you roar like a Baranga?' This word appears also as a family surname, as early as the seventeenth century, and as a place-name, a village called Barangi in the districts of Arges, Olt, and Cremenarii-Mostenii; in the last one the inhabitants are called *Barangesti*. There is also a Romanian

[1] *De Thematibus*, ed. A. Pertusi (Studi e Testi, 160), Vatican City, 1952, 90–1; cf. also J. P. Fallmerayer and M. E. Galanopoulos, Βίος Νίκωνος, Athens, 1933, 6–8; also K. Papar-rhigopoulos, Ἱστορία τοῦ Ἑλληνικοῦ ἔθνους, Athens, 1932, III, 465; and M. Vasmer, *Die Slaven in Griechenland.*

[2] A. Philippide, *Barangii in istoria Românilov*, Bucharest, 1916, esp. 16–28.

jest, *Baranga flamanda*, Bulg. Баранга гладина, 'hungry Varangian', used of hearty eaters, which is contracted to Барагладина, 'gipsy'. Whether this jocular name reached Romanian from Bulgarian, or vice versa, is not certain, but the contracted form had completely lost any contact with its origin, and is now only used as a sarcasm analogous to the Mod. Eng. *gyppo* or *diddy* [didicoi]. The probability of the word coming into Romanian from mediaeval Greek is fairly high. What is not likely is the author's original argument that Romanian produced a *b* for *v* mutation.[1]

[1] That is the author's argument, see the Icelandic edition, 308. Professor Robert Browning maintains, with much weight, that this is not possible.

9

Some individual Norse and English Varangians and travellers to Byzantium

This chapter is something of a ragbag, in that it attempts to gather up such evidences from non-Byzantine sources as can be found about Varangians and which are not of a clearly fictitious nature. The bulk of these come, not surprisingly, from Norse sources, and the reliability of these has, naturally enough, been severely impugned in recent years, most notably by Professor P. H. Sawyer.[1] Whatever is found in them, therefore, must always be treated with considerable caution, since they suffer from the double defect of not being certified copies of Public Record Office documents and also, at least in their oldest surviving manuscript versions, many years, indeed some centuries in several cases, later than the events they treat of and their own, often shaky, sources. Nonetheless, there is good reason to believe that a considerable amount of material in them is based on fact and, as Professor J. H. Delargy has shown, it is unwise to distrust an oral tradition wholesale, since where it has been possible to check its descent in recent years, it has very often been found to carry an anecdote, a piece of verse or a longer narrative over remarkably long periods with considerable accuracy.[2] In the interests of attempted completeness, therefore, the evidence of such sources as have not already been drawn upon will now be put together here with such caveats as befit individual cases, excepting the evidence of runic stones and other archaeological material, which will be dealt with in the next chapter.

In terms of chronology the first Varangians to be found in the literary sources are Þorkell leppr Þjóstarsson and his companion Eyvindr

[1] P. H. Sawyer, *The Age of the Vikings*, 2nd ed., London, 1971, 13 and 37ff.
[2] J. H. Delargy, 'The Gaelic story-teller', *Proceedings of the British Academy*, XXXI (1945), 178–220.

Bjarnason, both allegedly East Icelanders. These two are described in *Hrafnkels saga* as having been in Byzantium, Þorkell stating *hefi ek... farit út í Miklagarð, en em handgenginn Garðskonunginum*, 'I have been... to Byzantium, and am bound to serve the Emperor', while Eyvindr is said to have been a sailor *ok nam staðar í Miklagarði ok fékk þar góðar virðingar af Grikkjakonungi*, 'he stayed in Byzantium and received good honours from the King of the Greeks'. These events were computed by Guðbrandur Vigfússon as having taken place before *c.* 945, i.e. in the reign of Romanos I.[1] There is however a snag to this, as Professor Sigurður Nordal has shown with very strong arguments indeed that *Hrafnkels saga* is a work of fiction, nor have earnest attempts by 'fundamentalist' scholars succeeded in rebutting his proofs.[2] We may therefore pass these two by without further exertion.

A little later in time there appears Gríss Sæmingsson, who has rather more respectable backing, in that he appears in *Hallfreðar saga*, *Vatnsdæla saga* and the more austerely historical *Landnámabók*. Gríss is described as farming at Geitaskarð in Langadalur, and *Hallfreðar saga* observes *hafði hann verit allt út í Miklagarð ok fengit þar miklar sæmðir af stólkonunginum*, 'he had gone all the way to Byzantium, and received great honours there from the Emperor' (the last two words are missing in some MSS, but if they belong to the original text then we may infer that Gríss is being described as having served with distinction in the Byzantine forces). Gríss is an important figure in the life of Hallfreðr; Kolfinna, the poet's beloved, is married to him by force at her father's will, and Gríss is described on that occasion as being of middle age, his sight somewhat impaired, but otherwise strong and active. If the chronology of the saga has a solid base in fact, then this wedding will have taken place in 970 or 986, most likely in the latter year. Gríss is then described as owning a weapon of great splendour, a gold-inlaid spear (ch. 4) and his sword is spoken of as *þat er Garðskonungr hafði gefit honum*, which backs the surmise that the words *af stólkonunginum* are part of the original text. Vigfússon reckons him to have been in Byzantium *c.* 970–80,[3] but a passage in the text can give us a firmer indication than the purely chronological calculations as to when he is likely to have been there (if the saga has a factual base).

---

[1] *Hrafnkels saga*, ed. J. Jóhannesson (Íslenzk Fornrit XI), Reykjavík, 1950, 97–133; cf. also G. Vigfússon, 'Um tímatal í Íslendinga sögum', *Safn til sögu Íslands að fornu og nýju*, I (1855), 407–8.

[2] S. Nordal, *Hrafnkatla*, Reykjavík, 1940 (English translation by R. G. Thomas, *Hrafnkels saga*, Cardiff, 1958). Guðbrandur Vigfússon also came to this conclusion near the end of his life, see *Origines Islandicae*, ed. G. Vigfússon and F. Y. Powell, Oxford, 1905, II, 194 and 488–90.

[3] *Hallfreðar saga*, ed. E. Ó. Sveinsson (Íslenzk Fornrit VIII), Reykjavík, 1939, 144; cf. Vigfússon, 'Tímatal', *Safn til sögu Íslands að fornu og nýju*, I (1855), 446ff.

After his homecoming in the year 1000, Hallfreðr challenged Gríss to a duel, but on the night before the fight he dreamt that King Olaf Tryggvason came to him and advised him not to fight, as Gríss 'has prayed God that the man with the better cause may win'. The King then told him the truth, that Hallfreðr's cause was the worse one, as he had lain with Gríss's wife Kolfinna and composed a libel on him; accordingly the King counsels him to refrain from fighting, and to compound with a fine for his quarrel, saying that in the morning he will meet men who will bring him news which he will feel of greater importance than a duel. It turns out as Hallfreðr dreamt; he meets travellers the next day who tell him of King Olaf's fall in the battle of Svoldr; he reacts to this with great grief, goes home and lies down to mourn. People remark to Gríss that Hallfreðr is behaving in an unmanly way, but Gríss replies: 'Not so; I received less honour from the Emperor, yet the worst news I had was when I lost my lord, for the love of a retainer to his lord is great.' Accordingly, the two are wholeheartedly reconciled.[1]

Not only is this passage a fine description of a noble man towards his opponent, it is also very likely that it was remembered in men's memories until the author of the saga wrote it down because of the reason for Gríss's reaction. It is true that by current calculations[2] the story was written down around 1220, rather more than two centuries after the events described in it, but we must remember that both Hallfreðr and Gríss were men of considerable standing in their day, and their verses (especially Hallfreðr's) were well known in the twelfth and thirteenth centuries, and the saga is founded on them to a large extent. It is very likely, therefore, that the author was using a good source for his tradition here in this anecdote, perhaps even a verse by Gríss from which he took the matter (though, in view of the preference shown by saga-writers for reproducing verses in place of prose summaries, the reviser is less sanguine than the author about this). If therefore Vigfússon's reckoning is correct, and Gríss served in the Varangians or with the precursor to them between 970 and 980, there is a very good Byzantine backing for this calculation, in that in January 976 came the death of John Tzimisces, one of the most glamorous of all the Eastern Emperors, and, especially, one greatly loved by the army, whose loss a good soldier, such as we can judge Gríss to have been from the saga, would have mourned greatly. It is possible of course, without any great extension of the chronology, to regard the anecdote

---

[1] *Hallfreðar saga*, 192.
[2] *Hallfreðar saga*, Introduction, lxxviii; see also S. Nordal, *Um íslenzkar fornsögur*, Reykjavík, 1968, 118–19.

as a reference to the murder of Nicephorus II in December 969, but this is less likely on various grounds; for one thing Nicephorus, though a great general, and as such highly respected by his men, did not inspire affection in the way that the more glamorous Tzimisces did, for another, at best Gríss could only have been a very short time in the army by then, whereas the whole remark breathes the tones of the veteran soldier grieving for a well known and warmly loved commander.

The next, in terms of saga chronology, is Finnbogi, the eponymous hero of the late *Finnboga saga ramma*.[1] Finnbogi is given a very adventurous life by the author, which includes a reference to his travels to Greece, where he meets a King John, from whom he received such kindness, and his nickname *rammi*, 'mighty'. There is little doubt that even if the saga names a real person, as it stands it is pure romance. In its present form it has Finnbogi, who by internal calculation should have been born 925–31, visit the Emperor 'John' at eighteen, a clear impossibility, as the only tenth-century Emperor of that name was John Tzimisces, but an indicator of the *terminus post quem* of the anecdote, as in the fourteenth and fifteenth centuries there were a number of Johns on the throne, three of whom, John V, John VI and John VIII, acquired a certain amount of Western European attention.[2] There is then little reason to believe the entire story to be anything other than a fabrication of common-stock anecdotes.

The next Icelandic Varangian who crops up in Western sources is the brother of Gunnar of Hlíðarendi, usually known as *Kolskeggr*, 'Coalbeard'. It is however worth noting that *Landnámabók* refers to no brother of Gunnar by this name, giving them as Hjörtr, Helgi, Hafr and Ormr skógarnefr.[3] Hjörtr and Ormr skógarnefr are mentioned in *Njáls saga*, but Helgi and Hafr are not, while in their place is mentioned Kolskeggr, 'a mighty man and strong, a good and safe man in all things' (ch. 19). He is first mentioned as his brother Gunnar's companion on viking expeditions in the East, where it is stated that Gunnar fought a viking named Coal-beard who owned a sax, an excellent weapon, while his brother Hallgrímr owned a noted spear. The two sons of Hámundi slew these vikings and took their weapons, Gunnar the spear and Kolskeggr the sax. It is not impossible, therefore, that this brother's original name was either Helgi or Hafr, and that he acquired the other name through the attribution of the sword, or

---

[1] *Finnboga saga ramma*, ed. H. Gering, Halle am Saale, 1879, 39ff.

[2] Cf. J. Gill, *The Council of Ferrara-Florence*, Oxford, 1962; G. Ostrogorskii, *A History of the Byzantine State*, 2nd English ed., tr. J. M. Hussey, Oxford, 1968, 510–66 and refs. there.

[3] *Landnámabók*, ed. J. Benediktsson (Íslenzk Fornrit I), Reykjavík, 1969, 353.

simply because he possessed a huge black beard; be that as it may, he became known to all subsequent Icelanders simply by this attributive, so much so that he is never given any other name in *Njáls saga*. Since, however, *Njáls saga* differs from *Landnámabók* in this respect, there can be little doubt that the latter is more likely to be right about his real name.

Of the affairs of Kolskeggr after the death of Gunnar we are told in the saga (ch. 81);

> We now turn our story to Kolskeggr; he arrived in Norway and stayed in Vík all that winter. The next summer he went to Denmark, and entered the service of King Svend Forkbeard, and received great honours from him. Then one night he dreamt that a man came to him, who was fair in colouring, and he felt that this man woke him up and said to him 'Arise and go with me.' 'What do you want with me?' asked Kolskeggr. The other replied: 'I will give you a wife, and you shall be my knight.' Kolskeggr felt that he agreed to this and thereafter he woke up. Afterwards he went to a wise man and told him the dream, which he interpreted as a portent that he would go to southern lands and become God's knight. Kolskeggr was baptized in Denmark, but could not rest there, so went to Russia and stayed there for a year, and went on after that to Byzantium and became a mercenary there. Later news was brought of him that he had married there and become a commander over Varangians, which he was until his death.

We must bear in mind that this passage has more of a fictitious appearance than much of *Njáls saga*, and so must be taken with considerable caution, but it is equally dangerous to reject oral tradition out of hand, especially in a story which bears all the hallmarks of most careful composition and a devoted assemblage of all that a very intelligent author could find in the way of reasonably reliable tradition. There is certainly no trace of any Helgi, Hafr or Kolskeggr in later Icelandic history that can be checked, and the events described in Kolskeggr's life after Gunnar's death are such as could very easily have happened, the more so as this kind of eastwards drift by adventurous warriors until they were absorbed into the golden ranks of the Byzantine army will have been so commonplace as to have been reported back with reasonable frequency. Certainly, when we have scraped off the hagiographical propaganda, what remains is in every way probable, namely that Kolskeggr Hámundarson eventually reached Byzantium and entered the service of Basil II. In the halcyon age of both the Empire and the regiment a good soldier who made his mark on one of Basil's numerous campaigns would be certain of promotion and of Imperial goodwill, and it is not at all impossible for Kolskeggr to have reached a commissioned rank – but this must obviously all remain conjecture.

Þorvaldr Koðránsson, the first Christian missionary in Iceland, will also have arrived in Constantinople in the reign of Basil II. From the surviving records we gather that after his missionary work in Iceland was ended he rambled about Europe as a merchant for a number of years, and then went on a pilgrimage to Jerusalem, being joined on this journey by the second unsuccessful missionary, Stefnir Þorgilsson. *Kristni saga* speaks as follows of this journey:[1]

The two travelled together far and wide through the world, all the way to Jerusalem, and thence to Byzantium, whence they went to Kiev along the Dnepr. Þorvaldr died in Russia, near to Polotsk; he is buried there on a mountain by the church of St John Baptist, and is regarded there as a saint. Thus says Brandr the Far-Travelled of him:

> Hefi ek þar komit
> Er Þorvaldi
> Koðránssyni
> Kristr hvíldar lér;
> þar er hann grafinn
> I háfjalli
> Uppi i Drafni[2]
> At Jóhannesskirkju.

There have I come where to Þorvaldr Koðran's son Christ gives peace; there he is buried on the high hill up on Drafn at St John's Church.

The shorter *þáttr* of Þorvaldr expands this passage a little, stating:

The Emperor himself received him with great honour and gave him many excellent gifts of friendship. He held the greatest dignity in the East, being sent by the Emperor to the land as a leader or governor over Russia or the Kingdom of Kiev. Þorvaldr Koðránsson built there an excellent monastery by a cathedral [lit. 'main church'] dedicated to St John the Baptist, and endowed it with ample property; this house was therefore known as Þorvaldr's monastery; he ended his life in that house, and he is buried there. The monastery stands under a high cliff named Dröfn.[3]

The mention of Stefnir Þorgilsson as Þorvaldr's travelling companion gives some indication as to the period of their travels. The various witnesses to the Christianization of Iceland state that Stefnir went abroad as a young man, was converted in Denmark, travelled with Þorvaldr far and wide, met King Olaf I (Tryggvason) in Ireland and accompanied him to Norway when he went there to seek the kingdom.[4] King Olaf sent him to Iceland to preach Christianity there in 996 or 997, from which we may deduce that the stay by Þorvaldr and

---

[1] *Kristni saga*, ed. J. Sigurðsson and G. Vigfússon (*Biskupa sögur*, Copenhagen, 1858–78, 1, 25–6).

[2] Another reading is 'einn í Drapni', 'alone in Drapn'.

[3] *Biskupa sögur*, I, 48–9.   [4] *Flateyjarbók*, I, 285–6.

Stefnir in Constantinople was appreciably before 995, the year in which Olaf I became King of Norway, and equally an appreciable time after Þorvaldr's departure from Iceland in *c.* 986. This fits in, as it happens, with the great Christianization drive of Russia caused by the marriage of Vladimir of Kiev and Anna the sister of Basil II and Constantine VIII. As a result of Vladimir's agreement to become a Christian, the Emperors sent a team of clerics to Russia in the new Princess of Kiev's train, and the decade after 988 marks the energetic proselytization by these missionaries. We may naturally discount the boast that Þorvaldr was the head of this mission, or some kind of Imperial Governor with supreme power over princes and potentates in the land, but as a veteran missionary he is sure to have been given a responsible post in the work; the more so since as a native speaker of Norse he could make himself understood more easily than the Greeks. Unfortunately, however, there are no Russian or Greek litarary sources to buttress these narratives, and so far the monastic foundations around Polotsk do not appear to have received any historical or archaeological examination.

We now come to two other possible Varangians from the reign of Basil II, but the source is even less reliable than the ones so far examined. These are Gestr (or Þorgestr) Þórhallason, and Þorsteinn Víga-Styrsson, who were, according to the editors of *Borgfirðinga sögur*, in Constantinople around 1011.[1] The story is in *Heiðarvíga saga*, which shares with *Svarfdæla saga* the unenviable position of being so severely mutilated by the accidents of time that large portions of the story are only known through even less reliable secondary or tertiary sources, such as the summary made by Jón Ólafsson from Grunnavík of the contents of the leaves of *Heiðarvíga saga*, which were burnt in the great fire of 1728. Jón's memory was capacious, but where it has been possible to check him, it has often been found to have been appallingly inaccurate, and so the following narrative, as recorded by him, though likely to be right in its main outline, may be wrong in even more individual details than the original. What has happened so far in the saga is: Víga-Styrr killed the father of Gestr for little or no reason, and Gestr slew him in revenge. This happened around 1007. Gestr's kinsfolk got him away overseas, but Þorsteinn the son of Víga-Styrr followed him to exact his revenge. An attempt on Gestr's life in Norway miscarried, and so Þorsteinn followed him to Constantinople, where Gestr has just joined the Varangians. At this point Jón Ólafsson's summary goes on:

---

[1] *Borgfirðinga sögur*, ed. G. Jónsson and S. Nordal (Íslenzk Fornrit III), 2nd ed., Reykjavík, 1955, cxxiv.

Þorsteinn had news of this, and so went the same summer to Byzantium. *Now it is the custom of the Varangians and Norsemen* to hold games during the day, and to practice wrestling. Þorsteinn entered the team, but Gestr did not recognize him, and was not on his guard against him. Þorsteinn went to wrestle with him, having a sax under his cloak *with which he struck at Gestr's head*, but missed and wounded him *not severely* on the shoulder; here the old saw *that he who is not due to die may not be killed* was proved, for Gestr was not badly hurt. The Varangians leapt up and wished to kill Þorsteinn at once for their law was that if one man attempted to take another's life, then he should lose his own for the attempt. *Gestr now prayed the Varangians* to spare Þorsteinn, and gave them half his property to pay for his life, telling them the whole story and begging for his release; some others joined in he request, *and those men who judged the case acceded to Gestr's plea when they knew of Þorsteinn's family*. Þorsteinn was now released, and Gestr asked him not to try to kill him again, the more so as he could see that he was not going to be able to do so, and further to remember that he had not killed Styrr without very good cause. Þorsteinn promised to do so, but asked Gestr in return never to come back to Scandinavia, which Gestr promised and kept his promise. After all this Þorsteinn had run out of money, and Gestr gave him some for the expenses of his journey, after which they parted friends...Gestr never came back to Scandinavia, but was thought to be a good man where he stayed; there is no mention of his having had any offspring. Þorsteinn settled down at Hraun after his father, and lived there for the rest of his life.[1]

The italicized words in this passage are, according to Jón Ólafsson, actual words from the lost original; Jón observes in his annotation that this is to be found in other works (*saepius eru Norðmenn distingueraðir frá Væringjum*), which suggests that the author of the saga itself understood that there were others in the Varangian guards besides Norsemen – the nationality of these others will naturally vary according to the accepted date for the composition of the saga, but in all likelihood he will have been thinking of either Russian Scandinavians, Slavs from Russia or Englishmen. The only point that could be taken as a direct indicator that Þorsteinn Víga-Styrsson had joined the regiment is the remark that he was allowed to take part in their games, but this is not necessarily a proof of it, as he might have been invited to take part as a visitor from Scandinavia. If there is truth in the entire story, then we may take it as certain that these Varangians were not a part of the Hetairia that formed Basil II's life-guards, as for them the conditions of entry and entrance fee were such that no one is likely to have entered it until proven by many years' true service, while it would be somewhat easier to enter one of the outside units.[2] A further point of interest in this story is the description of regimental discipline in respect of men bearing weapons on the field during peaceful games, which

---

[1] *Borgfirðinga sögur*, 243.   [2] See above, p. 26.

shows the necessity felt by the authorities for a strong curb on the impetuous Northmen with their preference for primitive revenge rather than legal means of redress.

Heiðarvíga saga states further that Víga-Barði Guðmundarson entered the Varangians, served three years with them, and fell in a battle at sea. The phrase used is that he was *í Garðaríki, ok gekk þar á mála ok var þar með Væringjum.*[1] This is of course not impossible if we take A. Stender-Petersen's attitude that the Norsemen of Russia were as much Varangians as the soldiers of Byzantium, but the continuation, that Barði and the Varangians *váru á galeiðum við her* makes the Byzantine service a much greater probability, especially as in the later days of Basil II there was much naval activity under such excellent commanders as Basil Boioannes, in which case *Garðaríki*, normally the name for the Principate of Kiev, is here a misnomer for the Empire.

Finally we may name an Icelandic source for this period which states that Eilífr son of Þorgils sprakaleggr, the brother of Earl Ulf the father of King Svend II (Estridsson) of Denmark, served in the Varangians (probably as their commander or at any rate in command of one of the units of the regiment) in the latter days of Basil II. Eilífr had been one of the principal leaders of the Danish invasion of England under Svend I (Forkbeard), being placed by the King in charge of London with a fleet of 60 ships. Shortly after Svend's death, however, the citizens of London revolted and drove the Danes out, Eilífr escaping with three or four ships back to Denmark, according to the not very reliable *Jómsvíkinga saga*.[2] According to the same authority Eilífr did not feel sure that Knud could recover England, and so left Denmark for Byzantium, where he is described as having gone to Constantinople, become commander over the Varangians and fallen in battle. Now none of this is particularly improbable, and if we may accept that Eilífr went east and became a Varangian, one of his status would be sure to take with him a company of young and adventurous warriors who would have joined the guards with their chief. We must remember, however, that there is a very strong case for an opposite argument from a British source, which indicates that Eilífr did not leave England until after the death of Knud the Great (1035), and that he then went not to Byzantium, but to Germania.[3] Jón Jónsson has suggested that this may mean that he went first to Wendland (i.e. to Jómsborg) and only

---

[1] *Borgfirðinga sögur*, cxxiv and 243–4.
[2] *Jómsvíkinga saga* (the version in *Fornmanna sögur*, ed. C. Rafn *et al.*, Copenhagen, 1825–37, xi, 158–62).
[3] *Brut y Tywysogion*, ed. J. Williams ab Ithel (Rolls Series), London, 1860, 38.

then on to Byzantium,[1] and if this is so, and he is the Eilífr who led
a military expedition in Wales around 1020, then this argues strongly
against the story in *Jómsvíkinga saga*, and Jón Jónsson's attempt to
reconcile the two cannot in any case be regarded as very convincing.

Grettis saga relates one of the most fascinating of all Varangian stories,
in the postlude describing the avenging of Grettir by his brother
Þorsteinn drómundr on the slayer, Þorbjörn öngull Þórðarson, one
which has even had the dubious privilege of being turned into a modern
novel (by the French novelist Hugues Le Roux).[2]

　　According to the saga, Grettir and Illugi were killed in Drangey in
the year 1031; at that time their elder brother Þorsteinn, Ásmundr's
son by his first marriage, was settled and had a house in Tunsberg in
Norway.[3] The saga gives him the nickname *drómundr*, and derives it
because 'he was thought to be rather slow in his reactions'. The editor
in the *Íslenzk fornrit* edition, Guðni Jónsson has, however, very
sensibly drawn attention to its more likely derivation, from the Norse
corruption *drómundr* for the Greek *dromon*, which would suggest that
Þorsteinn, like many Varangians of that period, saw a good deal of
naval service in the Varangians.[4] He is given no great prominence early
on in the saga, indeed the lordly Grettir teases him for his slender build
and appearance,[5] though it is stated early that he was 'among the tallest
of men, and a fine singer'.[6] We may note, however, the saga-writer's
art here, in that he has placed these elements at this point in order to
prepare for the final sequence of the story, where Þorsteinn is the un-
disputed hero.

　　We must note at this point that though the present *Grettis saga* is
regarded by literary historians and editors as from a comparatively
late part of the thirteenth century, i.e. some 250 years after the events
described, it appears to have been founded on an earlier life of Grettir
by Lawman Sturla Þórðarson (*c.* 1217–84), a scholar whose caution and
accuracy make him, like his uncle Snorri, from whom he must have
learnt a great deal of the historian's craft, an author to be treated with
respect. There can be little doubt that the point that Grettir was
avenged in Constantinople has come from Sturla, as did certain other
points which we shall note presently.[7]

　　The saga states that Þorbjörn öngull, being outlawed after the killing
of Grettir in 1031, went to Constantinople, whither he was followed by

[1] J. Jónsson, *Víkinga saga*, Reykjavík, 1915, 328.

[2] H. Le Roux, *Les aimants byzantins*, Paris, 1897.

[3] *Grettis saga*, ed. G. Jónsson (Íslenzk Fornrit VII), Reykjavík, 1937, 82.

[4] *Grettis saga*, 34, n. 4.　　　　　[5] *Grettis saga*, 137.　　　　　[6] *Grettis saga*, 34.

[7] Cf. S. Nordal, *Sturla Þórðarson og Grettis saga* (Studia Islandica 4), Reykjavík, 1938.

Þorsteinn drómundr. Both of them entered the Varangians, though
neither knew the other by sight; *Michael Katallakos was then King of
Mikligarðr*.[1] Before the regiment sets off on an expedition, an arms
parade is held, at which every member of the unit is to produce his
weapons. Þorbjörn produces the sax which he took from the dead
Grettir, and explains the dent in the edge, how it was caused when he
struck the dead man on the head with it. The weapon is now passed
among those present until it reaches Þorsteinn, whereon he strikes
Þorbjörn on the head with it and kills him. He is at once seized, for
'their law was at this time that anyone who kills another man should
lose nothing but his life for it'. Nonetheless he is placed in a dungeon,
and left to die there unless someone can be found to pay a ransom for
him. The apparent contradiction may be resolved by the help of
Heiðarvíga saga, in that we may assume that the same process took place,
the accused being permitted to defend himself, and after his defence
the Varangians, recognizing the power of the Norse code of blood-
feud, commuted the capital punishment for one of a substantial fine.
This would explain the curious statement that *gjaldkeri staðarins*, 'the
City Treasurer' was the official who actually incarcerated Þorsteinn;[2]
this personage will have been the official responsible for collecting
fines, and therefore empowered to imprison debtors who were unable
to pay off their mulcts.

The remainder is that curious episode which most Icelandic scholars
are unanimous in declaring fictitious to the extent of being a pure
romance, the story of the love-affair of Þorsteinn and Spes.[3] It begins
with Þorsteinn languishing in his dungeon, but keeping up his spirits
by hymn-singing which, as his magnificent voice carries through a vent
from the cell to the street, is heard by a noble lady with the Latin name
of *Spes*, who happens to be passing by. She is attracted by the singing,
makes enquiries about the singer, and then ransoms him and another
debtor in the same jail (the second debtor, who, like 'A Clergyman' in
Boswell's *Life*, never reappears, was presumably released to make the
act less suspicious, and more like a genuine act of pious charity for
poor prisoners). Subsequently love of music becomes a mutual physical
love, and Spes's husband, who bears the name of *Sigurðr*, starts becoming
suspicious. He makes several attempts to catch them *in flagrante delicto*,

---

[1] *Grettis saga*, 272.
[2] The notes by R. C. Boer in his edition of *Grettis saga* (Halle am Saale, 1900) are wrong in
that the Varangians never had a specific part of Constantinople under their control;
Guðni Jónsson, in his edition, observes correctly in this respect (296, n. 1) that it was
clearly the Varangians, not the 'City Treasurer', who judged Þorsteinn; the latter would
have had only an executive function.
[3] *Grettis saga*, 134; see also *ibid.*, 375, Genealogical Table I.

but Spes always succeeds in hiding Þorsteinn. In the end Sigurðr demands that she shall swear an oath of carnal innocence, and she agrees to do so. On the way to the church where she is to make her oath there is a filthy ditch; a poor beggarman offers to carry her across it to save her finest 'clothes from being soiled, slips and saves himself but grasps her up on her thigh under her skirts while staggering about. She then swears that no man has soiled her body 'other than my husband and that filthy beggar who put his muddy hand on my thigh when he carried me across the dike today'. This oath is accepted as good, Spes then behaves like a ferocious Norsewoman, divorces her husband and marries Þorsteinn a little later. We are told that by then Þorsteinn had become friendly with Haraldr Sigurðarson, who was by then in Constantinople and commander of the Varangians, and that Haraldr had acknowledged and let him benefit from their relationship (according to the saga they were third cousins).

From all this we can see that *Spesar þáttr* is a complex tangle of many strands, though it is possible to unwind this tangle to some extent. The story of the woman who deceives her husband, hides her lover in various ways from his pursuit and swears an ambiguously-worded oath, is a child fathered in many lands.[1] In Iceland it was well known from the translation of *Tristrams saga*, where Queen Isönd swears just such an oath,[2] and the tale of how Þorsteinn escapes from the fuming Sigurðr by being hidden under a pile of clothes, in a jewel-chest and finally by being let down through a trap-door to an escape-route to the sea has numerous European and Icelandic brethren. To English readers one need only point to a comic analogue of a somewhat later date, when Falstaff hides from Ford in *The Merry Wives of Windsor*, while the last method (the trap-door) is in all essentials the tale of Haraldr Sigurðarson and Maria (see above, p. 98), and Boer has drawn the conclusion of their relationship.[3] The present author is not of Boer's opinion, but would like to put forward another possible reason for the relationship, namely that it is as likely that the story about the trapdoor down to a cave giving on to the sea was a common element in Varangian love-tales which then became attached to various named persons, as is commonly the case with such tales, and in this instance two have survived about two men who happened to be both kinsmen

[1] Cf. E. Ó. Sveinsson, *Verzeichnis isländischer Märchenvarianten*, Helsinki, 1929, xxi; also Vasilevskii, *Труды*, I, 227–8, which adduces a Mongol parallel probably of Indian origin.

[2] *Tristrams saga*, ed. G. Brynjólfsson, Copenhagen, 1878, chs. 58–9; H. G. Leach, *Angevin Britain*, London, 1921, 188, refers also to the pre-Byzantine Greek romance of Clitophon and Leucippe, but though this tale was popular in Byzantine times, the influence of *Tristrams saga* is much more obvious here to the present author.

[3] *Grettis saga*, ed. R. C. Boer (see above, p. 203, n. 2), Introduction, xiii–xiv and xxvi–xxx.

and contemporaries in the Varangian service, King Haraldr and his cousin Þorsteinn drómundr.

It is clear that the names *Spes* and *Sigurðr* are out of the question as the real names of a Byzantine Greek husband and wife. As Braun notes in his commentary on Vasilevskii's remarks on this story, however, there is no reason why the husband could not have been a Norse merchant who had taken up residence in Constantinople, or else the name could equally well be a Norse translation of a Greek or Russian name with the *sigr*, 'victory' element, such as Nikolaos or Nikephoros.[1] The name *Spes* is even more likely to be a translation; in this case the Greek equivalent is less likely to be the source, as *Elpis* is not found used as a Christian name in the same way as *Hope* is in English or *Von* in modern Icelandic. On the other hand, in Russian all the three names of St Paul's divine attributes, Faith, Hope and Charity, *Vera, Nadezhda, Lyubov'*, are well-known female Christian names, and it is quite likely that Spes was a Russian lady by the name of Nadezhda.[2]

The author is certain that the *þáttr* is the story of true events overlaid with various fictitious anecdotes inserted by various tellers of the story on the Pooh-Bah principle of corroborative detail. The historical core he sees to be the following events: Þorsteinn drómundr was, as his nickname indicates, a Varangian. It is not at all unlikely that he had already arrived in Byzantium; he may even have been there for quite a long time before Þorbjörn öngull came to join the regiment, but only heard after a longish while of his brother's death, and then took steps to avenge him. He had a love affair with a Russian woman by the name of Nadezhda, who may well have got him out of his trouble when he killed Þorbjörn, and he may well have married her in the end and, as was common among religiously-inclined Byzantines and Russians, they may have ended their lives in the cloister. There is nothing either unnatural or unduly rare about any of these things in the Norse or Byzantine contexts respectively, though the total combination will have been sufficiently little known or understood in Scandinavia to attract quite an accretion of other travelling anecdotes on to the historical core before the *þáttr* was composed and eventually written down.

The next Varangian from our Northern sources is Bolli Bollason known as *prúði*, 'the gracious'. Much is made of his magnificence in

---

[1] Vasilevskii, *Труды*, I, 229.
[2] There is also the well-known St Spes (feast day of SS Fides, Spes and Caritas, I August); cf. *Heilagra manna sögur*, ed. C. R. Unger, Christiania, 1877, I, 369ff.; also *Acta Sanctorum*, Augustus, under I Augusti.

Laxdœla saga, especially in the separate *þáttr* about him which is attached to the end of the saga. Scholars have, however, united in regarding this *þáttr* as a thoroughly untrustworthy piece of romancing, and there can be little doubt that if, like much of the Bible, it is read in any other than a simple fundamentalist way, it becomes clear that its contents cannot be taken at their face value without some careful critical sifting, which we will now endeavour to supply.[1]

Bolli is reckoned in the chronology of the saga as born in 1006–7, and to have married Þórdís, the daughter of the chieftain Snorri of Helgafell, shortly before the latter's death in 1031. Insofar as it is possible to be certain about dates, these are both among the most easily ascertained,[2] but when it comes to correlating them with Bolli's Byzantine journey as described in *Laxdœla saga*, the matter becomes much more difficult. The saga maintains that this journey occurred shortly after his wedding, i.e. at the latest in 1031, as *Eyrbyggja saga*, the basic source of information on Snorri and his family, counts Þórdís among those of Snorri's children who married while he was still alive. If *Laxdœla saga* is correct, and Bolli was eighteen years old when he married, then the wedding should have taken place in 1024–5. We are told that Bolli and Þórdís got on well together, and a daughter was born to them named Herdís, who was to become the mother of a noteworthy flock of descendants. This Herdís went when a year old to be fostered by her grandmother, Guðrún Ósvífrsdóttir, and about the same time (i.e. 1026–7) we are told that Bolli went abroad, first for a year to the court of King Olaf II, then for another year in Denmark, and then to Byzantium, where he should have come in 1028–9 by this reckoning. *Laxdœla saga* then continues:

> He was there [i.e. in Constantinople] for a little while before he was able to gain a place among the Varangians; we have not heard it said that any Norseman was able to enter the mercenary service of the Emperor as quickly as Bolli Bollason; he was many years in Byzantium and was thought to be the ablest of men in all matters of bodily strength and skill, being always among the foremost [of the Varangians]. The Varangians thought a great deal of Bolli while he was in Byzantium.[3]

The saga then states that he returned to Iceland four years after his stepfather, Þorkell Eyjólfsson, was drowned (i.e. in 1030, as Þorkell was drowned in 1026). His homecoming is described thus:

> Then came a ship to Eyjafjörðr; it belonged to Bolli Bollason, and most of the crew were Norsemen. Bolli brought with him much money, and many

---

[1] For an assessment of previous criticism, see *Laxdœla saga*, ed. E. Ó. Sveinsson (Íslenzk Fornrit v), Reykjavík, 1934, Introduction, lix–lx, lxxii–lxxvi.
[2] *Laxdœla saga*, 226 (ch. 78).　　　　　[3] *Laxdœla saga*, 214 (ch. 73).

precious things that great lords had given him; he was so nice in his dress when he came back from this journey that he would wear no clothes except those made of fine stuff [*skarlat*] or velvet [*pell*], and all his weapons were inlaid with gold. He was named Bolli the gracious...Bolli rode from his ship with eleven companions; all his attendants wore clothes of fine stuff and rode on gilded saddles; they were all handsome men, but Bolli was by far the finest. He wore clothes of velvet which the Emperor had given him, and over them a cloak of fine red cloth; at his side he bore his sword *Fótbítr* [lit. 'footbiter']; its hilt was inlaid with gold, and so was the blade; he wore a golden helmet and had a red shield at his side on which was drawn a knight in gold (which he had brought from Byzantium);[1] he carried a short sword in his hand, as is common abroad, and wherever they rested for the night the women did nothing but to gape at the splendid adornment of Bolli and his companions.[2]

This homecoming is supposed to have occurred in 1030, and this certainly agrees with what *Laxdœla saga* also says about Bolli being for a year in Iceland before Snorri the Chieftain died,[3] while on his death-bed Snorri is said there to have committed the rule of his land and people at Tunga to him with the words 'I do not wish you to be less in dignity than my sons, nor is the one of my sons here now who I think is going to be the greatest of them, that is Halldór.' Here there is conflict with *Eyrbyggja saga*, a much more reliable authority on Snorri and his family, which states that Snorri the younger, son of Snorri the Chieftain, was born after his father's death, though, as Professor E. Ó. Sveinsson, the most recent editor of both sagas, has observed, there was nothing to preclude Bolli and Þórdís from administering the estate, and Bolli from taking care of the chieftain's duties, until young Snorri was of age to assume his responsibilities, and that this arrangement was set up with the agreement of the sons and kinsfolk of the elder Snorri.

The *Laxdœla saga* narrative has caused considerable scholarly disagreement. Vasilevskii has attempted to use it as proof that there were no Norsemen in the Varangian regiment before *c.* 1030,[4] but Bogi Th. Melsted, recognizing more clearly the lack of internal agreement in the saga's chronology, came to the opposite conclusion, that it must be doubtful whether Bolli Bollason ever got to Constantinople.[5] The

---

[1] Some MSS omit the words in brackets.   [2] *Laxdœla saga*, 224–5 (ch. 77).
[3] See above, p. 206, n. 2.
[4] Vasilevskii, *Труды*, I, 185–8. Braun, however, in his note upon the passage (in that place) observes that one can place little reliance on the saga's story of the expedition and of Bolli's Byzantine adventure (though there seems no reason to the reviser to doubt that Bolli did serve in Byzantium, even if we have no reliable information in what capacity he served).
[5] B. Th. Melsted, 'Ferðir, siglingar og samgöngur milli Íslands og annarra þjóða á dögum þjóðveldisins', *Safn til sögu Íslands*, IV (1908–15), 652.

present author feels, however, that there is some historical base to the episode. The story of Bolli's magnificence when he returned from abroad must have been very strong indeed to have survived in the fairly vivid form it takes in the saga, and therefore some truth must have lain behind it. Moreover, that Herdís is sent for fostering at such an early age strengthens the supposition of historicity. Finally we must remember that Úlfr Óspaksson, Bolli's close kinsman, and Halldór Snorrason, his brother-in-law, were men of the same age as he, and Varangians at a similar period; all this suggests to the author, therefore, that what is more likely is that Bolli did not leave Iceland until some time after Snorri's death in 1031, since if he went abroad in *c.* 1026, he could not possibly have been a Varangian 'for many years' as *Laxdæla saga* phrases it, but this is more likely in the 1030s. The author's opinion is, therefore, that Bolli went abroad about 1032–3, and returned ten to fifteen years later. This would in no way conflict with his end described in the saga, and would certainly give him time to earn the kind of wealth that permitted him something of the (obviously exaggerated) ostentation he displays in it on his return. There is also some slight backing for this view in a comment in *Sneglu-Halla þáttr*, where we are told that Bolli had been a member of Haraldr Sigurðarson's household, and that when the King heard the news of the death of two of his former courtiers he remarked of Bolli: 'The brave man will have fallen before warriors', while of Halli he observed: 'The poor devil will have burst on gruel', which, according to the *þáttr*, was true.[1]

We must not, of course, make too much of the historical reliability of *Sneglu-Halla þáttr*, but it does have one advantage over *Laxdæla saga* in that it is based upon the original poems of the poet it describes. There is nothing inherently improbable in Bolli's having been a courtier of King Haraldr's at some stage, or at any rate sufficiently close to him, e.g. as a direct subordinate in the Varangians, for people to feel they could regard him as a courtier of the King. It is equally probable that Bolli the brave may have ended his life in the same way as his father and many other heroic men in Iceland, and fallen before the spears of enemies. So, if the *þáttr* has some truthful base, we can reason that Bolli did *not* leave Iceland for his equivalent of the Grand Tour until after 1031. King Haraldr did not reach Byzantium until 1034 at the earliest, and we may note that as there were two other Icelanders as close to him (Úlfr and Halldór), the narratives are not likely to be completely fortuitous. It is the author's surmise that all three young men went on the tour together, and joined the Varangians together, whether before or after Haraldr's arrival, or else they joined his company in Russia,

[1] *Flateyjarbók*, III, 428; cf. also *Íslendinga þættir*, ed. G. Jónsson, Reykjavík, 1935, 248.

and followed him south to Byzantium. This is admittedly based on evidence that is largely conjecture, but in itself the psychological motivation is not at all improbable.

Úlfr Óspaksson and Halldór Snorrason are our next Norse Varangians in roughly chronological order, and both of them are sufficiently notable to warrant a fairly detailed examination. Here *Heimskringla* is our principal authority, and there is no particular reason to object to any of Snorri's statements. Firstly it is recorded there that Úlfr accompanied Haraldr and Halldór in the battle when Halldór was wounded in the face so that he bore the scar for the rest of his life. We are also told that Úlfr was with them when they were put in prison (see above, p. 87), and ch. 36 of *Haraldar saga* informs us that Úlfr and Halldór came with the King to Norway on his return there, while Úlfr is described in the next chapter in the following words:

Úlfr Óspaksson was in great favour with King Haraldr; he was a very wise man, a good speaker, forceful in action, loyal and simple in temper. King Haraldr made him his Chamberlain and found him Jórunn Þórbergsdóttir in marriage [the sister of Þóra who was the King's mistress]...King Haraldr gave Úlfr the rights and dignity of a Landed Man [nobleman] and lands to the value of 612 marks, as well as the governorship of half the province of Þrándheimr; so Steinn Herdísarson tells us in the *Úlfsflokkr*.[1]

Úlfr died in 1066, shortly before the King set out on his last viking expedition to England: 'King Haraldr stood over his grave and said as he walked away: "There lies he who was the most true and loyal of men." '[2] Úlfr was also a poet, and one of his verses is cited in *Heimskringla*, which bears probably a little on our study. The occasion of this verse was when the expedition to England was being prepared, and in discussion someone remarked that it must be difficult to get into the *wered* of the English Kings, where every man was the equal of two. Úlfr remarked:

> Esa stöllurum stillis
> Stafnrúm Haralds jafnan
> (Ónauðigr fæk auðar)
> Innan þörf at hvarfa,
> Ef, hörbrekka, hrökkva,
> Hrein, skolu tveir fyr einum
> (Ungr kendak mer) undan
> (Annat) þingamanni.

[1] *Haraldar saga* (in *Morkinskinna*, ed. F. Jónsson, Copenhagen, 1900), 113, and *Flateyjarbók*, III, 390; one stanza has survived from this poem, cf. FJ *Skjald* A I 409, B I 378.

[2] *Heimskringla*, III, 175.

The King's stewards need not worry about the place in the bows of King Haraldr's ship; I am not unwilling to earn money if two men, bright maid, will flee before one, though as a youth I was used to different things.[1]

Here the old Chamberlain is speaking from the fullness of his heart; in his youth as a Varangian he was certainly not accustomed to two men giving way before one.

His companion, Halldór Snorrason, is the Icelandic Varangian who is most popular in Norse sources, being in this respect close to King Haraldr himself. This is not surprising when we reflect that he is almost certainly the source for the bulk of the Icelandic tradition in respect of the King's Varangian career, and as far as we can see, he was the close companion of the King right through his eastern adventures in Russia and Byzantium, as well as for a while one of his courtiers in Norway. Halldór's long service is a factor which makes the statement of *Bolla þáttr* as to Bolli's long Varangian service more likely: if, as seems highly probable to both author and reviser, Bolli, Úlfr and Halldór went off on their foreign adventures together, they would have stayed together until they had made their fortunes, especially during the exciting and profitable period of the wars of Michael IV.

The episode known as *Íslendings þáttr sögufróða*, which we find both in *Morkinskinna* and the life of King Haraldr in *Heimskringla*, tells in an entertaining way of how 'King Haraldr's Itinerary' spread out from Halldór. The *Morkinskinna* narrative reads:

It so happened one summer that a young and likely-looking Icelander came to the King and asked for his help. The King asked him if he knew any art, and he said that he knew some stories. The King said that he would receive him into his household if he would entertain them at any time that he was called upon to do so, and he agreed to this and did so, and was popular with the court, who gave him clothes, while the King gave him a weapon to bear. In this way time went until Christmas, when the man became depressed, and King Haraldr asked him why. He said that this was because of his temperament. 'Not so', said the King; 'I can guess the reason. I guess that it is because you are running out of stories; you have entertained us through the year, no matter who asked you, and you are depressed that you are going to run out by Christmas.' 'It is even as you guess', said the other, 'there is only one story left to me now, and I dare not tell it, for it is the story of your eastern adventures.' The King answered: 'That is the story that I most of all want to hear, and now you shall not entertain at all until Christmas, for men are at work, but on Christmas Day you shall begin this story and tell some part of it, and I will so order things that the tale will last as long as the Christmas feast. There is much drinking at the feast, and entertainments have to be short, so you will not discover during your telling whether men like it

---

[1] FJ *Skjald* A I 403, B I 372; cf. also E. A. Kock, *Notationes norroenae*, Lund, 1923-44, § 806, and *Heimskringla*, III, 176, n. 46.

well or ill.' This went so, and the Icelander began the tale, and told a part of it, but the King bade him stop fairly soon. After this drinking began, and the court discussed how great was his nerve to tell the story, and also whether the King liked it. Some thought the story well told, but others were less impressed. In this way the days of Christmas passed; the King insisted that the story received close attention, and because of his supervision of the narration the story lasted as long as the festivity. Then, on Twelfth Night, when the story was ended earlier in the day, the King spoke: 'Are you not curious, Icelander, how I like the story?' 'Lord, I fear that you may not' he replied. The King answered: 'I am quite pleased with it, it is no worse than the matter for it – but who taught you the story?' The Icelander answered: 'It was my custom in Iceland to go each summer to the Althing, and there I learned each year some part of the story from Halldór Snorrason.' 'It is no surprise then', said the King, 'that you knew the story so well, and this will be your good fortune; be welcome with me now and whenever you wish to stay with me.' The King gave him a good sum of money to buy things with, and the young man became a man of note.[1]

This short, but impressive, story is very important in our study. It demonstrates how Halldór Snorrason brought so much news of the adventures of King Haraldr and his companions in the East that there formed from it a whole saga, the *Útferðarsaga Haralds konungs*.[2] There can be no reasonable doubt that this narrative told a true story of the principal events that befell them, but, to us of the twentieth century, it is clear as the day that much of the narratives in *Heimskringla* and the other Kings' Sagas about Haraldr III in the east is a pack of fictitious anecdotes culled from the more fantastic side of folklore and subsequently fathered on to him.[3] This makes it abundantly clear that the *Útferðarsaga* was never written down, or else that if it was written, the MS was lost before *Morkinskinna*, *Fagrskinna* and Snorri's other sources were composed, and only a few of the anecdotes of the *Útferðarsaga* remained uncorrupted in oral tradition; one such is the note of Halldór's scar, where it is stated categorically that he brought this story back with him to Iceland.[4] Moreover, this chapter in *Heimskringla* has a very different tone from the other; thus it contains Halldór's harsh responses to Haraldr. It begins with the narrative of how the Varangians besieged a town and could not capture it. The defenders opened the gates to anger them, and lined up on the city walls to hurl jeers at them. In reply Haraldr had his men play unarmed games outside the city for some days. The story now continues:

---

[1] *Morkinskinna*, 199–200; *Fornmanna sögur*, VI, 354–6.
[2] See Jón Jóhannesson's introduction to the *þáttr* (Íslenzk Fornrit XI, cxii–cxiv).
[3] See above, Ch. 4; also J. de Vries, 'Normannisches Lehngut in der isländischen Königs-saga', *Arkiv for Nordisk Filologi* 47, 51ff.
[4] *Heimskringla*, III, 79; Schlumberger, *L'Épopée byzantine*, III, 246.

These Icelanders were named, who were with King Haraldr, Halldór, son of Snorri the Chieftain – he brought this story back to Iceland – and Úlfr Óspaksson, son of Óspakr the Wise; both these men were among the strongest and bravest of men, and were very dear to Haraldr; both of them had taken part in the games. After some days the citizens wanted to show more spirit, and so they appeared unarmed on the city walls, but left the gates open. When the Varangians saw this they dressed so for the games one day that they carried swords under their cloaks and helmets under their hoods. After they had played for a while they saw that the defenders were not suspicious of them, seized their weapons quickly, and ran towards the gate. When the defenders saw this they went to meet them, fully armed, and a battle began in the gateway. The Varangians had no defensive armour except that they wrapped their cloaks round their arms; they were therefore wounded, and some fell, while all were in grave danger; Haraldr and the force left in the camp now sought to help his men, but the garrison had climbed the walls and they shot arrows and hurled stones at them, and a fierce battle ensued, so that those who were striving in the gate felt that it was taking longer for the rescuers to come than they could wish. Then, as Haraldr advanced into the gate his standard-bearer fell, and he said 'Halldór, take up the banner.' Halldór took up the pole and answered unthinkingly: 'Who is going to carry a banner for you if you follow it as feebly as now?' This was more a remark in anger than truth, for Haraldr was the bravest of men. They now fought their way into the town, where a hard struggle ensued, which ended in Haraldr's victory and the capture of the city. Halldór was badly wounded, having a great wound in his face, the scar from which remained with him as long as he lived.

The author is of the opinion that this anecdote comes from the original *Útferðarsaga*, whether oral or written – or at the very least from Halldór Snorrason himself. *Morkinskinna* has this incident occur in the course of another siege, which was resolved by the 'dead commander' trick (see above, p. 72).[1] Now Stender-Petersen has pointed out[2] that Frontinus tells a rather similar story about Cato when he besieged the Lacetani,[3] when the siege was completed by his having the *maxime imbelles* of his auxiliaries advance unarmed up to the walls, whereupon the defenders made a sortie and chased them, when Cato sent other soldiers who had remained hidden nearby into the now defenceless town. There is an obvious likeness between the two tales, but the *games*, which are Snorri's most weighty point, and which are so peculiarly a Norse phenomenon, are a very strong factor in favour of the authenticity of the tale, as is indeed Halldór's angry outburst in the gate; both these points suggest a direct descent from him, as does the very fact that the cautious Snorri admits the story in this form and not

[1] *Morkinskinna*, 76.
[2] Stender-Petersen, *Die Varägersage als Quelle der altrussischen Chronik*, Aarhus, 1934, 86–7.
[3] Frontinus, *Strategemata*, ed. G. Gundermann, Leipzig, 1888, 103.

the other. It is of course virtually impossible to determine now how much of the collection of anecdotes about other Varangians which are fathered on to Haraldr in *Morkinskinna* originated from Halldór, but the probability is that these were not in the original *Útferðarsaga*, but were later added on to it.¹

Halldór is assumed to have been born between 1000 and 1010,² the son of the great Snorri the Chieftain Þorgrímsson, and his third wife, Hallfríðr, the daughter of Einar Þveræingr, and so descended on both sides from some of the noblest blood in Iceland, while both his father Snorri and his maternal grandfather Einar were noted wise men. His best description is that in *Heimskringla*:

Halldór was the largest and strongest of men, and the most handsome of men; King Haraldr testified of him that he was one who showed least emotion at violent news, whether good or bad, and whatever danger he met made no difference to his equable temper; he neither slept less, ate less nor drank less than was his custom for it. Halldór was a slow and laconic speaker, open and sharp in temper, and not given to flattery, which the King took ill, as he had with him plenty of other men of noble birth who were more servile in behaviour. Halldór stayed but a little time with the King, but went back to Iceland, set up house in Hjarðarholt, dwelt there to old age, and became an old man.

Landnámabók states that he married Þórdis Þorvaldsdóttir from Langadalr, the sister of Þórarinn the Wise, and two daughters are mentioned, Þórkatla, the ancestress of the Sturlungs, and Guðrún, the ancestress of the Vatnsfirðingar. He is also stated to have had two sons, Snorri and Birningr, and is considered to have returned to Iceland in 1051.³

Besides these sources, there exist two short and rather unhistorical *þættir* about Halldór, neither of which is of any interest to students of Varangica, except in so far as they are both based on what was clearly a strong tradition of Halldór's short temper and sharp tongue.⁴ Also, the last passage of the second *þáttr* has a tone which suggests that it may be the narrative of a true occurrence. King Haraldr sent word to Halldór that he should 'send him foxskins to make a covering for his bed, for the King felt he wanted warmth. Now when the King's message first reached Halldór it is said that he remarked "The cock is getting old", but he sent him the skins.'⁵ It is doubtful whether King Haraldr would have asked a friend's gift from a man who had

---

¹ E. Ó. Sveinsson thinks (*Laxdæla saga*, Introduction, xc) that very few have done so.
² *Laxdæla saga*, Introduction, lxxxv ff.
³ On Halldór's return and his family, see *Laxdæla saga*, Introduction, lxxxvii ff.
⁴ The best edition of both *þættir* is that of E. Ó. Sveinsson (Íslenzk Fornrit v, Reykjavík, 1934).
⁵ *Halldórs þáttr Snorrasonar*, ed. E. Ó. Sveinsson (see note 4 above).

insulted him as Halldór is made to do in the *þáttr*, but the conclusion suggests that the old Varangian comradeship had not been entirely lost after Halldór left Norway. Snorri, a descendant of Halldór's daughter, was in an unusually favourable position in an age when oral anecdotes were better preserved than today to obtain reliable traditions of his ancestor, and his conclusion was that Halldór lost favour with Haraldr once the latter had become King and shown his appreciation of the Byzantine preference for courtly deference, as he could not curb his outspokenness, but that he left Norway nonetheless in Haraldr's good graces, and in Iceland he kept up the King's reputation no less loyally than the more courtly-tongued poets.

One more Varangian from the period of Haraldr Sigurðarson is a certain Erlendr, whose paternity is not stated, nor yet his nationality. This person occurs in *Morkinskinna*, where he is said to have consulted Haraldr for a cure for his wife's madness,[1] and Haraldr discovered that the woman was being visited by some man who came to her each night, bedded her and gave her precious gifts. To cure her Haraldr had a cross of gold blessed and told the woman to offer it to the man in return. She did this, whereon he vanished and did not come back. By his learning Haraldr found out that this was an evil man who lay on gold and had become a dragon. Accordingly he searched out the local dragon's den, and had a great fire kindled outside it, whereon a huge snout appeared, but they could do nothing to the dragon. The next night a farmer in the neighbourhood dreamed a man came to him, asked for the loan of his ship, and said he would leave him the hire in the bows. The farmer agreed, and the next morning he went down to his ship and saw that it had been used in the night, and found a large gold cup in the bows; this was supposed to have been the evil being, who took this form of transport out of the area. Erlendr's wife recovered her health in full, and the man was never seen again.

The story is an obvious folktale, and we need not take any notice of any of its constituents except one: this is that near the quarter of St Mamas, where the Russians were expected to dwell in Constantinople, there was in the Middle Ages a river which, though normally small, ran fiercely in the spring rains, especially from February onwards. It was spanned by a bridge on twelve arches, and on it was the figure of a dragon in bronze. Popular belief said that there was a dragon in the river, or in a cleft nearby, and that it was given sacrifices. Even though the statue on the bridge had been destroyed long before Haraldr came to Byzantium, it is by no means impossible that the belief in the dragon

---

[1] *Morkinskinna*, 60–2; *Flateyjarbók*, III, 291–2.

lingered on in popular superstition,[1] and folktales have been known to take more unlikely routes around the world!

We must also remember that in *Morkinskinna*, and in the longer *Haraldar saga*, we are told that Már Húnröðarson, father of the later famous chieftain Hafliði Másson (of *Þorgils saga ok Hafliða*) was a company commander in the Varangians when Haraldr Sigurðarson first joined them pseudonymously as 'Nordbrigt'; Már had suspected that the newcomer was of royal birth, tried to fish the truth out of Halldór Snorrason and failed, while Haraldr himself refused to talk to him and, the saga says, 'he left Byzantium and felt that nothing was more likely than that some great things would soon happen'.[2] Gustav Storm maintained that the whole anecdote was highly suspect because of Hafliði's age (†1130), as he held him to have been born *c.* 1070–80, and that it was therefore impossible for his father to have been in Constantinople around 1035.[3] On the other hand, Bogi Th. Melsted has brought forward powerful arguments to the effect that Hafliði was born not later than 1055, and this makes the possibility of Már being a Byzantine commander in 1035 much greater.[4] It is most unlikely that Már commanded all the Varangians, since then Haraldr and his companions would have been obliged to reveal the truth to him, but he may well have been the commander of a company not normally stationed in the capital; we must also remember that, as Munch has pointed out, Hafliði his son was married to Halldór Snorrason's sister's daughter, and it is quite possible for some family traditions from both Már and Halldór to have been preserved in his family and that of Sturla Þórðarson.[5]

The next known name is that of Þormóðr Indriðason (or Ásgeirsson).[6] He is supposed to have arrived in Byzantium around 1064. This man was an Icelander on one side of his family, had been in Norway in the retinue of Prince Magnus, son of King Haraldr III, and later avenged his kinsman Koðrán Guðmundarson by killing his slayer, Hallr Ótryggsson. Hallr had been a member of Haraldr III's court, and he wanted to have Þormóðr executed, but Prince Magnus succeeded in reconciling the two, after which Þormóðr went first to Denmark and

---

[1] On the dragon and its image, see D. A. Banduri, *Imperium Orientale*, Paris, 1711, I, pt. iii, 58 and 87.

[2] *Flateyjarbók*, III, 290–1; *Morkinskinna*, 60.

[3] 'Harald Haardraade og Væringerne', *Norsk Historisk Tidsskrift*, 2 Række, IV, 359, 364.

[4] B. Th. Melsted, 'Ferðir etc.', *Safn til sögu Íslands*, IV (1908–15), 773–6.

[5] P. A. Munch, *Samlede Avhandlinger*, Christiania, 1873, I, 509.

[6] His story is in *Heimskringla*, III, 165. *Ljósvetninga saga*, ed. B. Sigfússon (Íslenzk Fornrit x), Reykjavík, 1940, 103, calls him 'Þormóðr Ásgeirsson, kinsman of the men of Möðruvellir', while *Flateyjarbók*, III, 376, states 'Þormóðr was first cousin once removed to Guðmundr Eyjólfsson the father of Koðrán'.

then to Byzantium. The *Flateyjarbók* text of *Haraldar saga* continues his adventure:

Þormóðr wished to become a soldier, but the Emperor thought that he was too small and said he would not be able to do a man's job. Then one day, as the Emperor stood on a balcony he saw how an enormous bull was led along for slaughter, and how Þormóðr hewed its head off with such force that it fell to the ground far away. The Emperor spoke: 'Need we despair that he will strike other big things beside bulls'; he now accepted Þormóðr into his army, and he served him for a while.

This anecdote is also in *Morkinskinna*.[1]

What there is of fact in it it is now impossible to say. The killing of Hallr is mentioned in connection with Haraldr's campaign against Earl Hákon Ívarsson in 1064. If Þormóðr did go to Byzantium, he is likely to have arrived there at the end of the reign of Constantine X or the beginning of that of Romanos IV, in which case he will have been an Icelandic representative in the battle of Manzikert, and may even have fallen there in the general débâcle, but all this can only be surmise.

The same applies to one Eldjárn from Húsavík, who appears in *Morkinskinna*, though his patronymic is not mentioned.[2] We are told that he composed a rude verse on a certain Sir Guipard when on a sea-voyage to England; the knight was furious at the verse, and sued Eldjárn, who denied the charge and defended himself before the court in England and declaimed to it a verse which he had made on Guipard's brave conduct in the battle of Foxerne (but all the Norsemen, though not the judges, knew that Guipard had been nowhere near this battle, and the verse was the most acid satire). Eldjárn was found not guilty; *Morkinskinna* says of him that he was 'previously come from out in Byzantium', and that this incident occurred about 1100. This does not of course constitute a direct claim that Eldjárn had been a Varangian – he could just as well have been a merchant or a pilgrim – but if he was we may take it that he will have served under Alexius I, possibly as a subordinate to our next personage from the west.

Our previous discussion of the commander Nabites has shown that he is as likely to have been an Englishman (General Wulf?) as a Norseman (Úlfr, Örn or Haukr). On the other hand Þórir helsingr, the commander of the regiment in the reign of John II, and a leader in the Emperor's great victory at Beroë, must clearly have been a Scandinavian – the most likely nationality is Swedish from the nickname, but we have no other evidence as to his identity than this anecdote, and so must be content to

---

[1] *Flateyjarbók*, III, 376; *Morkinskinna*, 233–4.   [2] *Morkinskinna*, 325.

rest the matter there. On the other hand we know somewhat more of our authority for Þórir's commandership, the Varangian who gave Einar Skúlason his information, Eindriði ungi, 'the Young'.

From what we can make of Snorri's words in *Heimskringla*, Eindriði the Young was a Norwegian nobleman.[1] The name suggests that he might have been of the family of Einar þambarskelfir, though P. Riant, arguing from the lack of a known patronymic, suggests that he was of low birth, made his way up by energy and ability, and learnt falseness and vanity from his contact with the Byzantines.[2] This is the wildest conjecture, even in a field where conjecture has to work on an unusually slender substratum of facts, for from what is known of Eindriði, he was evidently a rich and respected man, both in Norway and Byzantium. He is particularly mentioned in connection with the pilgrimage of Earl Rögnvaldr kali, whom he met and with whom, as we have seen, he had a difference of opinion which has resulted in his gaining a poor reputation because of the obvious partiality of the author of *Orkneyinga saga* for the Earl;[3] there is little doubt in the author's and reviser's minds that it has also influenced Briant's judgement unduly. On the other hand, as we have pointed out, Eindriði was clearly showing a superior knowledge of Mediterranean conditions when he took his forces with the least possible trouble to Constantinople to strengthen his master Manuel I's army instead of risking it on a harebrained run down to Palestine. Eindriði appears to have been in Norway on a visit to King Ingi I in Bergen in 1148; from the eventual outcome it is not unreasonable to assume that Manuel had sent him, as a senior officer in the regiment, possibly near to retirement (if he had been in active service himself in 1121, he will have completed a quarter of a century in the Imperial service by that time, and so been an admirable envoy for this purpose), on a recruiting expedition to Scandinavia. However it may be, Eindriði clearly decided not to spend his retirement in the east, for he is found back in Norway a few years later. There he supported King Hákon II (herðibreiðr) and later Sigurðr Markúsfóstri, until he was killed at the instigation of his old enemy from Earl Rögnvaldr's pilgrimage, Erlingr skakki. Eindriði is given one good witticism in *Heimskringla*; when Erlingr was said to be approaching with an overwhelmingly superior force before the battle of Véey, where King Hákon fell, Eindriði remarked: 'Too near the nose, said the old man when he was hit in the eye.'[4]

There also occurs in a Byzantine connection a certain Grímr rusli, although there is no suggestion that he was a Varangian. This person

[1] *Heimskringla*, III, 378.   [2] Riant, *Skandinavernes Korstog*, Copenhagen, 1868, 34.
[3] See above, p. 155.   [4] *Heimskringla*, III, 381.

is the man with whom the Princess Kristín, the daughter of King Sigurðr I, and wife of Erlingr skakki, forsook her husband and went to Byzantium 'where they stayed a while and had a number of children'.[1] Riant surmises that this was because Kristín was angry with Erlingr for the killing of the Haraldr who was said to be her illegitimate son by King Sigurðr II (munnr).[2] It is most likely that the two spent their time in Byzantium during the reign of Manuel I, as the last known Varangian of the Comnenian period appears to have done; he is Eiríkr Sigurðarson, supposed son of King Sigurðr II, and putative brother of King Sverre, and therefore usually named Eiríkr the King's Son. Eiríkr had travelled far in the East, and even bathed in the Jordan,

and had a burning candle in his hand, and he and his men said that before he entered the water he said that God would let the candle come burning out of the water 'if I am a true son of King Sigurðr', and they said that he walked out of the river with it still burning...He was a very courteous man and knew many things well, a small man in stature, and not fair of face.[3]

King Sverre permitted him to undergo a trial by iron to prove his paternity, and this succeeded well, whereon the King 'accepted Eiríkr's kinship well and made him a lord within his court. Eiríkr was a popular man and the most unassuming of men; he looked best after his own men of all the lords.' Eiríkr stayed with Sverre, and proved a good, but not over-lucky soldier, and it is clear that Sverre did not always like him, though he seems never to have doubted his loyalty. After the fall of Magnus III (Erlingsson) in 1184,[4] Eiríkr is said to have asked to be allowed to govern some part of the kingdom, and when King Sverre refused his request, he went on a viking expedition to Esthonia and raided widely in those parts to make money. On his return to Norway there were various accounts of his journey, and King Sverre gave him the title of Earl, and the Upplands to govern. Shortly afterwards Eiríkr died of sickness, as did his wife and son 'and many said that evil men had practised treachery on them and taken their lives'.[5]

After the fall of the Comnenian dynasty the last Norse or other Varangian soldiers mentioned by name before the collapse of the undivided Empire in 1204 are the three messengers sent in 1195 to recruit for the hard-pressed Angeli. These are Hreiðarr (or Reiðarr) sendimaðr, Pétr illska and Sigurðr grikkr Oddsson, though there is no absolute certainty as to their having actually served in the regiment. In the case of

[1] *Heimskringla*, III, 407.   [2] Riant, *Skandinavernes Korstog*, 36.
[3] *Sverris saga*, ed. G. Indrebö, Oslo, 1920, 64; *Flateyjarbók*, II, 586.
[4] *Sverris saga*, 120; *Flateyjarbók*, II, 636.   [5] *Flateyjarbók*, II, 635.

Hreiðarr, he was clearly in one capacity or another on the staff of Isaac II and Alexius III in turn; the latter sent him to Norway with the letter we have already referred to to King Sverre. *Sverris saga* described the mission as follows:[1]

There was a man of Vík named Hreiðarr, who had been long out of the country, and had travelled far. He came that summer to Norway with letters and the seal which is called *gullbóluskrá* ['chrysobull']. This seal the Emperor Kirjalax had sent to King Sverre, while the letters stated that Sverre should send ten hundred [i.e. 1200] good soldiers to the Emperor. Kirjalax had also sent to Denmark...the man who was called Pétr illska with a similar missive, and a third man to the King of the Swedes.

Hreiðarr is supposed to have pressed the matter hard with the King. Sverre delayed his answer, but in the spring he refused to accede to the Emperor's request as he expected to be at war with the Danes; nonetheless he permitted Hreiðarr to recruit any sons of farmers or merchants if they wished to go. 'Hreiðarr gathered a company of sorts and travelled round the country', but he did not take his levy to Constantinople, but joined Bishop Nicholas and the Baglar, and assisted them in the civil war over the next year, being one of the most effective of the Baglar leaders, holding Tunsberg for a long time against King Sverre, though at length he had to surrender. The King took him back into favour, and nursed him in his illness; shortly afterwards Sverre himself went down with his fatal illness, and both of them lay on the King's ship, 'where the King had Hreiðarr given all the nursing and help that he himself received, and talked often with him. Hreiðarr was a wise man and knowledgeable in many things.'[2] Nevertheless, after Sverre's death, Hreiðarr rejoined the Baglar; how highly he was thought of by both sides can be seen from the fact that he married Margrét, the daughter of King Magnus III, when she lost her first husband, Philip of Veigini. Later on, Hreiðarr also played a considerable part in the acknowledgement of Hákon (IV), Sverre's grandson, as King after the untimely death of his father Hákon (III). In 1211 he left Norway with his wife to visit Jerusalem, and went on thence to Constantinople, but whether he entered the service of Henry of Flanders or Theodore I in Nicaea there is no indication. According to the annals, he died in 1214.[3]

There is, however, a problem concerning Hreiðarr which has to be taken into account when attempting to estimate his Varangian (or, more precisely, Byzantine) career. In the Icelandic annals there is an

---

[1] *Sverris saga*, 133; see also *Flateyjarbók*, II, 646–7.

[2] *Sverris saga*, 193; *Flateyjarbók*, II, 699.

[3] For the texts relating to Reiðarr in Iceland, see *Oddaverja annáll* (*Islandske Annaler*, ed. G. Storm, Christiania, 1888) under the dates 1176, 1211 and 1214, and other annals in the same edition under 1175; cf. also Riant, *Skandinavernes Korstog*, 36.

entry (in MS AM 421, 4to) against the year 1175 'Hreiðarr the Messenger came out [to Iceland]. He was sent by Sverre to enquire whether the Icelanders would accept his rule.' According to Storm, this MS, which is a conflation of several older annals from originals that are now lost, was written around 1650, and derives from the annalist Björn Jónsson from Skarðsá.[1] Storm also maintains that it is *alt tilsat med selvstændige hypoteser*, 'all full of unsubstantiated assertions', one of which is this entry, and there is much to be said for his argument, though it cannot be taken as unreservedly as he intends it to be.

It is of course perfectly clear to us that this *reason* for Hreiðarr's visit must be wrong, since in 1175 Sverre was still a young deacon in the Faeroes, and had not yet become a pretender to the throne of Norway, much less so absolute a King that he could send a messenger to Iceland to attempt to obtain the sovereignty over its people. Nor is there much point in substituting Magnus III or his father Earl Erlingr for Sverre in the entry, as Norway, still shaken by the reverberations of the thirty years of civil war that had flared up at intervals ever since the death of Sigurðr I in 1130, was not a power of which the Icelanders, prosperous and at the height of their century of comparative peace, took any notice. Yet there is little doubt that a Hreiðarr did come to Iceland in 1175, even if subsequent annal-compilers mistook his errand, and in the light of our man's career, there is at least one other possible reason for his coming. By 1195 our Hreiðarr was clearly a person of standing and ability, as witness the fact that Alexius III (or Isaac II) entrusted him with a vital recruiting errand for the crumbling Empire. Twenty years earlier, he may therefore well have come from the same source, as an envoy from Manuel I to gather men to help the Emperor in his projected Turkish campaign which was to founder so disastrously at Myriocephalum. He would no doubt have gone via Norway, and would very likely have been recommended by Earl Erlingr and King Magnus to try his luck among the Icelanders – unfortunately there is no record now of whether he succeeded or failed, or of how many (if any) recruits from Norway and Iceland fell in the pass at Myriocephalum. Needless to say, this surmise of the author's can be no more than a possible interpretation, and in the very tenuous state of the source material it is not pressed by the reviser, but for want of a better one it is presented here.

We know nothing more of Pétr illska than this one note in *Sverris saga*, neither of who he was, nor of what success he had with his errand to Knud VI. Bearing in mind the references to *Dani* in the military encounters between the Latins and the forces of Alexius III and

[1] *Islandske Annaler*, Introduction, li ff.

Alexius V, it is not unlikely that Pétr was the messenger who brought with him a really substantial help. The Thanks to the successful rule of King Knud and his great lieutenant, Archbishop Absalon, Denmark was a strong and successful realm in the 1190s and the happy associations with the Empire in the past, as attested by Saxo, are quite likely to have induced the King to permit a force of some substance to be recruited in his domains, but once again this can only be speculation on probabilities.

The last person to be mentioned here, other than Harry the Englishman who got himself into woman-trouble in the days of Andronicus II (see above, p. 174) is Sigurðr grikkr Oddsson, who is mentioned in several places in *Sturlunga saga*. His nickname, and his activities in the civil wars of the Sturlungs, make it very probable that he was a Varangian at some stage of his career. We find him first of all mentioned in connection with the burning at Lönguhlið in 1197, where we are told that he took up a court case of a killing which was spoiled for him in the court;[1] according to the saga he returned shortly before this date, and was singular among returned Varangians in that he came back poor and without any gain from his service in the East. His subsequent career certainly suggests that as a Varangian he would have been unlikely to obtain any great advancement. Taken under his protection by a North Iceland chieftain, Hákon Þórðarson of Laufás, Sigurðr repaid him by cuckolding him, being caught three times by Hákon in bed with his wife. Later Sigurðr joined a party that attacked Hákon, and when the latter was caught by his enemies and no one else would strike the blow, Sigurðr killed him.[2] Against this unsavoury incident, however, must be placed another, more creditable one. Sigurðr was in the retinue of Þorgrímr alikarl and Þorsteinn Jónsson when they were on their way to seek revenge for the burning of Önundr the skewer. They went to attack Kálfr Guttormsson, Sigurðr's friend, at Auðbrekka, 'then Sigurðr grikkr left them and got Kálfr into sanctuary in church, and said that he would defend him while he could stand'.[3] In all probability he will have died some little time afterwards, most likely before the battle of Víðines in 1208, where we are told that Sveinn Jónsson sveitarbót took part in the fighting and had 'the sword called *Brynjubítr* which Sigurðr grikkr had brought from Byzantium'. It is of course perfectly possible that Sveinn had also been a Varangian, and that Sigurðr had left him the sword on his death – we are told that Sveinn was noted for his strength and had hit out powerfully with the sword at Víðines. The sword will definitely have been a Byzantine one, obtained

---

[1] *Sturlunga saga*, ed. K. Kålund, Copenhagen, 1096–11, I, 198–9.
[2] *Sturlunga saga*, I, 214.   [3] *Sturlunga saga*, I, 216.

by Sigurðr during his service among the Varangians; it certainly was a noted weapon, for it later came into the possession of Þorvarðr Örnólfsson of Miklagarðr in Eyjafjörðr,[1] from whom Sturla Sighvatsson seized it by force when he would not sell it.[2] From the dates that we have, Sigurðr grikkr (if he went to Byzantium) will have returned some time before 1197 – in all probability in 1195 or 96, and therefore served in the Varangians under either the last two Comneni or Isaac II Angelos.

[1] There are to this day three farms in Iceland named *Mikligarður*, one in Saurbæjarhreppur in Eyjafjörður, one in Seyluhreppur in Skagafjörður, and one in Saurbæjarhreppur in Dalir; notwithstanding the much-publicized theories on on Icelandic place-names propagated by Professor Þórhallur Vilmundarson, it is far from impossible that one or all of these may have been given the name in memory of the Great City of the Byzantines.

[2] *Sturlunga saga*, I, 318–19.

10

Runic inscriptions concerning Varangians

Up to the days of the Comnenian Emperors the greater part of the
Varangians were Swedes, and in Sweden have been found a number of
runic stones which bear the names of various men who died in Byzantium, and had these stones raised in their memory. How frequent the
journeys to the Empire will have been in the tenth to the twelfth centuries we may see from the old Swedish legal codes, where there are
provisions for inheritance for men who were resident in Greece. The
older manuscript of the code states that no one may receive an inheritance (in Sweden) while he dwells in Greece, while the younger
code determines that no one may inherit from such a person as was
not a living heir when he went away. There are similar enactments in
the older Norwegian *Gulaþingslög*, 'but if (a man) goes to Greece, then
he who is next in line to inherit shall hold his property'.[1] The composition of the *Västgötalag* is usually attributed to Askell, brother to Earl
Birger of Bjälbo, who was lawman of Västgötaland in 1219–25, but
many of their enactments were obviously much older when they were
codified, and this is one of these. The younger code, which is reckoned
to be from between 1250 and 1300, adds a number of points, but the
interesting thing is that, even when one allows for the naturally con-
servative temper of lawyers, the Norwegians and Swedes felt it necessary to retain these enactments so late in time.

We must of course recognize that the Swedish travellers to Greece
who are commemorated on the runic stones need by no means all have
been Varangians; some will have gone on other errands, as merchants,
pilgrims, or quite simply as trippers who died there while on their
journey. The danger of such a journey may be recognized from the

---

[1] *Norges gamle Love*, ed. R. Keyser and P. A. Munch, Christiania, 1846–8, I, 26.

fact that there are examples of folk who had such commemorative stones erected *before* they set out; one such is a stone from Stäket, whose inscription was still extant in the seventeenth century but has now vanished. This inscription was read and copied out by Aschanaeus, and has been edited by Elias Wessén, and reads (in translation): 'Ingirún Harðardóttir had runes graven for herself; she would go East and out to Jerusalem. Fótr carved the runes.'[1] Yet even with this proviso we may say with certainty that more than a half of these surviving runic carvings are for men who went into military service in Byzantium, were Varangians, and died in the East; it is stated of some that they gathered riches there for themselves or their heirs.

Most of the runic stones are from Uppland, as is to be expected, as Roslagen (the *Róðrslög* from which most of the Rūsi originated) lies there, and it was there that it was most common to start one's journey across the Principate of Kiev to Byzantium. We will now list them in alphabetical order of location, following Wessén's edition and Liljegren's supplementary collection. The texts are given here in English, while the originals are given in the notes.

(1) A stone at the church in Angarn. 'Over Tóki who died "out in Greece"; raised by his sons Þegn (Þiagn?), Gautdjarfr (?), Sunnhvatr (?), and Þórólfr.'[2]

(2) A stone from Broby in the parish of Täby 'Raised by Astrid over her husband Eysteinn (Øystein) "who visited Jerusalem and died in Greece".'[3]

(3) Another stone from Broby on Jarlebanka 'he died in Greece'.[4]

(4) A stone in Droppsta, Odensala parish, over a man, the father or brother of the man who raised the stone over a traveller to Greece who 'died in Greece'; the name is so worn as to be illegible.[5]

(5) A stone from in Ed, Ed parish, on the church path: 'Rögnvaldr had the runes carved after his mother Fastvi, daughter of Ónæmr. Died at Eiði (Aeði). God rest her spirit. Ragnvaldr had the runes carved. Was in Greece, was in command of soldiers.'[6] The form of the runes suggests that the stone was erected shortly after 1050; Otto von Friesen also points out that this Rögnvaldr was probably in a similar position to that held by Haraldr Sigurðarson, though it is possible that he commanded Varangians outside the City.[7] Wessén makes the point that the name Ragnvaldr (Rögnvaldr) is not normally a peasant name, but was more usual among noble houses in the Viking period.[8]

---

[1] E. Wessén, *Upplands Runinskrifter* (Sveriges Runinskrifter VI–X), Stockholm, 1940–58, III, 4ff. (hereafter referred to as U with the number of the stone added).

[2] U 201 'furs uti krikum'.   [3] U 136 'is suti iursalir auk antaþis uti krikum'.

[4] U 140 '....la.ba...han antaþis i kirikium'.   [5] U 446 'hon tu i krikum'.

[6] U 112 'rahnualtr huar a griklanti uas lis foringi'.

[7] O. von Friesen, *Upplands runstenar*, Stockholm, 1913, 56.

[8] E. Wessén, *Upplands Runinskrifter*, I, 161.

(6) Another stone from Ed, now in the Ashmolean Museum.¹ 'Þorsteinn had a mark made after his father Sveinn and his brother Þórir. They went out to Greece – and after his mother Ingibjörg. Öpir carved.' Wessén considers that the two men died on the way east, but there is no clear-cut evidence for this, nor that they were Varangians.

(7) Two stones from Hansta (mod. Hägerstalund) in Spanga parish; one of them is now on the Skans in Stockholm.² 'Gerðarr (Garðarr) and Jörundr had these stones raised after their nephews, Ernmundr and Ingimundr. These stones are raised after the sons of Inga. She became their heir, while they Gerðarr and his brother became her heirs. They (the younger brothers) died in Greece.'

Wessén considers that these two, Ernmundr and Ingimundr, in-herited their father's property, probably the farm of Hansta, after which they became Varangians and died in Greece, whereupon their mother Inga inherited the property, and in turn, on her death, Gerðarr and Jörundr, her brothers and heirs, raised the monument to their nephews, possibly because they had acquired fame. The carver's name was Véseti.

(8) A stone in Husby in Lyhundra parish.³ 'Eiríkr and Hákon and Ragn-hildr [raised this stone for Önundr the brother of Hákon and] Eiríkr and son of Ragnhildr, but he died in Greece. God and the mother of God save his soul.' The missing part is conjectured by von Friesen.⁴ The inscription is supposed to be done by Ásmundr, a noted rune-carver. Braun thinks that the inscription refers to the sons of Eymundr the Old, son of King Ólafr Skautkonungr.

(9) A stone in Lissby in Täby parish.⁵ '[Sveinn?] and Úlfr had stones raised for Hálfdán and for Gunnarr, their brothers. They died east [in Greece, or *perhaps*, in Garðar (Kiev)].' It is uncertain because of the fracture whether this stone really refers to Byzantine travellers.

(10) A stone at Lövsta in Bällinge parish,⁶ raised by a woman named Fastvi after Garðarr and Gautrekr, her sons – one died in Greece'.

(11) A stone in Skepptuna church, Skepptuna parish,⁷ over Fólkbjörn Fólkmarsson, 'who died also in Greece', raised by his father.

(12) A stone in Smedby, Fresta parish,⁸ over Ketill 'Greece farer', raised by his daughter Ingiþóra.

(13) A stone from Tillinge church,⁹ raised by Véfar for his brother Guð-mundr, 'who died in Arabia (Serkland)'. This might be an Ingvar stone (see below, p. 228) but it could also simply be a stone over a Varangian who died or was killed on service in Asia.

(14) Stones from Täby Church and Fittja, Täby parish.¹⁰ 'Guðlaug had [stones raised for Holm]a, her son and for herself. He died in Longo-

¹ U 104 'þir huaru hut til krika'.   ² U 73 'kiaþar b.repr.þir to i kirkium'.
³ U 540 'hon uarþ (tau)þr a kriklati'.
⁴ O. von Friesen, 'Hvem var Yngvar enn víðförli?', *Fornvännen*, 3 (1910), 199–209.
⁵ U 153 'þair antaþus aust...um'.   ⁶ U 1087 'onar uarþ tauþr i girkjum'.
⁷ U 358 'sar itaþis uk miþ krkum (sá er andaðiz út með girkjum)'.
⁸ U 270 '...faþur sin krikfarn.k...'.   ⁹ U 785 'han uarþ tuþr a srklant'.
¹⁰ U 133/U 141 (a) 'kuþ: luk.lit...a sun sin auk at sik sialfa.han to a lankbarþa l...ti';
    (b) 'kuþluk lit staina at hulma sun sin han to a lankbarþa lanti'.

bardia.' The most likely reason for this stone is that it commemorates a Varangian who died in the Normanno-Byzantine or Byzantine–Saracen wars in Southern Italy.

(15) Stone in the cathedral at Uppsala,[1] raised by a number of men, over an Ingifastr 'who went to Greece'. Öpir was the carver.

(16) Stone from Ulanda Bridge in Tillinge parish.[2] 'Kar had this stone raised for Mursi [? Horsa] his father and Kappi [Kabi?] for his brother-in-law. He made much money for his heirs out in Greece.' This is most likely a Varangian monument; Brate thinks the inscription is from *c.* 1070.

(17) Stone from Vedyxe, Danemark parish,[3] raised for Viðbjörn who travelled to Greece. Ásmundr Kárason was the carver.

(18) Stone from Väster Ledinge, Skederyd parish.[4] 'Þorgerðr and Sveinn had this stone raised for Ormgeirr [and Ormúlfr and Freygeirr (Froygæirr)]. He died in Sila in the North, but the others out in Greece. God help their souls and spirits.' Wessén interprets this inscription as follows: that since Þorgerðr is named first, Sveinn is sure to be her son, as if he had been her husband or her brother, his name would have come first. Accordingly, Þorgerðr's husband was either Ormgeirr (Ormeir?) or Freygeirr. Sophus Bugge thinks that Freygeirr was an Upplander, most likely from Skederyd. He and two others, Ormgeirr(?) and Ormúlfr, probably his elder brothers, went as leaders of a company of Norsemen to Byzantium and became Varangians; Ormgeirr and Ormúlfr died in Greece, but Freygeirr returned with a retinue of companions who had followed him out to the East. This expedition appears to be mentioned on various runestones raised in their memory; Freygeirr himself fell in Sila (now Osel).

(19) Stone in Ärentuna, in the district of Norunda,[5] raised by Ljótr the shipmaster over his sons, among whom was Jöfurr (Iufari) who 'came home to Krikhafnir...' (i.e. went to Greek havens and home again). This is probably a memorial to a merchant.

(20) Stone in Åshusby, Norrsunda parish, now in the church at Norrsunda.[6] 'Tófa and Hemingr had this stone raised after their son Gunnarr, but he died out in Greece. God and the Mother of God help his soul.' Most probably a Varangian memorial.

(21) Stone in Örby, Skepptuna parish;[7] the name is illegible: 'he fell in Greece", hence most probably a Varangian.

There are also some noteworthy runic inscriptions in Södermanland, which we now list, following the edition of the inscriptions by E. Brate and E. Wessén.[8]

[1] *U* 922 'at ikifast sin sturn maþr sum for til girkha ut'.

[2] *U* 792 'far aflaþi uti krikum arfa sinum' (cf. E. Brate, *Svenska Runinskrifter*, Stockholm, 1922, 65–6).   [3] *U* 956 'stniltr lit rita stain þino abtir uiþbiurn krikfara buanta sin'.

[4] *U* 518 'þir antrir uti krikum'.

[5] *U* 1016 'sturþi (k)nari kuam hn krikhafnir haima tu...'.

[6] *U* 431 'hon uar tau(þ)r mir krikium ut'.   [7] *U* 374 'hon fil o kriklontr'.

[8] E. Brate and E. Wessén, *Södermanlands Runinskrifter*, Stockholm, 1924–36 (hereafter referred to as *Sö*).

(1) Stone from Djulefors, Stora Malm parish, in Oppunda district.[1] 'Inga raised this stone for Ólafr [Ulaif] her heir; he fought in the East and died in Longobardia'; this Ólafr was probably a Varangian in the Byzantine South Italy campaigns (see above, no. 14).

(2) Stone from Grinda in Spelvik parish, Rönö district.[2] 'Guðrún raised the stone for Héðinn, who was the nephew of Sveinn, he was in Greece, drew gold. Christ help [his] spirit.' This Héðinn was probably a Varangian officer.

(3) Stone from Gripsholm, Kärnbo parish, Selebo district.[3] 'Tola had this stone raised for his son Haraldr, the brother of Ingvar. Bravely they went far for gold, gave the eagle [food] in the East, died south in Arabia [Serkland].' This is probably one of the stones that refers to Ingvar's journey along the Volga to the Caspian Sea (see below).

(4) Stone from Lundby, Lid parish, Rönö district.[4] An Ingvar stone (see below) raised by Spjóti and Hálfdán the sons of Eyvindr for their brother Skarði 'in Serkland lies the son of Eyvindr'. This Skarði had perhaps been one of the companions of Ingvar who reached Byzantium and entered the Emperor's service, though this is by no means certain (see later in this chapter).

(5) Stone from Nälberga, parish of Svärta, district of Rönö.[5] 'Vésteinn, Ögmundr, Guðverr raised a stone for their father Böðúlfr, man of might. He with the Greeks *varþ tu o þum þa*.' The last four words are of uncertain meaning; the most probable one is that they refer to a shortened form of a place-name, and Magnus Olsen has surmised that this was Ptolemais in Syria, which is referred to in Abbot Nikulas's *Leiðarvísir* as *Þolomaiða*.[6] This Böðúlfr has most probably been a Varangian.

(6) Stone from Rycksta, parish of Råby, district of Rönö.[7] 'Þrýríkr [Þrurikr] raised a stone to his son, brave man. Óleifr went to Greece, divided gold...'. Bugge surmises[8] that the *Þrurikr* of the stone should be *Þrýríkr*; accordingly this Ólafr Þrýríksson has been a Varangian officer, as the words *gulli skipti* suggest.

(7) Stone from Skåäng, parish of Vagnhärad, district of Hölebo.[9] 'Gnúpa had this stone raised to her brother Guðleifr. He died *austr at þingum* [prob. "in action in the East"]'.' This suggests that Guðleifr was a soldier, either in the service of Jaroslav the Great of Kiev or else as a Varangian in Constantinople.

(8) Stone in Strängnäs, near the Cathedral there.[10] 'Ei[ríkr had this] stone raised [to Ingvar and Haraldr], sons of Eymund[r]. They died] south in Serk[land].' Von Friesen has filled in the gaps according to F. Brand's

---

[1] *Sö* 65 'han austarla arþi barþi auk o lakbarþi lanti (antaþis)'.
[2] *Sö* 165 'uar han i krikum iuli skifti'.
[3] *Sö* 179 'þair furu trikila fiari at kuli auk austarlar: ni kafu tuu sunnarla a sirklanti'.
[4] *Sö* 131 'fur aust hiþan miþ ikvari o sirklanti likr'.
[5] *Sö* 170 'han miþ kriki uarþ tu o þum þa'.
[6] M. Olsen, 'Et "græsk" stedsnavn i et svensk runeindskrift', *Festskrift tillägnad Hugo Pipping*, Helsingfors, 1924, 411–18; cf. also *Leiðarvísir*, in *Alfrœði Íslenzk*, ed. K. Kålund, Copenhagen, 1908–18, I, 21.   [7] *Sö* 163 'for ulaifr i krikium, uli sifti'.
[8] E. Brate and S. Bugge, *Runverser*, Stockholm, 1887–91, 179.
[9] *Sö* 33 'han antaþis austr at þikum'.   [10] *Sö* 279 'air(rikr?) (hagg)ua (stain) (s)uni'.

reconstructions.[1] The stone is probably an Ingvar stone, and possibly refers to the same men as the Gripsholm Stone.

(9) Stone in the cathedral church at Strängnäs.[2] 'Hallví[?] had the monument made after [N.N.], brother of Úlfr. They went to the East with Ingvar, [and died in] Arabia.'

(10) Stone in the parish of Tumbo. '...died in[3] Greece'. Most likely a monument to a dead traveller to Greece.

(11) Stone in Västerby, parish of Tumbo, district of Väster Rekarne.[4] 'Ozurr (?) and Ern [raised a stone to] their father. He died in Greece.' The name of the man to whom the stone was put up is lacking, but he will have been in Greece.

(12) Stone in the church at Ytterjärna, district of Öknebo.[5] '[X. raised] this stone to Geir...[was] deceased out [in Greece].' The reading of the runes is doubtful, but it is likely that this Geirr was a Varangian.

Stones 3, 4, 8 and 9 are all raised in memory of men who went journeying with Ingvar the Far-travelled, a Swedish chieftain who travelled down the Volga to the Caspian Sea and had many fights on the way, but died of plague in 1041 according to his (very fanciful) saga and Icelandic annals.[6] According to the saga one of his companions, Valdimar, reached Byzantium with one ship,[7] and it is quite probable that these men entered the Varangians and some fell in battle with the Turks in the East, in the *Serkland* of the stones, though we must reflect that this term is as likely to have been used of the Caspian region as of the Sultanate of Rum in Asia Minor. It is generally assumed that this Ingvar was from Södermanland, as most of the memorial stones to his followers are found there, some sixteen in all, while six are in Uppland and two in East Götland. It is worth noting, however, that one piece of description comes so near to the reconstructed method of the emission of Greek fire as to have the reviser seriously considering it a fossil recollection of actuality, brought back by Ingvar's followers.[8]

There are two runic stones in East Götland which may be noted in our present context.

---

[1] O. von Friesen, *Upplands runstenar*, 206ff.

[2] *Sö* 281 'þir au(st)...miþ ikuari o sirklat(i)'.   [3] *Sö* 82 'þuþr (i) krikum'.

[4] *Sö* 85 'han antaþis uti krikum'.   [5] *Sö* 345 '(ua)er e(nta)þr ut (kr)k(um)'.

[6] *Yngvars saga viðförla*, ed. E. Olson, Copenhagen, 1912, lxxviff. Dr Olson's careful and cautious assembly and analysis of the archaeological material then available well repays scrutiny; cf. also *Annales Islandiae* (Arnamagnæan ed.), Copenhagen, 1847, 42, *Islandske Annaler*, ed. G. Storm, Christiania, 1888, 108.
There is also an excellent survey of the Ingvar stones in E. Wessén, *Historiska runinskrifter*, Stockholm, 1960, 30–46, where an attempt is made to balance the claims of stones, saga and annals against one another.   [7] *Yngvars saga*, 31.

[8] *Yngvars saga*, 20–1; see J. Haldon and F. Byrne, 'A possible solution to the problem of Greek Fire', *BZ*, 70 (1977), 91–9. One other Ingvar-stone, not listed either in Olson's edition of the saga or the Icelandic edition of this book, is *U* 837, Alsta, Nysätra Parish, whose inscription was read by Wessén and Jansson 'k.kulmk...rs liþ. kuþ hialbi...'. The editors think that the first gap read *Ingvars lið*. Other Ingvar-stones recorded in the

(1) Stone in the old church at Högby, district of Göstring.[1] According to E. Brate this stone dates from c. 1020. It was raised by Þorgerðr (þukir) to her uncle Össur, who died 'east in Greece'. On the reverse of the stone Ösurr is said to have been Gullason, one of five brothers, now all dead – one of them, Ásmundr, fell in the battle of Fyrisvalla (c. 984 or earlier).

(2) Stone in the churchyard at Harstad, parish of Väderstad, district of Göstring.[2] This is raised by Ásgautr and Guðmundr over Oddlaugr, farmer of Haddastadir (haþistaþum) who died in Greece. The inscription is not, however, unambiguously military, and this Oddlaugr may well have been a pigrim and not a Varangian.

There are two stones in Småland with a Byzantine interest.

(1) Stone in Tuna, parish of Ryssby, district of Sunnerbo.[3] This was raised by Tumi to his brother Össurr, 'he who was King Haraldr's shipman'. If this was Haraldr III of Norway, then we may be sure that this Össurr was a Varangian; the editor of the Småland inscriptions is, however, of the opinion that the King Haraldr in question was King Harold I of England (Harefoot). This is of course perfectly possible, but the probability of a Swede going East rather than West when going out adventuring is much higher, and we are inclined to favour a Varangian explanation.

(2) Stone from Erikstad, parish of Vittaryd, district of Sunnerbo.[4] 'The stone is raised by...nuir to Steinn, her son, who...died east in Greece.'

One inscription of a possible Byzantine interest is found in Västermanland.

Stone in a ruined church in Stora Ryttern, raised by Guðleifr (Kuþlefr) to his son Slakvi 'dead east in Karusm'. The editor, Dr S. B. F. Jansson, has pointed out that the most likely solution of the place-name is *Khovaresm*, which was the name of a fairly powerful Turkish state in mediaeval Central Asia, and we may guess that Slakvi went there either as a merchant or as a Varangian, i.e. in the retinue of a Byzantine ambassador to the ruler of Khoresm, or else as a captive from some frontier skirmish between the Khorasmians and the Empire.[5]

---

edition of the saga, but not originally considered by Dr Blöndal, are now U 644, U 654, U 661, U 778 and U 1143; as none of them adds anything significant to the evidence, they are now merely noted for the record.

[1] E. Brate, *Östergötlands runinskrifter*, Stockholm, 1911, no. 81; (front) 'eataþis austr i krikum'; (back) 'aitaþis asur austr i krikum'.

[2] Brate, *Östergötlands runinskrifter*, no. 94; 'taþr i kirkium'. See also S. B. F. Jansson, *The Runes of Sweden*, London, 1962, 59–60. Professor Jansson suggests that King Harold I (Harefoot) of England, son of Knud the great, and not Haraldr III of Norway, is the Haraldr of the stone.

[3] R. Kinander, *Smålands runinskrifter*, Stockholm, 1935–61, no. 42; 'þan ar uar skibari hrls kunuks'.

[4] Kinander, *Smålands runinskrifter*, no. 94; 'im itaþisk outr i krikum'.

[5] S. B. F. Jansson, *Runstenen i Stora Rytterns kyrkoruin*, Västerås, 1943.

One stone is found in West Götland:

> The churchyard at Kölaby. 'Agmund raised this stone for his cousin Asbjörn and Asa for her husband, who was Kolbein's son; he died in Greece.'[1]

The most famous of all Varangian inscriptions, however, is the marble lion from Piraeus. This statue stood in the time of the Empire at the entrance to the harbour of Piraeus, but when Francesco Morosini captured Athens in the Turco-Venetian war of 1668, he had it removed to Venice as a memorial of his victory, and had it placed in front of the naval stores where it still stands. Late in the eighteenth century the Swedish scholar and envoy Johann David Åkerblad noticed that there were runes carved upon this lion, and published an article on them[2] which formed the basis of C. C. Rafn's later study (for which, however, Rafn had fresh plaster casts made of the inscriptions).[3] It is also said that the eccentric Danish archaeologist M. F. Arendt went on a special journey to Venice in 1809 to read them, but failed to do so.[4]

The question was reopened some time after Rafn's death by the Swede Oscar Montelius[5] and the Dane Sophus Bugge;[6] in 1875 they came individually to the conclusion that the shapes of the runes indicated that they were similar to late Swedish runes, and that they were therefore carved by a Swedish Varangian around 1050, who was probably from Uppland. Shortly afterwards Ingvar Undset made a close examination of all the carvings,[7] and the painter J. F. Hansen made an exact drawing of them all according to his direction, which is now in the custody of the Swedish Academy of History and Antiquities in Stockholm. He was followed by H. Kempff in 1894, who published a study of the problem,[8] and by F. Sanders, who had a fresh plaster cast made. His study caused a minor controversy with Kempff.[9] Bugge then made a personal visit in 1897 to Venice to examine the runes,

---

[1] H. Jungner and E. Svärdström, *Västergötlands Runinskrifter*, Stockholm, 1958–70, no. 178; 'uarþr tuþr i krikum'.
[2] J. D. Åkerblad, 'Om det sittande Marmorlejonet i Venedig', *Skandinavisk Museum* II (1800–3), 1–12.
[3] C. C. Rafn, *Antiquités de l'Orient*, Copenhagen, 1856, 81ff.
[4] Rafn, *Antiquités de l'Orient*, 16.
[5] See next reference, 98 n.
[6] S. Bugge, 'Run-inskrifter pa marmorlejonet från Piræus', *Kungliga Vitterhets Historie och Antiqvitets Akademiens Månadsblad*, IV (1875), 97–101.
[7] I. Undset, 'Runlejonet i Venedig', *Kungliga Vitterhets Historie och Antiqvitets Akademiens Månadsblad*, XIV (1884), 19–23.
[8] H. Kempff, *Piræuslejonets runristingar*, Gävle, 1894–5.
[9] F. Sanders, *Marmorlejonet från Piræus*, Stockholm, 1896; for his continued quarrel with Kempff, see Kempff, *Piræuslejonets runristingar*, II, *passim*, and Sanders, *Runinskrifter*, Stockholm, 1898.

and published a popular version of his findings some ten years later.[1]

Unfortunately, all these weighty investigations are completely without substance, and mostly based on the ingenuity of the investigators. As Rafn's explanation is the most detailed, and because of the great reputation which he has enjoyed as a scholar, his results have been taken as gospel by various historians, though there is no external substantiation possible for them. Rafn read as follows (in normalized spelling).

On the right side of the lion:

Hákon vann, þeir Úlfr ok Ásmundr ok Aurn hafa þessa; þeir menn lagðu á, ok Haraldr háfi, of fébóta uppreistar vegna Grikkjaþýþis. Varþ Dálkr nauðugr í fjarri löndum. Egill var í faru med Ragnari til Rúmaníu...ok Armeníu.

Hákon won, they Úlfr and Ásmundr and Aurn have these; these men inflicted, and Haraldr the Tall, vast fines because of the rebellion of the Greek folk. Dálkr went unwilling to distant lands. Egill was journeying with Ragnarr to Rumania...and Armenia.

On the left side of the lion:

Ásmundr hjó rúnar þessar, þeir Ásgeir ok Þorleifr, Þórþr ok Ívar, at bón Haralds háfa, þó at Grikkir (of) hugsaþu (ok bannaþu).

Ásmundr carved these runes, they Ásgeirr and Þorleifr, Þórðr and Ívar, at the request of Haraldr the Tall, though the Greeks thought [and forbade] it.

Rafn thought that 'Haraldr the Tall' was Haraldr Sigurðarson, and that he had put down an attempted rebellion in Piraeus in 1040 with his Varangians. On the other hand, Byzantine sources do not mention any such rebellion, and it is most likely Rafn's imagination, and the entire solution is highly suspect; nor are Kempff and Sanders's attempts any more successful, any more than Bugge's, who thinks that the runes were carved by 'Úlfungr's men' in memory of one Hákon, who died in the port, and in revenge for whose death many Greeks were put into slavery; Ásmundr, Ármundr and Karl did the carving.

Another personal examination, by the Swedish archaeologist S. Söderberg, led that investigator to conclude that the runes were far too worn to be legible, odd words apart.[2]

Nevertheless, two more recent scholars have conducted investigations on the carvings which have given results that may be looked at in all seriousness. The earlier attempt was made by Erik Brate, who

---

[1] S. Bugge, *Populærvidenskabelige Foredrag*, Christiania, 1907, 98ff. The actual notes on which the lecture was based are now in the library of the Kungliga Vitterhetsakademien, Stockholm.   [2] S. Söderberg, 'Reseberättelse', *Månadsblad* xix (1891), 128.

examined the lion itself, Hansen's drawings and Sanders's plaster casts.[1] His conclusions were that the runes were carved in memory of 'Horsa, a good farmer', and that Swedes from Roslagen, Áskell, and others (?Þorleifr) carved them. Brate also concluded that this *Horsi* was the same man as was commemorated on the Ulanda Stone (see above, p. 228); admittedly the stone reads *Mursi*, but Brate reckons that this is a slip by the carver. Von Friesen considers that the stone was carved by a well-known rune-carver by the name of Bali (Balle), or by someone who copied his style. The oldest carving by this person is from *c.* 1050–60; hence Brate concludes that the runes on the lion of Piraeus date from the reigns of Constantine X (1059–67) or Romanos IV (1067–71).

Brate's study was criticized by Haakon Shetelig in 1923 after an independent personal examination of the lion itself.[2] Shetelig agreed with most of Brate's conclusions, but read a few additional runes. His conclusion was also that the carving was the work of three men; his work was also supplemented by a note by Magnus Olsen, who maintained that all that could be read with certainty was ...*i hafn þisi*... [...*u ru*]*nar at*.... then (probably) an illegible man's name, and lastly *m biki i*[? *sem bjuggu i*]. Both Shetelig and Olsen are of the opinion that it is now no longer possible to see with any certainty the names of the person or persons in whose honour the runes were carved, nor those of the carvers.

The last investigation is one done by E. Moltke, who communicated his results privately to the author in a letter which is published here with his consent in a slightly abbreviated translation.

When I examined the Piraeus lion in 1930 it became clear to me that it was hopeless to expect to read any of the carving on the right side, even though some of the runes were still visible on it, being carved deeply and clearly, because the inscription as a whole has been so damaged by vandals (particularly by bullets which have cut small, hemispherical indentations) that only a few connected words can be read, though this, together with its decoration, sufficed to enable me to make a definite decision as to the type and the period of the runes. Accordingly, I concentrated on the inscription on the left side, as I considered that there was more hope of a definite result there. I therefore took slanted-light photographs of both sides and also obtained a papier-mâché impression of both inscriptions. These photographs and papier-mâché impressions are now in the custody of the National Museum in Copenhagen.

As to the condition of the inscriptions at the present time, they are of course badly affected by weathering (as well as because of vandalism) and as the surface of the marble appears to be both soft and crumbled, I have

[1] E. Brate, 'Piræuslejonets runinskrifter', *Antikvarisk Tidsskrift för Sverige*, xx (1919), 3.
[2] H. Shetelig, 'Piræuslöven i Venezia', *Fornvännen* 16 (1923), 201–21; cf. also reply by Brate, *ibid.*, 222–4, and note by Magnus Olsen, *ibid.*, 221.

grave doubts as to whether they were appreciably more legible when Åkerblad viewed them. I base this opinion both on my general knowledge of rock textures and on the description given by the excellent archaeologist M. F. Arendt, that shortly after 1800 the runes were 'so worn that no one can read them'.

The two inscriptions, on the left and the right side of the lion, are carved by two rune-masters at different times. The inscription on the undecorated band on the left side is the older: it is most like the runes on the undecorated stones from Uppland from around 1000; as on these, the crossed through *a* and *n* runes are found, but not the runes with a stroke only through one side, which were taken up from the older special Swedish futharc later.

The inscription on the right side is of the common Uppland type of runes from about 1075, like the clean 'figure-of-eight' type carved by Öper. The *a* and *n* runes with a stroke through the middle are used, and in the word *þair* there occurs the later form of the *r* rune, which came late into the futharc.

Strangely enough, the inscription on the left side begins with a row of reversed characters, which probably read that two men...ulfr and Smidr (?) did something *i höfn þessarri* ('in this port'). The actual beginning is now gone, and it is not now possible to state whether ...*ulfr* is an independent name *Úlfr* or the second element of a longer name.

...ulf uk smi ( ) (r)   ...an i hafn ( ) þisi

After this comes a short gap, and then an inscription with ordinary, rightward runes, though it is not possible to read *with certainty* any characters other than the following:

..nar at ha...narþ....þum( ) il nanfarin (the end is perfectly legible) and this cannot really be made to yield any sense.[1]

The author himself also examined the lion *in situ*, and has come to the conclusion, without being a professional runologist, that because of the advanced state of decay of the inscriptions, all that can be said about them with any certainty has been said by Dr Moltke, in which conclusion the reviser, after patient study of the various impressions and photographs now in Copenhagen and Stockholm, joins him.

The last inscription that needs to be considered in this study is the carving, or rather graffiti found on the gateway of the Bukoleon palace. These are illustrated by Mambourg and Wiegand,[2] who deduce that they are from early in the thirteenth century, basing their conclusion on the shapes of the shields, which they assume to be the arms of the men on guard there. If these scrawls are runes, then they should be band-runes, and if they are, one may with a certain amount of uncritical benevolence read the name *Karkr* or *Krákr* on one of them, but the author is of the opinion that this is not runes at all, but merely doodles by the guards on duty.

[1] Private letter from E. Moltke to S. Blöndal, 7 September 1944.
[2] E. Mambourg and T. Wiegand, *Die Kaiserpaläste von Konstantinopel zwischen Hippodrom und Marmarameer*, Berlin, 1934, 8.

Select Bibliography

PRIMARY

Acta et diplomata graeca, ed. F. Miklosich and J. Müller, Wien, 1860–90.

Anna Comnena, *L'Alexiade*, ed. B. Leib, Paris, 1937–76.

Anon., Λόγος νουθετητικός, ed. V. G. Vasilevskii and V. Jernstedt, St Petersburg, 1896.

Constantine VII, *De Administrando Imperio*, ed. G. Moravcik and R. J. H. Jenkins, London, 1949–62.

De Ceremoniis Aulae Byzantinae, ed. J. J. Reiske, Bonn, 1828.

De Ceremoniis (chh. 1–83 only), ed. A. Vogt, Paris, 1935–40.

De Thematibus, ed. A. Pertusi, Rome, 1949.

Georgius Cedrenus, *Historiarum epitome*, ed. I. Bekker, Bonn, 1839.

Georgius Pachymeres, *De Michaele et Andronico Palaeologis*, ed. I. Bekker, Bonn, 1835.

Gregorius Bar-Hebraeus (Abulfaradh), *Chronicon Syriacum*, ed. P. J. Bruns and G. G. Kirsch, Leipzig, 1789.

Íslenzk Fornrit, ed. S. Nordal *et al.*, Reykjavík, 1933– .

Játvarðar saga, ed. J. Sigurðsson, Copenhagen, 1852.

John VI, Cantacuzenos, *Opera*, ed. L. Schopen, Bonn, 1828–32.

John Cinnamus, *Epitome rerum*, ed. A. Meineke, Bonn, 1838.

John Zonaras, *Annales*, ed. M. Pinder and T. Büttner-Wobst, Bonn, 1841–97.

Leo the Deacon, *Historiarum libri X*, ed. C. B. Hase, Bonn, 1828.

Michael Psellus, *Chronographie*, ed. E. Renault, Paris, 1926–8.

Morkinskinna, ed. F. Jónsson, Copenhagen, 1900.

L. A. Muratori, *Scriptores rerum historicarum Italicarum*, Venice, 1724–51.

Nicetas Choniates, *Historiae*, ed. I. Bekker, Bonn, 1835.

Den norsk–islandske skjaldedigtning, ed. F. Jónsson, 2nd edn., Copenhagen, 1920–2.

Orkneyinga saga, ed. S. Nordal, Copenhagen, 1915.

Повесть Временных Лет (Полное Собрание Русских Летописей I), ed. E. F. Karskii, Leningrad, 1926–9.

Pseudo-Codinus, *De Officiis*, ed. J. Verpeaux, Brussels, 1967.
Recueil des historiens des Croisades, Paris, 1841–1906.
Robert de Clari, *La conquête de Constantinople*, ed. P. Lauer, Paris, 1924.
Saxo Grammaticus, *Gesta Danorum*, ed. J. Olrik, H. Raeder and F. Blatt, Copenhagen, 1931–57.
Stefan Asochik, *Histoire d'Arménie*, transl. E. Dulaurier and F. Macler, Paris, 1883–1917.
Sveriges runinskrifter, ed. H. Hildebrand *et al.*, Stockholm, 1900– .
Sverris saga, ed. H. Indrebø, Oslo, 1920.

SECONDARY

J. B. Bury, *A history of the Eastern Roman Empire*. London, 1912.
The Cambridge Medieval History, vol. IV, 2nd edn., ed. J. M. Hussey, Cambridge, 1964–6.
F. Chalandon, *Les Comnène*, Paris, 1900–12.
J. Gay, *L'Italie méridionale et l'empire byzantin,* Paris, 1909.
A. Karlgren, *Dneprfossernes slaviske Navne*, Copenhagen, 1947.
K. Krumbacher, *Geschichte der byzantinischen Litteratur*, 2nd edn., München, 1897.
G. Ostrogorskii, *A history of the Byzantine state*. 2nd English edn., transl. J. M. Hussey, Oxford, 1968.
P. Riant, *Skandinavernes Korstog og Andagtsrejser til Palæstina*, Copenhagen, 1868.
S. Rozniecki, *Varægiske Minder i den russiske Heltedigtning*, Copenhagen, 1914.
S. Runciman, *A history of the Crusades*, Cambridge, 1951–4.
G. Schlumberger, *Un empereur au Xe siècle: Nicéphore Phocas*, Paris, 1890.
   L'épopée byzantine à la fin du Xe siècle, Paris, 1896–1905.
A. Stender-Petersen, *Die Varägersage als Quelle der altrussischen Chronik*, Aarhus, 1934.
   Varangica, Aarhus, 1953.
A. A. Vasilev, *Byzance et les Arabes*, Brussels, 1935–51.
V. G. Vasilevskii, *Труды*, St Petersburg, 1908–15.

Index